Comparative Research Methods

Edited by
DONALD P. WARWICK
York University

SAMUEL OSHERSON
University of Massachusetts

PRENTICE-HALL, INC., Englewood Cliffs, N.J.

Library of Congress Cataloging in Publication Data

WARWICK, DONALD P comp.
  Comparative research methods.

  (General sociology series)
  Includes bibliographical references.
  1. Social science research—Addresses, essays, lectures. I. Osherson, Samuel, joint
comp. II. Title. [DNLM: 1. Research. 2. Social sciences.
H 62 W299c 1973]
H62.W285   300'.7'2   72-6899
ISBN   0-13-153940-X

PRENTICE-HALL SERIES IN GENERAL SOCIOLOGY
NEIL J. SMELSER, *Editor*

10 9 8 7 6 5 4 3 2 1

PRINTED IN THE UNITED STATES OF AMERICA

PRENTICE-HALL INTERNATIONAL, INC., *London*
PRENTICE-HALL OF AUSTRALIA, PTY. LTD., *Sydney*
PRENTICE-HALL OF CANADA, LTD., *Toronto*
PRENTICE-HALL OF INDIA PRIVATE LIMITED, *New Delhi*
PRENTICE-HALL OF JAPAN, INC., *Tokyo*

Contents

Preface

This work grows out of the graduate seminar on Comparative International Studies offered in the Department of Social Relations at Harvard University from 1967 to 1971 and the Department of Sociology in 1970–71. Donald Warwick directed the course while Samuel Osherson was an early student. The major criterion used in selecting the articles was their success in this context. Four cohorts of students, representing some twenty countries, were kind enough to provide critical commentaries on the selections used each year. The introductory chapter has also profited from the seminar discussions. We are thus heavily indebted to the fifty-plus participants, and wish to express our gratitude for their assistance. Several visiting lecturers were also a source of stimulation and inspiration. Among these were Renée Fox, David McClelland, Alex Inkeles, Ezra Vogel, John Whiting, William Goode, and William Foote Whyte. Finally, we wish to acknowledge the cheerful and generous assistance of Elinor White, then administrative assistant of the Harvard Comparative International Studies Program, in the preparation of the manuscript.

D.P.W./S.O.

Introduction

Whatever their differences on other matters, social scientists aspire to universality of generalization in their theories. Few do not smart if their work is labeled "culture bound" or "ethnocentric." Even the animal psychologist hopes that his findings will not be vitiated by national differences in rat populations. If progress in the social sciences were measured by lip service to ideal norms, all would be well on the comparative front. Yet even a cursory review of standard texts in sociology, psychology, anthropology, and political science reveals that aspirations for cross-cultural generalization have far outrun achievement. Sociology and psychology are just emerging from a period of *de facto* ethnocentrism. Even now it is difficult to find an introductory text in either field that pays serious attention to comparative analysis. Methods courses are even worse. A student can pass through a year-long course without any awareness that research techniques may have to be modified in other cultures. Political science has fared somewhat better, especially in the field of comparative politics. But here, too, cross-national generalizations have been seriously hampered by the lack of adequate theory and by the heavy emphasis given to Great Britain and Western Europe. As the pioneer in cross-cultural research, anthropology could scarcely be called ethnocentric. Its position on cross-cultural generalization, however, is not much better than in its sister disciplines. The main problem is that, until recently, single-culture ethnographic studies have virtually dominated social anthropology. Only rarely have anthropologists studied the same variables with the same methods, including the same ethnographer, in different cultures.

Our aim in this volume is to provide materials that might help new as well as experienced social scientists to correct this situation. We have tried to include articles that would be intelligible to a beginning student and of interest to the veteran researcher about to try his hand at a comparative study. Our hope for this volume is twofold. First, we would like to encourage more social scientists to carry out comparative research, if only on a small scale. The theoretical importance of such research is discussed in Chapter One and we would only add our conviction that there can be no social science which is not comparative. Emile Durkheim has stated this point very well for sociology: "Comparative sociology is not a particular branch of sociology; it is sociology itself, in so far as it ceases to be purely descriptive and aspires to account for facts." Second, our hope is that comparativists of the future will learn from the mistakes of the past. Some of the studies done to date have been grandiose and ill-conceived. Teams of researchers, armed with stock questionnaires and general instructions for sampling, have set out for countries with which they were only remotely familiar. Efforts of this sort have produced some interesting findings, but they have also contaminated the research environment and sometimes created a sense of despair. In other instances, studies have paid little heed to the core concepts guiding the research, or have stumbled on technical matters such as questionnaire design and translation.

This twofold aim explains the alternating currents of optimism and pessimism running through the volume. On the pessimistic side several of the articles, including parts of our introduction, focus heavily on problems—what can go wrong with a study. This emphasis is quite deliberate. We see social science as a cumulative effort in which one can and should profit from the errors of others. At the same time, we are moderately optimistic about the future of such research, and have tried to include articles which represent this view. The report on the Jamaica Human Fertility Investigation (Ch. 12) provides concrete evidence that high-quality survey research can be carried out in very trying circumstances. The articles by Frey (Ch. 11), Mitchell (Ch. 10), and Berreman (Ch. 13) also lend varying degrees of support to an optimistic view. Our personal experiences, Warwick in Latin America and Osherson in Tunisia and Denmark, run in a similar direction. In short, we hope that more social scientists will be willing to experiment with cross-societal comparisons, but that they begin their forays on an informed and manageable basis.

The book does not address all of the issues arising in comparative research, nor does it cover all of the methods available. The core issue considered is equivalence—how to study the same problem in different societies and cultures. We see this as the central theoretical and methodological question raised by cross-societal comparisons. Part II explores various facets of conceptual equivalence. Gunnar Myrdal (Ch. 3) shows how research on national development may be seriously biased by concepts and emphases imported from Western societies. Savage, Leighton, and Leighton (Ch. 4) approach the problem of equivalence from the standpoint of mental disorders. The articles in Part III deal with ways of attaining equivalence of measurement. In Chapter 5 Przeworski and Teune discuss some of the difficulties of attaining equivalence in cross-national surveys, and suggest a method for resolving them. Schuman follows with an article on the "random probe," a technique developed in his research on Pakistan. Part IV takes up the more specific questions of linguistic equivalence and translation. Both Anderson (Ch. 7) and Deutscher (Ch. 8) show how language and culture are tightly interwoven, and caution against an overly mechanical view of translation. Part V illustrates the problems and possibilities of comparative research as they arise with two methods: survey research and participant observation. The five articles in this section consider the assets and liabilities of each method, and present concrete illustrations drawn from "live" studies. We had hoped to include more material on participant observation and other qualitative methods but found it difficult to locate brief articles that were genuinely comparative in focus. Some that were tried in the seminar were rejected as too technical, unreadable, or otherwise inappropriate for this volume. Though the result may seem to be a lopsided emphasis on survey research, it is emphatically not our intention to endorse any single method. In fact, we argue in Chapter 1 that many of the difficulties encountered in comparative research could be greatly reduced by creative *combinations* of methods.

PART I

COMPARATIVE RESEARCH METHODS: AN OVERVIEW

1

Comparative Analysis
in the Social Sciences

DONALD P. WARWICK AND SAMUEL OSHERSON

The use of systematic observation across societies as a basis for generalizing about human behavior is as old as Herodotus (ca. 495–424 B.C.)
and as new as data banks. Though the past century has witnessed an
enormous increase in the scope and complexity of cross-societal comparisons, and in the sophistication of the technology available for such analyses, the method itself has a venerable history. A brief review of the ebb
and flow of comparative analysis will help to place its present development in perspective.[1]

The *Nine Books of History* by Herodotus were perhaps the first to
give systematic attention to such subjects as comparative geography, anthropology, and government. Book II, for example, discusses certain similarities and differences between the Egyptians and the Greeks:

> 80. There is another custom in which the Egyptians resemble a particular
> Greek people, namely the Lacedaemonians. Their young men, when they
> meet their elders in the streets, give way to them and step aside; and if
> an elder comes in where young men are present, these latter rise from
> their seats. In a third point they differ entirely from all the nations of
> Greece. Instead of speaking to each other when they meet in the streets,
> they make an obeisance, sinking the hand to the knee.[2]

Thucydides (ca. 460–400 B.C.) also made numerous comparative observations in his writings on the Peloponnesian War. He noted at one
point that while it was the policy of Athens to exact tribute from her
allies, Sparta refrained from this practice, securing subservience instead

---

[1] The following historical summary draws upon F. Redlich, "Toward Comparative Historiography," *Kyklos*, 11 (1958), 362–89, and an earlier version of the essay
by Neil Smelser published in this volume.

[2] *The History of Herodotus*, in *Great Books of the Western World*, ed. R. M.
Hutchins (Chicago: Encyclopaedia Britannica, Inc., 1952), VI, 65.

by establishing oligarchies among them (Book I, 19). Probably the most ambitious comparative project carried out in classic antiquity was that directed by Aristotle (384–322 B.C.). Foreshadowing contemporary research on comparative government, he and his students gathered and analyzed 158 political constitutions. A broad concern with cross-societal differences in government, including specific attention to constitutions, is apparent in the *Politeia*. The other major contribution of the classic period, which came much later, is found in the *Lives* of Plutarch (A.D. 46–125). Though the various biographies are often treated as single case studies, even the table of contents underscores the comparative thrust of the work. The first three titles are *Theseus, Romulus,* and *Theseus and Romulus Compared*; this pattern of Graeco-Roman comparisons continues throughout the book.

Though there were undoubtedly many examples of comparative analysis between the second and eighteenth centuries, the next peak of activity came during the era of Romanticism. This was the period in which Alexander von Humboldt (1769–1859) carried out his pioneering work in comparative geography, and in which major breakthroughs were seen in comparative anatomy. Particularly important because of its close relation to contemporary social science was the research of Franz Bopp (1791–1867) in comparative philology. Though it had long been known that the Indo-European languages were related to each other, Bopp was perhaps the first to show that the structural features common to these languages formed a partial language in itself—a protolanguage.

Several developments from 1850 on provided the proximate impetus to cross-cultural comparison in sociology and anthropology. One was the comparative study of religion, especially the monumental series by Max Müller, *The Sacred Books of the East*. The same period saw a steady flow of publications on comparative politics and law. The two major intellectual landmarks of this era, however, were the rise of classic evolutionism and Marxist theory.

Led by Tylor, Frazer, and Spencer, the classical evolutionist point of view came to dominate sociology and anthropology in the late nineteenth and early twentieth centuries. The work of these men was comparative in the broadest sense of the term, extending across space and time. Beginning with the assumption that all societies pass through similar states, the evolutionists used data from "primitive" tribes of their time to reconstruct the earliest stages of civilization as well as the cultural trajectory followed to the present.

After World War I the evolutionists came under heavy attack from several sides. Anthropologists, such as Boas, Malinowski, and Benedict, challenged the assumption of unilineal evolution, with the West standing at the top of a scale of "progress." Reacting against the comparative excesses of the evolutionists, these writers moved away from a cross-cultural methodology. Specifically, Boas and his followers in the "historical" school of anthropology contended that there were *no* general laws of culture and that the task of the profession was to seek the unique patterning of culture within single societies. Malinowski's functionalism, in turn, emphasized the tendency of culture traits to form a unique, coherent whole. His approach also led to the intensive study of single societies, and a suspicion of multicultural comparisons. For her part, Ruth Benedict took direct aim at the notion that the values and institutions of the Western industrial societies made them more advanced than primitive peoples. Arguing strongly for cultural relativism, she and many others held that comparisons between societies, especially on an absolute scale of values, should be avoided.

Despite their ideological differences, nineteenth-century Marxism and evolutionism were very similar in their reliance on cross-cultural historical evidence. Both schools posited the existence of a fixed and universal set of stages, and both relied heavily on historical materials. Thus it is not surprising that intellectual Marxism met many of the same objections that were hurled at the evolutionists. With the wane of these two approaches and the bitter attacks launched on their use of cross-cultural materials, comparative analysis moved into the background in the period between the two world wars.

A number of events since 1940—including the wartime demands for intelligence on "foreign" peoples—have helped to restore an interest in comparative research. One was a notable decline in the intellectual appeal of cultural relativism and classical functionalism. On the positive side, all the social sciences, including psychology, have developed theoretical and methodological perspectives which are conducive to cross-societal comparisons. A comparative perspective on society and culture has been an essential component of the neo-evolutionary theories in anthropology, especially those of Leslie White, Marshall Sahlins, Elmer Service, and Julian Steward. Similarly, the "cross-cultural method" developed by George Murdock and his associates has provided a major stimulus to comparative research. The compilation of large amounts of diverse ethnographic data in the Human Relations Area File at Yale has permitted scholars to follow Murdock's lead in seeking statistical relationships between various aspects of society, culture, and personality. The modern structural anthropology of Claude Levi-Strauss has also opened new avenues of cross-cultural analysis. The same can be said for the work of the sociological functionalists, especially Parsons and Eisenstadt. These writers have adopted a neo-evolutionary orientation emphasizing the increasing differentiation of structure and specialization of function within societies—topics that are inherently comparative.

In addition to these shifts in theoretical perspectives, several other developments have contributed to a heightened awareness of the need for cross-societal comparisons. One was the formation of "regional studies" programs on areas considered to be of vital importance to the major powers. Many grew out of wartime work related to intelligence or other military needs. One result was that dozens of previously unexposed social scientists were introduced—by instruction or osmosis—to the language, culture, and history of Asia, Africa, and Latin America. Area studies programs at many universities also helped to foster a spirit of interdisciplinary collaboration by bringing together representatives of various fields in joint teaching and research efforts. A by-product of this exchange was an increase in comparative studies combining variables from several disciplines, such as sociology, economics, and psychology. Moreover, the recent emergence of several dozen new nations, with far-reaching implications for the foreign policy of the Western powers, has provided a significant extra-academic impetus to international studies. These and other factors, including greatly increased travel, have made the present generation of social scientists more aware of the ethnocentric biases and unquestioned generalizations built into their concepts and theories. Relationships once assumed to be universal have been shattered on the proving ground of the non-Western world. As a result there is now a more cautious and less grandiose attitude in theory construction, and a renewed quest for explanations that will stand the test of varying sociocultural conditions.

THE COMPARATIVE METHOD

Is there, or should there be, a distinctive *comparative method* in the social sciences? Robert Marsh argues, for example, that comparative sociology should be regarded as a separate field because its data and objectives are distinct from analysis limited to a single society.[3] While the data may be different, it is difficult to see how the objectives of comparative sociology differ from those of the field at large. Closer to the mark is Oscar Lewis's comment that "comparison is a generic aspect of human thought rather than a special method."[4] The difference between the com-

[3]R. M. Marsh, *Comparative Sociology* (New York: Harcourt, Brace & World, Inc., 1967), esp. Chap. 1.
[4]Oscar Lewis, "Comparisons in Cultural Anthropology," in *Readings in Cross-Cultural Methodology*, ed. F. W. Moore (New Haven: Human Relations Area Files Press, 1961), p. 55.

parative and the noncomparative wings of a social science discipline thus lies more in the range of variation considered than in a distinctive methodology.

Comparison in its broadest sense is the process of discovering similarities and differences among phenomena. Rather than being a second-order activity tacked onto more basic cognitive processes, comparison is central to the very acts of knowing and perceiving. As Ernst Cassirer observes:

> All the intellectual labor whereby the mind forms general concepts out of specific impressions is directed toward breaking the isolation of the datum, wresting it from the "here and now" of its actual occurrence, relating it to other things, and gathering it into some inclusive order. . . . By this process of running through a realm of experience, i.e., of discursive thinking, the particular receives its fixed intellectual "meaning" and definite character. It has definite appearances according to the ever-broadening contexts in which it is taken.[5]

Viewed as a fundamental operation in human thought, comparison is essential to any effort at social scientific analysis. Smelser (Chapter 2) points out that the aim of any science is to account for variation in empirical phenomena by specifying the conditions under which this variation occurs. For example, political scientists have long been interested in discovering the conditions (independent and intervening variables) that will account for certain directions of voting (dependent variable). A hypothesis is a proposed relationship between two or more variables, such as social class and party preference in voting. Comparison is involved in testing any hypothesis, for the investigator must hold some conditions constant (parameters) while allowing others to vary. In the example cited two parameters might be accuracy in the printing of the electoral ballots and the honesty of the officials supervising the elections (conditions that cannot be treated as constants in some countries). The essential analytic task is to seek out similarities in the relationship between two variables (social class and voting) under different conditions (electoral districts), with other conditions held constant. While comparison of this type is required to test any hypothesis, the complexity of the task increases when the range of observations is extended to include more than one society or culture, or the same society or culture at different points in time. When the scope of analysis is broadened in this way new challenges arise: the constants of one society must be treated as variables in another; the definition and measurement of variables may have to be modified to meet

---

[5]Ernst Cassirer, *Language and Myth*, trans. Susanne Langer (New York: Dover Publications, Inc., 1946), pp. 25–26.

shifting cultural conditions; hypotheses may have to be reworked, and so on.

In short, we use the term *comparative method* to refer to social scientific analyses involving observations in more than one social system, or in the same social system at more than one point in time. This definition would include a comparison between France and England in 1700, France in 1970 and England in 1900, or England in 1650 and England in 1972. We emphasize that our definition is not linked to any specific research *methodology*. Cross-societal comparisons may be based on historical analysis, survey research, small-group experimentation, use of aggregate data, participant observation, content analysis, or any other selection from the panoply of social science methods.

Advantages for Theory and Research

The assets of cross-societal comparison can be seen most clearly by relating this approach to the core requirements of theory building and theory testing. Using this yardstick, we would suggest five major benefits.

First, to be useful, social-scientific theory must be built upon clearly defined and culturally salient concepts and variables. Experience with cross-cultural research leaves little doubt that some concepts, such as "civil service," refer to phenomena that are not universally present even in the larger nation-states. Others, such as "industrialization" and "urbanization," often turn out to be multidimensional composites rather than unitary variables. William Goode's *World Revolution and Family Patterns*, an admirable example of comparative sociological research, shows that the relationship between industrialization and the nuclear family is much more complex than the British-American experience would suggest. Closer analysis indicates that "industrialization" embraces various subdimensions and that these are not related to each other in the same ways. Even with concepts such as "divorce," the need to achieve equivalent indices from one society to the next forces the social scientist to clarify the exact meaning of the concept.

Second, theories should cover the full range of behavior to be explained (dependent variables), and the full range of the explanatory conditions (independent variables) under consideration. Cross-cultural comparisons are clearly necessary for this task, for there is no single culture that covers the full range of behavior on all the variables central to a theory. Studies that confine themselves to a limited range of phenomena, whether the topic be political stability or personality disorders, may generate theories that are simply misleading. We cannot assume that the pattern of correlations obtained in the West, where the range of behavior may run from 3 to 5 on a 10-point scale, will hold up when the research is extended to cover the full spectrum of conditions or events.

Third, all theory aims at generality in the relationships postulated between variables. Here, too, cross-cultural comparison is essential, for there is no other way to determine the generality of findings than to test them in all relevant cultural settings. For example, political sociologists have long been interested in the relationship between social class and voting participation. One of the early findings in this field was that workers in the United States and Great Britain have a lower rate of electoral participation than the middle class. Cross-national research has demonstrated that this relationship is far from universal, even in the Western democracies.[6] Cities such as Vienna and Berlin are marked by relatively high rates of turnout in working-class districts. While these post-factum observations are helpful, the most direct road to generality of theory is through studies in which cultural, personality, and societal characteristics are systematically varied. Studies of this type require not only sound training in existing theory and sophistication in research methodology but sufficient familiarity with the societies in question to know *which* variables should be systematically varied in which situations.

Fourth, social scientific theory strives for comprehensiveness tempered by parsimony. A good theory is one that accounts for all the phenomena it sets out to explain with the least number of concepts and propositions. Comparative analysis may contribute to this goal by stimulating the search for new and/or simpler hypotheses about the relationships between variables. Sometimes, as with the advent of the evolutionary, diffusionist, or functionalist schools in anthropology, relatively new explanatory principles emerge. Cross-cultural research may thus have a heuristic function, serving as a source of hypotheses and theories. Similarly, one of its most valuable contributions may be to put pressure on the researcher to reduce proper names to more basic analytic factors, especially characteristics of total systems. For example, "in Germany and Sweden, better-paid workers are likely to be class conscious, whereas in Britain, the United States, and Australia, the less well-paid workers are class conscious."[7] This finding can be interpreted in several ways. One is simply to attribute the variation to "national differences"—West European countries are distinct from Anglo-American nations. This approach, however, says nothing about the kinds of causal factors sought by social science theories. A more productive approach would be to search for char-

[6]Cf. R. Bendix and S. M. Lipset, "Political Sociology," *Current Sociology*, 6 (1957), 79–99.

[7]A. Przeworski and H. Teune, *The Logic of Comparative Social Inquiry* (New York: Wiley-Interscience, 1970), p. 26.

acteristics of the two sets of nations that can be conceptualized as basic social scientific variables, such as status inconsistency. As Przeworski and Teune point out:

> The basic assumption is that names of nations, or of social systems in general, are treated as residua of variables that influence the phenomena being explained but have not yet been considered. Thus such concepts as "culture," "nation," "society," and "political system," are treated as residua of variables, which can be incorporated into a general theory. . . .
> If we accept the residual nature of names of social systems, we can then attempt to replace these names by variables. When we find that societies differ with regard to a particular characteristic, we can ask what it is about these societies that causes this difference.[8]

If comparative research sometimes aids the goal of comprehensiveness by suggesting more parsimonious explanations than previously existed, more often its contribution is that of specification. A well-designed cross-national study will typically find that a general hypothesis must be qualified to take account of varying patterns of conditions in the societies observed. This point is illustrated in the following hypothetical theory of political mobilization:

> Political mobilization depends upon exposure to mass media, membership in political organizations, and political socialization through the family; in those systems that have a regulated market, political mobilization depends upon individual mobility; in systems with free markets, political mobilization depends upon market involvement; if parties compete, it depends upon individual income; in addition, in India it depends upon the size of the community and in Chile, upon religiosity.[9]

While this set of multiple-contingency hypotheses offers scant consolation to those seeking neat theoretical explanations of social reality, it begins to approximate the complexity of political phenomena.

Fifth, comparative research often has a subtle and diffuse but generally salutary impact on the individual scholar's approach to theory and research. One common effect is a heightened sensitivity to the differential salience and researchability of concepts in varying cultural settings. For example, social psychologists may discover that research subjects in Latin America are less accustomed than U.S. students to standard laboratory methods. Some subjects may question their presence in "artificial" surroundings; others may not believe the instructions given by the experimenter or may provoke an argument over the procedures used. Com-

---

[8]*Ibid.*, p. 29.
[9]*Ibid.*, p. 85.

parable problems may arise because standardized personality or intelligence tests are much less common and accepted in Latin America than in the U.S. or Canada. Such experiences should make the social scientist more aware of both cultural differences and his own assumptions, whether in defining concepts, deciding on the suitability of a research method, or interpreting his findings. In other words, cross-cultural research experience may help to develop an apperceptive radar alerting the individual to cultural constants and variables.

CORE ISSUES IN COMPARATIVE ANALYSIS

Certain basic problems arise in comparative analysis whether the method of research is the sample survey, participant observation, historical analysis, or some other approach. These are (1) conceptual equivalence; (2) equivalence of measurement; (3) linguistic equivalence; and (4) sampling. These issues are brought into sharpest focus by the sample survey, which will be the major example in the following discussion. The article by Smelser (Chapter 2) provides insight into similar problems arising with historical and economic data, while the essay by Berreman (Chapter 13) suggests numerous sources of nonequivalence in ethnographic research.

1. Conceptual Equivalence

The most basic theoretical question in comparative analysis is whether the concepts under study have any meaning or equivalent meanings in the social units considered. Concepts may differ, first of all, along the dimension of *universality-specificity*. At a very general level some notions, such as "mother," "incest," "socialization," and "illness," can be regarded as applicable to all known cultures. This statement does not solve the many definitional questions surrounding these terms, nor does it lay to rest the related controversies about just what is universal. To state the point negatively, with concepts such as these the investigator has at least some hope of isolating constant reference points for cross-societal comparisons. Other concepts have meaning in many but not all cultures. The construct "federal bureaucracy" may provide a perfectly valid focus of comparison for nation-states, but it loses meaning when the analysis shifts to tribal or other less-differentiated social units. Finally, some concepts, such as "arctic hysteria," may be bound to specific cultures and may thus be of limited value for cross-societal analysis. However, even this concept could take on more general meaning if it were generalized to a present-absent (1–0) scale. A study could then be launched to explain why arctic hysteria is present in Eskimo cultures and absent from others. In Chapter 2 Smelser notes that a similar strategy was followed by Max Weber in his comparative research on the relation between religion and economic activity.

A second aspect of conceptual equivalence is *definitional comparability*. A major challenge of comparative research is to provide conceptual definitions that have equivalent, though not necessarily identical, meanings in various cultures. We will later consider problems of measurement arising even with concepts that meet this requirement. Inattention to definitional comparability has been a prime source of ethnocentric bias in cross-national research. Gunnar Myrdal (Chapter 3) underscores the distortions that have resulted from an uncritical application of Western concepts and theories to the nations of South Asia.

> When we economists, working within this tenacious but variegated and flexible tradition of preconceptions that admittedly are not too badly fitted to our own conditions, suddenly turn our attention to countries with radically different conditions, the risk of fundamental error is exceedingly great. This risk is heightened by the dearth of empirical data on social realities in the underdeveloped countries of South Asia, which enables many biases to be perpetuated that might be questioned and corrected if concepts and theories could be exposed to the challenge of concrete facts. The problem is compounded by another consequence of the Western-biased approach. When new data are assembled, the conceptual categories used are inappropriate to the conditions existing: as, for example, when underutilization of the labor force in the South Asian countries is analyzed according to Western concepts of unemployment, disguised unemployment, and underemployment. The resulting mountains of figures have either no meaning or a meaning other than that imputed to them. Empirical research then becomes faulty and shallow, and, more important, in the present context, less valuable for testing the premises latent in the Western concepts that have guided the production of new statistics. The very fact that the researcher gets figures to play with tends to confirm his original, biased approach.[10]

In a similar vein, Smelser (Chapter 2) highlights the conceptual difficulties involved in arriving at a satisfactory definition of *economic*.

The importance of comparable definitions is well illustrated in cross-cultural studies of mental disorders. The extensive research of Alexander Leighton and his associates on the relation of culture to mental disorder suggests that some psychiatric definitions derived from Western cultures are not necessarily applicable to other societies. In Chapter 4 Savage, Leighton, and Leighton review the standard diagnos-

[10]Chapter 3, p. 91.

tic criteria for psychiatric disorders in the light of cultural variations in symptoms. They comment as follows:

> As phenomena, the disorders are patterns of behavior and feelings that are out of keeping with cultural expectations and that bother the person who acts and feels them, or bother others around him, or both. Since, however, different cultures are by definition different systems of standards and expectations, it follows that what may be disturbing in one culture may be regarded as desirable in another.[11]

Both the methodological approach and the conclusions of this article are of interest for comparative social science.

Moving beyond this general approach, Leighton and several colleagues carried out a specific inquiry into conceptions of mental disorder among the Eskimos. The research team concluded that certain psychiatric terms used in the United States, including *mental deficiency* and *senility*, do not have exact counterparts in Eskimo culture. They note, however, that there are clusters of behavior comprising the syndromes of mental deficiency and senility, as defined by the American Psychiatric Association manual, but that their meaning is different than in the United States.

In general, the Leighton team found that patterns of symptoms commonly recognized as psychiatric disorders in the United States are divided by the Eskimos into two categories. The first consists of *psychologically expressed disorders*—personality characteristics reflected in an individual's thought patterns and overt behavior. Thus some members of this culture are considered "too much nervous" or "easy to get afraid." The indigenous explanations for these disorders ranged from magic and witchcraft to scientifically derived observations about genetic or physiological causation. The second category was *psychologically derived disorders*—physical sensations or disturbances of mood linked to psychological experience. Too much worrying, for example, was sometimes seen as the cause of "heart beating too much." Thus the Eskimos seem well aware of "psychiatric problems" and can differentiate mental or psychic malfunction from organic disturbances. Their classification of disorders differs from that seen in the United States, however, and their etiological explanation of symptoms places greater emphasis on the role of magic and witchcraft. The authors conclude:

> Although their psychiatric vocabulary varied in many respects, our subjects recognized disabilities that correspond to the whole range of major types of disorders identified in psychiatry. Even though the labeled

[11]Chapter 4, p. 100.

categories were different in terms of omissions and elaborations, they described the symptoms we commonly associate with senility, neurotic reactions, and so on. . . . In other words, there was no difficulty in differentiating between genuine pathology and socially useful behaviors that bear
some resemblance to psychopathology.[12]

The Murphy and Leighton study also touches on a final aspect of
conceptual equivalence: the *identifiability* of concepts in cross-societal
research. This is essentially a question of how an applicable concept
"surfaces" in a given culture—what are its outcroppings? This question,
of course, applies as much to equivalence of measurement as to conceptual equivalence. At one extreme is the situation in which a concept,
such as "mother," is readily identified both linguistically and observa-
tionally in almost every culture. At the opposite extreme are those cases
in which a concept can be considered theoretically salient, but where it
is not reflected fully or directly by the local language and thus must be
inferred from behavior. Among the Eskimos, for example, there is no
general term for *mental deficiency*, but members of this culture are at
least somewhat aware of the phenomena to which it refers. Under these
conditions the observer might have to infer deficiency from such indications as slow speech, poor performance in hunting and other valued activities, and slow advancement in school (where applicable). Wide variation in the identifiability of a core concept in comparative research not
only presents formidable problems of measurement—our next topic—but
also of interpretation.

2. Equivalence of Measurement

Beyond choosing variables that can be given comparable conceptual
definitions in the societies under study, the cross-cultural researcher faces
the further challenge of developing equivalent indicators for his concepts. Comparative research shares with all social scientific research the
normal difficulties of moving from theoretically meaningful concepts to
their empirically observable manifestations. However, special problems
are added by the fact that the transition is easier in some social units
than in others. Experience thus far suggests five overlapping problems
related to equivalence of measurement: differential researchability, and
comparability of stimuli, context, response, and reliability-validity.

RESEARCHABILITY. A critical difficulty in cross-societal studies is
that even theoretically applicable concepts may differ in their *salience* to

---

[12]J. M. Murphy and A. Leighton, "Native Conceptions of Psychiatric Disturbances," in *Approaches to Cross-Cultural Psychiatry* (Ithaca, N.Y.: Cornell University
Press, 1965), pp. 97–98.

a culture as a whole, or to specific subgroups within the society. Thus the notion of "looking for work," a key element in international studies of unemployment, may fall outside the experience of tribesmen and peasants in many parts of the "Third World."[13] The problem of irrelevance is especially acute in opinion surveys asking about the "national legislature," "public affairs," and other topics presuming awareness of national political units. Questions about concepts on which respondents have essentially no information or opinion may produce answers, but these are likely to be a better index of culturally defined response norms than of individual attitudes.

For example, a national probability sample survey carried out in Peru in 1970—the first in that country—contained various experimental items designed to measure traditional versus modern attitudes.[14] Among these was a set of questions containing a series of statements followed by three possible response categories: agree (*de acuerdo*), more or less agree (*más o menos de acuerdo*), and disagree (*en desacuerdo*). Field experience, especially in the rural areas of highland Peru, revealed several problems with these items. First, some of the concepts used in the statements were unintelligible to a segment of the respondents. One item read: "A person cannot change his own destiny." The interviewers reported that the word used for destiny or fate (*destino*) meant nothing to individuals with little education, while it was confusing to better-educated respondents. An even more serious problem arose from the response scale. Among the least educated, the very idea of ordering one's responses on such a scale was puzzling. To make matters worse, many did not understand the meaning of *acuerdo* and *desacuerdo*. The result was a series of "agree" responses which seemed to bear no relation to the content of the statements. As one interviewer put it, "some of the people answered just to answer."

A second barrier to researchability lies in the *unwillingness* of respondents or informants to discuss sensitive topics, such as politics, sexual behavior, income, or religion (see Chapters 10–13). In some cases, as in rural Peru, this reaction may stem from an unfamiliarity with the notion of research in general, or with a specific method. Because of its

---

[13]In this example serious questions could also be raised about the adequacy of the *conceptual* definition used in international comparisons. Unemployment is typically defined as a situation in which a person above a minimum age (such as fifteen) is out of work and looking for work. Phrased in this way the concept shows a decided bias toward urban-industrial conditions and against the life situation of the peasant.

[14]In September 1970 Donald Warwick prepared an evaluation of the fieldwork in this survey based on travel and detailed interviews with the field staff. The report was submitted as a memorandum to the Centro de Estadística de Mano de Obra (CEMO), Lima, Peru. The examples cited here and in subsequent pages are drawn from this evaluation.

short duration and the rapid-fire succession of questions, the sample survey often poses the greatest problems in this regard. In the Peruvian study many respondents openly expressed fears that the results would be used to increase taxes, expropriate property, force them to move from land to which they did not have legal title, or bring them harm in other ways.

The point to be emphasized is that difficulties in researchability may vary enormously from one society to another. In the United States it is not particularly difficult to obtain information on party preference and voting behavior; in many Latin American countries questions on these topics, where meaningful, arouse very strong suspicions. In the Peruvian survey, which came at a time of forceful governmental intervention in many spheres, questions about the military government were almost a total failure. One item asked: "Suppose that the government did something that you considered wrong and unjust; what could you and others like you do to stop it?" Many respondents bristled at this question, and some simply refused to answer. Others looked angrily at the interviewer and said: "What would *you* do?" This pattern of selective sensitivity is seen in other areas as well. Mitchell (Chapter 10) notes that ". . . it is said to be extremely difficult to obtain religious information in Moslem Pakistan, but relatively easy to do this in Hindu India. In some African areas, as well as in other parts of the world, there is reluctance to talk about dead children and the number of people in a household—obstacles to demographic researchers. In the Middle East there is reluctance to discuss ordinary household events, and Chinese businessmen in any country are reported to be especially secretive about any and all facets of their work and political lives."[15]

Finally, the researchability of a concept may vary because respondents are *unable* or *unaccustomed* to discuss it. This problem arose in a study of adolescents in Denmark:

> The socialization of adolescents is a problem faced in every society and we reasoned that all socializing agents—including teachers—would act to examine and rationalize their influence. Accordingly, we approached the Danish teachers for cooperation on the premise that they would acknowledge the desirability of being analytic about teaching and the characteristics of their students. The first hint that this premise was not accepted by Danish teachers occurred during the pre-test phase of developing the research instruments to be used with the teachers. Despite their apparent willingness to cooperate, the Danish teachers claimed that they were unaccustomed to considering analytically matters of adolescent interactions and could express no judgments or opinions. Indeed, despite strenuous

[15]Chapter 10, pp. 215–16.

efforts, only 30% of the Danish teachers completed the research materials in the study proper, forcing us to abandon this component of the investigation.[16]

The Peruvian study mentioned earlier provides a clear illustration of the inability of some respondents to grasp certain methodological techniques. The case in point involved the self-anchoring "ladder scale of aspirations" developed by Hadley Cantril and his associates. The survey question was introduced as follows:

> Here is a picture of a ladder. Suppose that the top is the best possible life for you, and that the bottom is the worst possible life for you.

The respondent was then asked to indicate his present position on the ladder, where he was five years before, and where he expected to be within five years.

Several problems arose with this scale, all related to an inadequate frame of reference. Some individuals had great difficulty in moving to the hypothetical level required. After repeating the question two or three times and still drawing no response, several interviewers (contrary to instructions) attempted to explain what might be meant by the "best possible life" and its opposite. The addition of concrete detail occasionally helped to break the deadlock. A few respondents, however, especially the illiterates, were totally unable to comprehend the task held out for them. One peasant in southern Peru seemed to understand the first of the three questions and pointed to one of the rungs to indicate his present position. However, when asked, "Where were you five years ago?" he replied, "In Ayacucho [an Andean city]."

COMPARABILITY OF STIMULI. A critical lesson learned from comparative research to date is that different indicators are often needed to tap the same concept in different cultures. If *intelligence* is defined as the ability to adapt effectively to the society in which one lives, the appropriate indices of adaptation will be different in rural Africa and urban United States, and perhaps even in different regions of each country. A United States test might use the following item to measure the ability to detect similarities and differences between objects: "What is the difference between a screwdriver and a wrench?" This same item will be a weak predictor of intelligence in a society that uses neither. This does not mean, however, that all items must be culture-specific. Smith and Inkeles claim that their OM scale, a sociopsychological measure of in-

[16]G. S. Lesser, "Advantages and Problems of Cross-Cultural Research," mimeographed (Harvard University, 1967), pp. 7–8.

dividual modernity, makes effective use of identical or near-identical items in six countries.

> We cannot leave the subject, however, without noting that from some points of view the derivation of a short scale to test modernity, however practically useful, is of only limited importance compared to some of the things we may note only in passing. To us the most fundamental of these observations lies in the evidence we find of the trans-cultural nature of the human psyche. We consider it notable in the highest degree that a pool of some 119 attitude questions and some 40 related informational and behavioral items should show such extraordinarily similar structure in six such diverse countries—and even more than that number of cultural groups. If we had started with the same theory and the same pool of items, but then devised a *separate or distinctive* scale of modernity for each of the six countries, the result might be interesting, but would not be compelling. Yet to find that in all six countries basically the *same set of items* both cohere psychologically and relate to external criterion variables in a strictly comparable fashion is, we believe, a finding of the first importance. It strongly suggests that men everywhere have the same structural mechanisms underlying their socio-psychic functioning, despite the enormous variability of the culture content which they embody.[17]

Unfortunately, the experience of other comparative studies does not provide a similar basis for optimism about the use of identical stimuli in very diverse cultures.

Since the question of equivalence in stimuli is particularly acute and visible in survey research, let us focus on this method. In general, four major options are open to the survey researcher for ensuring maximum cross-cultural equivalence in such stimuli as questionnaire items: (1) study design, (2) preliminary exploration, (3) flexible question format, and (4) the identity-equivalence procedure.

Study Design.   One effective approach to equivalence lies in a study design involving collaboration between knowledgeable members of all the participating societies. Duijker and Rokkan have suggested the following typology of organizational designs in cross-national research based upon the degree of collaboration with local researchers (repetitive vs. joint development) and the timing of the study (concurrent vs. successive):

> *Repetitive–successive:* the design, instructions, and research instruments are developed in one setting and then repeated in other cultures or nations.
> *Joint development–successive:* the design, instructions, and research in-

---

[17]D. H. Smith and A. Inkeles, "The OM Scale: A Comparative Sociopsychological Measure of Individual Modernity," *Sociometry* (1966), p. 377.

struments are the result of common decisions among participants from the several cultures; the study is tried first in one setting and then repeated in others.

Repetitive–concurrent: the design etc. are developed in one setting, usually by one investigator or organization, and the study is then carried out simultaneously in several cultures or nations. For example, an opinion survey might be designed by a U.S. sociologist, and then "farmed out" for simultaneous field work in the U.S. and several European countries.

Joint development–concurrent: the design etc. are arrived at jointly by collaborators from various cultures, and the study is carried out more or less simultaneously in these cultures.[18]

Although the practical problems involved in the last alternative (joint development–concurrent) are formidable, it is probably the most direct avenue to equivalence. The joint development–successive design also shares these advantages, but the study loses some degree of comparability from site to site because of the time lag involved. The success of the joint development design assumes, of course, that qualified investigators are available in each culture, that they are familiar with the cultural variations in their own societies, and that they are willing to work with others to hammer out a common and comparable design. These conditions are not always present.

Preliminary Exploration. In many cases a collaborative design will be either impractical for financial reasons or impossible because of the lack of trained social scientists in the societies under study. Such may be the case, for example, when the cultural units to be compared are peasant societies rather than nation-states. What can be done to promote equivalence of measurement under these conditions?

One option that is sometimes overlooked is to become as familiar as possible with the cultures through ethnographic reports, travelers' accounts, and the like. Such secondhand information is no panacea for equivalence, but it may suggest fruitful hypotheses and, perhaps more importantly, rule out or qualify others that do not fit.

Another fruitful type of preliminary exploration involves the collaboration of nonnative experts on the cultures to be investigated. This method was used by Savage and his colleagues (Chapter 4) in their research on the cross-cultural identification of mental disorders. The core problem facing this group was the following: "If we start with our traditional Western definitions of disorder and the criteria by which we recognize them, how far can we go with these into other cultures with some

---

[18]H. C. J. Duijker and S. Rokkan, "Organizational Aspects of Cross-National Social Research," *Journal of Social Issues,* 10 (1954), 8–24.

hope of being able to identify comparable phenomena?"[19] To explore this question the authors brought together anthropologists familiar with disparate cultural groups, such as the Rundi of Burundi, the Eskimos of St. Lawrence Island, and the Gilbert Islanders. By pooling their observations the research team was able to draw some tentative conclusions about the cultural generality of the major mental disorders found in the United States. This approach, which might be termed surrogate participation in other cultures, has much to commend it in the early stages of study design.

In the case of the sample survey, once the questions have been written much can be learned about their equivalence by *in situ* pilot testing. Pretests can be used to evaluate not only the adequacy and comparability of the survey questions but also the sample, the interviewers, the effectiveness of the field organization, the likelihood of controversy arising from the study, the rate of refusals and the reasons for them, the length and cost of the interviews, and the general appropriateness of the method to the problems under investigation. The temptation is always great, especially in complex cross-national studies, to rely on "swivel-chair" pretests carried out by experts in the research office. An abundance of sad experience shows, however, that office discussions are no substitute for live contacts in the field. Among the questions that might be considered in cross-national pretests are the following:

> Do the respondents understand what the study is about? After a reasonable "warm-up," do they feel comfortable in answering the questions? How is the study interpreted locally, and how are the interviewers located within the social structure (e.g., tax collectors, conscription agents, unidentified flying objects)?
>
> Is the wording of the questions clear? Do the respondents draw the same meaning from them as the study directors intended? Are the answers obtained in the various sites adequate for the purposes of the study? Is there sufficient detail? Are some cultural groups much more talkative or reticent than others? In the case of open-ended items, is there so much variation in the frames of reference within and between cultures that the responses will be difficult to code and analyze?
>
> Are there regional differences *within* the societies in the interpretation of the questions? Are there local expressions that should be incorporated to avoid ambiguity?
>
> Which items or sets of items are most difficult for the respondents to answer? Do these differ from culture to culture? Which seem to produce irritation, confusion, or embarrassment? Which seem to be regarded as irrelevant or even comical?

Pilot tests carried out *in situ* are usually expensive and time-consuming, especially in far-flung cross-national surveys. Nevertheless, they may

---

[19]Chapter 4, p. 101.

spell the difference between the success or failure of a comparative study. Most critics would agree that the well-known study of Almond and Verba, *The Civic Culture*, could have been much improved by careful and intensive pretesting.[20] Investments made at this stage typically pay handsome dividends not only in cross-national comparability but also in reduced headaches during the analysis stage. A month spent in pretesting may literally save years of tortuous analysis.

Flexible Question Format. The social scientist can never assume that a set of questions developed in one society can be translated and exported intact for use in other cultural settings. The perils of using identical stimuli modified only by translation are illustrated in *The Civic Culture*. A cardinal failing of this pioneering study was that the survey questions were developed in America by Americans for export to the other countries involved: Great Britain, Germany, Mexico, and Italy. Social scientists from these countries were not intimately involved in choosing the concepts and developing the questions, nor was there adequate pretesting. The major emphasis throughout was on arriving at items that were formally identical rather than functionally equivalent in meaning from society to society. As a result it is often difficult to determine whether the national differences reported in the findings stem from variations in national political cultures, from different meanings attached to the questions in the five countries, or from other irrelevant factors.

In certain situations it may be possible to approximate an identical set of items by choosing relatively universal problems for investigation and then allowing some flexibility in the question format used in each society. Inkeles and his colleagues adopted this approach in their six-nation study of individual modernity.[21] Their questionnaire represents, in effect, a compromise between wholly identical items and completely different indicators tailored to each cultural situation. The items were constructed by choosing themes judged to be salient in each country, such as holding political office, and then writing a stock question format which could be adapted to local conditions. For example:

C1–13 What should most qualify a man to hold high office?
　　　　1. Coming from (right, distinguished or high) family background
　　　　2. Devotion to the old and (revered, time honored) ways
　　　　3. Being the most popular among the people
　　　　4. High education and special knowledge[22]

[20]G. Almond and S. Verba, *The Civic Culture* (Princeton, N.J.: Princeton University Press, 1961).
[21]Smith and Inkeles, "The OM Scale."
[22]*Ibid.*, p. 372.

In any given society, such as in Chile, the wording was modified to reflect national or regional usage while still maintaining the general idea suggested by the response option. While this approach is clearly an improvement over the use of formally identical items in all cultures, it is subject to at least two limitations. First, it assumes that the entire dimension being measured, such as holding office, is equally salient and researchable in all the cultures involved. It may be that the concept of holding high office is highly salient and perfectly understandable in urban Chile, but less so in rural Nigeria. Second, the substitution procedure assumes that the alternatives are equivalent in meaning from culture to culture. To take a hypothetical example, it is possible that the notion of a "distinguished family background" in culture A carries a somewhat different connotation from the phrase "high family background" that is chosen for culture B.

The Identity-Equivalence Procedure.   In many if not most comparative studies preliminary investigation will suggest the need for indicators containing some items that are identical in all the cultural units and some that are specific to local conditions. We may find, for example, that the concept of *political action* is meaningful in the United States and Europe but that the pattern of salient *activities* differs in each country. Przeworski and Teune (Chapter 5) suggest the following as equivalent political activities in the United States and Poland:

United States	**Poland**
Contribute money to parties of candidates	Fight for execution of economic plans
Place sticker on car	Attempt to influence economic decisions
Volunteer help in campaigns	Join a party

To capture both the general and the specific elements at work in this situation, the authors suggest an empirical procedure called the *identity-equivalence* method. In brief, it operates as follows. First, the investigator attempts to develop questions measuring the relevant concepts in each country or culture. Some of these may be identical from society to society, others different. Second, a questionnaire is constructed which contains a large pool of items appropriate to the situation in each country. Items that would appear absurd in *any* of the social units to be studied are eliminated. Third, the entire questionnaire is administered in each setting. Each respondent answers every question, even those included because of their salience to other societies. Fourth, statistical analysis is carried out to isolate the *identical* items—those that "hang together" in similar ways across all the cultural units. Fifth, the analysis is extended to identify items with *equivalent* cross-cultural validity, that is, those that correlate highly with the identical items in one country but not others. For example, "placing a sticker on one's car" may be highly related to a general factor of participation in the United States, but in no other country. On the basis of this analysis, indices are constructed which include both identical and equivalent items for each country.

While as a general approach the identity-equivalence procedure is helpful in developing culturally sensitive indicators, it suffers from two major limitations. Most importantly, it requires respondents to answer a series of questions that may seem, if not foolish, at least irrelevant. In the example cited, one wonders how a Pole would regard a survey question asking whether or not he put a bumper sticker on his car, and how an American would view a query about fighting for the execution of economic plans. Yet the procedure seems to require that all questions be asked in all countries so that appropriate statistical tests can be made. The cost of this requirement may be that respondents become irritated with the whole questionnaire and thus answer with reduced seriousness and attention. Also, the procedure might force the investigator to omit certain items that were highly relevant for one or two cultures on the grounds that they would be considered foolish in others. The technique might be more useful if any item that would be considered irrelevant in any culture were eliminated from the core questionnaire, and if culture-specific items were added for use in single social units. This modification would make it more difficult to develop scales through the usual statistical techniques, but it might produce gains in validity and equivalence.

COMPARABILITY OF CONTEXT. The equivalence of measurement in field research will depend in good part on the comparability of the situations in which information is gathered. In any study involving contact with people, a question or a field observer becomes a "stimulus" in a specific spatiotemporal, political, and perceptual context. Thus the same survey questionnaire or the same participant observer may become quite different research stimuli as circumstances change from one setting to another. Berreman (Chapter 13) provides a vivid account of the way in which an ethnographic team was perceived in a Himalayan village, and of the implications of shifting perceptions for the research process. He writes: "The ethnographer comes to his subjects as an unknown, generally unexpected, and often unwanted intruder. Their impressions of him will determine the kinds and validity of data to which he will be able to gain access and hence the degree of success of his work."[23]

[23]Chapter 13, p. 284.

The situational forces bearing most strongly on personal interviews are the time and place of contact, the presence of "third parties," the attitudes toward the study in the surrounding community, and the sequence of the interviews. The place at which the interview is carried out may be psychologically significant because of the fears or associations evoked in the respondent. Cross-national employee surveys carried out in a factory manager's office may elicit attitudes different from those completed in a union hall. Moreover, in some cultures a male-female interview carried out in complete privacy may generate anxiety in the respondent (as well as the interviewer) and may cast suspicion on the entire study. The timing of the interview will also affect the willingness of respondents to participate, and sometimes their ability to provide certain types of time-linked information.

One of the greatest problems in cross-cultural surveys is the presence of "third parties" during the interview. In the 1970 national survey in Peru it was estimated that individuals other than the respondent were present in at least 50 percent of the interviews.[24] In some cases the audience consisted of seven or eight relatives and friends. In his report on the fieldwork in this study, Warwick noted several problems arising from this situation. First, there were numerous instances in which higher-status individuals tried to interject answers for the respondent. A typical case was seen in interviews with domestic servants carried out in the presence of their employers. With some questions the *señora* of the household would say, "What does she know about that?" or "She doesn't know anything—why are you asking her that?" With questions on the employee's income and social benefits, on the other hand, the *señora* would insist on providing the information herself, with obvious possibilities for distortion. Second, because the sample design called for interviews with all residents fifteen years of age and over, there was a great risk of group norms on responses to opinion questions. One interviewer reported a situation in which the head of the household, who was interviewed first, apparently instructed his children, who were to be interviewed the next day, on the proper answers to questions about ideal family size. Third, the presence of "third parties" seems to have placed some respondents under pressure to disguise or distort their answers in the direction of prevailing expectations. This problem has been reported in many studies. The effect of outside observers, however, is not always negative. As Mitchell (Chapter 10) points out, "in studies seeking information rather than attitudes, third parties may help keep the respondent honest and also help him to remember the requested information. In other instances, especially with women and younger people, respondents may refuse to be interviewed unless a third person is present."[25]

[24]These examples are drawn from the report cited in footnote 14.
[25]Chapter 10, p. 220.

Further discussion of the problem of "third parties" can be found in Chapters 10, 11, and 12. The point to be underscored in this discussion is that *variations* in the influence of these observers can be a major source of nonequivalence in comparative research.

Community attitudes toward the research may also influence decisions to participate as well as other facets of the interview. When the research is carried out in hostile territory, both the interviewer and the respondent may be highly guarded in their communications. Similarly, in communities showing a high degree of polarization along racial, ethnic, or political lines, the validity of the information may be severely curtailed if the interviewer identifies or appears to identify with one or another faction. Similar problems arise from the sequence in which the interviews are conducted. In traditional communities the interviewer is often advised to begin with the highest-status individual in the sample, and also with those who are most willing to participate. The legitimacy afforded by such high-status contacts may help to secure cooperation in the rest of the community. The danger, however, is that the message endorsing the interviewer may also contain information on the proper responses to delicate questions. Though these situational factors are difficult to control in advance, they should at least enter into the final reckoning on equivalence of measurement.

COMPARABILITY OF RESPONSE. Even questions that are identical in meaning and comparable in context may elicit different patterns of responses for reasons unrelated or only slightly related to item content. One factor known to influence both the quantity and the quality of responses is *differential loquacity*. Mitchell (Chapter 10) notes, for example: "If one examines marginals from studies conducted in Malaysia, one will notice that the Chinese, when compared with the Indians, have a much higher proportion of 'no answers' to pre-coded questions and fewer answers to open-ended questions. One of the reasons for this is that the Chinese are quite reticent, whereas the Indians are loquacious. This creates problems in comparing the two groups; and, of course, if the Chinese, the Indians, and Malaysians are treated as a single national sample, the Chinese will be underweighted and the Indians overweighted."[26]

Nonequivalence may also result from *differential response styles* in the several cultures. A response style is a tendency to choose a response category, such as "yes" or "agree," regardless of an item's content.[27] The

[26]*Ibid.*, p. 216.

[27]Cf. L. G. Rorer, "The Great Response Style Myth," *Psychological Bulletin*, 63 (1965), 129–50. This article summarizes much of the literature dealing with "response sets" and challenges some of the conclusions which have entered into the conventional wisdom of psychometrics. Like most articles in this field, however, it does not even raise the problem of response styles in cross-cultural research.

response style of *acquiescence* has received the greatest attention in methodological research. It is seen when respondents choose a disproportionate number of positive answers, especially "yes," "agree," and "true." Serious problems of interpretation arise in cross-cultural studies if respondents in one society are more prone to acquiescence than those in others. Two specific issues merit attention in this regard. First, are there aspects of the culture itself that predispose an individual toward one or another response category, irrespective of his "true" opinion? Second, in a given study are there factors related to response sets, such as education and social class, that vary across the samples? For example, Landsberger and Saavedra present data showing that in Chile acquiescence is highest in the least-educated strata of their sample.[28] If education and similar factors are the only sources of differences in response styles, the problem of comparability between societies can be handled by the usual statistical controls. If, however, there are genuine cultural differences, or if there is an interaction between culture and education, life will become complicated for the data analyst. In our view the most effective solution to the problem of response styles is prevention—avoidance of such question formats as "agree-disagree," which are highly susceptible to distortion.

COMPARABILITY OF RELIABILITY AND VALIDITY.   A central goal of all social research is to obtain accurate measurements of the phenomena under study. *Accuracy* may be defined as the generalizability of the measurements taken to all the measurements that might have been taken of the concept in question (cf. Chapter 9). In comparative research the question of accuracy is complicated by the need to establish generalizability for each cultural group. Some of the challenges involved have already been discussed in connection with equivalence of measurement.

Traditionally, a distinction has been drawn between two aspects of accuracy: reliability, or the consistency of a measure with itself, and validity, or the extent to which a set of observations measures what it purports to measure. Following Cronbach, Rajaratnam, and Gleser, we may recast these concepts as follows:[29] Reliability is the generalizability of a measure to other measures of the same phenomenon obtained with the *same* method, such as psychological tests or rater's judgments. Validity, in turn, is the generalizability of a measure to other measures of the same phenomenon obtained with *different* methods. Thus a paper-and-

[28]H. Landsberger and A. Saavedra, "Response Set in Developing Countries," *Public Opinion Quarterly*, 31 (1967), 214–29.

[29]L. J. Cronbach, N. Rajaratnam and G. C. Gleser, "Theory of Generalizability: A Liberalization of Reliability Theory," *British Journal of Statistical Psychology*, 16 (1963), 137–63.

pencil test of intelligence would be reliable if it correlated highly with a similar test made up of comparable but different items; it would be valid if it correlated reasonably well with a student's school performance, the ratings of knowledgeable observers, or other appropriate external criteria.

In cross-cultural research one of the most difficult tasks is to determine if a given measure, such as an attitude scale, shows equivalent reliability and validity across the units studied. Various approaches are open for assessing reliability. One possibility is to use standard statistical techniques, such as variance formulas, to compare the internal consistency of the items in the various cultures. This approach was adopted by Smith and Inkeles in their questionnaire study of individual modernity. Using the Spearman-Brown formula, which is based on average item-to-test correlations, they found that the reliability coefficients were roughly similar in the six countries covered by their research. Other formulas found in works on psychometrics could be used for the same purpose.[30] The problems of assessing reliability are more complex when the method of data gathering is participant observation. Even here, however, it would not be unreasonable, when possible, to have two observers keep an independent record of the major phenomena under investigation. Though this suggestion would obviously be difficult to implement in many ethnographic situations, the availability of at least two sets of observations for each culture studied would permit a gross calculation of reliability.

The usual method of assessing validity is to determine the relationship of a measure to some outside criterion thought to capture the same underlying trait. In comparative surveys, correlations can be computed between each major indicator of a concept and theoretically meaningful outside criteria. In their six-nation survey, Smith and Inkeles sought evidence for the validity of their individual modernity scale in its relationships with various social factors thought to be vehicles of modernization, including education, urban experience, and occupational history. In general, the stronger the relationships and the closer their patterning resembles that suggested by the guiding theory, the greater the case for validity. It should be emphasized, however, that validity can never be measured simply or directly; there is no one "validity coefficient." Ultimately the case rests upon a judgment about the appropriateness of a set of relationships between a measure and other variables. A significant feature of cross-cultural studies is that the pattern of relationships suggesting high validity may vary from situation to situation. Assume, for

[30]See J. C. Nunnaly, *Psychometric Theory* (New York: McGraw-Hill Book Company, 1967), esp. Chap. 7; and J. P. Guilford, *Psychometric Methods* (New York: McGraw-Hill Book Company, 1954), Chap. 14.

instance, that there are two measures of religious orthodoxy, one for Latin American Catholics and the other for Middle Eastern Moslems. A high correlation between the "Catholic" scale and church attendance would be evidence of validity in Latin America. An identical correlation between Latin American orthodoxy and religious observance in the Middle East might well be considered negative evidence for its validity. In short, decisions about the equivalence of reliability and validity can never be made in a mechanical fashion. The investigator must have an intimate knowledge of each culture in which he is working and must ultimately make a qualitative assessment of the "fit" between theoretical predictions and his data. Chapter 6 discusses an inventive approach to the assessment of accuracy in cross-cultural surveys. This is the "random probe technique" developed by Howard Schuman in his research on Pakistan.

3. Linguistic Equivalence

The problems of attaining linguistic equivalence through translation have received more attention from social scientists than any other aspect of cross-cultural research. A decade ago the question of translation was typically treated in quasi-mechanical fashion as a subtopic of equivalence in measurement. Heavy emphasis was placed on finding the right words to arrive at constant stimuli for use in diverse cultures. From the late forties through the mid-sixties the techniques for carrying out this process grew in sophistication, but the emphasis remained the same—on words. Now, partly as a reaction against the rigidities of the first approach, the pendulum has swung from words to "meaning." Deutscher (Chapter 8) argues that the primary aim of translation should be conceptual equivalence rather than strict lexical comparability. Some even hold that translation itself is a waste of time because it directs attention to words rather than ideas. We will return to this question after reviewing some of the issues at stake.

DIMENSIONS OF EQUIVALENCE. One of the challenges as well as frustrations in cross-cultural research is that, on the one hand, there are numerous demands for equivalence that must be met simultaneously and, on the other, one is never quite sure if he has met them. In the present instance we can point to six dimensions of equivalence confronting the social scientist concerned with conceptual-linguistic comparability.[31] The first is *lexical meaning*—the significance attached to the vocabulary itself, as distinct from grammatical construction. Some of the more common

[31]The following discussion draws on S. Ervin and R. T. Bower, "Translation Problems in International Surveys," *Public Opinion Quarterly*, 16 (1952), 595–604.

lexical problems in translation include the absence of objective referents (one society may not have a word for an object existing in another); untranslatable concepts, such as "nice"; and varying affective overtones elicited by similar words in different languages. Second, languages show great differences in *grammatical meaning*. A major obstacle to completely prearranged translation in cross-national surveys lies, for example, in varying syntactical requirements. As Ervin and Bower observe: "The grammar of some languages requires commitment as to the sex and social status of the speaker or hearer, or statements about location, agency, possession, sources of information and aspects of time which are not necessary in English. On the other hand some information is included in English which is not necessary in certain other languages. In either case, translation into an understandable form of the other language involves the introduction of pseudo-information or the loss of information."[32] Third, the quest for linguistic equivalence must pay due regard to the differential effects of *context*. This is an especially important consideration in survey research where it has been shown that such contextual factors as question sequence and the distribution of response alternatives (e.g., four favorable, one unfavorable vs. two favorable, three unfavorable) can have major effects on the findings.[33] It is generally recognized that the order of items in a survey questionnaire should also take account of the expectations, logic, and limitations of both the respondent and the interviewer—and these will almost certainly differ according to culture. An effective opening question in Boston, such as "How long have you been living in the Boston area?," may be totally ineffective when applied in Bangkok. Similarly, the entire sequence of questions may have to be changed in different areas, even within the same country, to provide for a smoothly flowing interview. Fourth, specific attention must be paid to the relationship between language and *response styles*. As noted earlier, it is quite possible that opinion questions worded in the typical "agree-disagree" format may be more conducive to an acquiescent response style (yea-saying) in one society than in another, even if the items are judged equivalent by the usual standards of translation. Fifth, and very critical, "correctly" translated linguistic stimuli can differ in their overall *salience* to the culture. The problem of equivalent salience arises not only with verbal stimuli but with such seemingly culture-free instruments as the Rorschach or the Thematic Apperception Test (TAT). As Anderson points out in Chapter 7, the challenge with the latter tests is to arrive at a faithful reproduction of their ambiguity in

[32]*Ibid.*, pp. 597–98.
[33]See S. Payne, *The Art of Asking Questions* (Princeton, N.J.: Princeton University Press, 1951).

each culture. Sixth, a major problem in some surveys consists of attaining *equivalence of scale points.* In his study of Israel, Blanc found it difficult to arrive at exact equivalents for scale markers indicating intensity of response, such as "many," "very many," "too many," "much," and "too much."[34] The issue of "linguistic markers" is discussed further in Chapter 8.

APPROACHES TO LINGUISTIC EQUIVALENCE.   How, then, can the conscientious social scientist deal with the problems of conceptual-linguistic equivalence? Given the many difficulties just noted, it is very easy to abandon all hope for the future of cross-cultural research. The tendency to despair is sometimes unwittingly reinforced by initiates in the field who wish to maintain an aura of mystery about comparative research, and perhaps keep poachers from their favorite preserve. However, the situation is neither as desperate as the extreme relativists would have it nor as simple as suggested by early attempts at translation.

The procedures for translation have shown marked improvements over the past three decades. In some of the earliest comparative surveys the "commonsense" approach to translation involved the use of bilinguals: one would read the questionnaire and translate it into his native language, with perhaps some cross-checking by another. This method came under attack as specialists in linguistics pointed out that (1) bilinguals in general may use their native language differently than monolinguals in the same society and (2) there are several types of bilinguals, each of which may have its own style of translation.[35] The next step, representing a major advance in research methodology, involved the use of "back-translation." In this case the questionnaire is translated from language A to language B by a native speaker of language B, then from B to A by a native speaker of A, then from A to B by a third party, and so on until discrepancies in meaning are clarified or removed. This procedure is illustrated in Gerald Lesser's comparative study of adolescents in Denmark and the United States:

1. The original questionnaires . . . were translated into Danish, then another translator independently translated this Danish version back into English.

2. Original and re-translated English versions were then compared and discrepancies clarified and corrected.

3. A second Danish version was then pre-tested in interviews with in-

[34]H. Blanc, "Multilingual Interviewing in Israel," *American Journal of Sociology*, 62 (1956), 205–9.

[35]See, for example, C. E. Osgood and T. A. Sebock, "Psycholinguistics: A Survey of Theory and Research," Supplement to *Journal of Abnormal and Social Psychology*, 1954.

dividual adolescents, with probes used to assess the meaning of the questions to them.

4. Based upon this pre-test information, the Danish questionnaire was again revised and then back translated, this time into English and once again into Danish.

5. Field interviewing in small groups then constituted the next trial phase.

6. A final back translation was performed.[36]

For a time it seemed as if back-translation was the sovereign and lasting remedy for the ills of linguistic equivalence. But before long, this technique also fell victim to sharp criticism. Deutscher (Chapter 8) states the objections very well:

> The back translation procedure does indeed guarantee that the words translate accurately or reveal that they do not. But back translation can also instill a false sense of security in the investigator by demonstrating a spurious lexical equivalence. Since language is a cultural artifact, it must be assumed that the question is being addressed to peoples who are immersed in two different cultural milieux. To the extent that this is so, it is not sufficient to know simply that the words are equivalent. It is necessary to know the extent to which those literally equivalent words and phrases convey equivalent meanings in the two languages or cultures. . . .[37]

Anderson (Chapter 7) suggests that the discrepancies produced by the various cycles of back-translation might be treated as a source of new items rather than as obstacles to be eliminated. That is, the different versions of questions produced by independent translators could be used as a basis for constructing alternative forms of the questionnaire. From the standpoint of test reliability and validity, the technical advantages of this approach are considerable. As he states: "Back-translation, when used as an iterative procedure with a new translation for each iteration, will produce a population of items in each language with heterogeneous and random errors. A random sample of items in each language, or use of different versions with randomly selected subsamples of subjects, should provide equivalence save for random error."[38]

Ultimately the issue of linguistic equivalence is inseparable from the theory and concepts guiding the study, the problems chosen, and the research design. Very often difficulties in translation are more the result of a poorly conceived study than of inadequate techniques. The following suggestions are offered with an eye to setting the problem of linguistic

[36]Lesser, "Advantages and Problems of Cross-Cultural Research," p. 13.
[37]Chapter 8, p. 167.
[38]Chapter 7, p. 159.

equivalence within the broader framework of conceptualization and research design.

1. One of the most effective aids to linguistic equivalence is a research problem that is salient to the cultures involved. Most of the articles published on translation, including those in this volume, emphasize the esoteric and the difficult cases. However, many studies present relatively few problems of translation. In general, the closer a concept is to the everyday life of a people, the fewer the problems of language. Questions about housing construction, migration, the more obvious aspects of occupations, children, and the like are relatively easy to deal with precisely because they require little abstraction from common experience. On the other hand, items dealing with public opinion, political affairs, international relations, and the like almost universally present difficulties of translation in the developing countries, in good part because of their limited salience.

2. The primary emphasis in translation should be on conceptual equivalence—comparability of ideas—rather than formally identical words in each culture. Perhaps because of a deeply embedded stimulus-response tradition in the field of psychological testing, social scientists using questionnaires seem to have been overly mechanical and rigid in their approach to translation. The underlying assumption has often been that if the stimuli, that is, the questionnaire items, were rendered formally identical through translation, their impact on the respondent would also be identical. This overemphasis on strict linguistic comparability is seen not only in studies drawing upon several languages but even in cross-national research using the same language in different countries. One of the authors had the experience a few years ago of participating in a debate in which a Chilean participant in a cross-national survey insisted that Chilean Spanish be preserved in a questionnaire to be used in Peru, even though it contained several expressions not understood by most Peruvians. Her argument was that it would be better to lose meaning in the interests of preserving formal equivalence.

3. Many problems of translation can be avoided by *advance* familiarity with the cultures to be studied. This point was raised earlier with regard to equivalence of measurement, but it applies as well to translation. A good portion of the difficulties seen to date stem from the fact that questionnaires were originally designed for use in one culture and then "farmed out" for replication elsewhere. The random probe technique (Chapter 6) is a helpful adjunct to interpretation when this type of design is unavoidable, but it would be much better to carry out the probing in advance and use the resulting information to construct more meaningful and translatable items.

4. Back-translation remains one of the most helpful tools open to the cross-cultural researcher, especially when used creatively. One example of such creativity is seen in Hudson's study of the Middle East and the United States.[39] When discrepancies arose in the initial back-

[39]B. Hudson, M. K. Barakat, and R. LaForge, "Problems and Methods of Cross-Cultural Research," *Journal of Social Issues*, 15 (1959), 5–19.

translations, Hudson used them as a basis for further field interviews aimed at clarifying the meaning attached to his terms in English and Arabic.

5. Whether or not successive back-translations are used, conceptual-linguistic equivalence can be improved through extensive pretesting of the research instruments in the local culture. Especially important are *qualitative* pretests in which respondents are asked not only for their answer but for their interpretation of the item's meaning.

In sum, conceptual equivalence, equivalence of measurement, and linguistic equivalence are tightly interwoven and should be treated as a single fabric. Some of the more glaring weaknesses in existing cross-cultural studies arise from a tendency to separate these issues and treat them in a piecemeal fashion.

4. Sampling

Sampling is a procedure in which a fraction of a group is chosen to represent the total population about which generalizations will be made. It is customary in the social sciences to think of sampling mainly in the context of selecting individuals or households for a sample survey. However, in comparative cross-cultural research, sampling may occur in various ways, including the following:

1. *The selection of research sites.* One of the first questions arising in cross-cultural research concerns the population of units about which generalizations are to be made. Does it include all societies in existence at the time of the study? all societies that have ever existed? all contemporary nation-states? all peasant villages now in existence? and so forth.

2. *The choice of research methods.* In many studies it is possible to approach the problem selected through two, three, or more research methodologies. The fact that an investigator chooses one means that he is, in effect, sampling from the universe of available methods and that his choice may lead to different findings than if he had selected another approach.

3. *The selection of population elements.* The individuals, households, or other units to be studied within a given society.

4. *The choice of indicators used to measure the major concepts.* This decision is, of course, related to the research methodology selected. In survey research we can conceive of a fairly large universe of items reflecting an underlying dimension, such as authoritarianism. By choosing only some of these, the investigator is relying on sampling.

5. *Combining indicators into indices.* The process of index construction involves a decision about which of the various indicators of a given concept are *most* representative of that concept. Here the investigator

may turn to such empirical procedures as factor analysis, or he may use his own expert judgment as the basis for selection. In either case he is choosing a sample of a larger population of units and using it to represent the whole.

The basic question emerging from this overview concerns the population about which the researcher wishes to generalize, whether it be people, nations, methods, or findings. While all the issues raised are important considerations in comparative research, two are particularly deserving of attention in the planning stages: (1) the selection of countries or societies—the first stage of sampling, and (2) the sampling of population elements within societies or countries.

THE SELECTION OF COUNTRIES OR SOCIETIES.   One of the more curious aspects of cross-national surveys is the tendency of investigators to apply stringent standards of probability in drawing samples within the societies and to ignore these same standards in choosing the societies themselves. On the basis of the cross-national studies conducted to date, it is safe to conclude that this first stage of sampling is often far from random—despite the *post hoc* rationalizations sometimes accompanying the research report. Many human considerations enter into decisions about research sites. The most commonly cited constraints are transportation costs, accessibility, availability of research sites, and other questions of convenience. Unfortunately, decisions relying heavily on such criteria may skew the sample in the direction of the more wealthy nations, for ease of transportation and quality of research facilities are correlated with economic development. Climate and living conditions for the researcher and his family, including schools, housing, and sanitation, may also affect the choice of sites—as will the touristic possibilities within the country and nearby. Thus Mexico and Chile have been popular sites in Latin America, while Paraguay, Ecuador, and Bolivia have been left to the ethnographers. Closely related to the "touristic bias" is the character of the cultures in question. Some investigators (or their wives) may prefer the more exotic flavor of the East, while others prefer milieus departing only slightly from their own. More subtle preferences may also come into play, especially feelings of religious, ethnic, or ideological affinity with a region. North American social scientists have often been partial to countries billed as "democratic," such as Nigeria in the early 1960s, and have avoided others tainted by authoritarianism, including Spain and Portugal. Similarly, Jewish investigators seem more likely than non-Jews to select Israel, while Catholics may incline more toward Latin America and sons of Protestant missionaries toward the Far East. Fads, traditions, and the reward structure within the social science professions may also be important, if unrecognized, influences on decisions about national units. Comparative politics and international relations have long shown a marked predilection for Western Europe and the United Kingdom, while specialists in demography have been more intrigued with India. All these human factors may sharply reduce the degree of randomness present in the first stage of sampling.

The problems of interpretation created by arbitrary and inadequate first-stage sampling are well illustrated in *The Civic Culture*.[40] A major weakness of its sample design is that the population of nations about which generalizations were to be drawn is never given a precise definition. The authors indicate that the study focuses on "the culture of democracy," but they provide neither an exact conceptual definition of democracy nor an operational "sampling frame" of nations judged to be democratic. The procedures followed in selecting the countries were also far from random, and not entirely clear. The authors state that "our comparative study of political culture includes five democracies—the United States, Great Britain, Germany, Italy, and Mexico—selected because they represent a wide range of political historical experience."[41] While the exact range of political-historical experience encompassed by the study is left undefined, several specific reasons for the selection of these five nations are given: the desire to compare the oft-contrasted United States and Britain on a series of variables; the German state's history of extensive power and control over the citizenry during its predemocratic phase; and the fact that Italy and Mexico are representative of "less well-developed societies with transitional political systems."[42] These criteria suggest a rather variegated sampling frame, including such dimensions as prior comparative research, certain types of historical experience, degree of economic development, and, within the less-developed societies, the character of the present political systems. However, even accepting the then-current population of "democratic" nations as a sampling frame, we would still have to conclude that the nations chosen were a very skewed sample. All five are Western nations, three of them European. While no country can be considered in any sense "typical" of developing nations, Mexico and Italy certainly seem very improbable choices. Even within the pale of Latin American nations the "Mexican case" is considered to be most unrepresentative, especially because of its revolutionary history, the presence of a virtual single-party system, and its proximity to the United States. Apparently no attempt was made to include a non-Western democracy, such as Japan, India, the Philippines, or Nigeria. At one

[40]Almond and Verba, *The Civic Culture*.
[41]*Ibid.*, p. 37.
[42]*Ibid.*, p. 39.

point Sweden seems to have been preferred over Mexico but was eliminated in midstream. The authors provide no explanation for this shift,
nor do they comment on why the entire democratic tradition of Scandinavia is completely excluded from the sample. It thus seems that considerations of convenience and a series of fortuitous events, rather than a
predesigned sampling scheme, led to the selection of the five countries
covered in this research. As a result the generalizability of the findings
to other nations is simply unknown.

SAMPLING WITHIN SOCIETIES. The problems of sampling within
single societies, whether they be nation-states or other units, are more
familiar, but still greatly complicated by the demands of cross-societal
comparisons. Four of the most common and vexing problems are (1) the
use of noncomparable or low-quality sampling frames, (2) the differing
selection procedures, (3) the overrepresentation and underrepresentation
of population elements, and (4) the high or varying nonresponse rates.
All these difficulties can again be illustrated in the Almond and Verba
study.

Sampling Frames: In their study Almond and Verba utilized a
"repetitive-concurrent" approach in designing the samples. That is, sampling procedures were designed and carried out independently by a local
research agency within each nation studied. This meant that no one
agency was responsible for overseeing the sampling procedures followed
and for ensuring comparability between the countries. A critical difference between the samples drawn in the five nations lies precisely in the
sampling frames used. A *sampling frame* is some type of list or other
device serving as the operational definition of the population under
study, such as enumeration records, electoral registers, or lists of employees. In the United States a probability sample was obtained by
dividing the country into metropolitan and nonmetropolitan areas, and
then into smaller localities. Census tracts within the larger cities and
census enumeration districts within the smaller municipalities were used
to select the dwelling units in which interviews were to be carried out.
In Mexico, on the other hand, the sampling frame was limited to cities
of ten thousand or more inhabitants. The country was divided into five
urbanization strata according to population size, and then specific cities
were randomly selected from each. The final stage of sampling, the
selection of households, was carried out through the use of town maps.
The German sample began with two strata, one representing communities with two thousand or more inhabitants, the other communities with
less than two thousand. After communities were selected from these
strata, the households to be contacted were drawn from a central regis-

trar of inhabitants. In both England and Italy the sampling frame consisted of electoral registers of *individuals* rather than lists of households. It is clear that a sample fulfilling stratified, multistage probability requirements in most of the design can lose its probability aspect in the last stage—the choice of individuals or households from the sampling frame. Mitchell (Chapter 10) writes:

> There are obvious differences in sampling units based on voting registers and those based on households; the former may consist primarily of men who are highly politicized, whereas the latter might also include a much higher proportion of all adults in the total universe. . . . Often the average size and complexity of the household differs in different parts of the interviewing area. . . . In these cases the sampling units and nations used to select respondents may overweight certain portions of the population and alter the selection probabilities of various segments of the universe.[43]

The quality of the materials forming the sampling frame may further introduce noncomparability and error into the samples. In the Almond and Verba study, the United States frame seems to have been of the highest quality, since it was based on reliable census information. It is likely, on the other hand, that the Mexican frame was of dubious quality, given that it relied on town maps which were probably outdated in many cases.

Selection Procedures: The comparability of samples in cross-societal research can be further reduced by the use of different procedures for choosing households or respondents. In some countries strata may be filled through the use of probability methods at each step, while in others quota samples are used (e.g., standing on a corner and interviewing ten males between the ages of thirty-five and forty-five). Thus it is not enough for a researcher to show that in each country the proportion of individuals falling into a given category in the sample, such as males over forty, is the same as in the national census; much depends on how these individuals were actually chosen.

The following quotations suggest considerable variation in the selection procedures used in *The Civic Culture:*

> *Italy:* As regards the population of twenty-one and over, the random selection was made by means of systematic sampling from the general electoral registers. It was considered preferable to use these registers and to avoid an intermediate selection from a few electoral areas, in order to obtain the widest distribution of the sample within the territory of the commune, and, consequently, maximum variability of the persons interviewed. . . .

[43]Chapter 10, p. 208.

As regards the sample of persons between the ages of eighteen and twenty-one, it was not possible to make a selection by means of official records of population. An empirical system of selection was therefore adopted, by which the interviewers selected persons exclusively from families or the houses of electors selected at random. This system, though not a strictly random one, made it possible almost completely to eliminate the risk of bias due to the selection by the interviewer; . . .[44]

United Kingdom: For each polling district a systematic selection of individuals was made: that is, names were taken at fixed intervals. This procedure gives a well-spread sample of electors, but special provision had to be made to obtain a sample of nonelectors.

For two of the polling districts in the selected constituency twenty names were selected (by dividing the total number of electors by nineteen and taking half the remainder as a starting point).

For the other polling district thirty-two names were selected in a similar manner, but of these, twelve were treated as samples of households, and all electors living in those twelve households were listed. At these households attempts were made to interview only a nonelector. Whenever more than one nonelector was found to be living in a single household, the birthday rule was used to select the one to be interview [*sic*]: that is, the nonelector whose birthday was nearest to the day of the interview. In this way a proportion of nonelectors in each constituency was to be obtained.

For electors the required quota was twelve interviews per polling district. To achieve this, the interviewers were instructed to first attempt to contact fourteen of the twenty names selected for each polling district. The remaining six names were to be used as reserves in case of refusals and noncontacts.[45]

Germany: In the selected households all members aged eighteen years and older were listed in unique order of succession. From this list the person to be questioned was determined, again by the use of random numbers. Substitutions were not allowed.[46]

These passages point up various inconsistencies in the methods adopted for choosing respondents. In both Italy and the United Kingdom electoral lists served as the sampling frame, while the procedure of systematic selection (including every 3rd, 5th, 10th, or nth name) was used as the basis to pick individuals. Also, in both countries households of electors were used in arriving at a sample of nonelectors. In Italy, however, this sample was limited to persons between the ages of eighteen and twenty-one and was chosen by an "empirical system of selection." In the United Kingdom the sample of nonelectors included individuals from a broader age range and was drawn by a different and seemingly more complex procedure. It is not clear from the discussion whether the inter-

[44]Almond and Verba, *The Civic Culture*, p. 512.
[45]*Ibid.*, pp. 517–18.
[46]*Ibid.*, p. 510.

viewers in the United Kingdom decided which fourteen of the twenty names were to be interviewed or whether this decision was made in the field office. The first policy would introduce further differences between the Italian and the British samples. In any event serious questions would have to be raised about the procedure of choosing a sample of nonelectors from the households of electors. It is doubtful that this group is representative of all nonelectors in the country. In general, the procedures described here illustrate the pitfalls of complete decentralization and "farming out" of sampling in cross-national research.

Final Representation of Population Elements: The comparability of cross-societal studies may be further reduced by research procedures leading to an oversampling of some groups and an undersampling of others. Such differences may arise from variations in sampling frames and selection procedures, as already suggested, or from the differential accessibility and participation of various categories of respondents. In the Almond and Verba study, women account for 64 percent of the Mexican sample, while census figures (1960) indicate that the corresponding figure for cities of ten thousand or over is 52 percent. Experience with surveys in many parts of the world suggests that women are generally more available for interviewing than men. However, there may also be important intranational differences in the accessibility of respondents. In the more urbanized areas men are normally away from home during the day, while in rural areas they may be easier to contact because of the proximity of their homes and work places.

Response Rates: Closely related to the preceding problem are differences in the overall response rates of sample surveys, that is, the percentage of completed interviews, refusals, not-at-homes, and so forth. In *The Civic Culture* the figures for *completed interviews* were as follows:

United States	83.3%
United Kingdom	59.0
Germany	74.0
Italy	74.0
Mexico	60.0

When the completion rate for a survey falls below 80 to 85 percent, there is usually cause for serious concern about the generalizability of the results. The reasons are simple: persons who refuse to participate in a survey, or those who are consistently not at home, often differ in nonrandom ways from participants. Participants may be more talkative, more cooperative, more affluent, or better educated than those who refuse. The problems posed by high nonresponse rates are compounded in cross-national surveys such as the Almond and Verba study. Here the reader must ask not only if a completion rate of 50 or 60 percent seriously jeopardizes the representativeness of the Mexican and British samples but how the differences between these and the other rates affect the interpretation of the results. In some cases, for example, variations attributed to national political systems may, in fact, stem from biases introduced by different response rates. Further discussion of sampling problems can be found in Chapters 9, 10, and 11 of this volume.

THE CHOICE OF RESEARCH METHODS

A final question which should be raised explicitly concerns the rationale for choosing one or another methodology of comparative research. In many situations the dictates of professional precedent are so strong that this question never arises. Anthropologists are expected to use ethnographic methods, sociologists and social psychologists the survey or their version of participant observation, and so on. As the social sciences acquire greater experience in interdisciplinary collaboration, however, several points are becoming clear. First, the methodological traditions associated with the various disciplines have great value and should not be discarded. Each approaches social reality in a different way, and each produces "valid" data—within limits. Second, in many cases the methods chosen to study a given problem are not the most appropriate for the phenomena at hand. Sample surveys, in particular, are often mounted when simpler methods of data collection would produce the same or better results. Third, comparative research would often be enormously better if several methods were used simultaneously.

In Chapter 9 Warwick lays out five criteria which can be used to carry out a benefit/cost analysis of a given research method: (1) appropriateness of the method to the problem at hand; (2) accuracy of measurement, including quantification, replicability, qualitative depth, and control over observer effects; (3) generalizability of the results; (4) administrative convenience; and (5) avoidance of ethical and political difficulties. Warwick then uses these criteria in contrasting two methods commonly applied in comparative research—survey research and participant observation. The following chapters illustrate the assets and liabilities associated with each method. In Chapter 10 Mitchell presents an overview of the obstacles encountered in many cross-national surveys and the problems that they pose for comparative analysis. Frey (Chapter 11) gives a detailed account of his efforts to survey the attitudes of peasants in Turkey. The discussion covers sampling, selection and training of interviewers, pretests, and actual fieldwork. Back and Stycos (Chapter 12) offer another example of survey research, in this case a study of human fertility in Jamaica. Their discussion is particularly helpful in showing the fears aroused by a survey of this type, as well as the strategies available for gaining rapport. Finally, Berreman (Chapter 13) gives one of the most detailed and vivid accounts on record of the interactions of a researcher and the researched population in an ethnographic study.

It is fitting to conclude this essay with an appeal for more innovative combinations of methods in comparative research. Many of the problems reviewed here stem from an exclusive or excessive reliance on single methodologies. Certain of the limitations noted in survey methods, for example, would be much less serious if the study also contained extensive qualitative information on the societies covered. An example of a highly fruitful combination of survey and ethnographic methods is seen in the research of William Foote Whyte and his associates at the Institute for Peruvian Studies in Lima. Their approach capitalizes on the strengths of both methods. Teams of anthropologists are sent to rural communities to carry out their usual round of observations. At roughly the same time interviewers enter the community to administer an attitude survey touching many of the same points covered in the ethnographic observations (e.g., exposure to mass media, interpersonal trust, and fatalism). Then both teams come together to compare their independent observations and to explore any differences that emerge. The great advantage of this methodological marriage is that it provides the analyst with additional sources of information for interpreting the findings, and immediate evidence on the validity of the data. Other fruitful combinations would include historical and survey data, historical and ethnographic data, and content analysis applied to ethnographic observations. In fact, almost any mixture of existing methods would offer possibilities for reducing the difficulties noted in this essay. We would hope that a comparable essay written ten years hence would be able to address the costs and benefits of mixing methods in comparative research. At present this type of innovation is in its infancy.

2

The Methodology of Comparative Analysis

NEIL J. SMELSER

COMPARATIVE ANALYSIS AS SCIENTIFIC INQUIRY

Scientific inquiry arises in the first instance with the specification of a scientific problem. A problem is specified by identifying an observable range of variation in empirical phenomena and asking under what conditions this variation occurs. The range of variation in question (often referred to as the dependent variable, or outcome) constitutes that which is to be explained. The conditions (often referred to as the independent variables, factors, determinants, or causes), when organized into a theoretical framework, constitute that which is used to do the explaining.

The dependent variable may be represented as an empirical universal, displaying no empirical variation: as, for example, in the question, Why do all societies everywhere prohibit marriage between fathers and daughters? Or alternatively, the dependent variable may be represented

A brief note on the history of this essay is in order. In 1965 I composed a draft entitled "The Methodology of Comparative Analysis." I presented it in the summer of 1966 at the Institute of Comparative Sociology at Indiana University. Subsequently I abbreviated some of the material for presentation under the title of "Notes on the Methodology of the Comparative Analysis of Economic Activity" at the Sixth World Congress of Sociology at Evian in September 1966. This abbreviated essay was published in *Social Science Information* (International Social Science Council, April–June 1967), pp. 7–21; in the *Transactions of the Sixth World Congress of Sociology* (The Hague: Editions Nauwelaerts, 1968), II, 101–17; in UNESCO, *The Social Sciences: Problems and Orientations* (The Hague: Mouton, 1968), pp. 145–59 and in my book *Essays in Sociological Explanation* (Englewood Cliffs, N.J.: Prentice-Hall, Inc., 1968), Chap. 3. In the meantime, copies of the original mimeographed version had circulated among some of the participants in the program of the Institute of Comparative Sociology. Donald Warwick, one of the editors of this reader, used the mimeographed version in his course entitled "Theory and Methods of Comparative International Studies" at Harvard, and on the basis of his experience with it, asked me for permission to reprint a sizable portion of it in this reader. On receiving this request, I took the opportunity to make some minor revisions. What appears here is a revised version of about three-quarters of the original essay.

as a range of different possible values: as for example, in the question, Why do persons at different income levels turn out to vote in different proportions? In one respect it does not matter whether the dependent variable is represented as a universal or as varying empirically; in both cases a regularity in the range of variation is brought into question; in the former case this range happens to be zero. In practice, however, as we shall see, the way in which the dependent variable and the search for its conditions are characterized makes a great difference in the strategies that are chosen for comparative research.

Part of the enterprise of scientific explanation, then, involves the search for conditions to account for variations. By asking the question, Variations *in what?* we are able to gain a classification of the subject matter of the scientific discipline; economics, for example, studies variations in the production, distribution, and consumption of scarce goods and services. In the next section I shall classify in some detail the kinds of dependent variables that constitute much of the subject matter of the social sciences. At present I shall focus on the ways—or methods—by which independent variables are handled in the search for explanations.

For a given dependent variable, the number of conditions that may affect it is, at first sight, discouragingly great. An individual's ability to perform a simple task in a small-group setting is influenced most immediately by his intelligence, training, and motivation. These three immediate factors are further conditioned by his social class background, his ordinal position in his family, the presence or absence of others in the same room when he is performing the task, the behavior of the person assigning him the task, and dozens of other factors. The number of conditions influencing complex social aggregates, such as changes in the divorce rate over the past century, appears even more forbidding. The initial picture, then, is one of a *multiplicity* of conditions, a *confounding* of their influences on the dependent variable, and an *indeterminacy* regarding the effect of any one condition or several conditions in combination. The corresponding problems facing the investigator are to *reduce* the number of conditions, to *isolate* one condition from another, and thereby to *make precise* the role of each condition, both singly and in combination with other conditions. How does the investigator face these problems?

The general answer to this question is that he imposes some sort of *organization* on the conditions. One of the simplest ways of organizing conditions is seen in the distinction between *independent* and *intervening* variables. An example will show the power of this distinction. Examining a great amount of cross-cultural material, Whiting and Child found strong correlations between types of child-training practices and types of beliefs concerning the genesis of disease; for example, cultures that impose strict and early weaning on their children tend, in their belief systems, to attribute disease to "oral" causes such as poisoning.[1] In interpreting this association, Whiting and Child asserted that certain personality variables—such as fixations on traumatic childhood experiences, and typical defenses against the anxiety associated with these fixations—"intervene" between child training and adult beliefs. That is to say, the personality variables are dependent in relation to child-training practices, but independent in relation to adult beliefs Speculating further, Whiting and Child argued that child-training practices are themselves dependent on a society's "maintenance systems"—"the economic, political, and social organizations of a society . . . surrounding the nourishment, sheltering, and protection of its members."[2] The several classes of variables constitute a chain of independent, intervening, and dependent variables, as follows:

| maintenance systems | child-training practices | personality variables | projective systems |

The relationship among the variables, thus organized, is much simpler than a lengthy list of associations among every combination of variables.

The example also reveals that the distinction among independent, intervening, and dependent variables is a relative one and that the status of any given variable may change. For example, the variable "child-training practices" is dependent with respect to "maintenance systems" and "personality variables." Furthermore, while the variable "projective systems" is dependent in every respect in the example, these beliefs may themselves turn out to be important independent variables in relation to the institutionalization of the "maintenance systems." No given variable, then, can be considered as inherently independent, intervening, or dependent.

Another way of organizing conditions in scientific investigation is suggested by the distinction between conditions treated as *parameters* and conditions treated as *operative variables*. Parameters are conditions that are known or suspected to influence the dependent variable but, in the investigation at hand, are assumed or made not to vary. Operative variables are conditions that are known or suspected to influence the dependent variable and, in the investigation, are allowed or made to vary in order to assess this influence. By converting variables into parameters, most of the potentially operative conditions are made not to vary, so that the influence of one or a few conditions may be isolated and analyzed.

---

[1]John W. M. Whiting and Irving L. Child, *Child Training and Personality: A Cross-Cultural Study* (New Haven: Yale University Press, 1953).

[2]*Ibid.*, p. 310.

As we shall see presently, all methods of scientific inquiry—including the comparative method—rest on the systematic manipulation and control of parameters and variables.

Like the independent-intervening-dependent distinction, the distinction between parameter and operative variable is a relative one. What is treated as parameter in one investigation may become an operative variable in another. Suppose, for example, it is known that foreign trade is important in the determination of the national income of a society, but that calculation of the impact of foreign trade on the domestic economy is impossible unless certain internal relations—say, between private investment, government investment, and consumption—are also known. The investigator may begin by assuming that foreign trade is a parameter—i.e., that it does not exist, or that it is constant—and, by thus simplifying the determinants of income, may proceed to establish national income as some function of private investment, government investment, and current consumption. Having established these relations, he may then "relax" the restricting assumption about foreign trade and "allow" it to vary, thus tracing its impact on the known relations within the economy. In this final operation he has transformed the parameter into a variable. In the same operation he could also have transformed domestic investment into a parameter—i.e., assumed that it does not vary—in order to pinpoint the impact of foreign trade more precisely.

By continuously and systematically transforming conditions into parameters and variables, by systematically combining and recombining them, scientific explanation is refined and generalized. Moreover, when the investigator is able to assess the influence of the various conditions, in both their individual and combined forms, and express the relations among these conditions in some logical form—such as a series of equations—a systematic scientific theory is generated.[3]

The several methods of scientific inquiry differ according to the ways in which the conditions are converted into parameters and variables, respectively. Consider the following five methods:

1. The *experimental method* involves the direct human manipulation of situations to create parameters and variables. In a simple, classic experiment in the natural sciences, the investigator wishes to determine the effect of temperature on the boiling point of water. To assess this effect, he must be certain that a number of other conditions—for instance,

---

[3]Since my focus in this essay is methodological, I shall restrict the discussion of scientific inquiry to the manipulation and control of variables *with respect to empirical problems.* I shall omit any further discussion of the *formal* characteristics of scientific theory (logical structure of concepts, derivation of propositions, internal consistency, and so on), even though I recognize fully that these formal characteristics are as essential to scientific inquiry as are empirical procedures.

purity of the water and atmospheric pressure—are treated as parameters, that is, not allowed to vary. If he does not assure this, the precise relation between heat and the changing state of water will be "contaminated" by variations in these other conditions; and the investigator will not be able to determine the precise source of influence. If he does control for purity and atmospheric pressure, the investigator will discover the "principle" that water will boil at 212° Fahrenheit. To illustrate the relativity of the distinction between parameter and operative condition, it might be added that the investigator might well have decided to treat atmospheric pressure as the operative variable and heat and purity as parameters, or purity as the operative variable and heat and pressure as parameters. In this case he would discover another principle linking an independent variable with the changing state of water. In every case, the emergent principle or law or prediction is not a claim of empirical universality, but a conditional statement of regularity, involving a number of assumptions about parametric constants within which and only within which the regularity obtains.

In the social sciences the experimental method is limited mainly to social-psychological and small-group experimentation. Most often experimentation is conducted by establishing two groups—the experimental and the control—that are identical in respect to many known or suspected sources of variation, such as age, sex, intelligence, educational level, and socioeconomic background; these conditions shared by the two groups are treated as parameters. Then, with regard to the operative condition under investigation, the experimental group is stimulated, the control group not; this condition not shared by the two groups is treated as the operative variable. Viewed from a different perspective, the experimental method is a species of the comparative method; its distinctive feature is that the social units being compared are deliberately created by the investigator.

The experimental method has three advantages over other methods of scientific investigation to be mentioned presently. First, because the investigator is able to manipulate the *situation itself* (as contrasted with his being able to manipulate only by conceptual means the *data produced* by the situation), he is better able to isolate precise, relatively uncontaminated relations between independent and dependent variables. Second, for the same reason, he is able to measure these isolated variables and relations more effectively. Third, because he is able to control what comes "before" and "after" in the experimental setting—that is, because the variable of time can be manipulated—he is better able to ascertain which are the causal variables. Even with carefully conducted experimentation, however, the results are never completely certain because the investigator cannot finally determine that he has made all the possibly operative conditions but one into parameters.

Most data in the social sciences are historical; they are the precipitates from the flow of social life that transpires without controlled experimentation. Furthermore, even if the investigator actually wishes to establish control groups for the study of many social variables, he is prevented from doing so for many variables—such as suicide and crime rates—by ethical and practical considerations. The social scientist is therefore presented with given data; he is obliged to ask why these data are arrayed in a certain way and not in some other way.[4] And because the "some other way" cannot be concretized experimentally, it must be found either in another comparable but not controlled historical setting or in the imagination of the investigator. At the same time, however, the investigator wishes to observe the same methodological canons that govern the experimental method. Because of the character of his data, however, he must rely on one or more substitutes. What are these substitutes?

2. The *statistical method*, applying mathematical techniques to populations and samples of events containing large numbers, often achieves the same transformation of potentially operative conditions into parameters as does the experimental method. The main difference between the two is that experimentation does so by situational manipulation whereas statistical analysis does so by conceptual (mathematical) manipulation, which holds constant or cancels out sources of variation, or shows them to be actually inoperative.

The statistical method can be described in terms of the several advantages of the experimental method cited above. First, with respect to the isolation of independent variables, the statistical method proceeds by correcting for known sources of variation or by showing suspected sources of variation to be spurious. An example of correcting for variation can be taken from time series analysis in economics. Suppose we wish to trace the influences of the long-term trend of potato prices over several decades. We know that potato prices vary seasonally as well as year by year, but we do not wish to measure the seasonal variation. So we calculate the average seasonal variation for fifty years and cancel out seasonal fluctuations for each individual year by adding or subtracting the average seasonal variation from the actual prices. In this way we "correct for" seasonal fluctuations and presumably obtain a more accurate picture of

---

[4]In his methodological essay Weber defined the objectives of systematic historical investigation as follows: "We wish to understand on the one hand the relationships [among] historical events . . . and on the other the causes of their being historically *so* and not *otherwise*." Max Weber, *The Methodology of the Social Sciences*, trans. and ed. Edward A. Shils and Henry A. Finch (Glencoe, Ill.: The Free Press, 1949), p. 72. Italics in original.

uncontaminated long-term price trends. Suppose also that over the fifty-year period the economy has experienced a steady inflationary trend. To correct for this trend, we might deflate the potato price series by the rate of general price inflation. By these statistical operations we make *parameters* out of seasonal fluctuation and general inflation, and we are thereby enabled to relate trends in potato prices more precisely to other determinants of price changes. A similar sort of operation is frequently found in the sociological analysis of intergenerational mobility (defined as differences in occupational status between father and son). Some mobility occurs simply by virtue of structural changes in the occupational structure itself. If the tertiary sector is expanding, for example, more sons will necessarily move into service industries from other backgrounds. An investigator of mobility rates may wish to analyze other determinants than the changing occupational structure—determinants such as family size, ordinal position in family, or achievement motivation. To isolate these determinants, the investigator may calculate a mobility rate that is expected solely on the basis of structural changes alone, then subtract this rate from the gross mobility rate, and explain the difference by referring to other independent variables. In this operation the effect of changes in the occupational structure is held constant, or made into a parameter for purposes of further analysis.[5]

The strategy of ruling out possibly spurious relations and thus isolating genuine ones is illustrated by multivariate analysis as used in survey research. Suppose that in a national survey it is found that age is positively correlated with intolerance. Suppose also that level of education is found to be negatively correlated with intolerance. Since age and educational level are themselves correlated (above the age of completed education, young people are more educated than old people), it is impossible to know, on the basis of the two correlations taken alone, if either or both or neither is a determinant of intolerance. To determine this, a method of partial correlation is applied: Holding education constant, what is the apparent influence of age? And holding age constant, what is the apparent influence of education? By carrying out a succession of such operations, both on the two variables in question and on other variables that may be associated with them, the investigator makes parameters of a number of possibly operative conditions and arrives at a more precise account of the operative conditions.[6]

[5]For an example of a research on social mobility using this kind of statistical manipulation, cf. Natalie Rogoff Ramsey, "Changes in Rates and Forms of Mobility," in *Social Structure and Mobility in Economic Development*, ed. Neil J. Smelser and Seymour Martin Lipset (Chicago: Aldine Press, 1966), Chap. 7.

[6]For an extended exercise that used the variables of age, education, and various measures of intolerance, cf. Samuel A. Stouffer, *Communism, Conformity and Civil*

With respect to the measurement of variables, it is possible that statistical analysis will be based on finely measured and readily quantifiable data. If so, the statistical method will have the same advantages as the experimental method, in which it is possible for the investigator to control the measurement as well as the operation of the variables. In practice, however, statistical analysis in the social sciences rests on inferior measures. The general reasons for this are two: First, many variables in the social sciences (for example, complex attitudes) have proved more difficult to measure reliably than many variables in the experimental natural sciences. And second, in uncontrolled historical investigation, unlike controlled experimentation, the frame of reference of the data-producing actors or agencies (for example, the Census Bureau) is different from the frame of reference of the investigator; the data in question are not produced with an eye to any particular scientific investigation. Investigators often must therefore accept given measures rather than impose measures designed specifically for scientific purposes.

Finally, with respect to the possibility of controlling time as a variable, statistical analysis of historical data frequently operates at a disadvantage in comparison to the experimental method. Statistical manipulation is usually performed on two types of data, both of which make for difficulty of controlling time: First, with respect to data that are procured at a single moment in time (as with census data or cross-sectional survey data), temporal precedence cannot readily be established because all classes of variables—whether assumed to be independent, intervening, or dependent—must be regarded as occurring at the same moment. Second, with respect to data that have unfolded in the course of historical events, "before-after" inferences are difficult to make, and causal priorities are correspondingly difficult to discover.

Several strategies have been devised in the social sciences to overcome the difficulties of controlling time as a variable. One is the use of the time lag as an assumption and as a research procedure in investigating associations. This is used widely in the analysis of economic dynamics. In his theory of the trade cycle, for example, Hicks posited a time lag of three months between investment and the consumption effect of

---

Liberties: A Cross-section of the Nation Speaks Its Mind (Garden City, N.Y.: Doubleday & Company, Inc., 1955), pp. 89–108. Stouffer actually found both age and education correlated with intolerance, even after correcting for the influence of each on the other. For a brief general discussion of this method as applied to the wartime researches on the American soldier, cf. Patricia L. Kendall and Paul F. Lazarsfeld, "Problems of Survey Analysis," in *Continuities in Social Research: Studies in the Scope and Method of "The American Soldier,"* ed. Robert K. Merton and Paul F. Lazarsfeld (Glencoe, Ill.: The Free Press, 1950), pp. 136–41.

investment [7] In his analysis Hicks made no effort to apply this presumed time lag to any particular data to determine whether the data of investment and consumption unfold in keeping with the assumed relation and lag. Kalecki, in developing his theory of investment and business cycle, posited two time lags—one between investment decisions and actual investment in fixed capital, and the other between investment in inventories and the rate of change in the private sector of the economy. Then, assigning temporal values to these time lags, Kalecki proceeded to interpret the fluctuations of investment, gross product, and so forth, in the American economy between 1929 and 1940.[8] The nature of this operation is that the dependent variables (investment in the one case and change in production in the private sector in the other) are lagged systematically behind the independent variables (decisions to invest in the one case and investment in the other) with the assumption that changes in the independent variables will precede changes in the dependent variables. If, by assuming a lag, the data can be more plausibly interpreted than by assuming no lag, this creates a presumption in favor of the causal priority assumed in the theory.[9]

A sociological example of the attempt to establish causal priority by assuming a lag is found in the effort of Henry and Short to discover relations between fluctuations in the suicide rate and fluctuations in business activity. Beginning with Durkheim's assertion that extraordinary windfalls in periods of speculation are disorienting and give rise to anomic suicide,[10] Henry and Short predicted that if this were the case, suicide would be positively correlated, especially among males, with rapid increases in the business index. Examining their own data, Henry and Short found that in general, the trough, or low point, of male suicide was reached just *before* the peak of business expansion. The slight general increase of suicide just before the peak, moreover, was contributed primarily by the female, not the male rate.[11] This led Henry and Short to reject Durkheim's hypothesis relating business prosperity and anomic

[7]J. R. Hicks, *A Contribution to the Theory of the Trade Cycle* (Oxford: At the Clarendon Press, 1959), Chap. 2.

[8]M. Kalecki, *Theory of Economic Dynamics: An Essay on Cyclical and Long-Run Changes in Capitalist Economy* (New York: Rinehart and Company, 1954), Parts IV and V.

[9]For an example of an attempt to assign causal priority to factors in business cycles on the basis of temporal priority, or "leads," cf. Arthur D. Gayer, W. W. Rostow, and Anna Jacobson Schwartz, *The Growth and Fluctuation of the British Economy 1790–1850* (Oxford: At the Clarendon Press, 1953), pp. 531–50.

[10]Emile Durkheim, *Suicide*, trans. John A. Spaulding and George Simpson (Glencoe, Ill.: The Free Press, 1951), pp. 241–54.

[11]Andrew F. Henry and James F. Short, Jr., *Suicide and Homicide: Some Economic, Sociological and Psychological Aspects of Aggression* (Glencoe, Ill.: The Free Press, 1954), pp. 42–44.

suicide. Furthermore, the grounds on which they rejected it rested on the logic of the time lag: if prosperity were genuinely causal, suicide rates should have accompanied business activity upward, perhaps with a slight lag; but since the opposite relation held, the causal inference could not be drawn.

Another device for controlling time as a variable is the development of the panel method as a research tool. In its first thorough application, a sample of voters were interviewed repeatedly over a period of about six months in order to gain a measure of their changing voting intentions. In addition, the investigators gathered other data that might be relevant as determinants of changes in intention to vote (exposure to mass media, personal contacts, etc.). Because several observations of several different types of variables were made at different points in time, it is possible to determine whether changes in the presumed independent variables actually occurred *before* the dependent variable—in this case a change in voting intention.[12] If so, the investigators could be somewhat more confident in their assumption that the presumed independent variables were causal. The panel technique thus approximates the experimental method; the main difference is that in experimentation the investigator introduces the independent variable himself at an appropriate time, whereas in the panel method the investigator records its introduction, which he usually does not control. In both cases, however, an attempt is made to control the variable of time in order to facilitate causal inferences.[13]

3. Like the statistical method, the *comparative method* is a substitute for experimentation. It is employed in the analysis of historical data, the number of cases of which is too small to permit statistical manipulation. This method is most often required in the comparative analysis of national units, which are few, but it may also be used in comparing regions, cities, communities, and other sub-national units. Because of the restricted number of cases, the investigator relies on systematic comparative illustration.

Despite this restrictive feature of the comparative method, its logic is identical to the methods just reviewed in that it attempts to develop explanations by the systematic manipulation of parameters and operative variables. An example will reveal this identity. One of Durkheim's central findings in his study of suicide was that Protestants display higher rates of suicide than Catholics.[14] The variable that he employed to explain this finding was differential integration of the two religious groupings: Prot-

[12]Paul F. Lazarsfeld, Bernard Berelson, and Hazel Gaudet, *The People's Choice: How the Voter Makes Up His Mind in a Presidential Campaign* (New York: Columbia University Press, 1948), pp. 3–8.

[13]Kendall and Lazarsfeld, "Problems of Survey Analysis," pp. 142–45.

[14]Durkheim, *Suicide*, pp. 152–56.

estants, with their antiauthoritarian, individualistic traditions are less integrated than Catholics and hence less protected against self-destruction. On examining the countries on which his religious data were available, however, Durkheim noticed that the Catholics were in the minority in every case. Could it not be, he asked, that minority status rather than religious tradition is the operative variable in the genesis of lower suicide rates among Catholics? To throw light on this question, he examined regions such as Austria and Bavaria, where Catholics are in the majority; in these regions he discovered some diminution of the religious differences between Protestants and Catholics, but Protestant rates were still higher. On the basis of this examination, he concluded that "Catholicism does not owe [its protective influence] solely to its minority status."[15] In this operation Durkheim used no statistical techniques; yet he was approximating their use by means of systematic comparative illustration. He was making minority status into a parameter in order to isolate the distinctive influence of the religious variable.

The comparative method is frequently divided into two types, positive and negative. Another example—Max Weber's studies on religion and the spirit of rational bourgeois capitalism—will illustrate the difference. Given that certain societies (mainly in northwest Europe and North America) have developed the values of rational bourgeois capitalism, Weber asked what characteristics these societies had in common. In so doing he was using the *positive* comparative method—identifying similarities in independent variables associated with a common outcome. Then, turning to societies that had not developed this kind of economic organization (e.g., classical India, classical China), he asked in what respects they differed from the West. In so doing he was using the *negative* comparative method—identifying independent variables associated with divergent outcomes. By thus manipulating the independent variables and the outcomes, Weber built his case that differences in religious systems were crucial in accounting for the different economic histories of the various societies.[16] Translating Weber's comparative method into the language of scientific inquiry, Weber was making parameters of those general features shared by both the West and his oriental examples (for instance, he ruled out the influence of merchant classes by pointing out that both China and the West had these classes prior to the development of capitalism in the West); and he was making operative variables of those religious aspects in which they differed. The oriental societies that

[15]*Ibid.*, p. 157.

[16]Relevant works include by Max Weber *The Protestant Ethic and the Spirit of Capitalism*, trans. Talcott Parsons (London: George Allen & Unwin Ltd., 1948); *The Religion of China* (Glencoe, Ill.: The Free Press, 1951); and *The Religion of India* (Glencoe, Ill.: The Free Press, 1958).

did not develop rational bourgeois capitalist ideals are logically parallel to control groups (because the crucial variable was not operative); the countries of the West are logically parallel to experimental groups (because the crucial variable was present).

I shall reserve discussion of most of the problems presented by the comparative method until later in the essay. At present I shall review its characteristics in terms of the three advantages noted for the experimental method. First, with respect to the isolation of operative variables, the comparative method stands at a disadvantage to both the experimental method and the statistical method because the investigator can manipulate conditions neither situationally nor mathematically. He must rely on cruder methods of manipulating variables, such as illustrative replication at several empirical levels and deviant case analysis. I shall illustrate these methods extensively later. I might note, however, that the comparative method and the statistical method shade into one another with respect to the isolation of variables and associations among variables. As soon as the number of units becomes large enough to permit the use of statistical techniques, the line between the two is crossed. In his classic, *Social Structure*, Murdock compiled data on 85 societies from the Human Relations Area Files and acquired comparative data on 165 other societies from the general anthropological literature. Having an *N* of 250, Murdock could go beyond the method of systematic comparative illustration and use statistical methods such as Yule's Coefficient of Association and Chi Square.[17] With respect to cases that did not reflect the general patterns of association, however, Murdock saw the necessity of returning to systematic comparative illustration: "It [is] scientifically desirable to examine every negative or exceptional case to determine the countervailing factors apparently responsible for its failure to accord with theoretical expectations. . . ."[18] The investigator, then, must be prepared to shift back and forth between statistical and comparative methods according to the character of his data, particularly according to the number of available cases.

With respect to the measurement of variables, the comparative method suffers the same disadvantage as the statistical method, since most of the data that are available are historical data, precipitated or produced from social behavior that has transpired without reference to the scientific purposes of the investigator.

Finally, because of the qualitative character of much historical data, and because many of them have unfolded as a result of the ebb and flow

[17]George P. Murdock, *Social Structure* (New York: The Macmillan Company, 1949) pp. vii–x.
[18]*Ibid.*, p. ix.

of historical events, the comparative method suffers even more than the statistical method from the inability to control the variable of time and therefore establish definite before-after and causal relations. Some historical events—outbreaks of wars, assassinations of political leaders, natural catastrophes, and so on—do occur at definite times and do constitute definite breaking points around which we may speak of a "before" and an "after." But these kinds of events are not necessarily the most important ones from the standpoint of comparative historical investigation.

Two examples of the difficulties of establishing before-after and causal relations by using the comparative method may be cited. In interpreting the observed association between child-training practices and adult belief systems about the origin of disease, Whiting and Child held child-training practices to be independent variables, personality factors to be intervening variables, and projective belief systems of adults to be dependent variables. In reviewing their findings the authors speculated as follows: "Let us imagine for the moment that our findings are due entirely to an effect of adult personality characteristics upon child-training practices."[19] Since the authors possessed data relating only to the close association between child-training practices and adult beliefs—and no data concerning the temporal priority of either—this speculation seems as plausible as the psychoanalytic interpretation put forth by the authors. Whiting and Child realized this when they observed that "it is an unfortunate defect of the correlational method . . . that it can provide no conclusive evidence about the direction of causal relationships."[20] The authors were justified, then, in calling for further research on the clinical history of individuals, by means of which the time factor can be observed and by means of which temporal and causal priorities among Whiting and Child's variables may be better established.

A second example of the difficulties of establishing temporal and causal priority by using the comparative method is found in the controversies that have surrounded Weber's thesis on religion and the rise of capitalism. One criticism has held that the thesis lacks validity because "Europe was acquainted with capitalism before the Protestant revolt. For at least a century capitalism has been an ever growing collective force."[21] In two respects such a criticism is unfair to Weber. On the one hand, he insisted on the interaction among economic factors and ideas rather than the exclusive causal impetus on either side.[22] Also, Weber was mainly trying to establish a relationship between two sets of ideas—

---

[19]Whiting and Child, *Child Training and Personality*, p. 318.
[20]*Ibid.*, p. 319.
[21]Amintore Fanfani, "Catholicism, Protestantism and Capitalism," in *Protestantism and Capitalism: The Weber Thesis and Its Critics*, ed. Robert W. Green (Boston: D.C. Health & Company, 1959), p. 87.
[22]Weber, *The Protestant Ethic and the Spirit of Capitalism*, p. 23.

the Protestant "ethic" and the "spirit" of capitalism—rather than between Protestant ideology and capitalism in general. At the same time, the criticism does underscore the difficulties of sorting out precise causal relations among historical phenomena because of the problems of controlling time and discovering before-after relations.

Before considering the comparative method in more detail, I shall mention two other methods—the method of heuristic assumption and the case study method—that are widely employed in the social sciences.

4. The *method of heuristic assumption* is a crude but widely employed method of transforming potentially operative variables into parameters. The most familiar version of this method is the famous explanatory strategy of *ceteris paribus*—"other things being equal." Economists explicitly assume, for instance, that for many purposes of economic analysis various noneconomic factors—especially institutions and tastes—are "given," that is, to be treated as parameters. Economists have also traditionally assumed some version of the postulate of economic rationality: if an individual is presented with a situation of choice in an economic setting, he will maximize his economic position. By extensive use of this method, economic analysts have been able to reduce the number of operative variables and to create relatively simple and elegant models of economic variables; moreover, its use accounts in part for the degree of theoretical sophistication of economics.

Helpful and necessary as the method of heuristic assumption has been, it is inferior to experimentation, statistical analysis, and comparative analysis. The method of heuristic assumption rests on no situational or conceptual manipulation other than making a simplifying or convenient assumption. Seldom if ever are attempts made to establish the empirical validity of the assumptions or to "correct" for the degree to which assumptions are not valid. The method of heuristic assumption accomplishes by "making believe" what the other methods accomplish by situational or conceptual manipulation in the light of some known or suspected empirical variation. Nevertheless, this method provides the investigator the same kind of service as the experimental, statistical, and comparative methods—systematically to render operative conditions into parameters to merit the isolated investigation of a limited number of selected operative conditions.

Outside economics the method of heuristic assumption is as widely but not as explicitly employed. In an experimental small-group setting, for example, in which the influence of different leadership structures on morale is being studied, the investigator often makes use of a number of important but unexamined heuristic assumptions—that the subjects speak the same language, that they share many cultural assumptions, that they are more or less uniformly motivated to participate in the experiment, and so on. All these variables, if treated as operative, would influence the outcome of the experiment; but they are implicitly assumed to be parameters. To choose another example, studies of voting behavior often rest on the assumption that voting behavior takes place within an unchanging constitutional, legal, and electoral framework. This framework, if varied, would influence the rates and direction of voting.[23]

5. The *case study method* can be subdivided into two types: *deviant case analysis* and *isolated clinical case analysis*. The former is explicitly one type of comparative analysis, the latter only implicitly so.

The method of *deviant case analysis* can be understood only in relation to a more general statistical or comparative analysis in which some association has been established. The starting point, in fact, for deviant case analysis is "the empirical fact that no statistical relationship, particularly in the social sciences, is a perfect one."[24] In deviant case analysis, the investigator takes the instance or instances that are exceptions to the general trend and attempts to locate independent variables that set them off from the general trend. Methodologically, the method of deviant case analysis is parallel to the negative comparative method. The investigator takes two "groups" that differ in outcome (dependent variable) and attempts to locate differences in conditions between them (independent variable). In deviant case analysis, one "group" is comprised of the deviant case itself, and the other by the majority of cases expressing the general finding. The method of deviant case analysis is also a method of "reading backwards" to approximate the experimental situation. In experimentation the independent variable is varied between experimental and control groups to produce different outcomes. In deviant case analysis the starting point is the different outcomes themselves (as between the deviant case and the majority of cases); the investigator then "reads back" to determine the respects in which the conditions affecting the deviant case (the "experimental group" by parallel) differ from the conditions affecting all the other cases. The main difference between deviant case analysis on the one hand and experimental and comparative methods on the other is that the N of the deviant cases is always so small that it is difficult to know which of the many respects the deviant case differs from the majority of cases is the crucial one. For this reason deviant case analysis is not as powerful as the experimental, statistical, and comparative methods but must be regarded as a method of locating new

[23]Two criteria for the level of advancement of a science are the following: (1) The degree to which parametric assumptions are explicit rather than implicit. By this criterion economics is more advanced than the other social sciences. (2) The degree to which parametric assumptions are informed by knowledge that is acquired not merely by assumption but by other methods of scientific inquiry. By this criterion economics is not very advanced.

[24]Kendall and Lazarsfeld, "Problems of Survey Analysis," p. 167.

variables, which can be "established" more or less firmly only by the application of more powerful research methods.

An example of the usefulness of deviant case analysis can be found in a study of cross-cultural associations by Beatrice Whiting.[25] In a comparative analysis of the incidence of sorcery as a cultural explanation of the onset of disease, she hypothesized that in societies that had a delegated system of authority to mete out sanctions against murder, sorcery would not occur as an explanation of disease, whereas in societies in which murder was settled by retaliatory methods, sorcery would be widespread. Taking fifty societies as a sample, she found that the association between sorcery and the presence of a superordinate system of justice was significant in the predicted direction. Despite this strong association, it became apparent that "Africa was strikingly aberrant, all but three of the nine tribes sampled having sorcery as an important explanation for sickness and not coordinate but superordinate control." Taking the African cases as deviant cases, she decided to "[analyze the material] in more detail to see if some other variables could be discovered."[26] This is the essence of deviant case analysis. She discovered that among the Azande, justice is decided upon by oracles and chiefs, but the actual retaliation is executed by relatives of the slain party with permission of the chief. On the basis of this information Whiting "[reclassified] all tribes, distinguishing between superordinate justice and superordinate punishment," and recalculated a number of correlations on the basis of this more defined conception of social control.[27] In this case the method of deviant case analysis led to the refinement of the same variable—type of social control—that was important in the original association; it could also lead to the discovery of new variables.

Isolated clinical case analysis is not so intimately related to the analysis of notable exceptions to a statistical association. It is rather the investigation of an individual unit with respect to some analytic problem. Alvin W. Gouldner's study of the deleterious effects of managerial succession on worker morale in a gypsum plant is an example of such a clinical case study.[28] Yet insofar as the study is couched in a general conceptual framework and related to other general findings on formal organizations, it becomes explicitly a comparative study. When Gouldner, for example, related his findings to some of Max Weber's propositions about authority, he was pointing out that his particular case differed in certain respects from the general relationships claimed by Weber and was isolating cer-

[25]Beatrice Blyth Whiting, *Paiute Sorcery* Viking Fund Publications in Anthropology, No. 15 (New York: Viking Press, Inc. 1950).

[26]*Ibid.*, p. 85.

[27]*Ibid.*, pp. 86ff.

[28]Alvin W. Gouldner, *Patterns of Industrial Bureaucracy* (Glencoe, Ill.: The Free Press, 1964).

tain variables that might account for the difference. This procedure is identical to deviant case analysis and the negative comparative method. In a later case study, Robert Guest isolated and analyzed an instance of smooth and successful managerial succession in another plant.[29] In contrasting his results with those of Gouldner, and in attempting to isolate the variables that underlie the differences in the findings of the two studies,[30] Guest himself was bringing the negative comparative method to bear on the general relationship between authority and worker response implied in Gouldner's case study.

In this section I have attempted to show the basic continuity between the comparative method and four other methods of analysis—experimental, statistical, heuristic assumption, and case study—that are used widely in scientific inquiry. All these methods have two features in common: they are ways of organizing independent and dependent variables to produce scientific explanations; and they are ways of organizing independent variables into parameters and operative conditions to isolate, measure, and establish the causal role of specific independent variables. The methods differ considerably in scientific power, however, because they vary with respect to (a) constrictions regarding the number and kind of social units under investigation, (b) the ways in which the variables can be manipulated, and (c) the kind and amount of theoretical and empirical knowledge on the basis of which the variables may be manipulated.

LEVELS OF COMPARATIVE ANALYSIS

In this section we shall use three dimensions to develop a typology of levels of comparative analysis: (1) the dependent variables that typically enter the formulation of scientific problems, (2) the number of social units—one or more than one—involved, and (3) the static or dynamic quality of the comparison.

Types of Dependent Variables in Social Analysis

For any scientific explanation it is essential to have a conceptual framework by which the major dependent variables are to be described,

---

[29]Robert Guest, *Organizational Change: The Effect of Successful Leadership* (Homewood, Ill.: Dorsey, 1962).

[30]Robert Guest, "Managerial Succession in Complex Organizations," *American Journal of Sociology*, 68 (1962), 47–54. See also comment by Gouldner and rejoinder by Guest, pp. 54–56.

classified, and analyzed. Without such a framework the investigator cannot locate sources of variation that are scientifically problematical. With respect to this characterization of dependent variables, I hold an explicitly nominalistic position: that the dependent variables are not in any natural way "given" in social reality but are the product of a selective identification of aspects of the empirical world of social phenomena by the investigator for purposes of analysis.

With this philosophical position in mind, let me now identify several levels of dependent variables that constitute the subject matter for social analysis:

1. Variations in aggregated attributes of the population of a social unit.[31] Here I refer to what Lazarsfeld and Menzel termed "properties of collectives which are obtained by performing some mathematical operation upon some property of each single member."[32] The mathematical operation may be adding, percentaging, averaging, and so on. As examples of aggregated attributes of a population, we might mention proportions of persons of different ages, persons holding various occupations, persons professing various religious beliefs, illiterate persons, and so on. To pose scientific questions is to ask under what conditions variations in these aggregated attributes may be expected.

2. Variations in rates of behavioral precipitates in the population over time. Here I have in mind variations in rates of voting, religious attendance, crime, suicide, collective protest, and so on. To pose scientific questions is to ask under what conditions variations in these rates may be expected. While at this level, like the first, we are dealing with the properties of individual members, these characteristics are conceptualized as a *flow* of behavioral precipitates within a specified period of time rather than as a *stock* of attributes that may be said to characterize the population at a given point in time.[33] The difference may be illustrated by the following: To enumerate the proportion of Ph.D.'s in a population is to

---

[31]For purposes of the general discussion that follows, I do not have any particular kind of social unit in mind. The discussion could apply equally well to national units, social classes, communities, formal organizations, or families.

[32]Paul F. Lazarsfeld and Herbert Menzel, "On the Relation between Individual and Collective Properties," in *Complex Organizations: A Sociological Reader*, ed. Amitai Etzioni (New York: Holt, Rinehart and Winston, Inc., 1961), p. 427. Lazardsfeld and Menzel used the term *analytical* to describe these kinds of properties, but we would prefer to avoid the use of such a very general scientific term for this specific descriptive purpose.

[33]One of the most frequently studied units—individual attitudes as tapped by sample surveys—can, depending on the perspective of the investigator, be considered as either aggregated attributes or aggregated behavioral precipitates. On the one hand, attitudes may be regarded as more or less enduring characteristics of individuals, and their existence in a population may be treated as any other aggregate of attributes. On the other hand, the attitudes may be regarded as behavioral responses to the stimulus of a survey question, and their recording may be treated as a behavioral "rate."

identify an aggregated population attribute; to calculate the proportion of graduate students attaining Ph.D.'s in 1964 is to identify a rate of behavioral precipitates.[34]

3. Variations in patterned social interaction (also referred to as roles or social structure). To pose scientific questions is to ask under what conditions variations in structure may be expected. Our conception of structure is similar to what Lazarsfeld and Menzel refer to as "structural properties" of collectives—those properties "which are obtained by performing some operation on data about the relations of each member to some or all of the others."[35] In one sense the notion of social structure is very close to the first two types of dependent variations, since we often identify social structure by referring to regularities in the population's attributes and behavioral precipitates. In using the term "family structure," for example, we refer to the empirical facts that the same people—adult male categorized as husband and father, adult female categorized as wife and mother, and several young classified as son, daughter, brother, and sister—regularly sleep under the same roof, share economic goods, and so on. The difference between regularities in a population's attributes and behavioral precipitates on the one hand, and its social-structural arrangements on the other, lies in the ways the notions are conceptualized. Social structure, unlike the other two, is conceptualized on the basis of the *relational* aspects among members of a social unit, not on some aggregated version of attributes of behavior of the individual members.[36] Furthermore, in conceptualizing social structure, I assume that the relations among members are not merely fortuitous or statistical but are regulated by the operation of certain social forces. These forces are *sanctions*, including both rewards and deprivations, and *norms*, or standards of conduct that indicate the occasions on which various kinds of sanctions are applied.[37]

---

[34]Just as a stock is a resultant of past flows, so in many cases the aggregated population attributes (e.g., proportion of Ph.D.'s) is a resultant of past rates of behavior (e.g., incidence of attainment of Ph.D.'s). Or, to put the matter in the language of Parsons's pattern variables, accumulated past performances (or achievements) often become qualities (or ascribed characteristics).

[35]Lazarsfeld and Menzel, "On the Relation between Individual and Collective Properties," p. 428.

[36]Because of this fundamental difference between statistical regularities among individuals and social structure, I cannot agree with Leach when he characterizes social structure as follows: "The social structure which I talk about . . . is, in principle, a statistical notion; it is a social fact in the same sense as a suicide rate is a social fact. It is a by-product of the sum of many individual human actions, of which the participants are neither wholly conscious nor wholly unaware." E. R. Leach, *Pul Eliya: A Village in Ceylon: A Study of Land Tenure and Kinship* (Cambridge: At the University Press, 1961), p. 300. Leach here seems to be ruling out all trans-individual, relational characterizations of social action.

[37]Here again I must disagree with Leach when he says that "[social structure] is normal rather than normative." *Ibid.*, p. 300.

4. Variations in cultural patterns. Cultural patterns—values, world views, knowledge, symbols and so forth—supply systems of meaning and legitimacy for patterned social interaction. Examples of concrete cultural patterns are the Judeo-Christian religious heritage, the values of democratic constitutional government, the Baroque musical style, and so on. To pose scientific questions is to ask under what conditions variations in cultural patterns may be expected. Cultural patterns are examples of what Lazarsfeld and Menzel called "global" properties of collectives;[38] they are not based either on aggregated information about individual members of a social unit or on specific relations among the members but are properties of the collective considered as a whole.

What are the relations among these several types of dependent variables? We may attack this question at two levels, empirical and analytic. At the *empirical* level, these variables may influence one another (i.e., they may stand as independent variables to one another), and there is no fixed causal priority among them. For example, suppose that as a result of a disastrous war (such as the German onslaught on the Soviet Union in World War II), there is a great increase in the aggregated population attributes. Because of this change, however, we would also expect an increase in various sorts of behavioral precipitates as well (mourning, deification of the dead, scapegoating, etc.). Furthermore, as a result of these changes, both of which pose a threat to traditional family life, there might arise new, alternative institutional frameworks to supplement the family, for example, communal arrangements for the case of the orphaned. This would be a change in patterned social interaction. This hypothetical causal sequence shows the complicated feedback relations that characterize the several types of dependent variables at the empirical level.

At the *analytic* level, the several types of dependent variables stand in the following hierarchy:

Top

Bottom

Cultural patterns
Social structure
Rates of behavioral precipitates
Aggregated population attributes

The characteristic underlying this hierarchy is that as we move upward, more and more variables that have heretofore been treated as parametric have to be treated as potentially operative variables. This means that social analysis—including comparative analysis—becomes more complex because it becomes progressively more difficult to ignore certain variables. Let us illustrate this hierarchy by a running set of examples:

[38]Lazarsfeld and Menzel, "On the Relation between Individual and Collective Properties," pp. 428–29.

To begin with the movement of aggregated population attributes, it is more nearly possible to consider movements in these without reference to variations in motivated behavior, social structure, or cultural patterns. Suppose, for instance, we wish to trace the course of the size of the total population over a period of decades. In the first instance, the movement of this aggregate is a function of birthrates, death rates, and migration rates. Posing the problem in this way, it is possible to proceed without making any particular parametric assumptions about the psychological determinants of behavior, social structure, and cultural patterns. This is possible because we are operating at the level of explaining nonbehavioral attributes of aggregated members.[39]

Let us now move to the behavioral level, considering the fertility rate as an example. If we are to treat this as a behavioral rate, it becomes imperative to make, at the very least, some simplifying assumptions about the psychological causes of fertility. Suppose, for example, we wish to make the prediction that size of family is a direct function of the level of family income. Even this simple prediction introduces the psychological assumptions that people treat children as economic commodities and that they will have as many children as they can afford. This example shows that when we move to the explanation of behavior it is essential to treat psychological variables as intervening between various kinds of conditions and behavior itself. It is not, however, necessary at this level to consider social structural variables and cultural variables as problematical. Analysis of differential fertility rates can be performed under the restricting assumption that family structure itself is not undergoing change.

When we move to the social-structural level, it becomes more difficult to consider variables nonproblematical. If we are interested in giving an account of the impact of industrial changes on the family structure, we cannot assume that these changes can be analyzed while holding behavior within this structure constant. Changes in institutional structure *necessarily* involve changes in the behavioral precipitates from this structure. As we move up the hierarchy, therefore, a certain asymmetry appears. It is possible to analyze changes at the lower level without necessarily assuming changes at the higher levels, but analysis of changes at the higher levels necessarily makes the variables at the lower levels problematical. Correspondingly, the problem of the manageability of large numbers of variables becomes greater as we move up the hierarchy.

The highest level of analysis of change involves variations in cultural

[39]As we shall see, however, it may become necessary to inquire into the psychological, cultural, and social-structural determinants of some of the variables influencing these movements if we are to develop a fuller, more adequate explanatory account.

patterns. At this level, too, the logic of asymmetry holds. It is possible to investigate changes in social structure without necessarily making any assertions about changing cultural patterns, but analysis of changes in cultural patterns necessarily raises questions as to what is happening to these cultural patterns at the social-structural and behavioral levels. Because changes at the level of cultural patterns necessarily involve changes in the whole system, these changes cannot be investigated while considering other social variables to be nonproblematical. It is for this reason that changes in cultural patterns pose the most complex analytical problems, and why we know less about these kinds of change than we do about the more manageable processes at the lower analytic levels.[40]

The Number of Social Units

The distinction here is whether comparative analysis involves (*a*) the explanation of the state of a dependent variable at different times in the *same* social unit,[41] or (*b*) the explanation of the state of a dependent variable in *different* social units. An example of the first is: Why is the British homicide rate higher in 1964 than it was in 1934? An example of the second is: Why is the rate of drug addiction higher in the United States than it is in Great Britain?[42] Even though the first sometimes poses problems of comparability (in what respects is Britain the same social system in 1964 as it was in 1934, and in what respects not?), the difficulties involved in analyzing dependent variables within the same social unit over time are usually not as great as in comparing dependent variables in different sociocultural contexts. The reason for this is that it is relatively more permissible to treat various conditions as parameters within the same social unit than in different socio-cultural contexts. I shall develop this point below when considering the issue of cross-cultural comparability.

The Static or Dynamic Quality of Comparative Analysis

The difference between static and dynamic analysis is whether time as a variable is combined with the usual associations between independ-

[40]For further treatment of the notion of a logical hierarchy among components of social action, see Neil J. Smelser, *Theory of Collective Behavior* (New York: The Free Press of Glencoe, 1963), Chap. 2.

[41]For present purposes it does not matter which dependent variable—aggregated population attributes, behavioral precipitates, social structure, or cultural patterns— is under consideration.

[42]This comparative issue is posed by Edwin M. Schur in *Narcotic Addiction in Britain and America* (Bloomington: Indiana University Press, 1962).

ent and dependent variables. An example of static analysis would be to compare the crime rate in 1900 in the United States with the crime rate in 1960 without reference to the ups and downs of the movement between the two points in time. Even though static and cross-sectional, it is still possible that the analysis be explanatory; for example, in this example it would be explanatory if the analyst attempted to account for the different rates by reference to a number of independent variables influencing the crime rate in each time period—variables such as institutional disorganization, rate of immigration, police morale, behavior of welfare agencies, and municipal politics and corruption.

To make the example dynamic, it would be necessary to trace the *path* of change of the crime rate over time, not only accounting for the different rate at two different times but accounting for how it came to move along its path. This involves the systematic introduction of combinations of independent variables and the development of these combinations of variables into models of change. Because dynamic analysis introduces the problem of time, the path of change over time, and the mechanisms by which change over time is affected, it is more complex than static analysis.

A typology of levels of comparative analysis may be derived from these three dimensions. Table 1 represents this typology. A question for research is entered in each cell, with a reference to a study revolving around the research question. As we move downward and to the right in the table, comparative research becomes more difficult and complicated. At the upper-left-hand extremes of the table, it is more nearly permissible to treat sociocultural context, time, and higher-level variables as *parameters*. Moving downward and to the right, however, it becomes necessary to treat these parametric characteristics as *operative variables*. Dynamic comparative analysis of cultural changes in different social units is the most complex of all types of comparative analysis; each of the features considered as parametric from the standpoint of other levels of comparative analysis must now be considered as variable.

SOME METHODOLOGICAL PROBLEMS IN COMPARATIVE ANALYSIS

In the preceding sections I outlined both the quality of the comparative method as an explanatory tool and several levels of comparative analysis. In the process I referred at least implicitly to some difficulties that are peculiar to the comparative method. In this section I shall make these difficulties more explicit, add some new ones, and suggest some strategies for partially overcoming them.

The Problem of Comparability in Different
Sociocultural Contexts

Let me introduce the problem of comparability by recounting Rad-cliffe-Brown's statement of the advantages of the comparative method.[43] He began with a specific example—the existence of exogamous moieties named after the eagle-hawk and the crow in a certain region in Australia. Instead of concentrating on the specific historical factors which might account for the evolution of the division of this particular region, Radcliffe-Brown adopted the comparative strategy. He turned to other societies, both in Australia and elsewhere, and discovered that the division into opposed groupings based on animal identities is very widespread. By using this comparative strategy, Radcliffe-Brown substituted "certain general problems" demanding general explanations for "a particular problem of the kind that calls for a historical explanation." These general problems were, for instance, the problem of totemism—or the association of a social group with a natural species—and the "problem of how opposition can be used as a mode of social integration." By using this strategy, moreover, Radcliffe-Brown located general sociological variables that could be brought back to explain the particular division between the eagle-hawk and the crow moieties in Australia. Summarizing the advantages of his strategy, Radcliffe-Brown commented, "[the] comparative method is . . . one by which we pass from the particular to the general, from the general to the more general, with the end in view that we may in this way arrive at the universal, at characteristics which can be found in different forms in all human societies."[44]

In general I agree with Radcliffe-Brown's recitation of the advantages of the comparative method. In using the method, however, the investigator encounters three related methodological problems, all of which fall under the general heading "the problem of comparability": (1) Are the *events* and *situations* we wish to explain—the dependent variables—comparable from one sociocultural context to another?[45] How, for example,

---

[43]A. R. Radcliffe-Brown, *Method in Social Anthropology*, ed. M. N. Srinivas (Chicago: University of Chicago Press, 1958), pp. 126–27.

[44]*Ibid.*, p. 127. Radcliffe-Brown's account of these advantages is also summarized in Whiting's brief characterization of the advantages of the comparative method: "The advantages of the cross-cultural method are two-fold. First, it ensures that one's findings relate to human behavior in general rather than being bound to a single culture, and second, it increases the range of variation of many of the variables." John W. M. Whiting, "The Cross-Cultural Method," in *Handbook of Social Psychology*, ed. Gardner Lindzey (Cambridge, Mass.: Addison-Wesley, 1954), p. 524.

[45]In asking this question I refer *both* to comparing events and situations in different social units (e.g., United States with India) *and* to comparing events and situations in the same social unit over time (e.g., nineteenth-century America with twentieth-century America).

TABLE 1

Levels of Comparative Analysis

	Same social unit		Different social unit	
	Static	Dynamic	Static	Dynamic
Aggregated population attributes	What factors account for the different composition of the American labor force in 1870 and 1950?[1]	What institutional conditions underlie the steady population decline of rural Ireland?[2]	What factors account for the different shape of the age pyramids of the populations of India and the United States?[3]	What conditions account for the peculiar course of the "demographic transition" in Holland, as compared with most other Western countries?[4]
Behavioral precipitates	Why has the rate of church attendance been higher in mid-twentieth century America than in mid-nineteenth century America?[5]	Why has the American divorce rate shown a steady upward climb, with peaks around wartime periods, during the past century?[6]	Why are divorce rates lower in Australia than in the United States?[7]	What conditions account for the different rates of economic recovery of the United States after the Civil War, Russia after World War I, and Germany and Japan after World War II?[8]
Social structure	Why is the nuclear family stronger in Israeli collective settlements than it was a generation ago?[9]	By what processes did the British family become a more specialized social unit during the years of the Industrial Revolution?[10]	What are the conditions underlying unilateral cross-cousin marriage?[11]	Why did technological innovation proceed at a more rapid pace in the United States than in Great Britain during the nineteenth century?[12]
Cultural patterns "other"	Why have American values become more "other-directed" and less "inner-directed"?[13]	By what processes does a communitarian social experiment become secularized?[14]	What are the social conditions underlying the rise of extremist, totalitarian social movements?[15]	By what processes are revolutionary ideologies routinized after successful revolutionary overthrows?[16]

See page 67 for footnotes.

can crime rates of a century ago be compared with crime rates now? Were not recording procedures different then from now? Was not the social meaning of a crime different then from now? Or, turning to Radcliffe-Brown's example, how can we compare groupings such as moieties with one another when the social meaning and context of these groupings differ from society to society? (2) A more general way of posing these questions is the following: Do the general *dimensions* used to compare societies cross-culturally distort events and situations? For example, suppose we wish to compare the "political" aspects of two societies with different cultural traditions and types of social structures. In what sense is it appropriate to apply the word "political" to both the role of an African chieftain and that of an American legislator? In what sense are both "political" roles rather than some other kind of roles?[46] Or, to use Radcliffe-Brown's example, in what sense can social groupings such as moieties be interpreted as reflecting "opposition . . . used as a mode of social integration"? Certainly *some* general dimension is necessary for

[46]Elsewhere Radcliffe-Brown recognized the importance of this question when he asserted: "If we are to study political institutions in abstraction from other features of social systems we need to make sure that our definition of 'political' is such as to mark off a class of phenomena which can profitably be made the subject of separate theoretical treatment." A. R. Radcliffe-Brown, "Preface," in *African Political Systems*, ed. M. Fortes and E. E. Evans-Pritchard (London: Oxford University Press, 1955), p. xii.

Footnotes to Table 1:

[1]Philip M. Hauser, "Labor Force," in *Handbook of Modern Sociology*, ed. Robert E. L. Faris (Chicago: Rand McNally & Co., 1964), pp. 167–72.

[2]Conrad M. Arensberg and Solon T. Kimball, *Family and Community in Ireland* (Cambridge: Harvard University Press, 1954), Chap. 6.

[3]Kingsley Davis, *The Population of India and Pakistan* (Princeton, N.J.: Princeton University Press, 1951).

[4]William Petersen, "The Demographic Transition in Holland," *American Sociological Review*, 25 (1960), 334–47.

[5]Seymour M. Lipset, *The First New Nation* (New York: Basic Books, Inc., Publishers, 1963).

[6]P. H. Jacobson, *American Marriage and Divorce* (New York: Rinehart and Company, 1959).

[7]Lincoln H. Day, "Patterns of Divorce in Australia and the United States," *American Sociological Review*, 29 (October 1964).

[8]Jack Hirshleifer, *Disaster and Recovery: A Historical Survey* (Santa Monica, Calif.: The Rand Corporation, 1963).

[9]Melford E. Spiro, *Children of the Kibbutz* (Cambridge: Harvard University Press, 1958).

[10]Neil J. Smelser, *Social Change in the Industrial Revolution* (Chicago: University of Chicago Press, 1959), Chap. 8–10.

[11]George C. Homans and David M. Schneider, *Marriage, Authority, and Final Causes: A Study of Unilateral Cross-Cousin Marriage* (Glencoe, Ill.: The Free Press, 1957).

[12]H. J. Habbakuk, *American and British Technology in the Nineteenth Century: The Search for Labour-Saving Inventions* (Cambridge: At the University Press, 1962).

[13]David Riesman, Nathan Glazer, and Ruell Denney, *The Lonely Crowd* (New York: Doubleday Anchor, 1953).

[14]Charles Nordhoff, *The Communistic Societies of the United States* (New York: Harper & Bros., 1875).

[15]William Kornhauser, *The Politics of Mass Society* (Glencoe, Ill.: The Free Press, 1959).

[16]Crane Brinton, *The Anatomy of Revolution* (New York: Vintage Books, 1958), Chaps. 7–9.

comparative analysis; otherwise the investigator is tied to a principle of relativism that prohibits him from moving outside the confines of a single social unit.[47] But the truth of this general point does not answer the question of which particular comparative dimensions least distort the distinctive sociocultural meaning of events and situations, yet at the same time provide a general basis for comparison. (3) An even more general way of posing the problem of comparability is: How is it possible to compare different *social units* (or social systems) with one another? Does it make sense to compare a highly complex nation-state like the United States with a hunting-and-gathering tribe in Australia, when they appear to differ from one another in almost every respect?

The amount of difficulty posed by these questions rests in large part on *how adequately the investigator chooses and operationalizes his comparative dimensions.* Let me explore this criterion in some greater detail.

The first rule of thumb is that the investigator should avoid concepts that are so particular to a single culture or group of cultures that no instance of the concept can be found in other cultures. The concept "civil service," for example, is so closely linked to a bureaucratic administrative form that it cannot be instantiated in societies without a formal governmental apparatus. The concept "administration" is superior, since it is not bound so closely to particular forms of bureaucracy, but even this term is quite culture-bound. Weber's concept of "staff"[48] is even more helpful, since it can encompass political arrangements based on kinship and other forms of particularistic loyalties. "Staff" is more satisfactory than "administration," then, and "administration" more satisfactory than "civil service," because the former allow for more nearly universal instantiation.

Merely to select a dimension that is universally identifiable in principle, however, is not sufficient. Comparability also depends on *how* the dimension is identified in different sociocultural settings. Let me illustrate from the field of economics. Clearly the term *economic* is a concept that is universally identifiable in principle. All societies face the problem of scarcity of resources, and all societies must come to terms in some institutionalized way with this problem. All societies thus have an "economic problem" and manifest "economic behavior." To say this, however, is only to begin to identify economic behavior comparatively. It is also necessary to ask how, in terms of actual operations, economic behavior is manifested empirically.

[47]Clyde Kluckhohn, "Universal Categories of Culture," in *Anthropology Today: An Encyclopedic Inventory*, ed. A. L. Kroeber (Chicago: University of Chicago Press, 1953), p. 520.

[48]Max Weber, *The Theory of Social and Economic Organization*, trans. A. M. Henderson and Talcott Parsons (New York: Oxford University Press, Inc., 1947), pp. 329ff.

One convenient and widely used method of identifying "the economic" is to limit the empirical referents of the term—as did Alfred Marshall—to those aspects of men's attitudes and activities that are subject to measurement in terms of money.[49] From the standpoint of empirical precision, the monetary index has advantages. From the standpoint of encompassing economic behavior on a uniform and universal basis, however, the index has severe limitations. Even in our own society, many economic activities—housewives' labor, lending a hand to a friend, and so forth—are seldom expressed in monetary terms. In the case of economies based on subsistence farming and domestically consumed household manufacture, the limitations of the monetary index are even more marked, since many kinds of economic behavior—such as the production, distribution, and consumption of foodstuffs—never become monetized. In addition, the monetary index is limited when comparing a growing economic system with its past, since one of the characteristics of economic growth is the entry of an increasing monetization; therefore, if the monetary definition of *economic* is used, the rate of growth is inflated by the transformation of nonmonetized economic activity into monetized economic activity.[50]

Despite these limitations of the monetary index, it is frequently employed in international comparisons. Both scholars and laymen are familiar with the comparisons of per capita per annum income of the nations of the world, ranging from around several thousand dollars per capita for the United States to less than one hundred dollars for some underdeveloped countries. These figures are inadequate as comparative measures for at least two reasons: (1) Based on monetized aspects of economies, they underestimate the income levels of subsistence and other kinds of economies with limited monetization. (2) They involve translations of various currencies into dollar equivalencies, usually on the basis of current international currency exchange ratios. Since many of these ratios are "pegged" artificially and do not represent true economic exchange ratios, additional bias creeps into the comparative estimates.

Another definition of economic activity has been suggested by Po-

[49]Alfred Marshall, *Principles of Economics*, 8th ed. (New York: The Macmillan Company, 1920), Book I, Chap. 2.

[50]I should add that some definitions of economics do not limit economic activity to monetized activity. Thus Samuelson's textbook definition is ". . . the study of how men and society *choose, with or without the use of money,* to employ *scarce* productive resources to produce various commodities over time and distribute them for consumption, now and in the future, among people and groups in society." Paul A. Samuelson, *Economics: An Introductory Analysis,* 5th ed. (New York: McGraw-Hill Book Company, 1961), p. 6. Emphasis added.

lanyi, Arensberg, and Pearson.[51] Reacting against the tradition of formal economics, they argue that economic activity should be defined as that instituted process that results in a "continuous supply of want-satisfying *material* means." This materialistic definition introduces a bias precisely opposite to that of the monetary definition of economic activity—a bias in favor of the primitive and peasant societies. In such societies, it appears that most economic activity is devoted to a sort of material subsistence based on food, clothing, and shelter. In advanced market societies, however, in which expressive behavior, ideas, personalities, and other "nonmaterial" items have economic value, the formula of the "economic" as the "supply of want-satisfying material means" is not an adequate comparative measure. It is as illegitimate to try to force a physical or material bias on all economic activity as it is to impose a fully developed market analysis on all economic activity.[52]

Any encompassing definition and measurement of economic activity, I believe, must involve more than a convenient index of monetized activity, physical production, or some other concrete activity. It must involve a definition of the production, distribution, and consumption of scarce goods and services *in relation to individual and social goals*. Economists have long recognized this relational quality of economic activity in their preoccupation with the notion of utility as the basis of economic value; yet this preoccupation has been predominantly in terms of the wants of individuals, despite the tradition of welfare economics that has pursued questions of interindividual comparability and community welfare.[53] Furthermore, economists have generally tended to treat wants as "given" and therefore subject to no further analysis.[54] But in cross-cultural comparative analysis, wants cannot be taken as a parametric "given." The definition and measurement of economic activity—to be genuinely comparative—must take more direct account of societal goals. To arrive at an appropriate comparative definition of economic activity, we may assume that a society possesses a value system which defines certain goals as desirable for unit members of society at various levels. By a process of institutionalization, the appropriate channels for realizing these goals are specified. It is apparent, however, that all societies exist in an environment that does not automatically guarantee the *complete*

[51]K. Polanyi, C. M. Arensberg, and H. W. Pearson, eds., *Trade and Market in the Early Empires* (Glencoe, Ill.: The Free Press and The Falcon's Wing Press, 1957).

[52]For further development of this point, and further criticism of the formulation put forth by Polanyi *et al.*, cf. Neil J. Smelser, "A Comparative View of Exchange Systems," *Economic Development and Cultural Change*, 7 (1959), 173–82.

[53]See, for example, I. M. D. Little, *A Critique of Welfare Economics* (Oxford: At the Clarendon Press, 1950); and Jerome Rothenberg, *The Measurement of Social Welfare* (Englewood Cliffs, N.J.: Prentice-Hall, Inc., 1961).

[54]Above, p. 55.

and *instantaneous* realization of these goals. Hence an inherent part of the definition of the situation is that certain institutionalized attention be given to the supplies of various facilities required to attain the valued goal. Part of this attention is economic activity. The goals—and the institutionalized means for attaining them—may vary considerably; they may concern perpetuation of kinship lines, attainment of a state of religious bliss, territorial expansion, or maximization of wealth. Economic activity is defined as a *relation* between these goals and the degree of scarcity of goods and services. Indeed the definition of the "economic" aspect in any given society—and the structure of its economy—will be in large part a function of both the institutionalized values and the availability (or scarcity) of resources.

In suggesting this definition and measurement of the "economic," I am attempting to resolve a tension that is inherent in comparative analysis. This is the tension between the comparative operationalization of objective activities on the one hand and the comparative operationalization of subjective cultural meanings on the other. The investigator is pulled toward the former because measurement is easy and comparisons are handy; but as we observed in considering monetary and physical indices, the concept of the "economic" is distorted by relying on these objective measures. At the same time the investigator is pulled toward the latter because he wishes to respect and give adequate representation to what individual cultures themselves define as "economic." This position was clearly stated by Marcel Mauss, who characterized his own comparative methodology as follows:

> . . . since we are concerned with *words and their meanings*, we choose only areas where we have access to the *minds of the societies* through documentation and philological research. This further limits our field of comparison. Each particular study has a bearing on the systems we set out to describe and is presented in its logical place. In this way we avoid that *method of haphazard comparison in which institutions lose their local colour and documents their value.*[55]

Yet if the investigator adheres too strongly to this position, he soon ends in a position of radical relativism, which treats everything as "economic" that any society chooses to define as "economic"; and in this way the investigator loses his grasp on any general concept of "the economic" whatsoever. My suggested definition of economic activity—a definition that *relates* social values and meanings to scarcity of resources—seems to

[55]Marcel Mauss, *The Gift: Forms and Functions of Exchange in Archaic Societies*, trans. Ian Cunnison (Glencoe, Ill.: The Free Press, 1954), pp. 2–3. Emphasis added.

avoid the pitfalls of both the objectivistic position and the subjectivistic position. The investigator, in constructing definitions and measures for general comparative concepts, such as "the economic," must allow cultural values and meanings to *intervene* between the concepts and their measurements. He must begin by comparing systematically the value systems of different societies, then identifying and measuring—using a different set of operational rules for each society—the classes of activity that are "economic" (scarcity-oriented) in relation to these values. This procedure is certainly more plagued with problems of operationalizability than the comparison of market transactions. But I am convinced that comparative analysis cannot proceed further without striving to introduce social values and meanings into the comparative identification and measurement of general constructs; if it does not undertake this task, it will be plagued by uncorrectable distortions from the very outset of analysis.

In setting forth my definition of the "economic" as a comparative construct, I have raised a set of general philosophical and methodological issues that have persisted in the social sciences for some time. I refer to the tension between positivistic objectivism on the one hand—a position that would define concepts and indices without any reference whatsoever to human consciousness and meaning, and phenomenological subjectivism on the other—a position that would make concepts identical to the meanings that individual actors and groups impart to them. My position is that definitions and measurements of concepts must *both* be as objectively measurable as possible *and* take into account the meaning assigned to the concept by the actors under investigation. Individual and cultural meaning systems, in short, are to be treated as a kind of intervening and transforming variable that must be inserted between generalized concept and empirical index.

The tension between the use of a single objective index and the use of diversified culturally qualified indices for comparative purposes is also illustrated in the work of Almond and Coleman, who put forth several suggestions for the comparative study of political institutions and behavior.[56] Like many other political scientists, Almond and Coleman are discontented with the comparative potential of traditional concepts in political science—concepts limited to the complex constitutional and parliamentary political systems of Western society in the nineteenth and twentieth centuries; they do not find these concepts useful "for the comparison of political systems differing radically in scale, structure, and culture."[57] In their search for more general comparative categories, Al-

[56]Gabriel A. Almond and James S. Coleman, eds., *The Politics of the Developing Areas* (Princeton, N.J.: Princeton University Press, 1960).

[57]*Ibid.*, pp. 304. Compare their statement with Radcliffe-Brown's: "In the study of the simpler societies the anthropologist finds that the concepts and theories of

mond and Coleman turn to anthropology and sociology. But they are also wary of very general sociological definitions that identify "political" with concepts like "integration" and "adaptation." They fear that such definitions represent "a return to a dull tool, rather than an advance to a sharper one, for if in pursuit of the political system we follow the phantoms of integration and adaptation, we will find ourselves including in the political system churches, economies, schools, kinship and lineage groups, age-sets, and the like."[58] I suggest, however, that in order to encompass all political activities it *is* necessary to include and measure the activities of churches, lineage groups, and so on, since these social elements *are* significant politically. Of course, I am aware of the difficulty of assessing and measuring this political significance empirically. Almond and Coleman apparently do not wish to go this far; they venture an in-between definition of political activity, somewhat more general than traditional definitions, but still not exhaustively comparative in principle: ". . . the political system is that system of interactions to be found in all independent societies which performs the functions of integration and adaptation . . . by means of the employment, or threat of employment, of more or less legitimate *physical compulsion*."[59] Physical compulsion, like money, is something "hard," relatively easy to operationalize. But to assert that this kind of definition is adequate for comparative analysis of political behavior is erroneous; to be so, it would have to be more general, even if less readily manageable empirically.

The general tension between easy operationalizability and comparative adequacy has also made its appearance in theoretical discussions of structural-functional analysis, in particular in the discussion of the "postulate of indispensability." In general terms, this postulate holds that there are certain universal functional exigencies (such as the socialization of the young, the integration of diverse groups in society) which society faces *and* that there are *specific* social structural forms which *alone* serve these functions (structural forms such as the nuclear family for socialization and organized religion for integration, for instance). Thus the postulate of indispensability links specific institutional or behavioral indices with general social functions, just as the monetary definition of economic

---

political philosophers or economists are unserviceable or insufficient. They have been elaborated in reference to societies of a limited number of types. In their place, the social anthropologist has to make for himself theories and concepts which will be universally applicable to all human societies, and, guided by these, carry out his work of observation and comparison." "Preface," *African Political Systems*, p. xiii.

[58] Almond and Coleman, *The Politics of the Developing Areas*, p. 5.

[59] *Ibid.*, p. 7. Compare Radcliffe-Brown's definition, which is remarkably parallel: "The political organization of a society is that aspect of the total organization which is concerned with the control and regulation of the use of *physical force*." "Preface," *African Political Systems*, p. xxiii. Emphasis added.

activity links money transactions to the general concept of "economic." Objecting to the postulate of indispensability, Merton has asserted that "just as the same item may have multiple functions, so may the same function be diversely fulfilled by alternative items. Functional needs are . . . taken to be permissive, rather than determinant, of specific social structures."[60] In line with this position, Merton goes on to insist on the importance of concepts like "functional alternatives," "functional equivalents," and "functional substitutes." Here Merton is opting for general comparative concepts (functions) that encompass a wide variety of empirical manifestations (items). I agree with Merton's emphasis but recognize that in doing so I am creating a host of problems of operationalization when it comes to identifying the range of structures that fulfill general functions.

To conclude this general discussion, let me return briefly to one of the ways of posing the problem of comparability: How is it possible to compare very different social systems—such as primitive tribes and advanced industrial societies—with one another, since they differ so radically in so many different respects? In one sense I have already answered this question by asserting that if we choose comparative dimensions that are in principle universal, and if we work out principles of operational definition in accord with the variety of social goals and meanings to which these dimensions are related, one society is comparable with any other society. It would be possible to compare the political system of a hunting-and-gathering tribe with the parliamentary system of Great Britain if the right comparative categories and the appropriate operational definitions were chosen.

Above and beyond this general principle, I should like to suggest, as a matter of comparative research strategy, that given the present state of the art of comparative analysis, it is most fruitful to compare social units that do not differ so radically as tribal societies and complex industrial societies. It is more fruitful to study variations in societies that are very close to one another in many respects. For example, we feel it is more fruitful to analyze the differential incidence of suicide in Denmark, Norway, and Sweden, which are quite close in cultural traditions and social structure,[61] than it is to study the suicide rate of Denmark in relation to that of India, whose cultural traditions and social structure are vastly different. The reason I favor this research strategy can best be stated in

[60]Robert K. Merton, *Social Theory and Social Structure*, rev. ed. (Glencoe, Ill.: The Free Press, 1957), pp. 33–34.

[61]For a review of various attempts to explain the different suicide rates in the Scandinavian countries, as well as an independent attempt to develop an explanation of the differences based on psychoanalytic variables, cf. Herbert Hendin, *Suicide and Scandinavia: A Psychoanalytic Study of Culture and Character* (New York: Grune & Stratton, Inc., 1964), pp. 1–26.

terms of the earlier discussion of parameters and operative variables. If two or more societies have important independent variables in common —such as cultural traditions in the case of the Scandinavian countries—it is relatively more permissible to treat these common characteristics as *parameters*, and study the effects of other variables *as if* these common characteristics were not in operation. The ability to convert potentially operative variables into parameters is of general scientific utility.[62] By contrast, if two social units that differ in almost every respect are chosen for comparison, the investigator is less able to "control" sources of difference considering them as parameters. The more similar two or more societies are with respect to crucial variables, the better able the social scientist is to isolate and analyze the influence of other variables that may account for the differences he wishes to explain comparatively.

One final research strategy remains to be discussed under the heading of the problem of comparability. Traditionally it has proved burdensome to compare the *content* of a specific tradition of a given society with that of another. It is difficult, for example, to compare the French bourgeoisie of the middle eighteenth century with the American middle classes of the twentieth century—the commercial and industrial base of the two classes differ; they are lodged in different stratificational contexts (the French bourgeoisie in a relatively elitist system with an established, if weakening, nobility; the American middle classes in a relatively open, middle-class-dominated egalitarian system). Still more difficulties arise when culturally more remote social groupings—for example, traditional Indian Brahmins with the New England "Brahmin" class—are compared. In these examples the problems of comparability loom large.

One way of meeting these problems of comparability is to compare the relevant social groupings not in terms of content but instead with respect to certain *intrasocietal relations experienced by each, independent of the content of the traditions affecting these groupings.* For example, the historical investigations of Alexis de Tocqueville revealed that one of the characteristics of the French bourgeoisie in the mid-eighteenth century was what is currently termed "status disequilibrium" or "lack of status crystallization." The middle classes, having attained much in terms of wealth and education, were nonetheless held back from participation in terms of political responsibility, access to privileges and offices reserved for the nobility, and access to "high society." The dissatisfactions of these status discrepancies, moreover, were an important ingredient of the political alienation of the French middle classes.[63] Now, compare the American middle-class experience on this dimension. The American mid-

---

[62]Above, p. 45.
[63]Alexis de Tocqueville, *The Old Regime and the French Revolution* (Garden City, N.Y.: Doubleday & Company, Inc., 1955), Part II, Chap. 8.

dle classes—however we choose to define them—as a whole, do not appear to experience status discrepancies to the same degree as the eighteenth-century French bourgeoisie. Yet in the American middle classes there are subclasses that do experience lack of status crystallization—highly educated persons with low-paying jobs, members of underprivileged ethnic minorities with high-status occupations, and so on. Can these groups be compared with the French bourgeoisie? With respect to cultural traditions, common aspirations, and so on, the answer is mainly negative. But with respect to their relation to the stratification systems of the two societies, the groupings seem more readily comparable. Furthermore, they are comparable because the basis of comparison is on *common intrasocietal relations* rather than on *unique cultural and social experiences* of the social groupings under comparison.

Another example will show the advantage of analyzing relations rather than content in comparative studies. Let us suppose that we are investigating student unrest in the United States and in Latin America. Let us suppose further that the curriculum studied—law, medicine, liberal arts, and so forth—is an important determinant in the level of student political unrest in both countries. In mentioning this kind of determinant, however, we raise a number of problems of comparability. How is it possible to compare law students in the United States with law students in Latin America? The curricula differ in content; American law schools have a "vocational" emphasis, Latin American law faculties a "humanistic" emphasis, and so on. We might transcend such problems of comparability, however, by asking, instead, in what relation each curriculum stands to the occupational structure of the country in question, in terms of ease of entry. Here we are changing the criterion of comparison from the concrete subject matter to a relation between student experience and probable later experience in the occupational structure. And in changing the criterion, we push to one side the differences in content between the various curricula. Using the new criterion, we would predict that engineers in both the United States and Latin America would show little unrest as students because the transition between student training and adult occupational roles is smooth in both cases; we would predict that American law students, who move into law firms and other forms of practice relatively smoothly, would be less prone to unrest than Latin law students, whose legal training equips them for very few specific occupational positions in their countries; and we would predict that liberal arts students in both cases would be subject to high rates of unrest because in neither case is there an easy, unambiguous transition to adult roles. Such a relational criterion helps to bypass the embarrassing and possibly unmanageable problems of comparing different content.

The Problem of Many Variables, Small N

One of the distinctive features of the comparative method is its applicability to a number of cases which is too small to permit statistical manipulation.[64] This feature gives rise to several methodological problems. Suppose, for example, we wish to pursue the explanation of the differential incidence of unrest among students in Latin America. Suppose, furthermore, that we have arrived at satisfactory indices for terms such as "unrest" and "student." Explanation involves the attempt to account for why, in certain American countries more than others, and within these countries in certain types of universities more than others, and within these universities among certain types of students more than others, the level of unrest is relatively high. Suppose, finally, that we discover associations between several independent variables and student unrest: students from lower socioeconomic backgrounds are more prone to join protest movements; students living away from their parental home are more prone to protest than those living at home; humanities students are more prone to protest than students in vocational subjects; students whose friends are politically active are more prone to unrest than those whose friends are not; and so on through several dozen associations. Among these many associations, many correlations, which are important, which are genuine, which are spurious, and which are weak? The answers to these questions are not easy to determine, however, because the number of countries is so small. We have more variables than cases. It appears to be impossible to sort out the respective influences of these variables. Multivariate statistical analysis is out of the question, since the number of cases is so small. This problem is endemic in comparative analysis, especially when the units in question are national units.[65]

Faced with this limitation, the investigator may turn to a more indirect but very valuable method of establishing the salience or importance of a particular association. This method is the *replication of the suspected association at a different analytic level.* Let me illustrate this method first by a classical example. Durkheim's most highly developed example for altruistic suicide was the military. His general interpretation was that military personnel, in comparison with civilians, were more involved in a collective code of honor and therefore were more likely to

---

[64]Above, p. 51.

[65]When the number of social units is larger—for example, when we deal with "cultures" as defined by the Human Relations Area Files, or when we deal with subcultural units such as family units, firms, etc.—the "comparative" problem turns into a statistical problem, and various statistical techniques can be brought to bear to remove spurious correlations and isolate genuinely operative conditions.

sacrifice themselves in the name of this code. On this basis he predicted higher rates of suicide among military personnel than among civilians. The available suicide statistics tended to support his hypothesis. Even after he corrected for marital status, the differences between military and civilian personnel stood. It still might be argued, however, that Durkheim had not isolated the salient differences between military and civilians; after all, they differ in many other respects than in commitment to a code of honor; on the basis of the gross comparison between military and civilians alone it is not evident that the differential value commitment is the operative variable.

To support his own interpretation, Durkheim turned to the analysis of *intra*military differences in suicide. First he compared those with limited terms of service with those of longer duration, finding that the latter—presumably more imbued with the military spirit than the former—showed higher rates of suicide; next he compared officers and noncommissioned officers with private soldiers, finding that the former—again more involved in the military life—showed higher rates; finally, he found ·a greater tendency for suicide among volunteers and reenlisted men, that is, those who chose the military life freely. Summarizing these intramilitary findings, Durkheim concluded that "the members of the army most stricken by suicide are also those most inclined to this career. . . ."[66] By replicating at the intraunit level, Durkheim rendered more plausible the interunit relation (between military and civilian); in all the intraunit comparisons the association was in the same direction as in the interunit comparison.[67]

Let us return to the example of student unrest in Latin American countries. Suppose, after comparative investigation, we are able to rank-order a dozen countries in terms of general level of unrest among students. Suppose further than the hypothesis mentioned earlier—the smoother the transition from student role to adult occupational role, the less the likelihood of unrest—appears to be a plausible hypothesis in accounting for the rank-ordering. Those Latin American countries with educational systems "out of line" with occupational structures in terms of this transition appear consistently to manifest higher levels of student unrest. But with an N of 12, and so many other plausible hypotheses available, we cannot have much confidence in the "transition" theory. To further test this theory, we turn to replication again, both at more general and less general analytic levels. We might observe, for example, that in general, Latin American countries have a greater incidence of student un-

---

[66]Durkheim, *Suicide*, p. 233.

[67]For a discussion of Durkheim's study, with special reference to the problem of replication and statistical significance, cf. Hanan C. Selvin, "Durkheim's *Suicide* and Problems of Empirical Research," *American Journal of Sociology*, 63 (1958), 607–19.

rest than North American countries. In the latter, moreover, education tends to be more technical, vocational, and geared to specific occupational lines than in Latin America. This finding would be consistent with the comparisons *among* the Latin American countries themselves. At a less general level, we might attempt to locate unrest according to the same association *within* each Latin American country. Thus, within each country, engineering and architectural students appear to be low in unrest because as a rule they move easily into occupational positions; law students are very high because, in Latin tradition, they are trained in general education and not prepared for any particular occupational role; economics students intermediate with respect to future occupational chances should be intermediate with respect to level of unrest. *Within* the United States, students in engineering, medicine, and law—with relatively smooth transitions into adult occupational roles—should be politically quiescent, whereas students in the liberal arts should be more prone to unrest, even though the overall level of unrest is lower in the United States than in Latin American countries. Should these hypothetical replications turn out as anticipated, they would generate greater confidence in the "transition" theory which could not be strengthened, no matter how refined the analytic techniques, if we remained at the level of comparing Latin American countries among themselves.[68]

In some cases intraunit comparisons may prove more fruitful than interunit comparisons. The logic behind this assertion is the same as that underlying the earlier assertion that it is often more fruitful to compare social units that are similar to one another, since it is more nearly possible to treat these similar respects as parameters. Suppose, for example, we wish to carry out certain investigations on societies that differ from one another in terms of level of industrialization. Suppose further that Germany, a relatively industrialized country, and Italy, a relatively unindustrialized country, are the two units chosen for comparison. For many purposes it would be more fruitful to compare northern Italy with southern Italy, and the Ruhr with Bavaria, than it would be to compare Germany as a whole with Italy as a whole. The two countries differ not only in level of industrialization but also in cultural traditions, type of

---

[68]This example reveals that the method of successive replication is likely to turn up new and perhaps unexpected hypotheses at each level at which it is applied. For example, we came up with the hypothesis that law students in one country are likely to behave characteristically differently from law students in another because of the relation between the legal training and the adult occupational structure. This hypothesis is considerably different from the one that would have arisen if we had remained at the lower descriptive level and generated propositions about law students as a general class to be compared—e.g., the proposition that "law students are prone to a high incidence of political unrest." The method of successive replication, then, may prove to be a method of *discovering* new hypotheses as well as rendering known hypotheses to be more or less plausible.

government, and so on. In interunit comparisons these variables cannot be treated as parameters. If we were, instead, to pursue *intraunit* comparisons between those regions of Italy and Germany that are industrialized and those regions that are not, it is possible to treat these interunit differences as parameters and thus possibly pinpoint the factors determining the differential level of industrialization more precisely. Then, having located what appear to be operative factors in intraunit comparisons, it is possible to move to the interunit comparisons to ascertain whether the same differences hold in the large.

Important and advantageous as is replication at different analytic levels in increasing confidence in comparative findings, the investigator must proceed judiciously in its use. He must attempt to establish that the parametric conditions governing the interunit comparisons are as nearly alike as possible to the parametric conditions governing the intraunit comparisons. Otherwise the investigation of the large relation in the small, or vice versa, would be an investigation of incomparables, like any other inappropriate comparison.

The Search for Universal Empirical
Occurrences and Associations Versus the
Multivariate Analysis of Empirical Differences

Earlier I identified a major goal task of scientific analysis as the specification of conditions under which an observable range of variation in empirical phenomena occurs. In pursuing this goal the investigator engages in three types of activities: (1) identifying and specifying the range of variation of the dependent variable; (2) establishing empirical associations between other conditions (the suspected independent variables) and the dependent variable; and (3) establishing the causal or determining status of the independent variables. These three activities are essential ingredients of specific explanation.

I believe that in the past comparative investigators, under the apparently proper influence of the scientific norm to search for *general* findings, have been led to a preoccupation with the first two types of activities, and that this preoccupation has inhibited or deflected the third kind of activity. Let me illustrate:

With respect to the first type of activity, investigators have sought to identify *cultural universals*, or manifestations of some phenomenon in which there is no variation whatsoever. A notable example is the assertion of the universal existence of the nuclear family or the universal existence of the incest taboo.[69] The analytic problem then becomes one

[69]Norman W. Bell and Ezra F. Vogel, eds., *A Modern Introduction to the Family* (Glencoe, Ill.: The Free Press), p. 2.

of adducing the various "functions" of the nuclear family or the incest taboo, or reasons for its universal incidence.

With respect to the second type of activity, investigators have sought to establish *universal associations* between conditions and dependent variables. A notable example of this search is the "finding" of the Chicago school of the interwar period on the association between the urban-industrial complex and the nuclear family.[70] The argument goes roughly as follows: The traditional farm or peasant family is given a shock by the development of a commercial market structure, by the development of industry, or by the development of cities—usually, in fact, by some great social force involving an undifferentiated combination of all three. The immediate effects of this shock are to draw one or more family members into wage labor (separate from their household), thereby destroying the traditional division of labor, making the family more mobile socially and geographically, placing the family in a generally anonymous social environment, and perhaps destroying its economic base further by flooding the market with cheap, mass-produced commodities that compete with those previously produced in the domestic setting. The result is the small nuclear family that is mobile, neolocal, and isolated from many of its previous social connections and functions. Once this assertion of the universality of the connection between the urban-industrial complex and the isolated nuclear family is made, the research problem quite appropriately becomes one of establishing the empirical strength of the relation by examining different societies at different stages of economic and urban development.

Both these activities—the search for universal occurrences and universal associations—are essential ingredients of the scientific enterprise. Clearly, however, they are not the whole enterprise. Furthermore, these activities have frequently led to several types of relatively unproductive byways of research:

1. Research on the universality of some occurrence or association may stalemate in controversy over the precise degree of "universality" that exists. With respect to the universality of the nuclear family, for example, the assertion of its universality has stirred a number of little traditions of research—on the Nayar, the Israeli family on the *kibbutzim*, the lower-class Jamaican family, for example—that attempt to establish, in considerable empirical detail, that the nuclear family *does* or *does not*

---

[70]Relevant works are Ernest W. Burgess and Harvey J. Locke, *The Family: From Institution to Companionship*, 2nd ed. (New York: American Book Company, 1953); W. F. Ogburn and M. F. Nimkoff, *Technology and the Changing Family* (Boston: Houghton Mifflin Company, 1955); and Ernest R. Mowrer, *Family Disorganization: An Introduction to a Sociological Analysis* (Chicago: University of Chicago Press, 1927).

exist in some particular social setting. Such research has some value insofar as it either fortifies or chips away at the assertion of empirical universality; yet, focusing on this assertion, investigators tend to neglect to consider new variables systematically to specify the precise conditions under which the nuclear family is institutionalized in different ways. Research, in short, tends to focus too exclusively on the status of the dependent variable rather than on the connection between independent variables that determine variations in the dependent variable.

With respect to the universal association between the urban-industrial complex and the isolated nuclear family, a number of "negative findings" have also begun to accrue.[71] These findings tend to show that the isolated nuclear family sometimes antedates urbanization and industrialization and that various kinds of extended family structures persist after urban-industrial development. While these findings are valuable, they are limited to the status of the dependent variable itself; the research does little to specify, in a systematic way, any new conditions or variables by which we can account for the differences in family structure. This limitation stems, I submit, from too great a preoccupation with the *empirical* universality—or lack of it—of an association.

2. If an occurrence or association is to be described as genuinely universal, its characterization may have to be so general that many important sources of variation are compressed into a global concept. With respect to the incest taboo, for example, it is apparent that with few exceptions, father-daughter and brother-sister sexual intercourse or marriage are almost universally prohibited. But the form this prohibition takes, the degree to which it is generalized to other kinsmen, the severity of sanctions against it, the kinds and rates of deviance from the taboo—all these variations tend to be overlooked if the research becomes too exclusively focused on the simple universality or nonuniversality of incest. Raymond Firth, protesting against simple explanations of the "universal" incest taboo, has written, "I am prepared to see it shown that the incest situation varies according to the social structure of each community, that it has little to do with the prevention of sex relations, as such, but that its real correlation is to be found in the maintenance of institutional forms in the society as a whole, and of the specific interest of groups in

---

[71]For example, Gideon Sjoberg, "Family Organization in the Preindustrial City," *Marriage and Family Living*, 18 (1956), 30–36; John Mogey, "Introduction" to "Changes in the Family," *International Social Science Journal*, 14 (1962), 417; Eugene Litwak, "Occupational Mobility and Family Cohesion" and "Geographic Mobility and Extended Family Cohesion," *American Sociological Review*, 25 (1960), pp. 9–21 and 385–94; and Sidney M. Greenfield, "Industrialization and the Family in Sociological Theory," *American Journal of Sociology*, 67 (1961–62), 312–22. See also the brief but informative discussion by William J. Goode in *The Family* (Englewood Cliffs, N.J.: Prentice-Hall, Inc., 1964), pp. 108–16.

particular."[72] Yet these questions cannot be answered unless the starting point of analysis is with variations in family institutions and sexual behavior instead of the preoccupation with the universal or nonuniversal occurrence of these phenomena.

The focus on the relations between the urban-industrial complex and the individuated nuclear family has also tended to obscure important sources of variation on both sides of the relation. Certainly the variables of industrialization and urbanization should be separated for purposes of assessing their impact on the family. Furthermore, neither urbanization nor industrialization is an irreducible whole; several subtypes of each should be identified before any adequate statement of the relations between each and the family can be formulated. In addition, the "individuated nuclear family" is not a single entity; it also displays variations that demand classification and separate description of subtypes. If we introduce these kinds of complexity in relating the independent and the dependent variables, we are in a better position to establish the specific conditions under which urban and industrial variables will influence family variables than if we remain at the level of nonspecific universals. Of course, such refinement of variables involves a sacrifice of "universals" and "invariants" in the meantime, but in this case I consider the sacrifice to be an advantage.

3. Preoccupation with the universality of an occurrence or an association may lead to a concern with methodological problems that do not merit this concern. If, for example, the investigator defines his problem as essentially correlational rather than explanatory, he is likely to focus on what has been called the issue of "independence of cases." The issue is this: If two societies have been in contact with one another in the past and have borrowed various cultural traits, should not they be counted as one society in order not to "inflate" the significance of the occurrence of this trait?[73] In an early effort at cross-cultural correlation, Hobhouse, Wheeler, and Ginsberg formulated this issue pointedly:

> It may be asked whether in any cultural area—in any territory, that is, where the conditions of life are very similar, and where, though it is too large for direct intercourse between its parts, there is opportunity for institutions to propagate themselves in the course of generations by social contact—we ought to reckon distinct cases at all. Institutions and customs tend to propagate themselves indefinitely, and if we find, say, a certain

---

[72]*We, the Tikopia* (London: George Allen and Unwin Ltd., 1936), p. 340. Cited in Russell Middleton, "Brother-Sister and Father-Daughter Marriage in Ancient Egypt," *American Sociological Review* 27 (1962), p. 611.

[73]This kind of criticism has plagued cross-cultural research from the very beginning. John W. M. Whiting, "The Cross-Cultural Method," p. 528.

form of marriage all over a sub-continent, it may be that it has had a single origin, and ought on our principles be accounted one case rather than many. Thus we find a certain amount of polygamy—very variable it is true—common apparently, with one doubtful exception, to all Australian tribes. Shall we count this as upwards of thirty instances, or is it in reality only one instance?[74]

Murdock, in his ambitious correlational work on kinship structures, re-calculated some of his work on the basis of "culture areas" as well as "tribal and societal units" in order to overcome the problem of possible contamination partially.[75] This methodological problem of the independence of cases is important and relevant if we remain at the level of correlation alone. But with respect to explanation—which involves the manipulation of parameters and operative variables—this particular methodological problem recedes into the background; even more, the lack of independence of cases may become an advantage for comparative analysis. Suppose, for example, we wish to analyze the factors underlying polygamous customs in a number of Australian tribal societies that are "not independent" from one another in terms of origins and borrowing. The fact that these tribes have similar origins permits us to consider those features they have in common as parameters, and this in turn allows us to pinpoint the operative variables influencing polygamy much more precisely than if these societies were fully "independent." By focusing on association alone, and thereby making "lack of independence" only a methodological difficulty, we obscure the positive uses that common origins and common features can have for comparative analysis.

4. Preoccupation with empirical universals often leads to *ad hoc* "explaining away" of apparent exceptions to the universal by appeal to unanalyzed residual categories. To illustrate this, let us refer to Robert Michels's famous "iron law of oligarchy," which is an assertion of a universal empirical association. For his dependent variable Michels chose the degree of concentration of power in the hands of a few in complex organizations. As independent variables Michels identified various technical and mechanical features of organizations associated with its increasing size—the increasing difficulty of equal participation in decision making, coordination of the organization's activities, and so on. In addition, he singled out various psychological characteristics of the masses (for example, their tendency to submit to and become dependent on leaders) and psychological characteristics of leaders (for example, their tendency to develop a sense of their own indispensability) as independ-

[74]L. T. Hobhouse, G. C. Wheeler and Morris Ginsberg, *The Material Culture and Social Institutions of the Simpler Peoples: An Essay in Correlation* (London: Chapman and Hall Ltd., 1915), p. 11.
[75]Murdock, *Social Structure*, pp. ix–x.

ent variables. All these independent variables, according to Michels, work in the same direction: to consolidate the power of an elite corps of leaders who dominate the masses and are relatively free from influence by them. This iron law of oligarchy, Michels concluded, is an empirical universal.

Most of Michels's exposition in *Political Parties* was given over to the attempt to establish that the political parties and trade unions of the late nineteenth and early twentieth centuries were in fact subject to this iron law. At various points in his analysis, however, Michels was at pains to handle various apparent exceptions of his iron law. He usually treated these apparent exceptions in one of two ways:

a. He regarded the exception as unimportant or unreal. For example, with respect to the referendum—which, on the face of it, represents an upward flow of influence in the polity—Michels dismissed it with assertions such as "the history of the referendum as a democratic expedient utilized by the socialist parties may be summed up by saying that its application has been rare, and that its results have been unfortunate."[76] Again, with respect to leaders' threats to resign—an apparent departure from the iron law—Michels interpreted these threats as leaders' attempts to consolidate their own power by bullying the followers. Michels may be more or less correct empirically in these diagnoses; but whether correct or not, I do not consider his method to be adequate. His tendency in these examples, as well as elsewhere in his work, was to eschew systematic explanations of why such phenomena persist despite their apparent unimportance; rather he wrote apparent exceptions off simply as "non-data." I submit that this relatively unproductive kind of analysis is a by-product of an undue fascination with establishing the empirical universality of a proposition rather than analyzing the empirical variability around some posited analytic relation.

b. He introduced a new variable—without formally incorporating it into his theory—to account for the apparent exception. In places Michels used cultural and ideological variables in this way, even though he rejected such variables as unimportant elsewhere in his work. Speaking of the tendency of leadership to consolidate, Michels made the expected assertion that "with the institution of leadership there simultaneously begins, owing to the long tenure of office, the transformation of the leaders into a closed caste."[77] Yet a few sentences later he qualified: "Unless, as in France, extreme individualism and fanatical political dogmatism stand in the way, the old leaders present themselves to the masses as a compact phalanx—at any rate whenever the masses are so much aroused

[76]Robert Michels, *Political Parties* (New York: Dover Publications, Inc., 1959), p. 335.
[77]*Ibid.*, p. 156.

as to endanger the position of the leaders."[78] Here Michels was identifying something characteristically "French" that makes for an exception to the iron law. In another place, he noted the presence of an abundance of Jews among the leaders of the socialist and revolutionary parties, and he fortified this observation with the statement that "specific racial qualities make the Jew a born leader of the masses, a born organizer and propagandist."[79] Then he proceeded to describe in some detail these specifically Jewish qualities. From Michels's qualification it would appear that something distinctively cultural—something associated with Jewishness—would have to do with the consolidation of leadership, above and beyond the inherent tendencies in organization itself. Yet Michels tended to leave both these exceptions and the implicit cultural explanations merely hanging. They surround his theory as convenient categories that are mobilized to account for apparent exceptions or additions to the iron law. They give his theory an appearance of simplicity and neatness; but in reality he was relying casually on many more variables than were formally incorporated into his original formulation of the empirical universal.

I believe that these relatively unproductive byways of research are more likely to be minimized if the comparative investigator gives up the search for empirically universal occurrences and associations. Certainly it is necessary in scientific analysis to identify and specify the range of variation of the dependent variable; it is equally indispensable to determine the strength of the empirical association between the dependent variable and suspected independent variables as carefully as possible. But instead of allowing each of these procedures to turn into a search for universals (or statements of statistical distribution), the research should focus on the multivariate analysis of ranges of variation of the dependent variable. Certainly it is desirable—even necessary—to begin a study with the *analytic* assertion of universal association. But the research procedure should *not* be to attempt to discover only the degree to which this analytic relation holds empirically, but rather a statement of the conditions under which it may be expected to obtain empirically. The question of the exact degree of universality is left open; the question of the exact pattern of empirical variation is left open. Comparative analysis should ask what factors appear to be at work when the posited analytic association is not observed empirically. And this is done by the systematic introduction of new variables and the manipulation of parameters and operative variables according to the canons of statistical analysis and systematic comparative illustration.

[78]*Ibid.*
[79]*Ibid.*, p. 258.

PART II

CONCEPTUAL EQUIVALENCE
AND
CULTURAL BIAS

3

The Beam in Our Eyes

GUNNAR MYRDAL

ANOTHER SOURCE OF BIAS: TRANSFERENCE OF WESTERN CONCEPTS AND THEORIES

Another primary source of bias of special importance to the study of the underdeveloped countries of South Asia may appear to be more mechanical, a function merely of the rapidity with which we have undertaken massive research in a previously almost uncultivated field. As research must of necessity start from a theory, a set of analytical preconceptions, it was tempting to use the tools that were forged in the West and that, in the main, served a useful purpose there,[1] without careful consideration of their suitability for South Asia. Thus a Western approach became incorporated into the mainstream of the discussion of development problems in South Asia, both within the region and outside it. Indeed, Western theoretical approaches have assumed the role of master models. For reasons we shall go into at considerable length in the body of the book, a Western approach must be regarded as a biased approach. Let us attempt to understand how this transfer came to pass.

Economic theorists, more than other social scientists, have long been disposed to arrive at general propositions and then postulate them as valid for every time, place, and culture. There is a tendency in contemporary economic theory to follow this path to the extreme. For such confidence in the constructs of economic reasoning, there is no empirical justification. But even apart from this recent tendency, we have inherited from classical economics a treasury of theories that are regularly posited

Reprinted from Gunnar Myrdal, *Asian Drama: An Inquiry into the Poverty of Nations* (New York: The Twentieth Century Fund, 1968), pp. 16–26. Copyright © 1968 by The Twentieth Century Fund. Reprinted by permission of the publisher.

[1] Throughout this book I am making the generous assumption that the Western approach is fairly adequate to Western conditions. This might be an overstatement. In any case, this is a book on South Asia, and I have not felt it to be my task to go into a critical analysis of the use of Western concepts and theories outside the region I am studying.

with more general claims than they warrant. The very concepts used in their construction aspire to a universal applicability that they do not in fact possess. As long as their use is restricted to our part of the world this pretense of generality may do little harm. But when theories and concepts designed to fit the special conditions of the Western world—and thus containing the implicit assumptions about social reality by which this fitting was accomplished—are used in the study of underdeveloped countries in South Asia, where they do *not* fit, the consequences are serious.

There is a conservatism of methodology in the social sciences, especially in economics, that undoubtedly has contributed to the adherence to familiar Western theories in the intensive study of underdeveloped countries. Economists operate to a great extent within a framework that developed early in close relationship with the Western philosophies of natural law and utilitarianism and the rationalistic psychology of hedonism. Only with time has this tradition been adapted to changing conditions, and then without much feeling of need for radical modifications. That economists work within a methodologically conservative tradition is usually not so apparent to the economists themselves, especially as the tradition affords them opportunity to display acumen and learning and, within limits, to be inventive, original, and controversial. Even the heretics remain bound by traditional thought in formulating their heresies.[2] As circumstances, particularly political ones, changed, there was room for a shifting of emphasis and approach. When theoretical innovations lagged far behind events, such adjustments sometimes took on the appearance of definite breaks, as in the so-called Keynesian "revolution." The new thoughts were soon integrated into the traditional mold, slightly modified to better suit the environment, the changes which were in themselves largely responsible for inspiring fresh thinking.

Occasionally a breakthrough established new lines of thought that contrasted more sharply with tradition. The most important challenge came, of course, from Marx and his followers. But Marx, at the base of his constructs, retained much of classical economic theory. And gradually economists remaining within the fold incorporated large parts of what was or seemed novel in Marx's approach, not least in regard to the problems of development, as we shall see. For both these reasons we should not be surprised to find that the biases operating on Western economists often tend to converge with those conditioning economists in the Communist countries. These assertions will be exemplified in various contexts in this book.

[2]See Myrdal, *Economic Theory and Under-developed Regions*, pp. 229ff.

When we economists, working within this tenacious but variegated and flexible tradition of preconceptions that admittedly are not too badly fitted to our own conditions, suddenly turn our attention to countries with radically different conditions, the risk of fundamental error is exceedingly great.[3] This risk is heightened by the dearth of empirical data on social realities in the underdeveloped countries of South Asia, which enables many biases to be perpetuated that might be questioned and corrected if concepts and theories could be exposed to the challenge of concrete facts. The problem is compounded by another consequence of the Western-biased approach. When new data are assembled, the conceptual categories used are inappropriate to the conditions existing: as, for example, when the underutilization of the labor force in the South Asian countries is analyzed according to Western concepts of unemployment, disguised unemployment, and underemployment. The resulting mountains of figures have either no meaning or a meaning other than that imputed to them. Empirical research then becomes faulty and shallow, and, more important in the present context, less valuable for testing the premises latent in the Western concepts that have guided the production of new statistics. The very fact that the researcher gets figures to play with tends to confirm his original, biased approach. Although it is the confrontation with the facts that ultimately will rectify our conceptual apparatus, initially the paucity and flimsiness of data in underdeveloped countries leave ample opportunity for biases, and the continuing collection of data under biased notions only postpones the day when reality can effectively challenge inherited preconceptions.

The danger of bias does not necessarily arise from the fact that students from the rich countries in the West inevitably face the problems of underdeveloped countries in South Asia as strangers. If anything, the outsider's view has advantages in social research. There are two ways of knowing a toothache: as a patient or as a dentist, and the latter is usually not the less objective. The white Southerner's conviction that he, and he alone, "knows" the American Negroes because of his close association with them has been proved erroneous. The stranger's view may be superficial, it is true, but superficiality is not the monopoly of strangers; it is a matter of the intensity and effectiveness of research. There is thus no necessary connection between superficiality and the extent of bias. Indeed, biases in research have no relation to superficiality *per se.* They emanate

[3]"One ever-present problem is the possibility that a conceptual scheme will imprison the observer, allowing him to see only what the scheme directs him to see and ruling out other interpretations of data. It is readily admitted that this danger is implicit in all a priori thinking." (Richard C. Snyder and Glenn D. Paige, "The United States Decision to Resist Aggression in Korea: The Application of an Analytic Scheme," in *Administrative Science Quarterly*, Vol 3, No. 3, December 1958, p. 358.)

from the influences exerted by society, from our personal involvement in what we are studying, and from our tendency to apply approaches with which we are familiar to environments that are radically different. Biases can be present or absent as much when we are strangers to the country we are studying as when we are its nationals and as much when the research undertaken stretches over long periods and is conducted with a huge apparatus as when it is simply a journalist's attempt to put his impressions and reflections in order.

Nor are Western economists uniquely subject to the specific biases emanating from our methodological conservatism. Our confreres in the South Asian countries are afflicted as much, if not more, with them. Many have been trained at Western centers of learning or by teachers who acquired their training in the West. All have been thoroughly exposed to the great economic literature in the Western tradition. Familiarity with, and ability to work in accordance with, that tradition is apt to give them status at home. Their motivations for sharing in this bias are fairly independent of their political attitudes. Part of the explanation, as will be shown in the next section, is that application of the Western approach serves both conservative and radical needs for rationalization in the South Asian countries.

That the use of Western theories, models, and concepts in the study of economic problems in the South Asian countries is a cause of bias seriously distorting that study will be a main theme of this book. For the moment a few *obiter dicta* must suffice to outline this general criticism.

The concepts and the theory of unemployment and underemployment rest on assumptions about attitudes and institutions that, though fairly realistic in the developed countries, are unrealistic in the underdeveloped countries.

The neat division of income into two parts, consumption and saving, is realistic in Western societies where the general levels of income and a stratified system of income redistribution by social security policies and other means have largely abrogated any influence of consumption on productivity. This is not the case in the underdeveloped countries.

Marx's assumption, so widely adopted by Western economists, that the effects of industrialization and, indeed, of investment generally—in the final instance Marx's changes in the "modes of production"—spread quickly to other sectors of the economy and to institutions and attitudes, may be fairly realistic for Western countries, both now and when they started their rapid economic development. But as these "spread effects" are a function of the level of living and of the general culture, the assumption is not valid for most underdeveloped countries, particularly when the sectors of change are small in comparison with the total community. This should be obvious after many decades of colonial history during which the modern enterprises remained enclaves in a largely stagnating economy, but it is seldom given the recognition it deserves, either in economic analysis or in planning for development.

The lack of mobility and the imperfection of markets in underdeveloped countries rob the analytical method of aggregation of magnitudes—employment, savings, investment, and output—of much of its meaning. This conceptual difficulty is in addition to the statistical one already pointed out: that the data aggregated are frail and imperfect, partly because their categories are unrealistic.

The list could be made much longer, as will be seen in this book. Our main point is that while in the Western world an analysis in "economic" terms—markets and prices, employment and unemployment, consumption and savings, investment and output—that abstracts from modes and levels of living and from attitudes, institutions, and culture may make sense and lead to valid inferences, an analogous procedure plainly does not in underdeveloped countries. There one cannot make such abstractions; a realistic analysis must deal with the problems in terms that are attitudinal and institutional and take into account the very low levels of living and culture. The newest attempts to analyze education (and health) in terms of "investment in man" do not even state the problem in a rational way. The "non-economic" facts do not adjust smoothly to economic changes, but set up inhibitions and obstacles to them, so that often the "economic" terms cannot even be given a clear meaning. A practical corollary is the much greater need for coordination of planning in the "economic" and the "noneconomic" fields.[4] Acknowledgment of this important difference is frequently made by way of qualifications and reservations. But the basic approach, not least in regard to the problems of economic planning, has remained a rather simple application of Western concepts and theories.

THE WESTERN APPROACH SERVES DEEPER INCLINATIONS TO BIAS

The temptation to apply the Western approach was said above to be almost mechanical, a function of the speed with which research was be-

[4]"For all practical purposes growth and development in the less developed parts of the world seem to depend rather upon the speed and efficiency with which given attitudes and institutions can be and actually are modified and changed. Viewed in its truly dynamic dimension the process of economic growth and development is and always has been a problem of political and socio-cultural change." (K. William Kapp, *Hindu Culture, Economic Development and Economic Planning in India*, Asia Publishing House, Bombay, 1963, p. 69.)

gun in a nearly untouched field and our natural inclination to utilize research methods with which we were familiar. The urge to do so was the more impelling as no other kit of tools was available for bringing a semblance of order into the analysis of the complex conditions in South Asian countries. But the matter is not so uncomplicated. The appeal of the Western conceptual approach draws further strength from the fact that it is well fitted to the rationalization of opportunistic interests both in the developed Western countries and among the influential intellectual elite in the underdeveloped countries themselves.

Generally speaking, the Western approach abstracts from most of the conditions that are peculiar to the South Asian countries and are responsible for their underdevelopment and for the special difficulties they meet in developing. These conditions and difficulties are all of a type that South Asians and their foreign well-wishers must desire to forget. They were the features of the social structure that were prominent in the thoughts of the European colonial masters, both in their stereotypes and in their more sophisticated reasonings. Exaggerated emphasis on these impediments to development served their need for rationalization. It explained away their responsibility for the backwardness of colonial peoples and their failure to try to improve matters. Both the post-colonial ideologies and the ideologies of the liberation movements were deeply stamped by protests against that thinking. And so the pendulum of biases swung from one extreme to the other. The intellectuals in these countries want to rationalize in the contrary sense, and it serves their needs to make the abstractions implied by Western economists. Genuine sympathy, in addition to reasons of diplomacy, brought Western economists under the same spell of opportunism. The fact that what they were applying was established theory, which had been successfully used in the Western countries, made the entrance of this systematic bias the easier.

It was an approach that appealed to both radicals and conservatives in South Asia. The radicals, partly under the impact of Marx's thinking, were prone to exaggerate the rapidity of adjustment of the entire social system to changes in the "economic" sphere; conservatives, averse to direct policy intervention in modes and levels of living, attitudes, and institutions, welcomed an approach that placed these matters in the shadow. Concerning the radicals, we must also remind ourselves of the similarities, particularly in basic concepts, between Marx's and Western economic theorizing. These have already been referred to and are illustrated in many contexts in the ensuing chapters.

There are also differences in approach, however, and it should be clear that certain elements of Marx's economic speculation often seem to fit situations in South Asia much more closely than those in the rich modern welfare states of the West: for instance, the apparent existence of a "reserve army" of idle, or largely idle, workers; the existence and the increase of a dispossessed proletariat; the often frank exploitation of workers by employers; and the big and widening gap between a few rich individuals or families and the masses of very poor people. It is remarkable that very little fresh analysis of the problems of the region in Marx's terms is forthcoming, while essays in the Western pattern are abundant. We thus often find at the universities in South Asia economists who are strongly anti-Western in their sympathies and politically far to the left, even avowed Communists or fellow-travellers, but who are yet eager and proud to place the emphasis of their teaching on the latest abstract and formal growth models developed at Cambridge or Yale, and whose ambition is to write articles resembling those in the Western journals and, hopefully, to publish them there.

In attempting to understand this bent of mind of the radicals we must take into account the virtual bombardment of massive Western research on the underdeveloped countries in recent times, while the literary output on their problems in Communist countries has been small, polite, but uninspiring. An additional factor is, however, that pursuit of Marx's particular approach referred to above would inevitably have led to a consideration of "non-economic" factors. The competitive strength of the Western approach is, at bottom, that its abstractions give an optimistic slant to the thinking about the development problems in the underdeveloped countries of the region.

Optimism, and therefore approaches that make optimism seem more realistic, is itself a natural urge for intellectuals in South Asia. That all planning in the region tends to err on the side of optimism is rather palpably clear.[5] The leaning toward diplomatic forbearance in the Western countries fits equally well with biases toward unwarranted optimism among their economists. In Western countries, especially America, optimism is even prized, as a foundation for enterprise and courage; it is almost part of the inherited cultural pattern—what George F. Kennan once called "the great American capacity for enthusiasm and self-hypnosis."[6] In the contest for souls, it is felt to be to the interest of the West that the underdeveloped countries outside the Communist sphere have develop-

---

[5]India's First Five Year Plan would seem to be an exception, as it underestimated the growth of output. But the surpassing of estimates was largely due to unexpectedly favorable monsoons and other accidents. The targets in regard to the policy measures actually making up the plan, and in particular the investments, were not met.

[6]In the Soviet Union uncritical optimism is programmatic, and realism, when it does not lead to optimistic conclusions, is considered a "bourgeois" deviation; this constitutes one of the many similarities in cultural situation between the United States and the Soviet Union.

ment and be made to believe in it. In the West there is also a natural wish, and so a temptation to believe, that the underdeveloped countries in South Asia will come to follow policy lines similar to those of the Western countries, and that they will develop into national communities that are politically, socially, and economically like our own. For this reason, too, there is a normal tendency to use a Western approach in studying these countries, as to do so is to play down the initial differences and make such development appear more feasible.

The two main sources of bias in the Western countries thus strengthen each other in that their influences tend to converge. As we saw, the international power conflict and the tensions and emotions associated with it have influenced the study of the problems of the underdeveloped countries in South Asia in the general direction of diplomatic kindness and tolerance—again, provided that these countries are not on the wrong side in that conflict. Many of the conditions peculiar to these countries are highly undesirable; indeed, this is what is meant by their being underdeveloped. Therefore, the other source of bias with which we dealt in the last section—the tendency to use the familiar theories and concepts that have been used successfully in the analysis of Western countries—exerts influences in the same direction. For when using the Western approach one can more easily soften the bite of these peculiar and undesirable conditions.

We have wanted to stress the political urges behind these tendencies that affect research on underdeveloped countries in the region. But these tendencies have at their core a compassion that makes them almost irresistible. Quite aside from the cold war and the opportunistic tendencies to bias emerging from it, we of the West are by tradition disposed to be friendly to peoples in distress, once we begin to take an interest in their condition. And it is our earnest hope, apart from all selfish interests, that they will succeed in their development efforts. That we wish them to develop into national communities as similar to our own as possible is a natural ethnocentric impulse that would make itself felt in the calmest world situation. Perhaps it should be stressed again that the concern of the West about the possibility of Communist expansion in underdeveloped countries is also understandable, and from the viewpoint of our own interests valid. And these interests justify using our influence to stop it. Still less can one criticize the human sympathy that characterizes the Western attitude toward these countries.

Nevertheless, we must not let these understandable and genuine feelings influence our perception of the facts. It is the ethos of scientific inquiry that truth and blunt truth-speaking are wholesome and that illusions, including those inspired by charity and good will, are always damaging. Illusions handicap the pursuit of knowledge and they must obstruct efforts to make planning for development fully effective and successful. For this reason, the present book is intended to be undiplomatic. In our study we want to step outside the drama while we are working. We recognize no legitimate demand on the student to spare anybody's feelings. Facts should be stated coldly: understatements, as well as overstatements, represent biases.[7]

One more point should be mentioned before we leave this attempt to characterize briefly the forces tending to create biases in research on development problems in South Asia. As these biases engender an over-optimistic view of development prospects, they sometimes provide encouragement; but mainly they are apt to create undue complacency. In any case, a more realistic view makes it clear that *development requires increased efforts: speedier and more effective reforms in South Asia and greater concern in the West.*

A NOTE ON THE UNAVOIDABLE *A PRIORI*

Our criticism of the tendency to take the Western approach in studying the conditions and problems of the underdeveloped countries in

[7]In regard to issues that have been felt to be awkward and threatening—for instance, the Negro problem in America—biases toward forbearance and optimism have been quite general in the social sciences. A "balanced view" on such issues tends to be a view that soft-pedals difficulties and causes for worry. Understatements, though in principle just as damaging to the establishment of truth as overstatements, are considered more "objective" and certainly give more respectability. When working without explicit value premises, "the optimistic bias becomes strengthened, paradoxically enough, by the scientists's own critical sense and his demand for foolproof evidence. The burden of proof is upon those who assert that things are bad in our society; it is not the other way around. Unfortunate facts are usually more difficult to observe and ascertain, as so many of the persons in control have strong interests in hiding them. The scientist in his struggle to detect truth will be on his guard against making statements which are unwarranted. His very urge to objectivity will thus induce him to picture reality as more pleasant than it is." (Gunnar Myrdal, *An American Dilemma, The Negro Problem and Modern Democracy*, Harper, New York, 1944, p. 1039.)

"I have often observed that social scientists who are responsible for the publication of other authors' works or who utilize them in their own writings, when they apprehend biases, believe that these can be 'edited away,' by modifying certain expressions used or cutting out or revising certain practical conclusions drawn. Similarly, a general tendency toward understatement is observable in most social science literature. When an author has set down something which he feels to be unfavorable about a social class or a region, he looks for something favorable to say in order to 'balance the picture.' A 'balanced view,' a colorless drawing, is considered to be more 'scientific.' Particularly in governmental investigations great care is usually taken to spare the readers. The deliberate attempt that is made in such reports not to offend anyone will often make them difficult to use for scientific purposes. This tendency is, of course, not only ineffective in mitigating biases, but, even worse, it is itself one of the main types of bias in research." (*Ibid.*, p. 1043.)

Concerning the general problem of bias, see the same work, pp. 1035–45.

South Asia should not be understood as a denial of the right to start out with a theoretical preconception about how things are or, indeed, of the necessity of doing so. Questions are necessarily prior to answers, and no answers are conceivable that are not answers to questions. A "purely factual" study—observation of a segment of social reality with no pre-conceptions—is not possible; it could only lead to a chaotic accumulation of meaningless impressions. Even the savage has his selective precon-ceptions by which he can organize, interpret, and give meaning to his experiences. On a fundamental level modern social science is no different from the magical thinking of primitive man. Scientific data—facts estab-lished by observation and classification—have no existence outside the framework of preconceptions. Generalizations about reality, and their or-ganization within an abstract framework of presumed interrelations, pre-cede specification and verification. They constitute "theory" in research.

In strict logic a non-theoretical approach in scientific work is thus impossible; and every theory contains the seed of an *a priori* thought. When this theory is stated explicitly, we can scrutinize its inner con-sistency. This immanent criticism does not take us beyond the sphere of abstract logical relationships; it conveys nothing about empirical reality. But it is also a first principle of science that facts are sovereign. Theory, therefore, must not only be subjected to immanent criticism for logical consistency but must constantly be measured against reality and adjusted accordingly.

The two processes go together. As we increase the volume of ob-servational data to which we are led by our analytical preconceptions, our original theories are refitted in order to make sense of the data and explain them. This is the crux of all science: It always begins *a priori* but must constantly strive to find an empirical basis for knowledge and thus to become more adequate to the reality under study. This is also the reason why we can never achieve perfection—merely an approximate fitting of theory to facts. But there are differences in how close we can come to the facts. In the underdeveloped countries of South Asia, most of the crucial data are deficient in scope and reliability. Moreover, such data as exist are heavily prejudiced by inadequate preconceptions, and we must always be on guard against biases arising from this source.

Theory is thus no more than a correlated set of questions to the so-cial reality under study. Theory always has its essential function in rela-tion to research still to be carried out. As greater realism is approached, theory becomes better equipped to fulfill this function. "Pure" and un-restricted model-building *pro exercitio* may have its aesthetic or peda-gogical value, but it is a diversion from serious research.

What must be emphasized is that *all knowledge, and all ignorance, tends to be opportunistic*,[8] and becomes the more so the less it is checked and reconditioned by solid research directed to the empirical facts. Through wide and arduous travelling, which seldom means taking the shortest route, students undoubtedly will be forced gradually to correct their preconceptions, however deeply rooted in opportunism these may be. Until the approach is better tailored to reality, the data fail to fall into place, the facts rebel, and the logic is strained. In the longer time perspective I see no reason for pessimism about the study of the under-developed countries in South Asia. Inherent in all honest research is a self-correcting, purifying force that in the end will affirm itself.

An interesting parallel comes to mind—namely, the history of re-search on inherited group differentials in aptitudes, especially intelli-gence. This to me has always stood as one of the great monuments to the ethos of truth-seeking and its intrinsic quality of leading, in the end, to truer knowledge. The psychologists who more than half a century ago set out to measure innate differences in intelligence between whites and Negroes, men and women, rich and poor, had no doubt that such differ-ences existed and that they were pronounced. There is truth in the bibli-cal saying that "he that seeketh, findeth"; but if a scientist seeks what isn't there he will find it only as long as empirical data are scanty and the logic is allowed to be forced. As the researchers amassed their ob-servations and as they refined their tools for observation and analysis, they found what they had *not* been seeking and what, indeed, was con-trary to their preconceptions: the differences disappeared, or at least could not be scientifically established.

We shall in time come to see a similar change in the approach to the study of the underdeveloped countries in South Asia. The more we labor with these problems, the more evident will become the necessity to modify the analytical preconceptions that are now dominant. But this process of improvement can be speeded up if we help by scrutinizing our approaches for irrational influences that are working on our minds. This is why I have asked for greater interest in the sociology of knowledge. Such an inward turn of research interests would pay large dividends in more rapid scientific progress.

[8]Myrdal, *An American Dilemma*, pp. 40–42 *et passim*.

4

The Problem of Cross-Cultural Identification of Psychiatric Disorders

CHARLES SAVAGE, ALEXANDER H. LEIGHTON,
AND DOROTHEA C. LEIGHTON

The questions posed in the present chapter arise from the relationship of psychiatric disorder to culture. Psychiatric activities and ideas form a subpattern within the family of Western cultures, and the definitions of psychiatric disorders have their base in Western views about what human nature is or ought to be. As phenomena, the disorders are patterns of behavior and feeling that are out of keeping with cultural expectations and that bother the person who acts and feels them, or bother others around him, or both. Since, however, different cultures are by definition different systems of standards and expectation, it follows that what may be disturbing in one culture may be regarded as desirable in another. Thus the man or woman who in America is hospitalized for hearing voices or jailed for his sexual activities might have this behavior ignored, accepted, or even venerated in some other cultural group.

An extreme proponent of cultural relativity, using this line of argument, could deny the possibility of identifying and enumerating the same kinds of psychiatric disorder in markedly different cultures. Any pattern of behavior, so the argument might run, is healthy or sick only to the extent that it is so defined by a given culture. Certain patterns of behavior may be defined as psychiatric disorder in the West, but it does not follow that they will be so defined in another culture. Conversely, behavior patterns that we regard as normal or admirable may be defined in other cul-

Reprinted from Jane M. Murphy and Alexander H. Leighton, M.D., *Approaches to Cross-Cultural Psychiatry* (Ithaca, N.Y.: Cornell University Press, 1965.) Copyright © 1965 by Cornell University Press. Reprinted by permission of the publisher and the authors.

tures as abnormal. The greater the contrast, furthermore, between cultures, the more radical these discrepancies are apt to be. To speak, then, of "the same psychiatric disorder in two different cultures," is virtually self-contradictory.

Such an extreme view with regard to cultural relativity embodies two rather doubtful assumptions. One is that the possibilities for variation among cultures are limitless. The second, which is more or less necessary to the first, is that personality is infinitely plastic, that all of us as we begin life are capable of every form of human behavior and feeling. With regard to the first, despite the considerable variation evident among known cultures the range does not appear to be boundless. On the contrary, the evidence suggests that there are denominators and limitations common to all sociocultural systems. This applies not only to certain specific patterns such as the incest taboo, but also to larger functional attributes. There are, for instance, no cultural groups known that lack patterns of leadership and followership, or that have no set of rules regarding what is right and what is wrong.

In a similar way one may argue that the evidence available is against a theory of infinite plasticity in personality. It would seem more probable that there are some biological factors at work that influence the norms and deviations of personality found in any sociocultural group. Hence, from the point of view of psychiatry we may say that although cultures differ, there are some characteristics common to all cultures and hence also universal forms of deviance. The mentally deficient, the person who kills indiscriminately, and the person who exhibits uncontrolled excitement are possible examples.

If, however, one rejects an extreme view with regard to cultural relativity, he must also on the basis of available anthropological evidence reject a corresponding extreme of biological determinism. Some behavior pertinent to psychiatry is relative to culture, and cultural differences must enter to some extent into the definitions and perceptions of psychiatric disorders. The problem then is: If we start with our traditional Western definitions of disorder and the criteria by which we recognize them, how far can we go with these into other cultures with some hope of being able to identify comparable phenomena?

❖   ❖   ❖

This chapter attempts to point out a lattice of criteria whereby psychiatric disorders as they occur among adults may be recognized outside the European family of cultures. As noted in the first chapter of this book, a reason for this interest is the hope of discovering something about etiology. We want to use prevalence and incidence studies as a way of gathering evidence about what kinds of sociocultural factors influence the origin, the course, and the outcome of psychiatric disorders.

As soon as one begins to define the criteria of disorder, however, he becomes aware of an enormous number of difficult questions. They buzz about in the mind and in the air of discussion, coming and going from here and there, disturbing, insistent, and unconnected—or perhaps connected only dimly by unclear premises.

In part the problem arises from the language of psychiatry itself, which, although technical, is often neither precise nor consistent. Moreover, many of the terms for disorders and even symptoms imply theories of cause, so that it is difficult to separate reference to phenomena from reference to etiological ideas. This distinction is, of course, of fundamental importance when you wish to examine the phenomena in order to develop and check the ideas.

Another set of questions hovers around the matter of deviance and conformity. Deviance from cultural expectation is a characteristic common to most behavior recognized in our society as psychiatric disorder, and it would seem desirable as one criterion in any definition of disorder in another culture. By itself, however, deviance is far from being an adequate guide. The comment of Sapir[1] on the Indian, Two Crows, who denied that two and two make four was: "We suspect that he is crazy." On the other hand, perhaps Two Crows was a mathematical genius who had transcended the ordinary rules of counting. A person may also be considered as deviant by members of his cultural group as a result of accidental events; in some tribes, for instance, a man who had the bad luck to lose two wives and six children through sickness might be regarded finally as a witch, and hence deviant.

Turning the coin over, we must also observe that just as deviance from cultural standards is not sufficient evidence of psychiatric disorder, so conformity and adaptation are not sufficient evidence of its absence. It is possible for roles to be filled by persons whom we as clinicians would say were psychoneurotic or schizophrenic. In talking with Navahos we have noted that impairment from senility was not perceived as either illness or deviance, but rather a part of the expected behavior (role) of older people.

A similar problem arises from the fact that in the diagnosis of psychiatric cases there are sociological, biological, and psychological parameters, any one of which may predominate. This makes it impossible to describe psychiatric disorder in unitary terms and leads the diagnostician

---

[1]E. Sapir, "Culture and Personality," in *Selected Writings of Edward Sapir in Language, Culture and Personality*, D. G. Mandelbaum, ed. (Berkeley: University of California Press, 1951).

to jump from one level of discourse to another. For example, in defining illness we find ourselves with two different and divergent models, the one more or less traditional in clinical medicine, the other statistical. According to the medical view, if a person has *treponema pallidum* in his system he has syphilis and he is ill. Even if he is not contagious, and is not in any way impaired, he still has syphilis. Furthermore, if everyone else in the community has it so that deviance consists in not having syphilis, he is still considered ill.

This viewpoint also applies to conditions in which there is no recognized specific causal agent—for instance in diabetes, coronary thrombosis, and cancer. The center of disorder in conditions of this sort is considered to be the malfunctioning of some organ or set of organs. In cancer the disorder is in the growth characteristics of cells. It is thought probable, of course, that unknown factors are at work producing these malfunctions, and in some instances there may even be fairly well-founded theories. Cause in this sense, however, is not part of the diagnosis as it is in syphilis and tuberculosis. The agent as a critical factor in diagnosis is replaced by criteria for recognizing the pathology—blood sugar level, electrocardiogram reading, microscopic cell characteristics, and so on.

If we carry this model over into psychiatry then we would say with Knight[2] that a "touch of schizophrenia is like a touch of syphilis," or, if not syphilis, at least like diabetes. But to do this we must have criteria that point infallibly to pathology; they can be more complicated than the blood sugar or electrocardiogram but they must have at least a comparable degree of specificity. At times it almost seems that we have such criteria, but on closer scrutiny they tend to melt away.

A clinical example will serve as illustration. A young woman calls a psychiatrist, asking for an appointment. She complains of backache. She calls again and breaks the appointment, saying she is going south to see her doctor. She shows up for the broken appointment fifteen minutes early. She enters the office furtively. She wears dark glasses. Her hair is slicked back. She sits tensely on the couch and then moves over to a chair by the window. A dark flush creeps up over her neck and face. Even before she has said a word the conviction has formed in the psychiatrist's mind that she is an acute paranoid schizophrenic. She then relates that she has violated a taboo. She has been intimate with a piano salesman. She complains that he was a Communist, that the police are watching her, and that the doctors in a hospital where she was examined for ulcer symptoms have planted a radio in her stomach.

Even if she vomited a radio, many of us would still be inclined to

---

[2]R. P. Knight, "Borderline States," *Bulletin of the Menninger Clinic,* vol. 17 (1953), pp. 1–12.

cling to our original diagnosis. Are there not sufficient critical points evident so that one can say: this is schizophrenia, regardless? Yet all the immediate signs and symptoms which we interpret as schizophrenia could point just as well to panic. As a matter of fact, in this patient after two weeks of tranquilizers and psychotherapy all the schizophrenic indicators disappeared and have not returned over a period of several years. They could still recur, and the natural history of the case might eventually establish the patient as schizophrenic, but with periods of remission in symptoms. We know, however, from other cases that it is also possible that the symptoms will never return, or if they do they will again be of brief duration and related to stressful events.

We can go further and say that in some situations her behavior would not be regarded as symptomatic even of panic, but rather as realistic fear—if, for example, she lived in a police state in the midst of a stringent campaign against communism. The "radio in her stomach" might turn out to be an uneducated person's version of some medical maneuver involving the use of radioactive isotopes.

This example demonstrates how illusive the clinical model can be. The same problem occurs, of course, with diagnosis in other branches of medicine, and the difference is one of degree—but the degree in psychiatry is considerable. If psychoneurosis rather than schizophrenia were chosen for illustration, the problem would appear even greater. The idea of disease as a type of malfunction works well so long as the agent causing the malfunction, or a central aspect of the malfunction, or both, can be detected with a high degree of accuracy and reliability. In psychiatry we have difficulty meeting these criteria except where there is an organic condition. Usually what we have to deal with is malfunctional behavior. This immediately raises the question: "Malfunctional according to whom?" There are two broad types of possible answers: those according to cultural expectations, and those according to dynamic theories of psychiatry. If we lean heavily on the first of these, we are back again to the problem of deviance. If we lean on the other, we are building answers into the questions we wish to investigate.

The statistical definition of *normal* and *deviance* is easily explained and easily applied, but if employed independently of concepts about function and malfunction, it brings its own share of difficulties. Strictly applied, it would rule out the possibility of finding the majority of any cultural group to be neurotic. If it were utilized in this manner in other branches of medicine, tonsilitis, sinus trouble, and tooth decay would be obliterated as types of illness because most people have them. In some parts of the world malaria, hookworm, and vitamin deficiency would be similarly eliminated.

We have given here only a bare indication of the questions that can be raised. They are numerous, complex, and entangling; they are also slippery as to foundations and full of hidden premises. It is notable, too, that they cut across each other with introductory expressions such as "But if . . . ," "Suppose you should find that . . . ," "How about a case such as . . . ?"

Now, there are many possible "supposes" and "ifs" that do not exist in nature, and it occurred to us in due time that perhaps some of these were wrong questions. We turned from them, consequently, for the time being and took up a different approach.

What we did was to select one by one each entity recognized as a psychiatric disorder and then we tried to answer two questions: (1) By what criteria would I as a psychiatrist diagnose this condition in a person in our own society and culture? (2) Which of these criteria would I expect to remain employable in most other cultures as well? We did not seek general criteria that would distinguish all disorder from nondisorder, but only criteria for each recognized clinical entity such as mental deficiency, psychoneurosis, and obsessive-compulsive personality. Attention was concentrated on observable phenomena and, to the greatest extent possible, all definitions based on theories of psychological and sociocultural cause were avoided.

The review of criteria was conducted in the autumn of 1957 at the Center for Advanced Studies in the Behavioral Sciences in a series of weekly seminars. Four psychiatrists participated: the authors and Dr. David Hamburg. The guide employed in the deliberations was the 1952 *Diagnostic and Statistical Manual of Mental Disorders*, issued by the American Psychiatric Association. By January 1958 a set of criteria had been developed upon which the four psychiatrists could agree. Hamburg left the Center at this time, but the authors moved on to invite a group of anthropologists to participate in a continuation of the seminar, reviewing the criteria in the light of the cultural group with which each anthropologist was most familiar. The participants were Ethel Albert, Ward Goodenough, Dell Hymes, David Mandelbaum, Milton Singer, and Charles Wagley. The cultural groups that served as the main points of reference were the Rundi of Burundi (Africa), the Eskimos of St. Lawrence Island (Alaska), the Gilbert Islanders (Micronesia), the Navahos (American Southwest), the Tapirepé (Brazil), and the peoples of India.

In June 1958 the criteria were taken by Savage and A. Leighton to Many Farms, Arizona, and reviewed during a two-day session with Dr. Walsh McDermott and his staff, who had run an experimental clinic for Navahos during the preceding three years. Although the Many Farms Clinic was not concerned with psychiatric disorder as such, it had inevitably encountered some cases. The Navaho assistants, particularly the "health visitors," were a valuable source of comment.[3] The criteria offered in the following pages are the upshot of these several steps. . . .

PSYCHOSIS WITHOUT DEMONSTRABLE ORGANIC DISEASE

1. Schizophrenia

The diagnosis of this condition is vexatious because of the range of opinion among psychiatrists as to what should be included and excluded. At the Second International Congress of Psychiatry in 1957 the focus was on schizophrenia, and much disagreement was in evidence. The range stretched from people with intractable, incurable, irreversible illness to those who manifested only some autistic thinking.

It is, however, possible to select and specify a section within the range, and we have chosen what we believe to be the symptom complex that most American psychiatrists would accept. The criteria are:

A. *Delusions.* A delusion may be defined as a belief at variance with those beliefs or sentiments accepted in the cultural system to which the individual belongs.[4] An understanding of the beliefs characteristic of a culture is therefore mandatory. In most circumstances the presence of a delusion is presumptive evidence of psychosis, and where there is lack of indication pointing to other psychoses, the most likely possibility is schizophrenia. Further, a common feature is that schizophrenic delusions are directed against cultural sentiments and at the same time are strongly influenced by them.

As is evident, the concept of delusion is primarily a matter of cultural definition, and hence confronts us with the problem of cultural relativity. While there may conceivably be some delusions that would be false in all cultures of the world (for instance, that human beings have wings), it is apparent that an effort to catalogue these would not get us very far. It must be accepted that the content of delusions cannot be the basis of epidemiological comparisons between cultures. It would be a delusion if a man in our society were to believe that semen had wandered up into his head and caused his brains to deteriorate. In parts of India, however,

[3]W. McDermott, K. Deuschle, J. Adair, H. Fulmer, and B. Loughlin, "Introducing Modern Medicine in a Navaho Community," *Science*, vol. 131, nos. 3395 and 3396 (January 22–29, 1960), pp. 197–205 and 280–87.

[4]A. H. Leighton, J. A. Clausen, and R. N. Wilson, eds., *Explorations in Social Psychiatry* (New York: Basic Books, 1957), Editorial Comment to ch. 2 ("Paranoid Patterns" by J. S. Tyhurst), p. 69.

this idea is culturally acceptable, and apparently has considerable history in the East, being known in the Ming Dynasty in China. One is reminded of the belief formerly held in Europe that a woman's womb could move up into her throat and choke her. Delusions can, however, be detected against each culture's network of sentiments for defining reality. This means that as instances of sentiments that are out of keeping with culture, they can be counted in two or more groups that have different cultures.

It remains possible, even probable, that the character of the sentiment system in various cultures may exert a differential influence toward obscuring or revealing delusional behavior. Cultures vary not only as to topics, but also as to the degree of sharpness with which they define credibility. How big a problem this amounts to is something for investigation in particular cultures selected for study.

B. *Schizophrenic thinking.* Like dreaming, schizophrenic thinking is symbolic and wish-fulfilling. There is persistent misinterpretation and preoccupation with inner fantasies, so that the person seems to be out of touch with the world. The concrete and the symbolic are characteristically confused, as in the patient who said and literally meant he was "going up in an airplane to get perspective." Although the schizophrenic himself often makes extensive use of symbols, he has difficulty with other people's symbols and is apt to misunderstand metaphor.

This kind of thinking, so characteristic of schizophrenia, is hard to describe, yet recognizable after one has become acquainted with it. The quality of thought is very different from that shown by the person who is senile, mentally deficient, or slowed up by depression. At the same time, it can be expected to present grave problems for an American or European psychiatrist attempting its detection in a language and a cultural background not his own. For these reasons we do not regard it as a strong criterion, and yet we are disinclined to omit it altogether because of its frequency in cases of schizophrenia. It could, furthermore, turn out in some cultures to be less difficult to detect than we now imagine.

C. *Hallucinations.* Whereas delusions consist in false beliefs, hallucinations consist in false sensory perceptions. Auditory hallucinations—for instance, a voice speaking when nobody is there—are probably the commonest, but parallel disturbances of vision, smell, taste, body feelings, and touch also occur.

Cultural sentiments and definitions present some problems in the distinguishing of this phenomenon. In our own society few hallucinations are sanctioned or "believed in" except by some of the smaller religious sects. Among other societies, however, this may not be the case. Hearing voices and having visions may be an expected part of experience and take place on a basis that has nothing to do with schizophrenia or any other psychiatric disorder. One must distinguish, then, in part on the basis of the cultural acceptability and appropriateness of the hallucination. Duration provides another indicator. Many schizophrenic hallucinations are more or less continuous for years, whereas those that arise purely on a cultural basis are apt to have short duration or occur only from time to time as the situation demands.

So far as cross-cultural comparison is concerned, the remarks made in regard to delusions may be repeated here. It is not the reported voice or vision as such that can be counted and compared cross-culturally but the instances in which the voice or vision is out of keeping with the cultural framework.

D. *Schizophrenic actions.* Schizophrenia is primarily a disorder of thinking, but certain individuals develop related characteristic behaviors that are very striking: withdrawal, gesturing, posturing, or lying in a stuporous state. In time there may be habit deterioration and silly, scattered, superficial talk, with manic features but without the manic's wit. Unusual sexual activity may also occur such as chronic and open exposure and masturbation.

The cross-cultural applicability of this criterion scarcely needs comment. Although exceptional instances and possibilities can be pointed out, behavior of this type is usually recognizable as disordered in all the cultures with which we are familiar.

E. *Inappropriate affect.* This means showing emotion that is unsuitable for a given cultural context or failing to show emotion that is expected. Thus, there may be laughing when sadness or solemnity is called for, or there may be a chronic state of exhibiting little or no outward appearance of emotion. This latter is called "flattened affect," and although it is by no means a necessary part of the schizophrenic syndrome, it is sometimes very marked and arrests attention.

This criterion in general should not give too much difficulty across cultural lines. In India, where for many people the whole goal of life is to downgrade affect, there might be some special problems in distinguishing schizophrenic flattening from other kinds. This is not, however, something to be expected frequently in other cultures; and in any event, since the flattening is only one criterion in a syndrome, it could be evaluated along with others in reaching a conclusion as to whether a schizophrenic complex of symptoms was present or not.

F. *Personal history.* Several characteristics may be noted under this heading. One is that the age of onset is generally from the middle teens to the middle thirties. A first appearance of schizophrenic symptoms after forty is exceptional.

The mode of onset has two common alternative patterns. In one, a normal youth suffers a change of personality over a period of a year or so. Although the particulars of this change vary a good deal, it is usually so striking that everyone around the person takes note of it. "The last year in high school Jim got somehow strange. He was always one of the bunch before, but that year he was different. He kept more to himself, and he seemed to be doing a lot of thinking. He wasn't the same guy at all."

The other mode is one in which a person who has always been a bit rigid, withdrawn, proud, and uncompromising gradually accentuates these characteristics beyond the bounds of normal and then begins to show delusions and other frank manifestations of the disorder.

A third possibility is the sudden appearance of schizophrenia in its full-blown form, perhaps first being manifest in a state of excitement and fear. From clinical experience one would say this is much less common.

There do not appear to be any major and general cultural obstacles to our getting personal history data of this type. There are always chance and situational factors, in our own society and in others, that cause the completeness of history to vary from case to case. This does raise questions of case comparability, but it does not promise to be significantly greater cross-culturally than intraculturally.

Considering the schizophrenic criteria as a whole, and recalling again that they constitute a syndrome, so that one looks for a plurality and evaluates each item in relation to the others, it seems that in most cultures one could detect at the very least the level of impairment that we associate with hospitalization. This is confirmed by the fact that, so far as we know, schizophrenia has been found in every cultural group in which people trained in European psychiatry have worked. The problem lies in the gradation from obvious schizophrenia to conditions that are better described as eccentric or maladjusted. There is also the problem that most if not all cultures provide niches in which persons with some of the milder forms of schizophrenia can fit and in which the symptoms of the disorder are part of a role. Schizophrenic thinking expressed in poetry and painting is at times acceptable as art in our own society. We are not hereby diagnosing any artist as schizophrenic because of his abstract or symbolic style, or because of meanings we derive from psychiatric interpretation of his work. Rather, we take the matter from the opposite side and say that we have known schizophrenic patients who did find a market for their schizophrenic thinking and who did circulate in fashionable bohemian circles without their disorder being at first evident in this subculture. One patient in particular, known to one of us, was an outstanding and successful artist and just as outstandingly schizophrenic. This was eventually obvious to his colleagues when he went to live on top of a pillar like St. Simeon Stylites and then became mute.

It has often been suggested that what we call schizophrenia might well be an asset in the role of medicine man or Sadhu. Delusions, hallucinations, posturing, and symbolic utterances of unclear meaning might render the incumbent more rather than less effective. From both clinical and anthropological experience we are inclined to doubt very seriously that this often happens. The healer or priest role has its requirements and regulations, and the unusual behavior that goes with it nearly always has its particular context. The role is, in short, most often a highly integrated node in a social system. The schizophrenic's behavior and thinking are not that well controlled or adaptable, at least not in the kind of patients we commonly see. In fact one of the characteristics of the syndrome is the tendency to wander off all the established pathways of society and to break through its fences, no matter how self-defeating this may appear to be. And even where this countersocial or asocial behavior is not marked, the oddness of the schizophrenic may still be apparent to others of his social group even though he may be performing a role that utilizes some of his symptoms. Thus, one of the seminar members said that in India people will tell you that there are three kinds of Sadhus: the quacks, the real thing, and those who are touched in the head.

We may say again, therefore, that between the grossly evident and the almost normal is a considerable range, and the problem is to hit a similar cutting point for the people in any two cultures to be compared. This does not seem impossible, but it does require working out standards for particular cultures, and at present it is probably not possible for cultures in general.

2. Paranoid States

We suggest two criteria taken together as definitive of this condition.

A. *Delusions of persecution and/or grandeur.* The meaning of delusion has already been discussed, and the meaning of "persecution" is obvious. "Grandeur" refers to a role far more splendid, powerful, and important than one's actual role; the person who thinks he is Napoleon is the conventional example.

This criterion, then, involves delusions with a particular kind of content.

B. *Hostility toward others.* This is expressed in a tendency on the part of the subject to interpret the entire world in terms of hostility toward himself. Projection is a part of this interpretation—at least in the simpler sense of the word. That is to say, he reads into the acts of others hostile intentions against himself which are actually his own hostility toward them.[5]

Paranoid behavior is thought of most often as part of the schizophrenic picture, and yet it occurs widely in other disorders such as brain syndrome and depression. That it occurs alone as a chronic disorder with tremendous logical elaborations on the basis of a few false premises—*paranoia vera*—is a matter open to question. Many if not most psychiatrists believe that this does not happen, but that people who seem at first to have such a condition sooner or later develop additional symptoms of some disorder, usually schizophrenia. Occasionally they turn out not to be delusional at all but to have justification for their views.

Transient paranoid behavior is probably found from time to time in almost everyone. It seems human nature to blame others for what we do not like but find going on within ourselves. Few things are so painful as self-reproach and few are so relieving as righteous indignation.

With regard to cross-cultural identification, it has to be recognized that societies exist in which hostility, suspicion, and what we would call false beliefs of persecution (e.g., by witches) are exceedingly prevalent. Several familiar questions immediately arise. Are we to regard these sentiments and behaviors as cultural patterns which normal individuals learn through growing up in the society, or do we have instead a clinical paranoid state on a mass scale? And if it is a cultural pattern, how can one ever identify the truly paranoid in such a context?

It is easy to puzzle oneself into a state of paralysis by elaborating further questions along this line. The issue often seems the key obstacle to identification and counting of psychiatric disorders in any culture except our own.

But let us note several things. First, the question comes up in this major form with only one complex of psychiatric symptoms, and not with psychiatric disorder generally. Second, paranoid behavior as a clinical entity is a symptom complex which appears as a component in a number of different syndromes, most commonly schizophrenia. It is also seen transiently in people who are not psychiatrically ill. Third, our definition of a delusion is that it is a false belief *according to the standards of the believer's culture*. That a belief is false according to the standards of some other culture including our own does not therefore make it a delusion. Indeed, one of the features of the clinically observed delusion is its resistance to the conforming pressures of the social group. On the basis of these points, we think that culturally patterned sentiments and be-

[5]As is well known, Freud employed a much more complicated definition of projection.

havior reflecting hostility, suspicion, and what persons of our culture would call false beliefs of persecution, are not to be equated with a mass paranoid state in any clinical sense of the word. They can rather be considered as more closely related to a normal capacity for paranoid reaction together with the normal process of culture acquisition. It still remains possible that masses of people in a society could in a short time become hostile and delusional in terms of their own cultural standards. One can visualize this as happening at a time of great stress. Whether or not it should be regarded as normal or abnormal would depend on the results of examining the actual situation and on standards set for dealing with this particular phenomenon. But this is a special case, not one that is general in cross-cultural work. We may conclude, therefore, that the problem of mass paranoid state versus cultural pattern loses some of its formidable character if one breaks it down into more specific parts and is careful about definitions.

Let us return to the question of identifying paranoid symptoms in an individual where the cultural background gives prominence to hostility, suspicion, and beliefs of being persecuted. It is important again to keep in mind that the paranoid symptoms comprise only one of several components in the syndromes we are trying to distinguish. Thus if they were part of the schizophrenic syndrome, it would still be possible in many instances to make an identification through other delusions, hallucinations, schizophrenic thinking, withdrawal, posturing, inappropriate affect, or history of personality change. The problem is further reduced by recognizing that a delusion is such in terms of the culture in which it occurs. The conviction that one is bewitched is not a delusion in a witchcraft culture unless there is something about it that does not fit within the range of the accepted pattern.

It is here, of course, that one begins to get into borderline cases, and competent knowledge regarding the cultural range becomes important. Very often the question is not one of specific items as such, but of appreciation of oddity in how they fit together. This may be illustrated by a conversation one of us had with Dr. T.A. Baasher of the Clinic for Nervous Disorders in Khartoum North, Sudan.

A. Leighton asked Baasher how he would distinguish religious delusion from accepted belief among people coming to his clinic. Baasher replied that he could give no general rules, but he could illustrate it with a case he had seen that involved a murder. Some years ago there had been two religious leaders in the neighborhood of Khartoum who were great rivals. A follower of one of the men began to hear voices telling him to kill his master's rival. It seemed to him that the voices came from a divine source and he set out to execute their command. Since he did not know his intended victim by sight, he wandered from place to place relying on the voices to let him know when he had come upon the man. Several times he saw someone he thought was his target, but the voices said, "No." Eventually one evening he entered a village where a number of men were sitting under a tree talking. One was on a chair, playing with some little sticks. The voices said that this was the man. The religious follower protested that surely not, he was just a poor individual, not a great leader. The voices, however, said, "Don't you see? It's a disguise. Kill." So the follower speared him. Later the follower was arrested for murder and then sent to Baasher for examination.

"Now," said Baasher, "it is not out of keeping with this culture for a man to be extremely devoted to a religious leader, nor is it out of keeping for him to undertake to kill on his master's behalf, and of course he could make a mistake and kill the wrong man, as this disciple did. It is within the cultural range for a religious man to hear voices that tell him to do things, and for him to go and do those things. But the way all these elements fitted together in this case did not make sense. This is especially so since the two religious leaders in question had made up their differences and been friends for over a year prior to the murder. Item by item, there is nothing that was counter to the culture, but the whole reflected odd thinking, like the Knight's move in chess. I thought he was a paranoid schizophrenic from the story, and examination brought this out." . . .

SOME NOTES ON DIAGNOSIS

We have discussed the possibility of identifying symptom patterns and impairment cross-culturally, and we have concluded that if one selects particular cultures instead of trying to deal with cultures in general, he will probably be able to establish operational criteria that will permit the desired comparison at a useful and meaningful level of approximation. We also think that operational steps are facilitated if the detection of symptom patterns and the rating of impairment are used as a primary focus in cross-cultural estimates. At the end of the seminar it was the opinion of most participants, anthropologists and psychiatrists alike, that syndromes as a whole are manageable cross-culturally. When one takes up individual symptoms one by one, there is plenty of opportunity for postulating difficult situations and ground for arguments regarding feasibility, but when one considers the symptoms as components of syndromes, and takes the latter as the unit for counting, the task does not look so difficult. Although problematic cases will undoubtedly occur, we do not expect these to be so numerous as to cause serious statistical difficulty.

When one moves beyond symptoms and impairment to consider full diagnosis, especially with regard to the functional psychoses, the psychoneuroses, and the personality disorders, he must be prepared to meet considerable challenge. There are many subtleties in the diagnostic process that are bound to be affected by cultural differences. A constant awareness of these subtleties is necessary in any work that strives for accuracy and consistency, and it seems appropriate, therefore, to outline a few.

In the psychiatric interview, the patient influences the doctor and the doctor influences the patient; diagnosis is one of the complex resultants of this interaction. The diagnosis depends not only on the symptoms and manifestations of the patient, but also on the doctor's training, familiarity with the patient and his culture, and his attitudes toward the patient, which are in turn influenced by the patient's attitudes toward him. Very often the diagnosis reflects whether he likes or dislikes the patient, and whether he approves or disapproves of him. Unfortunately the hierarchy of values differs from doctor to doctor, from time to time, and place to place. "Sociopathic disorder," for instance, often implies dislike and disapproval. "Depression" is usually more flattering than "schizophrenia," which sometimes simply implies craziness.

The diagnosis may at times be a projection of the physician's personality onto the patient. This is apt to happen in rather obscure cases where the diagnosis is achieved empathetically, that is, by transient trial identification with the patient. Such identification is useful, but one runs the risk of confusing himself with the patient. To employ it skillfully one must have a thorough knowledge not only of the patient and his culture, but also of one's self and of one's own culture.

The psychiatrist who attempts diagnoses in another culture will be influenced by his attitude not only toward his patient but also toward his informants, his interpreters, and his anthropologist colleagues. The diagnosis will also be influenced by the attitudes of the informants and patients toward their own culture, toward Western culture, toward the psychiatrist, and toward mental disease in general.

A diagnosis then is the result of a relationship, whether it be a one-one relationship between psychiatrist and patient, or a more complex one between psychiatrist-interpreter-informant-anthropologist-patient. Spiegel[6] has described his difficulties in establishing relationships and doing interviews with the parents of disturbed children from American-Irish Catholic families of the lower income bracket in the Boston area. He had to learn a new language, a new set of values, and new modes of

[6]J. P. Spiegel, "Some Cultural Aspects of Transference and Counter-transference," *Individual and Familial Dynamics*, J. H. Masserman, ed. (New York: Grune & Stratton, 1959).

behavior. One is forcibly struck with the similarities between these difficulties and those found in dealing with psychotic patients. Yet these people were not psychotic, not patients, and not from another culture. These comparable problems of dealing with psychotics and people of other cultures can be described as essentially communication difficulties. The psychiatrist-anthropologist must maintain an orientation in his own culture, in the culture under study, and in the private world of the patient under discussion.

Our interest in culture, however, should not obscure the very important, and possibly common, masking effects that can arise from endemic illness such as tuberculosis. From the discussions at Many Farms one would suspect that the problem is not so much one of disentangling neurotic and psychotic complaints from native superstition and folklore as it is of disentangling such complaints from the organic background and perhaps from the tendency of unlettered peoples to express emotional discomfort in terms of aches and pains.

PART III

EQUIVALENCE OF
MEASUREMENT

5

Equivalence in
Cross-National Research

ADAM PRZEWORSKI AND HENRY TEUNE

How can valid comparisons be made in cross-national research when so many terms and concepts differ in their meanings from country to country? In this paper the authors argue and illustrate the significant claim that by using "equivalent indicators in different countries and relating them to "identical indicators," the validity of cross-national research can be safeguarded. Only by combining cross-national and nation-specific indicators can reliable and valid assessments be made.

Do you believe in God?" is in most cultures an ambiguous question. This ambiguity is multiplied when responses are recorded cross-nationally. How can a response be interpreted? In fact, there are great differences between the percentages responding affirmatively to this question in various countries. But what can be concluded? It is possible that an affirmative answer means that a person believes in God, that he believes in some superior being, or that he is affirming his affiliation with some institutionalized form of religion—that he simply declares an identification with a social group. What then can a social scientist do with the fact

Reprinted from Adam Przeworski and Henry Teune, "Equivalence in Cross-National Research," *Public Opinion Quarterly* (1966–67):*30*, 551–68. Reprinted by permission of the publisher and the authors.

The authors wish to express their gratitude to the International Studies of Values in Politics for creating this opportunity to work together.

This paper represents some preliminary work in preparation for a large-scale cross-national study supported in part by the Department of State and in part by the participating institutions.

that a higher percentage of Americans said "Yes" to this question than Frenchmen?[1]

Data of comparative character are now abundantly available. However, lingering doubts about the comparability, the meaning, and the validity of these data find expression in exchanges between scholars doing cross-national research. Attempts are being made to examine the nature of the difficulties and to build into research designs some ways of resolving questions of comparative validity. Some procedures for establishing the meaning, validity, or equivalence of concepts in cross-national research will be given in this paper. Analysis of cross-national data on values will demonstrate these procedures.

It is clear by now that the logic of comparative research does not differ from any other type of social science inquiry. Women are politically more conservative than men. Whether this relationship between sex and political conservatism is analyzed in one country or across countries does not change the logic of inquiry. Comparative research is social science research that goes beyond the borders of one country. To study something "comparatively" often means that at some stage countries become units of analysis. However, the very choice of countries as units of analysis threatens the validity of the findings. Accumulated experience leads to the expectation that most of the third, or intervening, variables that alter the character of examined relationships are to be found at the level of the nation-state. Concepts are expected to have different meanings in different countries. Relationships are expected to differ more between countries than within a single country. These differences are attributed to systemic variables. In the case of sex and conservatism, examples of these variables would be cultural traditions, histories of suffrage movements, party systems, and levels of education of women in comparison with men. The operation of these variables is expressed in such notions as "culture," "society," "political system," and the like. Thus, although logically not different from other studies, cross-national analysis requires research procedures that involve caution in order to yield validity in a more differentiated setting.

Since theory is built on relationships between general, abstract concepts, more than simple statements of relationship between single indicators of complex phenomena will be sought. Death rates may indicate governmental effectiveness, as Lipset argued, and voting may be an in-

[1]The data for France were gathered by the Institut Français d'Opinion Publique. These 1947 data are reported in Arnold M. Rose, *Theory and Method in the Social Sciences* (Minneapolis: The University of Minnesota Press, 1954), p. 107.

U.S. polls report a high proportion of affirmative answers to the question, "Do you believe in God?"

dicator of democratic participation.[2] But it would be naïve to assume that deaths and elections are equivalent components of the inferred concepts of governmental effectiveness and democracy in every country. For, although elections in the United States may be the core factor in democratic participation and in Africa every reduction in the mortality rates may indeed reflect the effectiveness of the government, death rates would most likely be a poor indicator of the effectiveness of the American government and elections would be of little significance in indicating the extent of democratic participation in Ghana.

When such abstract concepts as government effectiveness, democratic participation, the value of social harmony, or social stratification are compared, it is necessary to introduce some procedures for establishing the cross-national validity of the operational definitions. It is the problem of determining what are "intense partisanship," "social change," and a "one-party system." These constructs can and must be used for cross-national comparisons, but single, identical indicators can only rarely be assumed to signify the same complex phenomenon in all societies.

The critical problem in cross-national research is that of identifying "equivalent" phenomena and analyzing the relationships between them in an "equivalent" fashion. There are two conventional approaches to the problems of measurement in cross-national settings. One approach is to argue that intersocietal or intercultural differences are of a qualitative nature—that in each society the particular pattern of interdependent factors defines the functioning of each of the elements. Accordingly, abstracting particular "traits" from their peculiar structural-functional setting is not possible and cross-national measurement cannot have validity. For example, it is impossible to measure political integration in various countries, for cross-national differences in integration are believed to be qualitative or essentially different. In sharp contrast to this position, it can be assumed that single, identical indicators of various cultural traits, such as voting, have cross-national validity and meaning, and thus comparisons can be made in terms of these single standards, external to each of the cultures involved and free from the particular cultural setting.

The problems of equivalence in cross-national research are confronted at two stages of inquiry. The first stage is when an equivalent measure of a concept in various countries is necessary. A second stage occurs when cross-national data are being analyzed and it is necessary to remove the influence of extraneous phenomena, which are common but not equally relevant to the cultures involved. These two stages will be discussed in this paper. An example of the first case is assessing political

[2] S. M. Lipset, *Political Man* (New York: Doubleday, 1960).

participation in countries where the role of voting is substantially different. An example of the second is a research design on the relationship between political participation and community integration. If it is found that in all countries integration of political units depends on the level of economic development, then the influence of this factor has to be eliminated in testing the relationship between participation and integration.

GOALS OF COMPARATIVE RESEARCH

Most cross-national studies involve implicit or explicit comparisons of various countries with respect to some traits. In formal terms, description is an operation in which a quality or a parameter is ascribed to a specified unit of observation. Description results in a table where columns are properties and rows are entries of specific objects, whether these are individuals, societies, villages, or states. Comparative description is an operation of assigning a property or properties to two or more units of observation. For example, the governmental system of the United States is characterized as "presidential," while that of Great Britain is described as "parliamentary." This kind of comparative description comprises the vast bulk of statements made in courses in comparative government in American universities. It matters little how the tables are arranged, that is, whether the material is presented government by property (the United States has . . . and Germany has . . .) or is presented property by government (The executive in the United States is . . . , while in Germany it is . . .). The essential feature of comparative descriptions is the mention of specific units of observation. In cross-national description these are such units as cultures, nations, states, identified by name.

In scientific research the goal is not description in the sense mentioned above but rather a set of statements concerning relationships between or among variables. In addition to classifying, ranking, or scoring specific units on economic productivity, technological development, or some attitude such as "achievement," the relationships between these phenomena are examined. Thus productivity would be related to technology, or to attitudes, or to the social structure, or to a combination of these factors.

In formal terms, cross-national analysis is an operation by which a relationship between two or more variables is stated for a defined population of countries. In analysis, no proper names of societies or cultures are mentioned. The goal is not to "understand" Ghana or Cuba, not to describe Hitler, Stalin, Roosevelt, or Churchill, but to see to what extent external crises and internal control, military prowess and economic frustration, nationalism and persecutions, are related, and to know the generality of each relationship. Whether variables are related depends on the observations of Ghana, or Hitler. But these are the observations that are means to an end—the end of testing relationships between variables, even at the cost of obscuring some differences between specific units.

Even if it is discovered that a relationship holds for one group of countries but not for another, it does not follow that the specific units for which the relationship holds must be enumerated. If such a discovery is made, the inquiry should be directed toward identifying the third, or intervening, variable or variables that would account for this difference. If it is argued that the achievement motive explains economic productivity but the relationship holds only in societies that have a certain type of social structure, the hypothesis must be reformulated to read that the achievement motive in societies with high migration explains economic productivity.

These are the very kinds of discoveries, identification of intervening variables, that make cross-national analysis an essential part of the process of developing social science theory. From the point of view of scientific inquiry attempting to explain the variance of social phenomena, such concepts as "social system," "culture," or "political system" can be absorbed into the analysis as nothing but residuals of variables influencing the phenomenon being explained. To say that a relationship does not hold because of systemic or cultural factors is tantamount to saying that a set of variables, not yet discovered, is related to the variables that have been examined.

EQUIVALENT MEASURES OF IDENTICAL CONCEPTS

One crucial issue in cross-national research is the problem of equivalence of indicators used in various settings. As in any social science research, cross-national research requires measurement: an expression of a set of observations in a language, often numerical, of some standard. However, as was said earlier, the standards of one culture may not be applicable to another. Constructed concepts, derived from several operations or observations, are sociologically relative. And while manifestations of differences with respect to such concepts exist within each country, these seem especially frequent and marked at the cross-national level. The problems are empirical. For example, can the value of equality be measured by the same items in Great Britain and Japan? Can the intensity of social integration of local communities be measured through the same indicators in both the United States and India?

What constitute identical and what constitute equivalent measurements of the same concepts in various countries? This problem was given full attention by the authors of *The Civic Culture*[3] and can be illustrated by the research findings presented in that book. The methodological principle utilized in that study was to obtain equivalence by using identical stimuli in various countries. Thus the authors are careful to list all factors that may weaken the identical nature of the stimuli, such as linguistic and connotative differences, timing of interviews, and training of the interviewers. The procedure used in the study is acceptance of a single standard, assumed to have cross-national validity by virtue of its identity properties, as the sole indicator of such concepts as "partisanship," "national pride," "subjective competence."

In this study, partisanship was inferred from the answers to a question about whether an individual would object to his son or daughter marrying a member of a party different from his, and questions concerning his views of the members of opposite parties. The answers were used to say something about the degree of partisanship existing in the five cultures. As could be expected, only a trace of the sample of Americans said they would be displeased if their offspring married a "reactionary" Republican or a "pink" Democrat. But, in the European countries and Mexico, some people said they would be displeased.

To return to the opening question of this paper, what does a response to a question about the preferences of a parent for party affiliation of a prospective son- or daughter-in-law mean? Does it mean, as Almond and Verba claim, the psychological distance between parties, or perhaps the political distance between parties, or distance between classes, on which the party is based, or regions? Or perhaps it indicates that the person wants to participate in the marriage choice of his children—a norm in which there are substantial differences between cultures. Or what? The second measure of partisanship, used independently of the first one, is how positive and negative the individual feels about members of opposite parties. Some of the statements that were scored positive are "interested in defense and independence" and "intelligent people." Some negatively scored statements are "selfish people," "fascists," "imperialists," and "atheists." In Italy, where parties have taken a stand on God, one finds a set of respondents who state that members of a certain party are atheists. The Christian Democrats have this belief about the Communists. None of the Communists in turn believe this negative thing about the Christian Democrats, although a substantial portion of the Communists have a "neutral belief" that the Christian Democrats are "religious people." Now, what do cross-national comparisons of answers to this question mean? It is quite obvious that single, identical indicators do not

[3]G. A. Almond and S. Verba, *The Civic Culture* (Princeton, N.J.: Princeton University Press, 1963). In Chapter 2, attention is given to the problem of equivalence.

permit making equivalent inferences about such concepts as "partisan-ship."

In seeking equivalence in cross-national research one must go beyond the problem of identical stimuli. Single items are rarely sufficient to measure concepts at any level of analysis. The problem of whether a concept can be measured cross-nationally by a set of identical indicators is empirical. Although complete equivalence is probably never possible, attempts can be made to measure equivalence if they are based on a *set* of indicators or observations. The researcher must attempt to reconstruct the meaning of concepts in various cultures through an empirical procedure. Suggested below is a procedure that should permit the identification of identical and equivalent indicators in cross-national research.[4]

The task is to measure a property X in cultures C_1, C_2, ... C_n. As an example, let the property be political activity and the population of the countries consist of two units. The following assumptions will be made:

1. There are a number of indicators x^o_1, x^o_2, ... x^o_n that can be used to measure the property X in each culture.

2. A set of items X_k is common to all cultures.

3. For each culture C, there is a set of items X^o_{n-k} that is specific to the given culture.

From (2) and (3) it follows that

4. For each culture C, there is a set of indicators X^o that is composed of subsets X^o_k and X^o_{n-k}.

Two definitions based on the procedures for the analysis of homogeneity developed by Scott[5] are now necessary:

---

[4]Of the various models of measurement in the social sciences, the one used here is called the "domain generality model." This model proceeds to state a number of concepts, a domain of concepts, related to any attribute. Scores for individuals are based on the scope of acceptance of those concepts, admittedly a sample of all related concepts. This scope can be expressed as a proportion. It is in the context of this model that discussion about "functional equivalents" becomes meaningful. For a discussion of this model, as well as other models, and functional equivalence, see W. A. Scott, "Attitude Measurement," in G. Lindzey and E. Aronson, eds., *Handbook of Social Psychology*, rev. ed., forthcoming.

[5]W. A. Scott, "Measures of Test Homogeneity," *Educational and Psychological Measurement*, 1960, Vol. 20, pp. 751–757. W. A. Scott and M. Wertheimer, *Introduction to Psychological Research*, New York, Wiley, 1962.

$$HR = \frac{\sigma_t^2 - \Sigma\,\sigma_i^2}{(\Sigma\,\sigma_i)^2 - \Sigma\,\sigma_i^2}$$

where σ_t^2 = variance over subjects in total scale scores
σ_i^2 = variance over subjects in scores for each item
$\Sigma\sigma_i^2$ = sum of item variances over all items
$\Sigma\sigma_i$ = sum of item standard deviations over all items

5. Items x_1, x_2, ... x_k are defined as *identities* if the set X_k is homogeneous.

6. For each culture C, items $x^o_k + 1$, $x^o_k + 2$, ... x^o_n are defined as *equivalents* if they are correlated with the set X^o_k.

Homogeneity is defined as a weighted average inter-indicator correlation, independent of scale length.

In other words, those indicators which are intercorrelated in a pooled, across-country analysis are maintained to have identical cross-national validity with respect to a given concept and a given set of countries. Those indicators which are specific to each country and which are correlated with the identical indicators are maintained to have equivalent cross-national validity. An empirical test is the safeguard of identity, and the demonstrated identity is the safeguard of equivalence.

This procedure may be needed for methodological as well as theoretical reasons. It may be needed because identical indicators do not provide sufficient scale reliability. But, more importantly, it may be essential when it is reasonable to expect on empirical grounds that the meaning or the structure of a concept differs from country to country.

The concept of political activity will be used as a brief illustration for two countries. A set of common items hypothesized to be identical for both countries is the following: (1) Follow political news, (2) Vote in elections, (3) Attend political meetings, (4) Talk with friends about politics, (5) Try to be acquainted with political issues. Such items can be used for most countries. Let it be assumed that items (1), (2), and (5) compose a homogeneous set of identities. The concept of political activity constructed above is clearly insufficient, since there are great differences in the structure of political activity in the two countries. Let the two countries be the United States and Poland. In order to test this hypothesis, a set of items peculiar to the United States and one peculiar to Poland should be written:

United States	Poland
6_1 Contribute money to parties or candidates	6_2 Fight for execution of economic plans
7_1 Place sticker on car	7_2 Attempt to influence economic decisions.
8_1 Volunteer help in campaigns	
9_1 Testify at hearings	8_2 Join a party
10_1 Write letters to Congressmen in support of or against policies or programs	9_2 Participate in voluntary social works
	10_2 Develop ideological consciousness

The next step is to analyze all items separately for each country. Then those items which are correlated with the identity items for each country are selected as equivalents. For example, let these items be 6_1 and 10_1 and 6_2, 7_2 and 8_2.

In using this "identity-equivalence" procedure it is not necessary to begin with subsets of items specific for different countries. If one begins with a sufficiently large number of indicators, all items can be used in all countries, and the isolation of identities and equivalents can be done in the process of statistical analysis. Obviously, the items cannot be culturally absurd, for example, "place sticker on car" in a country where there are no cars or "fight for execution of economic plans" where there are no plans. In general, items specific for each country, X^c_{n-k}, can be viewed as those indicators which either have little or no variance in all but one country or are not correlated with items X_k in more than one country. For example, in Poland the item concerning placing sticker on a car would have no true variance; in the United States the item "develop ideological consciousness" would most likely have little variance. This is an alternative formulation of assumption (3) above.

EQUIVALENT AND IDENTICAL MEASURES FOR ASSESSING VALUES CROSS-NATIONALLY

Following are three illustrations of the development of identical and equivalent measures with actual cross-national interviews. The value scales were administered to 63 local political leaders in Yugoslavia, 60 in Poland, 119 in India, and 96 in the U.S.[6] The procedure follows the alternative of using all identical items for all countries and the identification of those items which scale cross-nationally, the identical items, in analysis. Items that correlate with the cross-national items only for certain

[6]The following were directly involved in the gathering of these data: From Yugoslavia: The Institute of Social Sciences in Belgrade—A. Vratusa, Director, S. Bosnic, Z. Puric, R. Marinkovic; Institute of Sociology and Philosophy in Ljubljana —J. Jerovsek and Z. Mlinar; from Sarajevo—S. Tomic.

From Poland: The Polish Academy of Sciences—J. Wiatr, K. Ostrowski, A. Przeworski.

From India: The Centre for the Study of Developing Societies—R. Kothari and D. L. Sheth; Indian Institute of Technology, Kanpur—K. K. Singh and A. Ashraf; University of Poona—V. M. Sirsikar.

From the United States: W. A. Scott, University of Colorado; S. Eldersveld, University of Michigan; J. Woodmansee, Wake Forest College. Those directly involved in the research at Philadelphia were T. M. Watts, R. Hunt, and P. Wehr. The director of the U.S. research is P. E. Jacob. We also wish to thank Harold Guetzkow of Northwestern University for his usually helpful criticism.

This, of course, is only a list of the principals. Many others, known to the authors, were also involved.

countries, according to the position of this paper, are equivalent measures, nation-specific measures of the same variables.

The items were designed to measure values. The values were: "social harmony," "material progress," "selflessness." A common set of items was written for all countries. Response categories were: (1) format A—"Generally agree" or "Generally disagree," (2) format B—"Should be a goal," or "Depends" or "Should not be a goal," (3) format X—"Very important to achieve," or "Somewhat important," or "Not important to achieve," (4) format D—"Very important to avoid," or "Somewhat important," or "Not important." In addition, there were some specific hypothetical questions in which closed choices were offered.

The items for assessing three values are listed below with the format used for the question and the direction of the scoring, where a plus indicates that "agree," "should be," "very important" response indicated the value, *ex hypothesi*, and a minus indicates that "disagree," "should not be," "not important" response reflects the value.[7] (Whether responding to the first alternative or to the last alternative reflects the value.)

Social Harmony

Scale	Format	Score	
Poland	A	+	1. It is desirable in reaching political decisions to reconcile as many conflicting interests as possible
Yugo. Poland	A	—	2. It is not necessary for leaders to try and smooth over conflicts that naturally arise in a community
None	B	—	3. To encourage argumentation and conflict, so that all issues can come to the surface
None	B	—	4. To fight for the realization of a goal, no matter who is against it
Identity	C	+	5. Cooperation
Identity	C	+	6. Avoidance of conflict
Identity	C	+	7. Maintenance of friendly relations among the people who have to make the decisions
Identity	D	+	8. Offending people
India	D	+	9. Making enemies
India Poland	D	+	10. Use of violence
None	D	—	11. Agreeing with everyone
None	D	—	12. Tolerating unreasonable points of view
U.S.	Special		13. Suppose a political leader here saw that a particular group in the community was tending to disrupt the general community consensus. What should he do? — (a) Allow the group to continue to dissent.

[7]All responses were scored dichotomously. In those cases where there were more than two categories of response, the dichotomous scoring was at the point closest to the median. This analysis was done at the University of Colorado under the general direction of W. A. Scott, S. Bosnic from Yugoslavia, and K. Ostrowski from Poland.

+ (b) Try to get the group to conform to the wider consensus.

0 (c) Try to get the majority to modify its views to meet those of the minority more closely.

None   Special   14. Suppose a political leader had a program for social action that would ultimately benefit the entire community. But it is strongly opposed by a substantial number of people, and the leader anticipates that enactment of the program would disrupt the community. What should he do?

— (a) Pursue the program even at the risk of disruption.

+ (b) Give up the program.

0 (c) Weaken the program to avoid conflict.

Material Progress

Scale	Format	Score	
Poland	A	—	1. A rising standard of living is not an important sign of progress
U.S.	A	+	2. The long-term economic development of the nation should be considered as its most important goal
None	A	+	3. As long as people are well off economically, one need not worry about other problems
Poland Yugo.	A	—	4. Hard work is not enough, success depends on one's connections
Yugo.	A	—	5. Just because a person can't get ahead economically, it is not his own fault
Identity	A	+	6. The future economic development of the nation should take precedence over immediate consumer gratification
India	A	+	7. One should encourage private enterprise among small industries
None	A	+	8. People who produce more should be paid more
Identity	C	+	9. Economic progress
Identity	C	+	10. Efficiency
Identity	C	+	11. Technical competence
India	C	+	12. Universal education
India U.S.	C	+	13. Working hard

Selflessness

Scale	Format	Score	
U.S. India Poland	A	+	1. A leader should not be concerned about his own status, only about doing a good job
India	A	—	2. No one should expect a political leader to be absolutely selfless in his actions

Identity	A	—	3. Only impractical idealists would sacrifice themselves for others
Identity	A	+	4. Sacrificing oneself for others is the highest value man can achieve
None	A	—	5. The individual's *own* welfare should be his first and foremost concern
Poland U.S.	B	+	6. Subordination of one's own self-interest in the interest of a higher cause
Poland	C	+	7. Doing one's duty as the job requires it, no matter how unpleasant
Identity	C	+	8. Sacrificing oneself for the benefit of others
None	C	—	9. Protecting one's own career
Yugo.	C	—	10. Obtaining recognition for one's achievements
None	Special		11. Suppose a leader is offered a job at a higher level, but it is one in which he could not be of as much service to the community. What should he do? — (a) Take the higher-level job + (b) Stay where he can be of maximum service to the community
Identity	Special		12. An official is requested by his superiors to move to another position where he can be useful, but the position is one of lower prestige than he enjoys at present. He refuses to move. Has he acted properly or not? + (a) Yes — (b) No

The interrelationships between these items or questions are presented in Tables 1 to 3.[8] The first matrix in each table is for all countries, the result of a pooled analysis of all respondents. This matrix is the cross-national identity set, established by the fact that these items scale for all respondents regardless of culture. The relationships between the identity items are given for each country in the other four matrices with the additional items that scaled with the cross-national identity items—the nation-specific items. The r is the mean correlation between items in the sets.[9] The items that scaled for specific countries are designated under "Scale" in the list of items given above.

[8]Because of the nature of this research and the nature of dichotomous correlations, it is difficult to get high correlations. Mean intercorrelations exceeding .20 are difficult. Because of the cross-national character of the data, achieving mean intercorrelations above the research average of .20 for homogeneous American respondents is even more difficult.

[9]The HR for each of these scales are the following: "material progress," .24: "social harmony," with two additional items excluded because of low variance, .15; "selflessness," again with two additional items not reported in the final identity set, .15. These additional items were excluded because of low variance, lack of conceptual clarity, or correlation with other scales. Some of these excluded items were added to the nation-specific set.

TABLE 1

Social Harmony (Identity set: r=.250)

Item	5	6	7
5			
6	.27		
7	.23	.27	
8	.12	.36	.25

Yugoslavia: $r=.146$

Item	5	6	7	8
5				
6	.07			
7	.05	.37		
8	.31	.22	.05	
2	.16	.04	.23	−.04

India: $r=.158$

Item	5	6	7	8	10
5					
6	.45				
7	.28	.15			
8	−.01	.15	.03		
10	.07	.19	.05	.23	
9	.04	.12	.02	.26	.34

Poland: $r=.239$

Item	5	6	7	8	10	2
5						
6	.39					
7	.21	.11				
8	.39	.50	.15			
10	.45	.53	.18	.52		
2	−.13	.04	.20	.13	.21	
1	.38	.21	.11	.15	.25	.04

U.S.: $r=.213$

Item	5	6	7	8
5				
6	.18			
7	.20	.35		
8	.12	.40	.36	
13	.03	.17	.14	.18

TABLE 2

Material Progress (Identity set: r=.185)

Item	6	9	10
6			
9	.06		
10	.11	.27	
11	.02	.30	.36

TABLE 2 (cont.)

Yugoslavia: $r=.228$

Item	6	9	10	11	5	4
6						
9	.04					
10	.27	.08				
11	.25	.41	.51			
5	.35	.31	.15	.33		
4	.14	.17	.17	.16	.08	

India: $r=.176$

Item	6	9	10	11	7	12
6						
9	−.08					
10	.21	.17				
11	.02	.33	.19			
7	.13	.05	.36	.02		
12	.26	.14	.22	.10	.02	
13	.17	.37	.28	.10	.16	.48

Poland: $r=.117$

Item	6	9	10	11	1
6					
9	−.07				
10	.31	.49			
11	.11	−.02	−.05		
1	.06	.12	.24	−.02	
4	.24	.09	.19	−.07	.14

U.S.: $r=.221$

Item	6	9	10	11	2
6					
9	.25				
10	.09	.35			
11	.25	.37	.38		
2	.13	.29	.22	.15	
13	.11	.16	.17	.23	.17

TABLE 3

Selflessness (Identity set: $r=.171$)

Item	3	4	8
3			
4	.26		
8	.09	.32	
12	.05	.12	.19

Yugoslavia: $r=.177$

Item	3	4	8	12
3				
4	.25			
8	.33	.35		
12	.13	.04	.16	
10	.15	−.01	.11	.26

India: $r=.137$

Item	3	4	8	12	2
3					
4	.30				
8	.09	.12			
12	.16	.09	.06		
2	.31	.18	.17	.10	
1	.17	.09	−.08	.21	.09

Poland: $r = .169$								U.S.: $r = .120$					

Item	3	4	8	12	1	6	Item	3	4	8	12	1
3							3					
4	.05						4	.05				
8	.01	.25					8	.31	.08			
12	−.06	.02	.16				12	.19	.08	.00		
1	.15	.12	.39	.00			1	.22	.20	.05	−.05	
6	.23	.36	.25	.08	.15		6	.20	.14	.11	.06	.16
7	.18	.08	.39	.08	.16	.50						

The tables show that the nation-specific items add to the international or cross-national identity scale items. In the case of "material progress," the means of the correlations are improved for Yugoslavia and the United States. Although, in general, the mean correlations are lower for the national tests of items—the identity items plus the nation-specific items—the number of items for each scale is substantially increased and thus the reliability of the scale is enhanced.

The scale scores for individuals on each of the national sets of items then, when corrected for scale length, can be treated as comparable scale scores across cultures or nations even though the items comprising the cross-national scale are not exactly the same. By this procedure longer, and thus more reliable, more contextually relevant, and thus perhaps more valid, items are acquired than by the conventional procedure of simply comparing responses to identical, single questions across cultures.[10]

[10]Equivalence can also be defined in terms of variances of scores. Let "relevance" of a given dimension to a society be defined as the variance of a set of items. Comparisons in terms of relevance can then be made across countries. If a random sample of the entire population is used, it can be said that the more similar the total variance of items X^c_n is to the total variance of items X^d_n, the more similar is the relevance of property X for the two societies. And inversely, for example, if one society highly shares a norm against cruelty to animals and another society is distributed with regard to this norm, we can say that for the first society this norm is irrelevant while for the other one it is relevant—naturally in terms of the definition accepted above. Interesting comparisons can be made by comparing the variance of identities with the variance equivalents for each culture. The ratio of the sum of total variance of identities and the covariance of identities and equivalents to the total variance of all items provides a measure of universality of relevance of a given property to a country.

This ratio, U(niversality) of R(elevance) would equal:

$$UR = \frac{\sigma_k{}^2 + 2\Sigma\sigma_i\sigma_k r_{ih}}{\sigma_n{}^2}$$

The same procedure can be applied to the example of integration for local communities. The modes of integration may be different in different countries. The integrative institutions, the structure of rewards and sanctions, the economic base, and the integrative symbols may differ from country to country. However, as long as some components of integration are common to the studied countries, identical and equivalent indicators can be found and measurement can proceed.

EQUIVALENCE OF CROSS-NATIONAL RELATIONSHIPS

A second approach to equivalence is to analyze relationships within countries and to compare them across countries. In the first step, a relationship is examined for within-country units. For example, one can study the relationship between the level of economic development and the level of integration of local communities. Individual country analysis will open a field for discovering the operation of intervening variables related to hypothesized relationships. Such analysis will result in a series of statements of relationships, one for each country. Examining the relationship between education and political activity, it may be found, for example, that the respective correlation coefficients are .84 in the United States, .93 in Germany, and .21 in Mexico. The question for comparative analysis is whether the relationship between these two variables is the same in the three countries.

The point is that if the hypothesis concerning the relationship between education and political activity is to gain cross-national confirmation, within-country relationships must not differ. Procedures for testing the hypothesis that correlations are not different in independent samples are available and should be applied to answer the question posed above. If correlations are not found to be different in various countries, it can

---

where

$$\sigma_k{}^2 = \text{total variance of identities}$$
$$2\Sigma\sigma_i\sigma_k r_{ih} = \text{covariance of identities and equivalents}$$
$$\sigma_n{}^2 = \text{total variance}$$

The larger the ratio, the more a society is divided over the items it shares with other societies. The smaller the ratio, the more a society is divided over items specific to that society. For example, if the UR for the United States with regard to political activity equals .50, it can be concluded that activities common to the United States and other cultures are as important in differentiating the American people as in other societies. If the UR for India with regard to the social integration of local communities equals .10, it can be concluded that factors specific to India are much more important in distributing local communities on the dimension of integration than are the factors common with other countries.

be inferred that either in none of the countries does a "third" variable influence this relationship or that in all of the countries the related variables operate in the same way. To use another language, there are no "systemic" differences with regard to this relationship in the observed countries.

Before a relationship can be said to hold cross-nationally, the question that must be answered, to restate the position, is whether or not the relationship between the variables is the same in all countries. Probably, the strength of relationships between variables will differ among countries. These differences should serve as a cue that other variables, present in different degrees of intensity, are interfering with the relationship being analyzed cross-nationally. The task is to eliminate the influence of these related, but extraneous, variables. In order to see to what extent a relationship is similar across countries, it is necessary to reconstruct the scores for variables, freeing them from the influence of extraneous factors.

The data provided in *The Civic Culture*[11] for the relationship between education and the "feeling of relative freedom to discuss politics" will be used to illustrate how scores can be reconstructed and why it is necessary to do so. The table provided in the book had to be slightly adjusted in our Table 4, because numbers of respondents do not add up in the original data. It should be recognized that this is a comparative description, not a statement of relationship between variables except in so far as the "political system" is interpreted as a variable—an interpretation inconsistent with the assumptions of this paper.

The goal is to compare the freedom to discuss politics independently of differences in educational levels among the countries. In other words

TABLE 4

Feeling of Relative Freedom to Discuss Politics, by Nation and Education[a]

			Education					
	Total		Primary or Less		Some Secondary		Some University	
Nation	%	(N)	%	(N)	%	(N)	%	(N)
United States	63	(969)	49	(338)	70	(443)	71	(188)
Great Britain	63	(939)	59	(593)	70	(322)	83	(24)
Germany	38	(940)	35	(790)	52	(124)	60	(26)
Italy	37	(991)	30	(692)	53	(245)	59	(54)
Mexico	41	(1,004)	39	(877)	54	(103)	54	(24)

[a]Numbers in parentheses refer to the bases upon which percentages are calculated.

[11]Almond and Verba, *op. cit.*, p. 122.

"political cultures" rather than educational levels are being compared. Let "some university education" be scored as 3, "some secondary education" as 2, and "primary or less" as 1. It is possible now to calculate an average educational level in each country. When the regression of "freedom to discuss politics" to education is analyzed and the means of "freedom to discuss" are adjusted, it appears that the original data are quite misleading. The original and the adjusted means are shown in Table 5.

If education is statistically controlled, it turns out that Great Britain and Mexico rank higher than the United States with respect to the felt freedom to discuss politics.

Since experimental designs are rarely possible in cross-national research, analysis of covariance seems to be the technique particularly appropriate for data analysis. This technique permits controlling for the operation of the intervening variables and therefore makes it possible to isolate particular variables from the networks of interrelationships specific to each country.

SUMMARY AND CONCLUSION

The problem of equivalence in cross-national research can be met with the two assumptions that indicators of similar variables are manifested in different ways for different populations and that the influence of third, or intervening, variables must be taken into account in the analysis of cross-national data.

The importance of controlling intervening variables has long been recognized in social research. Only in this way can the cross-national equivalence of relationships be established.

A sound procedure for establishing cross-national equivalence of identical concepts has not been part of the repertoire of the social scientist committed to analysis of data from other countries. Such a procedure has been presented in this paper with some examples.

TABLE 5

Original and Adjusted Means of Relative Freedom to Discuss Politics, by Nation and Education

Nation	Education	Freedom (Original)	Adjustment .345 $(x_i - \bar{x})$	Freedom (Adjusted)
United States	1.84	.63	.1578	.47
Great Britain	1.39	.63	.0034	.63
Germany	1.19	.38	−.0655	.45
Italy	1.36	.37	−.0069	.38
Mexico	1.11	.41	−.0931	.50

Cross-national measures, following the arguments presented here, will be composed of a cross-national, identical set of indicators and a set of nation-specific indicators. The cross-national and nation-specific indicators combined provide a scale for reliable and valid measurement of the same phenomenon in various countries. According to the proposed procedure, measurements of similar variables in different countries are said to be identical if the same, interdependent indicators are used to assess the same phenomenon. In other words, the measurement is identical to the extent to which the operations furnish homogeneous indices for all countries. Measurements for specific countries are equivalent to the extent to which the specific measures are related to the identical measures. By allowing the researcher to utilize different indicators in different countries, the identity-equivalence procedure permits him to take into account phenomena which otherwise might be considered "qualitatively" different and hence not measurable. By referring the equivalent indicators back to the identical indicators, this procedure introduces safeguards of validity—the guarantee that the phenomena examined in various countries constitute specific occurrences of a more general concept.

6

The Random Probe:
A Technique for Evaluating
the Validity of Closed Questions

HOWARD SCHUMAN

The familiar dilemma of open versus closed interview questions becomes especially acute when surveys are undertaken outside middle-class American society. Inevitable ignorance of the subtleties of another culture leads the researcher toward an open-ended approach, while his experience with the difficulties of channeling diverse free responses into a useful frame of reference and of coding enormous masses of verbal data encourages him to rely on closed questions. The method of "random probes" suggested here is intended to allow a survey researcher to eat his cake and still have a little left over.

Important sociological analysis is often based on a small number of "closed" survey questions.[1] To the survey analyst, and perhaps even more to the non-survey-oriented sociologist, doubts sometimes arise about whether a question carries the same meaning for respondents as for the

Reprinted from Howard Schuman, "The Random Probe: A Technique for Evaluating the Validity of Closed Questions," *American Sociological Review* (1966):*31*, 218–22. Reprinted by permission of the author.

The writer is indebted for advice and encouragement to Alex Inkeles, Director of the comparative project of which the Pakistan study was one part, and to David H. Smith, an Associate of the project. The project is an aspect of research on development undertaken by the Center for International Affairs, Harvard University.

[1]One among many examples is the use of a single question on aspirations in Alan B. Wilson, "Class Segregation and Aspirations of Youth," *American Sociological Review*, 24 (December 1959), pp. 836–845. One solution to the problem discussed here leads of course toward scaling, but few exploratory cross-cultural surveys develop unidimensional or even adequately reliable Likert scales. More often the focus is on individual questions or on small sets of very modestly intercorrelated items. There are few "scales" in the sociological literature for which the problem raised here would not be relevant.

social scientist who constructed it. This is particularly true when the respondents differ greatly from the investigator in education, cultural characteristics, or life chances. True, the process of analysis itself is intended to elucidate the sense of data, yet there is often a need on the part of both investigator and reader to hear the respondent's own voice, and this is doubtless an important reason why surveys make use of open-ended questions and why free responses often make up a significant part of survey reports.

As surveys are increasingly undertaken in non-Western countries the problem becomes both more salient and more important. Questions framed in English by middle-class American professors are translated into Bengali and put in formal fashion by educated and urbanized Pakistani students to illiterate peasants in East Pakistan. Is this a reasonable endeavor? The survey researcher, accustomed to being told "it can't be done," plunges ahead boldly, but even he at times must wonder whether his tables really mean what he thinks they mean. If he himself has wrestled with problems of translation, and realized the ease with which unwanted connotations are added and wanted connotations lost, he cannot help but be aware that wording can be equally meaningful to both parties without that meaning being shared.

One solution is to work largely with open-ended questions. But in addition to immense problems of translation and coding when large-scale surveys are involved, it is difficult to obtain sufficiently rich responses from individuals who are both uneducated and unused to expressing opinions. Moreover, the very variety of frames of reference produced by open-ended questions changes from asset to liability when one is attempting to classify all respondents in terms of single variables. Because of these difficulties, surveys continue to rely heavily on closed multiple-choice questions even in settings very different from the United States.[2]

In this paper I would like to suggest a simple technique for obtaining on a routine basis both qualitative and quantitative information on the meaningfulness and meaning of responses to closed survey questions. The approach is an obvious extension of interviewer probing, traditionally used in surveys to encourage more detailed answers to *open*-ended questions. Such probing has undoubtedly been used in pre-testing closed questions and perhaps has been tried in regular surveys; but it seems

[2]Cf., Gabriel A. Almond and S. Verba, *The Civic Culture* (Princeton: Princeton University Press, 1963), p. 46, where approximately 90 percent of the questions are closed. For a full discussion of the advantages of both open and closed questions, see P. F. Lazarsfeld, "The Controversy over Detailed Interviews—An Offer for Negotiations," reprinted in Daniel Katz, *et al., Public Opinion and Propaganda*, The Dryden Press, 1954.

never to have been developed and applied systematically. The technique is direct and simple: each interviewer is required to carry out follow-up probes for a set of closed items *randomly* selected from the interview schedule for *each* of his respondents. The probe does not replace the regular closed question in any way, but follows immediately after the respondent's choice of an alternative. Using non-directive phrases, the interviewer simply asks the respondent to "explain a little" of what he had in mind in making his choice.[3] The recorded comments (or occasionally lack of comments) are used by the investigator to compare the intended purpose of the question and chosen alternative with its meaning as perceived and acted on by the respondent.

Both the randomization method and its usefulness will be illustrated by describing its application in a complex attitude survey of 1000 factory workers and cultivators in East Pakistan in 1964. In addition to background and open-ended questions, the schedule consisted of 200 closed and quasi-closed items, mostly in the form of two to four forced alternatives.[4] Each interviewer was given a list of these 200 questions and shown how to select by a chance method ten items from the list prior to each interview. He was to probe these ten questions *regardless* of the respondent's general or specific level of understanding. (Interviewers were also instructed to probe under certain other circumstances, but different symbols distinguished random from other probes.) The essence of the method is to obtain probe material on a *random* sample of the 200,000 closed responses expected in the survey.

The selection of ten questions per interview results in a sample of ten explanations by *each respondent*, and these can be evaluated to provide a measure of his ability to understand the questionnaire as a whole. From exactly the same item evaluations, we simultaneously obtain on the average fifty randomly probed responses for *each question*; working with these across individuals gives us an evaluation for each of the two hundred items, indicative of how well *they* are understood.[5]

---

[3] Phrases used by the interviewer are: "Would you give me an example of what you mean?"; "I see—why do you say that?"; "Could you tell me a little more about that?" As with most probes, the exact wording is less important than the manner in which it is made. It is particularly important that the respondent's closed choice not seem challenged.

[4] Not all of the questions probed were completely closed. Some required brief free replies which were highly constrained by the form of the question (e.g., "Generally, how often during a day do you pray?"). Still others involved quite free responses (e.g., ten sentence completion items). In these latter it also seemed desirable to obtain probe material on a random basis to clarify the sometimes cryptic patterns of answers. Such open and quasi-closed questions are involved in the random selection procedure but are generally excluded from the quantitative scoring to be discussed here. Scoring was applied to 175 questions.

[5] To obtain similar follow-up qualitative information, Almond and Verba, *op.*

EVALUATING THE RANDOM PROBES
QUANTITATIVELY

The Pakistan random probe material has been evaluated question by question on a five-point scale by regular coders who first read the follow-up material blind, then used it to predict the respondent's original closed alternative, and finally evaluated the total "fit" between probe explanation and chosen alternative. The evaluation code, explanations, and point equivalents are shown below.

Code	Interpretation	Points
A	Explanation is quite clear and leads to accurate prediction of closed choice.	1
B	Explanation of marginal clarity and leads to accurate prediction of closed choice.	2
C	Explanation very unclear; cannot make any prediction about closed choice.	4
D	(a) Explanation seems clear, but leads to wrong prediction of closed choice; (b) Respondent was unable to give any explanation of his closed choice ("don't know"); (c) Respondent in course of explanation shifted his closed choice away from original.	5
(R)	(Explanation is simply literal repetition of closed choice; cannot judge respondent's understanding of question.)	(omit)

The point gap between "B" and "C" reflects the fact that "B" is close to "A" in meaning and implication, while "C" points to an essentially unsatisfactory explanation. The symbol "R" really indicates inadequate probing by the interviewer, since rote repetition of a chosen alternative by the respondent does not allow us to judge his understanding one way or the other. Such repetitions are excluded from score computations, but a separate count of them can be kept for both individuals and questions. In general, the evaluation scheme is conservative: some of the responses coded "C" may be due to inadequate probing or translation, and some

---

cit., reinterviewed in depth a ten percent sub-sample of their original survey respondents. Their method has the advantage of allowing construction of a stratified rather than simple random sample, thus insuring better representation for infrequent responses. On the other hand, it is very costly in time and money, and it may also lead to over-probing and to "second-thought" explanations rather different from those a respondent might have given in the original interview. Our method involves only slight additional costs in interviewing time and provides a more natural inflow of information for all questions and for all individuals.

proportion of the responses coded "D" for incorrect prediction may actually have involved mis-check during the interview.[6]

To obtain quantitative indices, the numerical scores for separate responses are summed separately for each individual and for each question, and the sums are divided by the number of scorable probes available in each case. The resulting averages constitute 1000 individual probe scores and 200 question probe scores.[7] For the Pakistan survey, the reliability of the scoring was estimated by having the necessary responses reevaluated independently for a random sample of 30 individuals and a random sample of 30 questions. Product moment correlations of 0.75 and 0.92, respectively, were obtained, indicating satisfactory scoring reliabilities for both types of scores. The higher question reliability is due to the larger number of responses on which question scores are based.

Both individual and question scores can be interpreted directly in terms of the meanings used in the original evaluation procedure. For example, a mean score of 3, whether for an individual or for a question, indicates understanding half way between the "B" and "C" levels. If an individual score, it becomes a signal that the respondent probably had a generally low understanding. This supplements interviewer comments and ratings with a more objective measure of comprehension. But the more important warning is a high *question* probe score, for it suggests ambiguity, lack of clarity, or unintended meaning for the question over the entire sample. This provides information not ordinarily obtained from interviewers, especially newly-trained interviewers in developing countries.

In the Pakistan study the median question probe score is 1.4; 87 percent of the closed questions have mean scores between 1.0 ("A" understanding) and 2.0 ("B" understanding). Thus most but not all of the questions fall within what would appear to be an acceptable range. On an individual basis, the median score is 1.4 and 87 percent of the respondents average between 1.0 and 2.0. A small but significant minority

---

[6]The major limitation of the quantitative evaluation scheme is its inapplicability to subtle grades of intensity. In general, on items that ask a person not only to select among qualitatively different alternatives but also to indicate his strength of feeling, only the former can be evaluated readily from probe material. Thus a response is evaluated as "A" if it is spontaneously worded, clear in meaning, and correctly predicts the respondent's basic closed choice among two or more possibilities—even though his intensity of feeling cannot be predicted.

[7]Since only ten out of two hundred responses were probed in each interview, there is sampling error in the sense that a given individual may have been probed by chance on a particularly easy or difficult set of items. Sampling error by question is less, since 50 respondents were probed on each question. The number of questions probed is limited not only by cost of evaluation (the present ratio produced $10 \times 1000 = 10,000$ free responses) but also by the need to avoid questioning too frequently a respondent's choices.

of respondents thus seem to have real difficulties with the questions—not surprising for a sample with generally low education—although it should also be noted that within the sample the correlation between individual probe scores and schooling is trivial (-0.10), and between the same scores and a verbal aptitude measure the relation is not much greater (-0.23). There are a few individuals with such low scores as to suggest that they contribute mostly random error to the study (22 persons score 3.0 or greater), but to a considerable extent error seems to be concentrated in a few questions. Questions and individuals are inextricably related, of course, because the unit of analysis is the single response to a single question, but it is of some significance that more than half the responses rated "C" or "D" are concentrated in only one-fifth of the questions.

QUALITATIVE USE OF RANDOM PROBES

Formal numerical scoring provides only a rough index of the general value of an item. The qualitative understanding gained by reading 50 responses to a question offers a much richer source of information on the way the question was perceived and the meaning of the closed responses it evoked.[8] The kinds of elucidation provided will be illustrated by several examples from a set of questions on religion.

In the Pakistan study two questions were included to determine whether Islamic religious obligations are interpreted by various sample groups to include achievement-related effort as an end in itself. The answers to these questions show excellent variation, intercorrelate well, are significantly related to a number of background variables, and are relevant to an important hypothesis. But the random probes suggest that the questions were reasonably well understood by less than half the sample. Most respondents reinterpreted them in ways that had little to do with their original purpose. This question, with a mean probe score of 2.3, is an example:

"Do you think that whether a man works diligently every day is:
1. An absolutely essential part of religion,
2. An important but not essential part of religion, or
3. Of little importance to religion."

A common interpretation is represented by the following probe response from a man who had chosen the first alternative: "My family depends

[8]In the Pakistan analysis, coders not only provided a score for each individual response but also wrote a brief holistic evaluation of each question on the basis of having read all fifty responses to it.

on me. If there is no food and empty stomachs [because of laziness], then I cannot give attention to prayer." Respondents who chose the third alternative tended to give even more distant explanations, for example: "It is not good to work hard everyday. It will ruin the health."

The minority of probed respondents (about two-fifths) who did appear to understand the question in the intended frame of reference (e.g., "Allah has written in the Koran that men should work hard each day") were more educated than average, as would be expected. For them the question can certainly be used. For the less educated in the sample, however, the question must at the very least be treated with caution, and empirical relationships discoverable with it should be subjected to special scrutiny before final interpretation is made. Indeed, some researchers may prefer to drop such a question altogether.

Quite the opposite type of case is provided by the following yes-or-no question, intended to determine whether ethical actions and religious actions are conceived as separable by certain of the groups studied:

"Do you think a man can be truly good who has no religion at all?"

When this question was first presented to local translators and interviewers, their reaction was unanimously negative. No ordinary man would understand the point of the question, they felt. Whatever might be the case among Westerners or among the University-educated, the average Pakistani Muslim would certainly see a non-religious man as by definition devoid of goodness. All agreed that the question could not lead to meaningful responses and should not be included.

It was included, however, and in fact produced about one third "yes" and two-thirds "no" choices. But was the question perhaps misinterpreted in some way? The random probes indicate that understanding was very good indeed (mean score 1.1). A typical probe explanation for a "yes" response was: "He may not believe any religion, yet he can render good offices to the people of the land." Another man said: "He may be good and his heart may be very pure, and he can help people anyway." The "no" responses were also to the point: "The man who has no faith has no idea of good and bad, so he cannot be good." "The person who has no religion, what good thing may be in him? He is wretched." More generally, of the 52 probes to this question, only one was coded as confused. It therefore seems quite reasonable to interpret Pakistani response patterns for the question much as one would for ordinary Americans.

The two questions discussed thus far have shown the usefulness of random probe material in reaching decisions about the inclusion or exclusion of questions for analysis. But probably the greatest value of this additional material comes from making the analyst aware of subtle changes in meaning that have occurred between question formulation and tabular analysis. Usually it is not a case of rejecting a question, but rather of bringing into clearer focus the impact the wording had upon respondents and thus interpreting response patterns in a more accurate way.

The following forced-choice question, for example, was intended to contrast material striving with concern for more spiritual ideals:

> "Some people say that the more things a man possesses—like new clothes, furniture, and conveniences—the happier he is.
>
> Others say that whatever material things a man may possess, his happiness depends upon something else beyond those.
>
> What is your opinion?"

This question produced a wide distribution of responses and was understood without difficulty. However, the Bengali phrase for "something else beyond those" was interpreted in a broader way than the limited religious idea conceived in constructing the question and attempted in translation. Those who chose the second alternative sometimes gave religious justification ("It depends upon God's blessing"), but even more frequently they gave other sensible non-material explanations for their responses:

> "Suppose a man has no child, whereas he has all other things; then he is not happy."
>
> "It depends on one's wife. If she is not good, one is not happy."
>
> "I may have much wealth but there are many enemies against me."

Clearly the question was well understood. But just as clearly it would be incorrect to use the question as a direct indicator of religious *vs.* secular orientation. The probe material here helps the analyst to understand more precisely what it is he has measured—which is, after all, the final goal of "validity."

This last illustration also indicates why the quantitative evaluation described earlier must remain a relatively crude index. For each question that was not understood exactly as originally intended, it becomes a matter first of judgment and then of convention whether the question is being "misinterpreted" or simply differently interpreted. In practice the decision is seldom difficult, but occasionally a set of scores would be considerably altered had a different convention been established.

Through qualitative and quantitative review of random probe responses the survey researcher has an opportunity to increase his own sensitivity to what his questions mean to actual respondents, and thereby improve his comprehension of the resulting data. At the same time, quotations become available that can offer emotional insight into a table representing answers from people he and his readers are attempting to understand.

Of course, the addition of random probes to a survey is no panacea. It does not reduce the need for careful pre-testing, or solve the problems of survey analysis, but it is a simple, inexpensive, and natural way of obtaining valuable free response material on a systematic basis. In research in other cultures—and under some conditions in one's own culture —it forms a useful supplement to standard attitude survey methods.

PART **IV**

LINGUISTIC EQUIVALENCE
AND
TRANSLATION

7

On the Comparability
of Meaningful Stimuli
in Cross-Cultural Research

R. BRUCE W. ANDERSON

In essence the problem of translation is one of equivalence and variance. The focus of this paper is on the problem of maximizing equivalence. Some existing data on translation equivalence are discussed in an effort to destroy some misconceptions and to indicate the needs for empirical data which will help the investigator answer the question: "How do we know we are asking the same question in two or more settings?" Six problem areas are discussed: (1) translation of non-verbal stimuli; (2) stimulus complexity and sample size; (3) stimulus ambiguity; (4) verbal stimuli; (5) back translation, an iterative approach; and (6) bilinguals and bilingualism.

Many investigators are led into cross-cultural research by accident, or as a result of the fascination of foreign things. Others see the crossing of national and cultural boundaries as essential for establishing universal laws of social behavior. Whatever the reasons, sociologists are frequently found making cross-cultural comparisons, and in doing so they come up against the problems of translation whether they are aware of it or not. Indeed, one could argue that part of the concern which sociologists have long manifested about the status of interviewers relative to that of interviewees may be viewed as pertaining to translation problems. In short,

Reprinted from R. Bruce W. Anderson, "On the Comparability of Meaningful Stimuli in Cross-Cultural Research," *Sociometry* (1967):30, 124–36. Reprinted by permission of the publisher and author.

A complete revision of a paper read at the annual meeting of the American Sociological Association, September 1966. The comments of James A. Black, Donald T. Campbell, Irwin Deutscher, Dell Hymes, and Robert F. Winch on earlier versions of this manuscript are gratefully acknowledged.

translation[1] is involved whenever research requires asking the "same" question of people with differing backgrounds. This is true whether the comparison involves societies using unwritten, tribal languages, nation-states using the "same" language (such as England and the United States), or subcultural groupings within a single society. Many of the differences involved at these various levels of linguistic "exoticism" are matters of degree, not of kind.[2]

Further, one may question the correctness of the assumption that the members of the same subculture do not require translation in order that they may understand each other. The frequency with which comments like "I'm sorry, but I don't quite see what you are driving at" occur leads the writer to suggest that this assumption is less valid than it at first appears. Another instance of "hidden need for translation" obtains in the one-culture study where the investigator is not a participant in that culture. Here the need is centered in the probable ethnocentrisms of the investigator and his probable implicit comparisons. Attribution of "home culture meaning" to "host culture stimuli" is the likely consequence of misguided disregard for translation in this context.

In essence the problem of translation is one of equivalence and variance. The focus of this paper is on the problem of maximizing equivalence. The concomitant minimization of variance is dealt with only indirectly. Several questions might be raised at the outset, among them: (1) How does one know he is asking the same question in different settings? (2) What is the minimal level of equivalence necessary for two questions to be considered the same? and (3) What criteria can be established for equivalence? There are no absolute answers to these questions, since the goals of each individual research project will be instrumental in defining criteria of equivalence.[3] Some existing data on translation equivalence and some areas where additional data would be desirable will be discussed below.

Much of the data to be cited is drawn from studies involving per-

---

[1]Since the meaning of "translation" may vary, it seems appropriate to provide a a definition of translation as "the replacement of textual material in one language . . . by equivalent textual material in another language" (J. C. Catford, *A Linguistic Theory of Translation, An Essay in Applied Linguistics*, London: Oxford University Press, 1965, p. 20). The principle is the same whether the replacement involves textual material in two "whole languages" or in two varieties (such as idiolects, or dialects) of the same language.

[2]See, for example, Einar Haugen's revealing article "Semicommunication: The Language Gap in Scandinavia," *Sociological Inquiry*, 36 (Spring 1966), pp. 280–97.

[3]Catford, *op. cit.*, discusses the nature of equivalence in translation. His approach, however, deals with formal linguistic criteria and is not *directly* relevant to the pragmatics of instrumentation for cross-cultural research.

sonality tests. The reason for this eclecticism is simply that psychologists have been more interested in translation problems, to date, than have sociologists.[4] Adopting this approach may be justified on the grounds that the specific stimulus content, *per se*, is irrelevant to the search for general guidelines for translation equivalence. The use of data involving personality tests has the added advantage of raising the question of "what is equivalent" more sharply than other types of data might. This question is, of course, logically prior to the question of "how much is equivalent."

Focus upon the locus of equivalence properly includes considerations of situational equivalence—such as administration conditions—which are peripheral to the present paper. It also includes the question of response equivalence. The *intra-societal* measurement with (assumed) equivalent stimuli which results in *variant* responses is typically taken as an indicator of individual differences only after some sort of validation. A common means of validating personality instruments is by comparison of responses made by subjects who exhibit behavioral differences. Similar findings in cross-cultural comparison are often assumed to indicate *cultural differences* without comparable concern for behavioral validation. If, on the other hand, *equivalent* responses are obtained from a multi-societal investigation they are often uncritically attributed to *cultural universals*. It will be noted that in either of these situations stimulus equivalence is assumed, and conclusions are based on the obtained response equivalence or variance. This paper will be concerned with response equivalence only when it can be used as an index of stimulus equivalence.

It is important to recognize that the question of translation equivalence is a special case of instrument validation. As in the case of other aspects of "the validity problem" the importance of the theoretical matrix within which the instrument in question is embedded should not be overlooked. The assertion that "the goals of each individual research project will be instrumental in defining criteria of equivalence," above, was intended to alert the reader to this fact. Given a single bivariate hypothesis

---

[4]But, see John Useem, "Notes on the Sociological Study of Language," *Social Science Research Council Items*, 17 (September 1963), pp. 29–31; Joyce O. Hertzler, *A Sociology of Language*, New York: Random House, 1965, pp. 128–31; and chapter 8 in Robert M. Marsh, *Comparative Sociology: Toward the Codification of Cross-Societal Analysis*, New York: Harcourt, Brace and World, 1967. Cf. Paul Bohannan, "Translation—A Problem in Anthropology," *The Listener* (May 13, 1954), pp. 815–16; Herbert P. Phillips, "Problems of Translation and Meaning in Field Work," *Human Organization*, 18 (Winter 1959–1960), pp. 184–92; and Joseph B. Casagrande, "The Ends of Translation," *International Journal of American Linguistics*, 20 (October 1954), pp. 335–40.

and a single question or instrument for measuring each variable, what can be concluded from findings which appear to support the hypothesis? The present writer is of the disposition that interpretation of such findings (without benefit of additional information) as supportive of the hypothesis, as supportive of the validity of the instrument(s) employed, or as supportive of both instruments(s) and hypothesis would be tenuous at best. The presence of translated instruments should serve to increase, rather than decrease, one's reluctance to accept such conclusions. In discussing ways of improving the quality of translations in the following paragraphs, the reader should understand that the techniques advocated are intended as complementary to traditional validational procedures, not as substitutes for them. Indeed, the use of "translation-equivalent forms" of research instruments provides one take-off point for application of the logic of validation suggested by Campbell and Fiske.[5] This will become particularly obvious to the reader familiar with their work in the discussion of "back translation," below.

The discussion of maximization of stimulus equivalence in cross-cultural research will focus on six problem areas: (a) translation of non-verbal stimuli; (b) stimulus complexity and sample size; (c) stimulus ambiguity; (d) verbal stimuli; (e) back translation, an iterative approach, and (f) bilinguals and bilingualism.

I. TRANSLATION OF NON-VERBAL STIMULI

A non-verbal personality test, such as the TAT or Rorschach, *appears* to avoid the problem of translation except with respect to instructions given during administration. Lindzey[6] rightly observes that differences in response language in cross-cultural testing by these techniques result in a shift of the location of the translation problem rather than its elimination. The Welsh Figure Preference Test[7] minimizes these problems of response translation by asking the respondent to indicate whether

[5]Donald T. Campbell and Donald W. Fiske, "Convergent and Discriminant Validation by the Multitrait-Multimethod Matrix," *Psychological Bulletin*, 56 (March 1959), pp. 81–105. Cf. Campbell's "Recommendations for APA Test Standards Regarding Construct, Trait, or Discriminant Validity," *American Psychologist*, 15 (August 1960), pp. 546–53, and Lee Sechrest, "Incremental Validity: A Recommendation," *Educational and Psychological Measurement*, 23 (Spring 1963), pp. 153–58; for additional remarks concerning this approach to validation.

[6]Gardner Lindzey, *Projective Techniques and Cross-Cultural Research* (New York: Appleton-Century-Crofts, 1961), p. 73.

[7]George S. Welsh, *Preliminary Manual: Welsh Figure Preference Test, Research Edition* (Palo Alto: Consulting Psychologists Press), 1959.

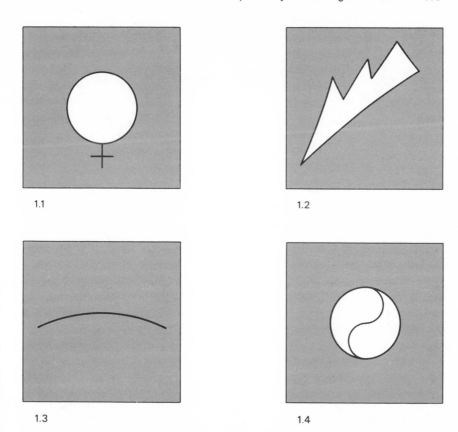

Figure 1. Pictures Adapted from the Welsh Figure Preference Test. (Published by Consulting Psychologists Press, Inc., Palo Alto, California. Research edition, Copyright 1949 by George S. Welsh, released for research use, 1959, by the publishers.)

or not he likes each stimulus—rather than asking for complex responses as with other "projective" tests.

Even with the Welsh test, where the problems of comparing verbal responses in different languages have been effectively eliminated by reducing the content of the responses to a binary choice situation, translation difficulties remain. Consider, for example, Figure 1.1 taken from this instrument. A biology student in any Western European society could clearly and unambiguously interpret this stimulus—and his liking or disliking of it would probably be influenced by his interpretation. Figure 1.2, on the other hand, has no clearly understood meaning to a Western European—yet an American Indian might well interpret it in terms of the

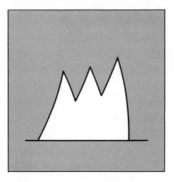

2.1 Mountains

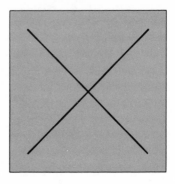

2.2 Trade

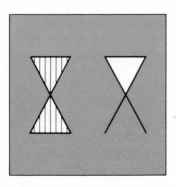

2.3 Dead Bodies

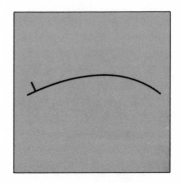

2.4 Morning, Sunrise

Figure 2. Pictures Adapted from "Pictography and Ideography of the Sioux and Ojibway Tribes of North American Indians" by William Tomkins. (In *Universal Indian Sign Language of the Plains Indians of North America* by William Tomkins. Published at San Diego, California, in 1929 by the author. The section from which these pictures are adapted is pp. 70–78 in this volume).

pictographic symbol for "mountain" as can be seen by comparison with Figure 2.1. It would be naive to assume that these and similar differences in interpretation which might obtain across societies would not influence responses differentially.[8] Thus, it must be concluded that the use of non-verbal measures changes the nature of the translation problem but does not avoid it.

[8]In this connection see Monica Lawlor's comparison of the responses made by English subjects to those made by West African subjects; "Cultural Influences on Preference for Designs," *Journal of Abnormal and Social Psychology*, 51 (November 1955), pp. 690–92. Cf. Margaret Naumburg, "Art as Symbolic Speech," chapter 17 in Ruth Anshen, *Language: An Enquiry into its Meaning and Function* (New York: Harper and Brothers, 1957).

II. STIMULUS COMPLEXITY AND SAMPLE SIZE

Hanks,[9] Geertz,[10] and others who have modified the TAT pictures in efforts to gain equivalence across cultures indicate awareness of the need to translate visual stimuli. To undertake the translation of a volume of prose requires a considerable familiarity with the subtleties of both languages involved—even to attain minimal readability. Similarly, modification of visual stimuli requires extensive knowledge of the responses which the original stimulus evoked in the base society and also of the stimulus which will have the same or similar meaning in the second society. Comparison of the sentence "I love you" with the *Kama Sutra* or of one of the Welsh Figure Preference Test "droodles" reproduced in Figure 1 with a TAT picture will immediately suggest one influence of stimulus complexity upon translatability. For the linguistically unsophisticated sociologist the task of finding an equivalent for the shorter, simpler stimulus appears intuitively manageable while the parallel task with more complex stimuli appears hopeless.

Associated with the problem of stimulus complexity is the size of the sample of stimuli. In general the more complex the stimuli the less practical it becomes to administer a large number of them. Thus the usual number of TAT pictures shown is twenty or fewer. If one out of these twenty pictures is inadequately translated—a situation which appears quite likely given the difficulty of the task—the five percent confidence level can no longer be applied to results, regardless of subject sampling procedures employed. Even if all stimuli were satisfactorily translated, the size of the stimulus sample might be considered too small to absorb latent random error. These criticisms imply acceptance of the premise that the original small sample was drawn randomly from some population of theoretically relevant stimuli. This assumption may also be questioned.

III. STIMULUS AMBIGUITY

It is a truism that a useful stimulus must be sufficiently ambiguous that it does not require a single response. One could posit a continuum

---

[9] L. M. Hanks, "Modified TAT's of Forty-Seven Thai Children and Adults," in B. Kaplan, ed., *Primary Records in Culture and Personality*, Vol. 1 (Madison: University of Wisconsin Press, 1956), as cited in Bert Kaplan, *Studying Personality Cross-Culturally*, (New York: Harper and Row, 1961).

[10] H. Geertz, "Modified TAT's of Thirty-three Japanese Men and Women," in B. Kaplan, ed., *Primary Records in Culture and Personality*, Vol. 2 (Madison: University of Wisconsin Press, 1957), as cited in Bert Kaplan, *Studying Personality Cross-Culturally*, (New York: Harper and Row, 1961).

of ambiguity ranging from questions such as "Are you male or female?", which permit but two answers, to stimuli like the Rorschach blots which permit a seemingly infinite variety of responses. The problem of the translator, noted by Jacobson[11] in his methodological note on the O.C.S.R. Seven-Nation Attitude Studies, is to faithfully reproduce the ambiguity from one language into the other. The difficulty of this task clearly varies directly with the extent of the ambiguity. How does one know with any certainty if the ambiguity is equivalent in two cultures when it is difficult to describe the nature of the ambiguity in other than purely mechanical terms (i.e., colored, symmetrical blots . . . etc.)?

From the foregoing it can be seen that ambiguity and complexity interact to increase the difficulty of meeting the requirement that equivalent versions permit the same range of responses. Even more difficult is attainment of stimuli which will produce translation equivalent responses with equal probability under controlled conditions. To reduce the problem of translating ambiguities the time honored procedure of precoding responses takes on new significance. A set of pre-determined forced choices can often be selected which will define a meaningful response universe in both societies, and the probabilities of the respective choices can be compared, providing data for a rather precise evaluation of the equivalence of ambiguity in the languages in question. With open ended questions, on the other hand, attainment of parallel "double-ambiguity" is virtually impossible. It might be noted in passing that the use of precoded response categories has the added advantages of facilitating use of larger samples of stimuli and of easing the task of employing statistical scoring techniques.[12]

IV. VERBAL STIMULI

It has been argued, above, that the use of visual stimuli merely modifies the problems of translation, but does not avoid them. With respect to the impact of stimulus complexity and ambiguity, and of the number of stimuli employed, upon translation equivalence attention has been fo-

---

[11]Eugene Jacobson, "Methods Used for Producing Comparable Data in the O.C.S.R. Seven-Nation Attitude Study," *Journal of Social Issues*, 10 (4, 1954), pp. 40–51. Catford, *op. cit.*, pp. 94–98, in distinguishing between various types of untranslatability remarks that "Linguistic untranslatability occurs typically in cases where an *ambiguity* [italics in the original] peculiar to the . . . [source language] text is a functionally relevant feature . . ." of the language in question. His explanation goes on to discuss sources of such ambiguity in considerable detail.

[12]See Paul E. Meehl's classic *Clinical Versus Statistical Prediction: A Theoretical Analysis and a Review of the Evidence* (Minneapolis: University of Minnesota Press, 1954).

cused on problems relevant for verbal and visual stimuli alike. In addition there are problems which are almost purely linguistic in nature. Thus, for example, the semantic range of, and overlap between, any two languages is likely to be uneven. The frequent and often necessary perpetuation of foreign words and phrases in English and other languages attests to this fact. These are often situations where nothing short of an extensive essay will adequately translate the meaning, as with *gemütlichkeit.*

Deutscher[13] provides an interesting illustration of the possible consequences of assuming that the words "friend, *freund,* and *amigo* are equivalent." He observes that, while the German term, *freund,* is limited to really close friends and the English term, friend, is applied to a broader circle of acquaintances, the Mexican usage of *amigo* includes both "direct address and indirect reference to strangers with whom the speaker may have had only the most casual and superficial encounter." The reliability with which these terms are "translation-interchangeable" is quite high. Given this fact, "the conclusion drawn from a hypothetical study of Germans, Americans, and Mexicans must be that Germans are a very unfriendly lot; Americans are quite friendly; and Mexicans are the most outgoing of all peoples when it comes to establishing friendships." Obviously the differences in semantic range noted by Deutscher serve to obscure any conclusions which one might wish to draw with respect to national character from such a study.

The punster's double-meaning provides an illustration of the difficulty encountered in cross-linguistic matching of ambiguities. Phonology is another purely linguistic phenomenon which may influence the translation process, as illustrated by the following excerpt from Catford:

> A Jew has been accused of horse-stealing, and, in court, the following exchanges take place:
>
> JUDGE: Did you steal a horse?
> INTERPRETER: Hot ir gestolen a pferd?
> ACCUSED: Ikh hob gestolen a ∧ pferd?
> JUDGE: What did he say?
> INTERPRETER: He said 'I stole a horse.'
>
> The point here is that the interpreter failed to take note of a feature of the accused's speech: namely the Yiddish rise-fall tone, ∧ , which occurs on the word *pferd.* Had he done so, his translation might have been 'What. Me steal a horse?'[14]

[13]Irwin Deutscher, "Asking Questions Cross-Culturally: Some Problems in Semantic Comparability—and Some Solutions," Syracuse, unpublished manuscript, December 1966.
[14]Catford, *op. cit.,* p. 54.

The presence of homonyms which may delight the comedian should be included among essentially linguistic phenomena which may cause the translator difficulty. Another is the differential frequency of translating equivalent terms. Thus, "nice" is the English term listed in a bilingual dictionary which approximates the frequency of the Danish word *hyggelig* most closely. It is also the least adequate of the possible translations given in terms of meaning equivalence. Yet another source of difficulty, familiar to all who have studied a foreign language in school, is differential grammatical organization. These problems lie beyond the scope of the present paper, for solving them would require considerable linguistic sophistication.[15] This paper seeks, rather, to point out some problems which the linguistically unsophisticated sociologist is likely to encounter in putting his propositions to cross-cultural test and to comment on various heuristics which have been developed for unraveling some of them.

The naive approach to verbal translation may be illustrated by the reports of Sundberg,[16] Lövaas,[17] and Gough and Sandhu[18] which pass over the problem with a casual reference to having had a native speaker (*of the non-English language*) do the translating and occasionally having a second bilingual independently check the job done by the first. These writers appear, from their reports, to consider that a person who can read English and who is a native speaker of some other tongue can pro-

[15]See Catford, *op. cit.*, and Charles E. Osgood and Thomas A. Sebeok, *Psycholinguistics: A Survey of Theory and Research Problems*, A Morton Prince Memorial Supplement to the *Journal of Abnormal and Social Psychology*, 49 (October 1954), expanded and reissued in book form by Indiana University Press, at Bloomington, in 1965. Illustrations of the linguistic difficulties encountered in translation may be provided at length. See, for example, Theodore Savory, *The Art of Translation* (London: Jonathan Cape, 1957), p. 14 (the absence of a precise French equivalent for the English word "home"); Robert Edward Mitchell, "Survey Materials Collected in the Developing Countries: Sampling, Measurement, and Interviewing Obstacles to Intra- and Inter-National Comparisons," *International Social Science Journal*, 17 (4, 1965), p. 677 (the difficulty involved in translating "aggressive"); Haim Blanc, "Multilingual Interviewing in Israel," *American Journal of Sociology*, 62 (September 1956), pp. 205–209 ("very many," "too many," and other phrases); William L. Hunt, Wilder W. Crane, and John C. Wahlke, "Interviewing Political Elites in Cross-Cultural Comparative Research," *American Journal of Sociology*, 70 (July 1964), p. 66 ("may or may not"); and Phillips, *op. cit.* ("angry," "strange," "day-dreams," and "a 'good' quarrel").

[16]Norman D. Sundberg, "The Use of the MMPI for Cross-Cultural Personality Study: A Preliminary Report on the German Translation," *Journal of Abnormal and Social Psychology*, 52 (March 1956), pp. 281–83.

[17]Ivar O. Lövaas, "Social Desirability Ratings of Personality Variable by Norwegian and American College Students," *Journal of Abnormal and Social Psychology*, 57 (July 1958), pp. 124–25.

[18]Harrison G. Gough and Harjit S. Sandhu, "Validation of the CPI Socialization Scale in India," *Journal of Abnormal and Social Psychology*, 68 (May 1964), pp. 544–47.

duce an equivalent to any English document in his native language. To add a second individual with similar qualifications to check the first ignores more problems than it solves as examination of some aspects of the nature of bilingualism, below, will make clear. A more sophisticated means of controlling the quality of translation should be considered before turning to the bilingual as a phenomenon.

V. BACK TRANSLATION: AN ITERATIVE APPROACH

One way in which a translation can be checked for equivalence is to ask additional bilinguals to start with the translated version and translate it back into the language of origin. Schachter[19] reports an application of the "back-translation" technique, but fails to make optimal use of the results. Having obtained one or more back-translated versions of the instrument in the source language the procedure indicated by Schachter was to "eliminate any differences." A more desirable procedure, first suggested to the writer by Donald T. Campbell, would be to recognize these as alternate forms which approach measurement of the same conceptual realm with somewhat different linguistic irrelevancies. These two, or more, measures might be used to generate added versions in each language through several iterations of the back-translation procedure. This process appears costly, and it undoubtedly is more so than a one-step translation, but it appears that the result would permit effective randomization of the effects of language and translation through the use of multiple forms. Further, if a complex personality inventory such as the California Psychological Inventory[20] is considered one item at a time the task of exhausting translators' ability to devise new versions, especially without access to other translations or instructions to do other than provide a "true" translation, appears relatively manageable.

Back translation, when used as an iterative procedure with a new translator for each iteration, will produce a population of items in each language with heterogeneous and random errors. A random sample of items in each language, or use of different versions with randomly selected subsamples of subjects, should provide equivalence save for random error.

[19]Stanley Schachter, "Interpretive and Methodological Problems of Replicated Research," *Journal of Social Issues*, 10 (4, 1954), pp. 52–60. Mitchell, *op. cit.*, indicates that there is "general agreement on how the actual translation of the questions should be made" and proceeds to describe the back-translation technique as discussed by Schachter. Cf. Casagrande, *op. cit.*

[20]Harrison G. Gough, *California Psychological Inventory Manual* (Palo Alto: Consulting Psychologists Press, 1957).

VI. BILINGUALS AND BILINGUALISM

Another approach to translation equivalence of stimuli suggested by Schachter[21] and used by Osgood and associates[22] in conjunction with back translation, uses response equivalence of bilingual subjects answering both language versions of the same instrument as an index of stimulus equivalence. Schachter's suggestion was that bilinguals respond repeatedly in both languages while iterative changes in the translated version were made until identical responses obtained. Osgood and his associates[23] apparently use this approach occasionally. An alternate use of bilingual subjects for validation is reported by the Psychological Testing Staff of Sears Roebuck and Co. in a mimeographed report.[24] Their data show that correlations between English and Spanish versions of the Guilford-Martin inventories administered in standard order with a five months time gap approach split-half reliabilities for the same scales. These data suggest that (a) the translation is reasonably equivalent to the original, and (b) that the persons responding "think similarly" in both languages.

The findings of Ervin[25] and of Lambert and his associates[26] raise issues which cast doubt on the underlying assumption that bilinguals "think similarly" in both languages. Ervin,[27] using the TAT, French bilinguals, counter-balanced order, and a shorter time gap, found systematic differences which could be derived from child rearing practices and French/American differences in value systems. While her findings may be criticized on methodological grounds, they are clearly suggestive of a

[21]Schachter, op. cit.

[22]Charles E. Osgood, W. K. Archer, and Murray S. Miron, The Cross-Cultural Generality of Meaning Systems, Appendices to a proposal submitted to the National Science Foundation, mimeographed, (Urbana: Institute of Communications Research, University of Illinois, 1962).

[23]Ibid.

[24]Sears Roebuck and Co., Psychological Testing Staff, National Personnel, A Comparison of the Spanish and English Versions of the Sears Executive Battery, mimeographed, October 12, 1955.

[25]Susan M. Ervin, "Language and TAT Content in Bilinguals," Journal of Abnormal and Social Psychology, 68 (May 1964), pp. 500–507. For additional discussions of bilinguals and bilingualism see Einar Haugen, Bilingualism in the Americas: A Bibliography and Research Guide (University of Alabama, 1956); and Uriel Weinreich, Languages in Contact (The Hague: Mouton and Co., 1966). Both of these sources contain extensive bibliographies.

[26]Wallace E. Lambert, "Measurement of the Linguistic Dominance of Bilinguals," Journal of Abnormal and Social Psychology, 50 (March 1955), pp. 197–200; and Wallace E. Lambert, J. Havelka, and C. Crosby, "The Influence of Language-Acquisition Context on Bilingualism," Journal of Abnormal and Social Psychology, 56 (March 1958), pp. 239–44, reprinted in Sol Saporta, ed., Psycholinguistics: A Book of Readings (New York: Holt, Rinehart and Winston, 1961), pp. 407–14.

[27]Ervin, op. cit.

"dual personality" in bilinguals. If such exists it is clearly impossible, on the basis of available data, to ascertain the presence or nature of its possible bias producing effects when using bilinguals either as translators or as subjects.

The Lambert studies of bilingualism suggest several variables which should be explored further in order to determine more clearly the nature and influence of bilingualism upon translation. First, these investigations suggest that the order of language learning may have important consequences for the type of characteristics exhibited by the bilingual. This suggests that the predominant utilization by American investigators of bilinguals who have learned English as a second language may introduce errors. Second, the Lambert studies indicate that bilinguals may have a dominant language, one which is preferred or which is easier for them to use. Linguistic dominance tends to be associated with the order of language learning, though this is not always the case. It also appears to be associated with a third dimension of bilingualism—coordinacy/compoundness. These two ideal types are most simply distinguished with respect to relative conceptual independence. If the bilingual utilizes a sort of "common set" of concepts which link his two languages together we term him a compound bilingual. If, on the other hand, such a link is absent and he uses the languages more or less independently, linking them for translation purposes by parallel responses to environmental stimuli, we term him a coordinate bilingual. Lambert and associates clearly indicate that separation of context of language learning increases conceptual independence—a finding which could account for differences between the Ervin data, obtained from persons who probably were coordinate bilinguals, and the Sears Roebuck findings based on a sample which may have included a significant proportion of compound bilinguals.

SUMMARY AND CONCLUSIONS

This paper raised a question which is basic to cross-cultural research: How do we know we are asking the same question in both settings? Its purpose was not to provide the answer, for at present there is none. Rather its goal was to discuss briefly some of the problems of translation in an effort to destroy some misconceptions and to place in sharper relief the needs for empirical data which will help the investigator answer this question. Many of the studies cited are as insightful as they are incomplete, as rewarding as they are inadequate. The need now is for rigorously controlled research which will pay heed to the different types of problems which have been discussed. One would hope that such research would take the form of self-conscious examination of the adequacy of the translations used in comparative research, as well as in the form of studies specifically directed at further elucidation of problems of translation.

8

Asking Questions Cross-Culturally:
Some Problems of Linguistic
Comparability

IRWIN DEUTSCHER

To do research we must know what we and our associates are talking about now. We must constantly ask ourselves: "What do these words mean? Why do I use them?" If we are reading research documents written by others, say a year ago, we must be sure we know what the words meant then. If we read a document written thirty years ago, full comprehension is almost a philological job, so rapid is the change in the connotation and denotation of terms.[1]

INTRODUCTION

The peculiar relationship between what men say and how they otherwise behave is, or ought to be, a focal concern of the social sciences. Theoretically the extent and nature of the relationship can be expected to vary under different conditions. Any act is an historical process, constructed by the actors as it unfolds. It is influenced in its construction by alterations of and redefinitions of the immediate situation in which actors find themselves at various points in the flow of action. From this symbolic interactionist perspective we anticipate that, to the extent that words and deeds occur at different stages of the act (in different situations), there is no theoretical basis for assuming that what people say correlates with whatever else they may do. The empirical evidence fits this theoretical

Reprinted from Howard S. Becker, Blanche Geer, David Riesman, and Robert S. Weiss, editors *Institutions and the Person* (Chicago: Aldine Publishing Company, 1968). Copyright © 1968 by Howard S. Becker, Blanche Geer, David Riesman, and Robert S. Weiss. Reprinted by permission of the publisher and the author.

[1]From "What's in a Name," Chap. 9 in Everett C. Hughes and Helen MacGill Hughes, *Where Peoples Meet: Racial and Ethnic Frontiers* (Glencoe, Ill.: The Free Press, 1952), pp. 130–44.

perspective. In fact, sometimes people do as they say, sometimes they do not, and sometimes they do the exact opposite.[2]

There is, in addition, good reason to believe that apparent discrepancies (or correlations) between words and deeds are frequently a spurious artifact of the inadequate technology of social science—more apparent than real. Our techniques for tapping the phenomena interfere with and impinge upon those phenomena in ways that distort our findings—we create static with our instruments.[3]

We are confronted with many serious problems in the methodological domain, but what is perhaps the most devastating gap is our unwillingness (and consequent inability) to come to grips with semantics: What do people intend to convey when they answer our questions or, for that matter, when they speak at all? What do people understand to be the intent and meaning of our questions? This is the dimension to which the present paper addresses itself—the dimension of language as it impinges upon our research and, inevitably, as it impinges upon human behavior itself. In the pages which follow we will explore and interpret some of the evidence which illuminates the way language is, in fact, the essential peculiarity of human behavior and human interaction.

There are two avenues through which social scientists can seek to understand human behavior: we can ask questions or we can observe action. These two avenues are not independent of each other. The process of asking questions and the manner of response is, in itself, overt behavior—a part of whatever social act is in process. This segment of the act is, in turn, related to other segments of overt action. As Mark Benney and Everett Hughes have put it, "the interview, as itself a form of social rhetoric, is not merely a tool of sociology but a part of its very subject matter."[4]

---

[2]For a preliminary statement of the problem of the relationship between what people say and what they do, see my "Words and Deeds: Social Science and Social Policy," *Social Problems* (Winter 1966), 13(3): 235–54.

[3]Attempts, in social psychology, to confront this issue have largely endeavored to avoid verbal sources of evidence rather than to treat conversation as data in itself. See, for example, Stanley Milgram, "Group Pressure and Action against a Person," *Journal of Abnormal and Social Psychology* (August 1964), 69(2): 137–43; Martin T. Orne, "On the Social Psychology of the Psychological Experiment: With Particular Reference to Demand Characteristics" *American Psychologist* (November 1962), 17(11): 776–83; Donald T. Campbell, "Factors Relevant to the Validity of Experiments in Social Settings," *Psychological Bulletin* (1957), 54(4): 297–312; Eugene J. Webb, Donald T. Campbell, Richard D. Schwartz, and Lee Sechrest, *Unobtrusive Measures: Non-reactive Research in the Social Sciences* (Chicago: Rand McNally, 1966).

[4]Mark Benney and Everett C. Hughes, "Of Sociology and the Interview: Editorial Preface," *American Journal of Sociology* (September 1956), 62(2): 138. It is possible to view the records men leave behind—written and otherwise—as a third avenue of understanding.

What problems need to be considered when comparable information is sought verbally from people who operate with different vocabularies, different grammars, and different kinds of sounds? In other words, what problems of comparability of meaning are introduced when questions are addressed to publics who vary in their everyday lexicon, syntax, and phoneme? This is a legitimate question to raise in respect to survey or interview research within any society in which linguistic variations exist. And, where social barriers occur, linguistic variations develop: among social classes, age groups, regions, ethnic groups, and between sexes or rural and urban segments of the population, to mention only a few possibilities.

These problems of communication are presented in an exaggerated form when truly different languages are involved, and when the intention is to pose identical questions and achieve comparable responses in those different languages. In order to dramatically highlight some of the linguistic issues which must also be present in domestic interviewing and survey research, we will take a close look at what is known to occur when comparable responses are sought to presumably comparable questions from publics who speak different languages.

ON LEXICAL EQUIVALENCE

The increasing number of survey researchers and opinion pollsters whose work requires that international comparisons be made are not unaware of the importance of achieving comparability of questions which must be asked in more than one language.[5] The technique which is widely employed to deal with this problem is called "back translation":

> There is general agreement on how the actual translation of the questions should be made. First, the original instrument is translated into the local language, and then another translator independently translates this translated version back into the original. The original and retranslated versions are compared and the discrepancies are clarified.[6]

Such a procedure can indeed be helpful in identifying semantic errors in translations. The manner in which it solves some problems while

[5]Curiously, this problem has been largely posed as one of comparability in *asking questions*, without a concomitant concern for comparability in *listening to responses*. Robert Weiss has suggested correctly that a concern with response equivalence (in contrast to question equivalence) in domestic research would have led to the development of an analogue to the back-translation technique discussed below. This analogue might take the form of studying the comparability of categories employed in coding open-end questions.

[6]Robert Edward Mitchell, "Survey Materials Collected in the Developing Countries: Sampling, Measurement, and Interviewing Obstacles to Intra- and International Comparisons," *International Social Science Journal* (1965), 17(4): 678.

simultaneously creating new ones is exemplified in the report of one field-worker in Thailand who was attempting to translate, not a complex survey instrument, but very simple sentence completion items which relate to basic human experiences. Analyzing the results of his back translation, Phillips concludes that:

> The results of this procedure, however, were so dismal that it was abandoned after a dozen items. That the majority of the translations were not coming through accurately was obvious, but the source of error could be discovered only after prolonged discussion. Items which originally read "He often day-dreams of . . ." or "Sometimes a good quarrel is necessary because . . ." appeared in the retranslated versions as "When he sleeps during the day he dreams of . . ." or "Sometimes a quarrel brings good results because . . ." (This last item later proved to be untranslatable. After much discussion, the translators decided that, although it was conceivable that an American might enjoy a quarrel for its cathartic effects, the notion would be incomprehensible to a Thai.)[7]

More recently Schuman has expressed concern over the problems encountered in a Pakistani study in which "questions were framed in English by middle-class American professors . . . , translated into Bengali and put in formal fashion by educated and urbanized Pakistani students to illiterate peasants in East Pakistan." Schuman asks, "Is this a reasonable endeavor?"[8] If the survey researcher "has wrestled with problems of translation, and realized the ease with which unwanted connotations are added and wanted connotations are lost, he cannot help but be aware that wording can be equally meaningful to both parties without that meaning being shared."[9] Although people may answer, we cannot always be certain of what it is they are responding to. An illustration of how different groups may provide similar response distributions for very different

[7]Herbert P. Phillips. "Problems of Translation and Meaning in Field Work," *Human Organization* (Winter 1959–60). 18(4): 190.

[8]Howard Schuman, "The Random Probe: A Technique for Evaluating the Validity of Closed Questions," *American Sociological Review* (April 1966), 31(2): 218. John M. Roberts has employed a tape recorder to assist in detailed analyses of back-translations; see Florence Rockwood Kluckhohn, "A Method for Eliciting Value Orientations," *Anthropological Linguistics* (February 1950), p. 9. Painstaking efforts to achieve comparability are also reported by Bradford Hudson *et al.*, "Introduction: Problems and Methods of Cross-Cultural Research," in Bradford Hudson (Ed.), *Cross-Cultural Studies in the Arab Middle East and United States: Studies of Young Adults, Journal of Social Issues* (1959), 15(3) 111. Raymond Fink has attempted back-translation through an intermediate language: see his "Interviewer Training and Supervision in a Survey of Laos," *International Social Science Journal* (1963), 15(1): 24. In a paper dealing with some of the same issues raised in this one, but focused on comparative problems in the use of psychological instruments, Anderson cites several examples of "the naive approach to verbal translation": see R. Bruce W. Anderson, "On the Comparability of Meaningful Stimuli in Cross-Cultural Research," *Sociometry* (June 1967), 30(2): 124–36.

[9]Schuman, *op cit.*, p. 218.

reasons, is found in Stoodley's report of comparative attitudes among German, American, and Filipino youth. On items related to authoritarianism, the democratically oriented Filipino youth sometimes respond in ways that distribute similarly to a German Nazi subsample. But in the light of the cultural contexts within which those responses are called forth, the similarity does not extend beyond the statistical distribution.[10]

The back-translation procedure does indeed guarantee that the words translate accurately or reveal that they do not. But back translation can also instill a false sense of security in the investigator by demonstrating a spurious lexical equivalence. Since language is a cultural artifact, it must be assumed that the question is being addressed to peoples who are immersed in two different cultural milieux.[11] To the extent that this is so, it is not sufficient to know simply that the words are equivalent. It is necessary to know the extent to which those literally equivalent words and phrases convey equivalent meanings in the two languages or cultures.

There are, of course, many instances in which the object denoted by a word is the same in many languages. Thus, the Frenchman says *chien,* the German *Hund,* the American *dog.* In this case the words differ but the referent seems to be the same. Is this always true? As Roger Brown poses the question, "Are the languages of the world a set of alternative codes?"[12] Are the sentiments called forth in actors who employ different words to refer to the "same" object necessarily the same sentiments? If not, can we then assume that simply because two words refer to the same object, they *mean* the same thing?

As clear as it is that denotations may be identical, it is equally clear that connotations may simultaneously differ. It has been observed, for example, that English *horse,* French *cheval,* and German *Pferd* may have different ranges of application and different semantic overtones.[13] Brown has pointed out that,

[10]Bartlett H. Stoodley, "Normative Attitudes of Filipino Youth Compared with German and American Youth," *American Sociological Review* (October 1957), 22(5): 553–61.

[11]The problem is further confounded by the fact that it must also be assumed that different sets of peoples are immersed in different *social* milieux. Language is not only a cultural artifact; it is also a social artifact. The manner in which commonly understood meanings emerge within specific social context and the manner in which ellipses convey mutually understood messages, is illustrated by the dialogue reported (and interpolated)l in Harold Garfinkel, "Studies of the Routine Grounds of Everyday Activities, *Social Problems* (1964); 11: 225–50.

[12]Roger W. Brown, *Words and Things* (Glencoe, Ill.: The Free Press, .1958), p. 19.

[13]John B. Carroll and Joseph B. Casagrande, "The Function of Language Classification in Behavior," in Eleanor Maccoby, Theodore M. Newcomb, and Eugene L. Hartley (Eds.), *Readings in Social Psychology* (New York: Holt, Rinehart and Winston, 1958), p. 19.

The German *Vaterland* is much like the American fatherland. The two words may have identical referents. If, however, we extend our notion of semantics to include all the contexts in which a word may be used—all the things said of it, all the adjectives applied to it, all the emotional slogans in which it appears—it will be clear that *Vaterland* and fatherland are not identical.[14]

Elsewhere, he notes that the French word *amie* is not quite the same as English "lady friend" or German *Freundin*. The word *amie* is more likely to designate a sweetheart than either of the other expressions, and yet it has a wider semantic range than English "sweetheart." "There will be French utterances containing *amie* for which 'lady friend' is an unlikely English substitute."[15]

Social scientists are rarely concerned with cross-cultural comparisons involving dogs or horses; they may sometimes be concerned with questions of nationalism—fatherland; they are very likely to exhibit interest in interpersonal relationships such as those involving kin, friends, and acquaintances. In order to insure a reasonable level of comparability, it is necessary that the distinctions made in interpersonal relationships by respondents be equivalent. An Israeli sociologist engaged in multilingual interviewing reports, for example, that "In trying to determine how close each respondent felt toward his best friend in the housing project, he was asked whether this person is a 'friend' or an 'acquaintance." Even assuming that the difference is easily rendered in languages of the Western cultures (Hebrew *yedid-makar*, French *ami-connaissance*, German *Freund-Bekannte*, Yiddish *Fraynd-Bakanter*), can we assume that they can be as easily rendered into the Arabic dialects?" As will be seen below, one cannot even assume that the differences are easily rendered in languages of the Western cultures.

Sociologists, being concerned with patterns of association and influence, with sociometric analyses, among other things, frequently employ in their instruments words such as "relatives," "neighbors," and "friends." The complexity and diversity of kinship terminology and kinship concepts has been thoroughly documented in the literature of ethnography;[17] clearly, a "relative" in one culture may or may not be a "relative" in an-

---

[14]Brown, *op. cit.*, pp. 259–60.

[15]Roger W. Brown, "Language and Categories," appendix to Jerome S. Bruner, Jaqueline J. Goodnow, and George A. Austin, *A Study of Thinking* (New York: Science Editions, 1962), pp. 310–11. Perhaps the closest expression we have in English would be the cumbersome "great and good friend," which appears appropriate only in reference to highly prominent persons and only in print.

[16]Haim Blanc, "Multilingual Interviewing in Israel," *American Journal of Sociology* (September 1956), 62(2): 206.

[17]For a study of kinship terminology in 250 societies, see George P. Murdock, *Social Structure* (New York: Macmillan, 1949). Paul Friedrich has meticulously documented the manner in which radical changes in kinship terminology occur with shifts in the social structure. See his "Linguistic Reflex of Social Change: From Tsarist to Soviet Russian Kinship," *Sociological Inquiry* (Spring 1966), 36(2): 159–85.

other. But important linguistic nuances may exist in the use of any term—even one which is reproduced with accuracy by the back-translation method. The word "friend," for example, translates easily back and forth with the German cognate "*Freund*." But is *ein Freund* in fact a friend? Hardly! For the German, the term is reserved for a very few intimate associates of long standing. For the American, the English cognate has a much broader reference to a much wider assortment of acquaintances. Incidentally, the Spanish word which would provide a reliable back translation for the English "friend" is *amigo*. Yet among Mexicans that term is employed both as a form of direct address and as indirect reference to strangers with whom the speaker may have had only the most casual and superficial encounter.

What are the possible consequences of an assumption on the part of the cross-lingual survey researcher, that the words friend, *Freund*, and *amigo* are equivalent? Because of the semantic variations among these three words—the different ranges of phenomena to which they refer—we would expect differential response rates to questions related to frequency and thus to any other questions which may be contingent upon frequency, e.g., extent of influence, source of information, relative standing among alternative reference groups, and so on.[18] But if it is assumed that the back-translation process guarantees a reliable degree of comparability, the conclusion drawn from a hypothetical study of Germans, Americans, and Mexicans must be that Germans are a very unfriendly lot; Americans are quite friendly; and Mexicans are the most outgoing of all peoples when it comes to establishing friendships. This observation on national character may or may not be correct, but the data from such a cross-lingual survey provide no evidence whatsoever on the matter.

ON MATTERS OF DEGREE: DISTINCTION AND CLASSIFICATIONS

Although the emphasis thus far has been upon the problem of simple lexical equivalence, the related problem of variability in the kinds of distinctions a language may facilitate or retard deserves careful attention. In an earlier paper, I raised the question of comparability in the distinction

[18]A casual perusal of readily available questionnaires employed by two reputable national and international survey research organizations reveals frequent use of questions such as the following: "How often do you talk about . . . with your friends? Very often, sometimes, never." "Is there anyone else, other than your family and friends, that you are likely to discuss . . . with?" "Some people spend most of their free time alone, some with their immediate family, some with friends, and so on. From the list on the card there, I'd like to know the way you most often spend your free time." The list referred to in the last example includes such alternatives as "With immediate family," "With other relatives," "With school friends," "With other friends."

between a simple affirmative or negative response: "Should we assume that a response of 'ja,' 'da,' 'sí,' 'oui,' or 'yes' all really mean exactly the same thing in response to the same question? Or may there be different kinds of affirmative connotations in different languages?"[19] I have since learned that "a simple English 'no' tends to be interpreted by members of the Arabic culture as meaning 'yes.' A real 'no' would need to be emphasized; the simple 'no' indicates a desire for further negation. Likewise a nonemphasized 'yes' will often be interpreted as a polite refusal."[20] And I have since been reminded of what every American college boy knows—that when a girl says "no," she doesn't necessarily mean "no"; as a matter of fact she may very well mean "yes."

Such semantic nuances in distinctions can create immense problems in the kind of research which requires that responses be coded into predetermined categories in order to facilitate comparisons. As an Austrian respondent informed one American interviewer, "every 'yes' has its 'however,' and every 'no' its 'if' "[21] David Riesman finds something of the Arab in English-speaking American college professors. On the basis of an analysis of their responses to precoded alternatives, he observes that "it sometimes happens that people torn between 'yes' and 'no,' will answer in one direction and then add qualifications in the other, showing for example that their 'yes' doesn't quite mean 'yes,' and may even lean toward 'no' "[22]

C. Wright Mills, stimulated by I. A. Richards' *Mencius on the Mind*, became intrigued over a quarter of a century ago with "the manner in which 'lack' of distinctions in a language limits thought. . . ." Regarding the Chinese word for "aged," "there is no distinction between age in chronological sense and the sense of an ethical pattern toward those who are old. . . . Thinkers of Mencius' period do not 'discuss or treat as open to discussion the rightness of paying respect to age as age.' "[23]

[19]Irwin Deutscher, "Words and Deeds: Social Science and Social Policy," *op. cit.*, p, 249.

[20]Edmund S. Glenn, "Semantic Differences in International Communication," *Etc.: A Review of General Semantics* (Spring 1954), 11(3): 164. The observation is attributed to one E. Shuby without further citation.

[21]William H. Hunt, Wilder W. Crane, and John C. Wahlke, "Interviewing Political Elites in Cross-Cultural Comparative Research," *American Journal of Sociology* (July 1964), 70(1): 66.

[22]David Riesman, "Some Observations on the Interviewing in the Teacher Apprehension Study," in Paul F. Lazarsfeld and Wagner Thielens, Jr., *The Academic Mind* (Glencoe, Ill.: The Free Press, 1958), p. 277, footnote 11. Elsewhere Riesman notes problems of differences in connotations of the same words among different segments of the academic population. See, for example, his discussion of the reaction to such phrases as "protest vigorously," on pp. 336–37.

[23]C. Wright Mills, "Language, Logic and Culture," *American Sociological Review* (October 1939), 4:5, reprinted in Irving Horowitz (Ed.), *Power, Politics, and Richards*, pp. 55–56. In view of the current situation in China, this example also

Sometimes, as with the Chinese case of age and respect, we may make distinctions in English which are not made in other languages, but it is equally possible for others to make distinctions which we choose to ignore. It might, for example, be difficult to obtain comparative data on the reading habits of Poles and Americans, since we have only one verb "to read" and there are at least twelve different Polish verbs which distinguish different kinds of "reading" from one another (e.g., to read: habitually, completely, aloud, to a group, the same thing, a meaning into a text, or to bury oneself in reading).[24] Perhaps more important is a parallel distinction found in French, German, Spanish and many other languages: *connaître* vs. *savoir, kennen* vs. *wissen, conocer* vs. *saber*. English, in spite of its shared linguistic heritage with those three languages, makes no such distinction. We employ the single verb "to know" for both of the senses indicated by the dual terms in the other languages. The inability of English speakers to easily make this distinction may have had serious consequences for methodological thought in the social sciences.[25]

The problem of categories is, unfortunately, not limited to dichotomous distinctions such as age-respect, friend-acquaintance, or yes-no. It enters into all matters of degree, including those kinds of attitudinal responses we like to arrange in scales. It is standard procedure among sociologists to provide response categories which assume in the minds of respondents a spectrum or continuum along which breaking points are arranged at regular intervals. Typically, response categories of the following types appear on questionnaires: "Do you ever . . . ? (always, frequently, seldom, never)," or "Do you approve of . . . ? (very much, somewhat, not much, not at all)."

There are several assumptions in this procedure which become especially tenuous within the context of cross-lingual research designed to provide cross-cultural comparisons. One problem is that different languages sometimes provide linguistic markers at different points on the continuum. Even if the extremities of a scale are comparable, one cannot

---

serves as a caution for those who are prone to linguistic determinism. Thinking and behavior can and do overcome linguistic restraints.

[24]Glenn, *op. cit.*, p. 174.

[25]In his efforts to clarify the distinction between "subjective understanding" and "objective cognizance," Tiryakian reminds his readers that it is reflected in the French and German distinctions cited here. See Edward A. Tiryakian, "Existential Phenomenology and the Sociological Tradition," *American Sociological Review* (October 1965), 30(5): n. 66, p. 687. Alfred Schutz goes to great lengths to spell out the difference between "knowledge of" and "knowledge about." Both John Dewey and William James laboriously spell out this important distinction between ways of knowing. However, positivistic and behavioristic science, which dominates American methodology, either ignores the distinction or treats it as spurious.

assume that the gradations in between are. In his Israeli study, Blanc found that "there was often no good way of rendering intelligibly the difference between an emphatic 'very many' and a plain 'many.' What is one to do, for example, if Arabic, like classical Hebrew, (but unlike modern Hebrew), knows no verbal distinction between 'many' and 'too many,' 'much' and 'too much.' "[26] Another cross-cultural survey reports that "it was not possible to find a French equivalent for 'may or may not' as a check-list response."[27]

In addition to providing differently located markers along the same continuum, languages may vary in the dimensionality with which a phenomenon is viewed—as in the Polish case of "reading." The Thais speak of anger not in terms of degree, but primarily in terms of the situations in which it occurs. They have a number of different words for "angry"; for example, angry at a person is one word and angry at an action is another.[28] English syntax, as well as that of the languages with which we tend to be familiar, dichotomizes number—views it bi-dimensionally, i.e., singular and plural. Chinese does not make this distinction at all, and, according to Carroll and Casagrande, some languages have four "numbers": singular, dual, trial, and plural.[29]

The fact that there are nearly universally accepted standards of measurement for some phenomena in the physical world can lead us to assume that the dimensions of such phenomena are universally perceived alike. The assumption is in error because the symbolic meaning of physical phenomena varies from culture to culture and that variability is reflected in language. It is true that we can measure and scale color, temperature, time, weight, and dimensionality in units which are expressed with perfect equivalence by scientists in any language. But those are not the terms of everyday discourse. Ethnographers and psychologists have been both confused and fascinated by the way primitive peoples classify standard color chips or yarns. If the language has one word for what we distinguish as brown and yellow or blue and green, then all of the brown

[26]Blanc, *op. cit.*, p. 206. See also Gerald Bronitsky, "Some Methodological and Meta-Methodological Considerations in Cross-Cultural Comparisons of Occupational Prestige Scales" (Indiana University, mimeographed, n.d.).

[27]Hunt *et al., op. cit.*, p. 66. A refreshing escape hatch to the problem of locating the scales people have in their heads (as over against imposing scales constructed by scientists), is suggested by Hamblin. Taking his lead from the psychophysical model provided by S. S. Stevens, Hamblin suggests that we employ "ratio measurement" in our social science scaling. See Robert L. Hamblin, "Ratio Measurement and Sociological Theory: A Critical Analysis" (Department of Sociology, Washington University, St. Louis, mimeographed, 1966).

[28]Phillips, *op. cit.*, p. 189.

[29]Carroll and Casagrande, *op. cit.*, p. 19.

and yellow chips get sorted into a single color group as do the blue and green ones.[30]

As important as the measurement of time may be to us, there are languages which do not conjugate verbs into tenses: The Navaho verb "must rigorously specify whether an act is in progress, or just about to start, or just about to stop, or habitually carried on, or repeatedly carried on."[31] And Dorothy Lee says that "the Wintu verb conjugates for validity rather than time. In naming an action the Wintu must describe his ground for believing in the action, the evidence for the action."[32] Thus, for example, the Wintu distinguish between direct visual evidence, hearsay evidence, and evidence on the basis of known regularity. Indo-European languages arbitrarily slice time into discrete tenses. In the indicative mode in English, we may refer to an event as occurring in the future, the present, the immediate past, or the distant past. It should be noted that the Frenchman, although employing the same syntactical device, slices time in ways which are not exactly the same as those employed in English. Unrelated languages, like Wintu, may not give time so salient a position in their syntax or may treat it very differently. The Guaraní Indians express time as a continuum rather than in discrete intervals. Their past tense is expressed with the suffix -yma pronounced more slowly as the temporal remoteness of the event increases.[33]

When an American truck driver complains to the waitress at the diner about his "warm" beer and "cold" soup, the "warm" liquid may have a temperature of 50° F., while the "cold" one is 75°. And a "thick" milkshake in Brooklyn is far thinner than a thin shake in St. Louis. The

[30]V. R. Seroshevskii, *Iakuti* (St. Petersburg: Royal Geographical Society, 1898); W. H. R. Rivers, "Vision," *Reports of the Cambridge Anthropological Expedition to Torres Straits* (1901), 2: 132. Both of these sources are cited by Roger Brown. Brown comments extensively on cultural variations in color perceptions and has reported some experimental efforts to explore it. See, for example, *Words and Things, op. cit.,* pp. 238 ff: "appendix," *op cit.,* pp. 279–80, 306; for a report on a study of English and Zuni differences in color classification and perception, see Eric H. Lenneberg and John M. Roberts, "The Language of Experience," *Memoir of the International Journal of American Linguistics* (1956), 22: 13.

[31]Clyde Kluckhohn and Dorothy Leighton, *The Navaho* (Cambridge: Harvard University Press, 1946).

[32]Dorothy Lee, "Conceptual Implications of an Indian Language," *Philosophy of Science* (1938), 5: 89–102. The quotation is from Brown, *Words and Things, op. cit.,* p. 254. If language forms determined cultural forms, then the Wintu should have been expected, because of this linguistic emphasis upon evidence, to develop a highly refined legal system and to have been led to emphasize the rational pursuit of knowledge. Their culture appears to emphasize neither.

[33]Brown, "Language and Categories," *op. cit.,* p. 280. A similar device is used by the American hipster. When he describes something as "way out," he expresses roughly how far out it is by how slowly he pronounces the vowel.

descriptive word is unrelated to the operational measure, because the word assumes a *normative* base which is unrelated to the arbitrary measurement base. Implied in the words is the assumption that beer "ought" to be no more than 40° F., and the assumption that soup "ought" to be no less than 85°. The terms "cold" and "hot" reflect departures above or below this cultural normative expectation. That, and not a thermometer, provides the linguistic standard. The standard for the same objects may well vary from culture to culture, from nation to nation, from region to region and, for that matter, within any given social unit—between classes, age groups, sexes, or what have you; what is "cold" soup for an adult may be too "hot" to give to a child.

LANGUAGE, CULTURE, AND THE INTERVIEW

Language, as a cultural artifact, is part of the larger cultural configuration in which it is found. This is the position formulated by the linguistic relativists, identified as the Whorf-Sapir hypothesis.[34] It is the position of the early twentieth century French school of sociology, which viewed language as the operational key to the sociology of knowledge.[35] It is intricately related to what anthropologists call "ethno-science."[36] It is a variant of what has come to be known as culture-personality theory. And, in a microcosmic form, it is not unrelated to the symbolic-interactionist and phenomenological traditions in social psychology.[37] Thus one prominent psycholinguist and social psychologist faces up to a compelling conclusion from the experiments on linguistic conditioning: the experiments "suggest that when an utterance becomes meaningful it causes us to take account of something beyond itself."[38]

The social psychologist's laboratory is an unexpected source of valida-

[34]See John B. Carroll (Ed.), *Language, Thought and Reality: Selected Writings of Benjamin Lee Whorf* (New York: John Wiley, 1956).

[35]A prime example is Marcel Granet's *La Pensée chinoise*, which provides the base for C. Wright Mills' analysis of "The Language and Ideas of Ancient China," in Horowitz, *op. cit.*, pp. 469–524.

[36]See, for example, W. C. Sturtevant, "Studies in Ethnoscience," in A. K. Romney and R. G. D'Andrade (Eds.), *Transcultural Studies in Cognition*, special publication of the *American Anthropologist* (June 1964), 66: 3, Part 2.

[37]Harold Garfinkel, building on the symbolic interactionist tradition, has pioneered in efforts to illustrate phenomenological theory in field situations. A number of such attempts are reported in his "Studies of the Routine Grounds of Everyday Activities," *Social Problems* (1964), 11: 225–50. Garfinkel describes the process he applies as "ethnomethodology." For a commentary on some of the more subtle differences between this sociological approach and the anthropological approach, see George Psathas, "Ethnomethodology and Ethnoscience," paper read at the meetings of the Eastern Sociological Society, New York (April 1967) mimeographed.

[38]Brown, "Language and Categories," *op. cit.*, p. 269.

tion both for the essentially cultural nature of language and for symbolic-interactionist theory. The research which led Brown to the conclusion just mentioned was conducted by behaviorists employing conditioning techniques reminiscent of Pavlov. Razran,[39] for example, showed his subjects words while they were eating, conditioning them to salivate at the sight of certain words. One of the original conditioned words was "style." Having conditioned his subjects, Razran proceeded to introduce a new series of words to them—including both "stile" and "fashion." Even though "stile" is similar to "style" in both appearance and sound and "fashion" is most dissimilar, conditioning was, in fact, generalized to "fashion" and not to "stile." The generalization appears to be semantic—related to meaning—rather than dependent upon visual or audio clues. Of equal importance is a follow-up experiment conducted by Riess,[40] this time with children as subjects rather than adults. With children, the generalization was to the homophone rather than to the synonym. It appears that the invisible and inaudible similarity between "style" and "fashion" which is learned through familiarization with language comes to supersede the less salient sensory similarities. For the child, "style" and "stile" resemble one another. This is not so for the adult, to whom language is meaning and who therefore generalizes his response from "style" to "fashion."

The marriage between ethno- and psycholinguistics has resulted in some cross-cultural experimental evidence regarding the impact of language on perceptions of the environment. Most frequently cited, although hardly as persuasive as the conditioning experiments, are two studies conducted by Carroll and Casagrande with American Indians. They view the idea of linguistic relativity as a special case of culture-personality theory.[41] In order to test the hypothesis that users of different languages have different mental experiences, they attempt to create designs which show some correspondence between the presence or absence of a certain kind of nonlinguistic response. Both studies require their Indian- and English-speaking subjects to sort images of actions into like categories. In the Carroll experiment, pictures are presented to adult Hopi subjects; in the Casagrande experiment, objects are presented to Navaho children. Both the pictures and the objects are designed to denote phenomena which are categorized differently in English and in the Indian languages. Carroll finds some association in the predicted direction between the language and the categories in which his pictures are placed, and Casagrande concludes that "we have shown that language patterning seems to

[39]G. H. S. Razran, "A Quantitative Study of Meaning by a Conditioned Salivary Technique (Semantic Conditioning)," *Science* (1939), 90: 89–90.

[40]B. F. Riess, "Genetic Changes in Semantic Conditioning," *Journal of Experimental Psychology* (1946), 36: 143–52.

[41]Carroll and Casagrande, *op. cit.*

be correlated with tendency to match objects on the basis of form rather than color or size."[42]

In fact, although significant differences are found in these studies, relatively small amounts of variance are explained. C. Wright Mills observed independently, and without recourse to formal experimental devices, that "the function of words is the mediation of social behavior."[43] In translating a string of words from one language into an equivalent string of words in another language, the cross-cultural researcher must fail in his efforts to achieve comparability when he fails to recognize that "a vocabulary is not merely a string of words; immanent within it are societal textures . . . "[44]

The fact that language reflects cultural values means that it must impinge upon definitions of the interview situation—a matter of no small methodological importance. Benney and Hughes define an interview, in part, as a relationship between two people where both parties behave as though they are of equal status for its duration, whether or not this is actually so. This kind of fiction is obviously going to come off better in some cultures than in others and among some segments of a society than in others. In their words:

> Anthropologists have long realized—if not always clearly—that the transitory interview, held with respondents who do not share their view of the encounter, is an unreliable source of information in itself. . . . Equally, the climate which makes widespread interviewing possible in the West today is itself relatively novel.[45]

The kind of cultural climate which tolerates a situation like an interview is "a fairly new thing in the history of the human race."[46] The interview is most generally seen as an encounter with a stranger. There are wide cultural variations in prescribed forms of interaction and language with a stranger. As we shall see below, there are equally wide variations in such particular concepts as "privacy," "security," and those matters which are considered to be of an intimate or personal nature.

[42]*Ibid.*, p. 31.

[43]Mills, "Language, Logic, and Culture," *op. cit.*, pp. 432–33.

[44]*Ibid.*, Mills, of course, combined his introspective evidence with "objective" historical evidence, e.g., it is at this point in his discussion that he cites the inability of the ancient Chinese to make any distinction between the concepts of age and respect. To the extent that Mills' analysis is correct, ancient Chinese is a most suitable language for public opinion or survey research. Would the frequent discrepancies between verbalizations and conduct noted in American research persist if English could be described as follows? "merely to pronounce its elements is to constrain one's self and one's conduct. In each word there dwells . . . a value-attitude and hence a sanctioned act. Each word in the language invited its users to feel that to speak is *to act or to react*" (p. 481).

[45]Benney and Hughes, *op. cit.*, p. 142.

[46]*Ibid.*, p. 142.

The ubiquitous Southeast Asian cultural value of "courtesy" has been described in detail by Emily Jones.[47] This "important and pervasive value" defines the interview situation in a manner which has a large potential for distorting supposedly "comparable" data. It can act as a deterrent to obtaining reliable information—either in response to formal questions or in an interviewing situation which is more open. From the perspective of the respondent, it is a cultural obligation to see to it that the interviewer is not distressed, disappointed, or offended in any way. And, to further complicate matters, should the interviewer be a product of this same culture, then he is likewise obliged not to distress, disappoint, or offend his respondents. This amiable definition, however, has its advantages as well as its drawbacks. For example, "To ask personal questions is well within the bounds of courteous behavior."[48]

Many different definitions of the interview situation may be subsumed under the gross cultural value which leads to courtesy bias. Mitchell suggests that a courtesy or hospitality bias is common in Asia everywhere from Japan to Turkey:

> The direction of the courtesy bias is different in different countries. For example, the humility of the Japanese is said to lead them to underevaluate their own achievements, class positions, and the like. On the other hand, some researchers in the Middle East claim that respondents there tend to exaggerate their achievements, class position, knowledge of the world, and extent to which they are modern rather than traditional. In practical terms, this means that the type of question-wording appropriate in Japan and the West would be inappropriate in Turkey and Iran.[49]

If courtesy is highly valued in some parts of the world, one might anticipate that the opposite would be true in other parts. There are certainly ethnocentric societies (and ethnic groups within societies), where all outsiders—including interviewers—are considered fair game for deception. Such a "sucker" bias is described by the Keesings in a study of elite communications in Samoa.[50]

[47]Emily L. Jones, "The Courtesy Bias in South-East Asian Surveys," *International Social Science Journal* (1963), 15: 1. The elements of the code are listed on p. 71.

[48]*Ibid.*

[49]Robert E. Mitchell, *op. cit.*, p. 681. In addition to Jones, Mitchell cites Mary R. Hollsteiner, *The Dynamics of Power in a Philippine Municipality* (Quezon: Community Development Research Council, University of the Philippines, 1963).

[50]Felix M. Keesing and Marie M. Keesing, *Elite Communications in Samoa, A Study of Leadership* (Stanford: Stanford University Press, 1956), cited by Mitchell, *op. cit.*, pp. 681–82. In a personal communication Robert Weiss has pointed out the relationship between the "sucker bias" and the process of "putting someone on." The respondent defrauds the interviewer by acting, for example, as someone the interviewer might imagine him to be. In fact, Weiss' observation can be extended to include the "courtesy bias" as well, since it too is a form of "put-on."

Although it may well be within the bounds of courtesy to ask personal questions in Southeast Asia, most other peoples set limits. Hunt reports that "even native French persons asked to help in translating interview questions could think of no discreet way to ask respondents their religious views."[51] Lerner remarks on the basis of his interviews with Frenchmen that the French equate security with privacy. It follows that if they permit a breach of their privacy for interviewing purposes, they view this as a self-breach of their personal security. His problem was not a matter of the validity of data obtained but a matter of obtaining it in the first place: "Most refusals were based squarely upon the feeling that such an interview was an unwarranted intrusion into their personal affairs."[52] Lerner found that the trick was to get a Frenchman started, "but, once started, how they talked!"[53]

Both Lerner and Hunt report types of resistance among Frenchmen which differ from the typical American survey experience. The traditional survey check-list or yes-no type of questions were regarded with suspicion by both Austrians and Frenchmen: "a relatively high proportion could not be persuaded to answer in the customary and familiar form used in almost all American surveys."[54] Europeans described such questions as "too brutal" and suggested that they smacked of American gimmickry. This differential definition is further confounded by the observation that the French regard as silly, frivolous, and unworthy of attention any question which requires a respondent to play a role (e.g., "What would you do if . . . "). Lerner interprets this within a culture-personality framework:

> Such questions are handled with greater facility by people . . . who are closer than the French are to other-directed personalities, and who, having a less stable or less rigid conception of themselves and their proper conduct in the world, show a more supple capacity for rearranging their self-system upon short notice.[55]

Lerner relates this observation to an earlier experience interviewing in the Middle East, where he found that the "traditionalists" were unable to answer such questions as "What would you do if you were presi-

[51]Hunt *et al., op. cit.,* p. 66.

[52]Daniel Lerner, "Interviewing Frenchmen," *American Journal of Sociology* (September 1956), 62(2): 193.

[53]*Ibid.,* pp. 187–88.

[54]Hunt, *op. cit.,* p. 65. Evidence of the consequences of such differential definitions is found in the proportion of completed forms returned from two subsamples who were asked to mail them. The request was met by 97 percent of the California legislature and by 62 percent of the lower Austrian legislature, p. 65.

[55]Lerner, *op. cit.,* p. 191. David Riesman has observed some of these identical reactions among certain types of American college professors. See Riesman, *op. cit.*

dent of Syria?" The "moderns," on the other hand, had no difficulty responding to questions which required them to take the role of a newspaper editor, the leader of their country, or a resident of another country.[56] *There are then cultural differences in both those things people are able to talk about and those things they are willing to talk about.*

We have already noted the inability to make discreet inquiries about religion among Frenchmen. This is also the case in Moslem Pakistan but not so in Hindu India. The Almond-Verba five-nation study reports that Italians seem reticent about political topics.[57] Middle-class Americans prefer not to be too specific about their incomes. And there are many people who consider sex-talk taboo.

In some African areas, as well as in other parts of the world, there is a reluctance to talk about dead children and the number of people in a household. . . . In the Middle East there is a reluctance to discuss ordinary household events, and Chinese businessmen in any country are reported to be especially secretive about any and all facets of their work and personal lives. In many countries, respondents are reticent about political topics in general and party preference in particular. On the other hand, it is by no means clear that family planning is nearly as sensitive an issue in the developing countries as might be expected.[58]

But the overriding cross-cultural problem remains that of differences in definitions of what must be perceived as an alien social situation by most peoples of the world—certainly by the less cosmopolitan and the more poorly educated. The American has had sufficient routine exposure to polls and surveys, both as consumer and respondent, to feel that he knows what they are. The same assumption cannot be made regarding other peoples in other societies. The study of the evolving social relationship between interviewer and respondent in various cultures is in itself an important sociological undertaking.

This discussion of culture and the interview assumes that language and culture cannot be divorced, "for language, in the full, is nothing less than an inventory of all the ideas, interests, and occupation that take up the attention of the community. In this extended sense, the study of lan-

[56]Lerner, *ibid.*

[57]Gabriel Almond and Sidney Verba, *The Civic Culture* (Princeton, N.J.: Princeton University Press, 1963), chap. 2, cited by Mitchell, *op. cit.*

[58]Mitchell, *op. cit.*, p. 675. Mitchell considers a number of related problems not covered in the present paper, including the difficulty in obtaining comparable sampling frames in different societies, the differential accessibility of the sexes as respondents in survey research in different countries, and the problem of intrasocietal ethnic differences. For example, his secondary analysis of marginal tabulations in several Southeast Asian surveys reveals large differences in Chinese and Indian responses, especially in the proportion of "no response."

guage cannot be distinguished from the general study of culture."[59] As Kenneth Burke would have it, "the names for things and operations smuggle in connotations of good and bad—a noun tends to carry with it a kind of invisible adjective, and a verb an invisible adverb."[60] Everett Hughes sums it up this way: "There is generally a great deal in a name, as Juliet plainly knew. Often it is more than a pointer; it points with pride, or with the finger of scorn."[61]

SOME SOLUTIONS

Two Southeast Asian experts reach diametrically opposed conclusions regarding the application of Western survey techniques in that part of the world. Wuelker concludes that "there seems to be some justification for doubting whether research methods elaborated in the West are in fact suitable for Southeast Asia . . . "[62] But Jones, after her penetrating analysis of the courtesy bias in Southeast Asia, insists that "the distorting effects of 'courtesy bias' can be overcome" and concludes that "the standard techniques of the West (with fewer adaptations than might be assumed necessary) are applicable to Southeast Asia."[63] One of her major solutions is that questions "be limited to those for which there is no obviously pleasing answer."[64] This is hardly a satisfactory solution for the social scientist, the opinion pollster, or the market researcher, all of whom are primarily interested in values, attitudes, opinions, preferences, aspirations, and the like. Mitchell attempts to sidestep anthropological critics of opinion studies with this same device: "these critics sometimes ignore the fact that survey research methods are used for gaining factual as well as attitudinal information." However, on the basis of his analysis of materials at the International Data Library and Reference Service at Berkeley, he concedes that they reveal "very high proportions of 'no answers,' 'don't knows,' 'no opinion,' neutral positions on attitude scales and undifferentiated responses to manifestly different questions. . . ."[65]

[59]Brown, *Words and Things*, op. cit., p. 260.

[60]Kenneth Burke, *Permanence and Change*, p. 244. Cited in Mills, "Language, Logic, and Culture," op. cit., p. 433.

[61]Hughes and Hughes, op. cit.

[62]Gabrielle Wuelker, "Questionnaires in Asia," *International Social Science Journal* (1963), 15(1): 37.

[63]Jones, op. cit., p. 70. She includes among these standard techniques, cross-sectional surveys, panel studies, mail questionnaires, and community studies.

[64]*Ibid.*, p. 71.

[65]Mitchell, p. 673. Mitchell acknowledges that it is not always easy to obtain reliable demographic data: "one study found no respondents earning less than ten (U.S.) dollars per month: another study found approximately 9 percent; and a third, which seems to be the most accurate, found 70 percent in this category" (p. 688). He attributes this discrepancy to errors in sampling, but elsewhere he observes that "one study in Africa discarded two-thirds of the sample" because the reported expenditures of these respondents exceeded their known income" (p. 674, footnote 2).

If the simple application of the back-translation technique is no solution to problems of comparability in cross-lingual research, then what is? Must we abandon such efforts? Hardly, for to retreat in that manner would be to abandon sociology, not only because a sociology limited to observations of those who speak our own language is no sociology at all, but because these same problems exist in interviewing within our presumably monolinguistic society. Most of the evidence cited in this paper comes from scholars who have gained firsthand familiarity with alien languages and alien cultures. Roger Brown wisely cautions that "there is a familiar inclination on the part of those who possess unusual and arduously obtained experience to exaggerate its remoteness from anything known to the rest of us."[66]

In the first place, sophisticated investigators are well aware of the fact that back-translation is not a simple ritualistic technique, but an arduous and creative process. Recall that after his "dismal" results, Phillips (quoted earlier) abandoned the process. Hudson provides a hint of the amount of effort which must be extended in his description of the painstaking procedure undertaken by his Middle East research team. His back-translations were accompanied by field interviews in both the Middle East and the United States, designed to explain discrepancies. "The emphasis of these interviews was on the meaning which had been placed upon the question and terms employed in the two languages."[67]

The quest, in this case, was for comparability in *meaning*. Presumably, lexical comparability of the friend-*Freund* type was not sufficient for the Arab Middle East research team. It is in this sense that Hunt and his colleagues feel secure in the comparability of the materials gathered in their European studies: "the problem of translating concepts from one culture to another . . . was solved in the light of researchers' experience and understanding of the particular system and culture they were studying. This means that 'operational equivalence' was perhaps less common than 'conceptual equivalence.' . . ."[68] Schuman describes what he calls a "random probe technique" for determining the validity of cross-cultural interview data. His interviewers probe on randomly selected questions from the questionnaire, in a continuous attempt to determine if the respondent's notion of what the question means is the same as that intended by the investigator.[69]

In his report of his effort at multilingual interviewing in Israel, Blanc recommends that care be taken to "translate accurately—not literally, not freely, but just 'accurately.'" In this sense, he suggests, anything can be

[66]Brown, *Words and Things, op. cit.,* p. 233.
[67]Bradford B. Hudson *et al., op. cit.,* p. 11.
[68]Hunt *et al.,* p. 67.
[69]Schuman, *op. cit.,* p. 216.

translated into any language.[70] There are, according to Blanc, several factors which ought to be considered when translating. Among them, we cannot assume that valid correlations exist between any two languages, the investigator must be familiar with the cultural context before constructing instruments, overprecise phrasing is generally untranslatable ("The quest for accuracy may defeat its own end."), and rephrasing of questions on the spot is virutally unavoidable.[71]

Mitchell describes pressure coming from overseas survey agencies to abandon any efforts at translation, replacing it by a process which would presumably provide conceptual equivalence:

> Considerable knowledge of the local culture and language is needed in order to gain conceptual equivalence. . . . Agencies in the field which are aware of this are becoming increasingly opposed to what some of them refer to as "canned questionnaires sent from the United States." They feel that a client's attempt to preserve the exact form of his questions, especially precoded ones, can only lead to major errors. One agency now insists that clients attach a paragraph of explanation or a *rationale* to each question submitted. Once the agency discovers the intention behind a question—that is, the kind of answer which is desired and how the question will be used—it formulates its own version.[72]

Two themes run through these various experiences and suggestions: (1) *it is imperative that the researcher be familiar with the cultural milieu of which the language is a part, and* (2) *efforts should be directed toward obtaining conceptual equivalence without concern for lexical comparability.* F. Kluckhohn adds the sage advice that the translation of concepts from one language to another is facilitated when the issue is salient in both cultures. In her description of an instrument administered in Spanish, Japanese, Navaho, Zuñi, and English, she reports that a common comment of respondents in all of the cultures was: "These are really important questions." As a result, Kluckhohn offers the following hypothesis: "the degree of success in the translation of ideas from one language to another increases in accord with the degree that the problems phrased are critical and generalized."[73]

This reasonable hypothesis might even be extended to suggest that it is wise to determine the salience of *the idea of having an opinion* on an issue, before attempting to assess that opinion among a people. One Southeast Asian expert has observed that "the ability to form their own opinions and express them is confined to comparatively small sections of

---

[70]Blanc, *op. cit.,* p. 205.
[71]*Ibid.,* p. 209.
[72]Mitchell, *op. cit.,* pp. 677–78.
[73]Florence Kluckhohn, *op. cit.,* p. 7.

the population."[74] It is even possible that in tradition-directed societies the mechanisms for opinion formation may be completely absent. Public opinion is, in the final analysis, a phenomenon of mass societies with specialized and differentiated publics. And, even if the mechanisms and the ability are present, the process of answering a question is also the process of making a decision. In any society only certain individuals are perceived as having a legitimate right to do that.[75]

Critics of surveys in the developing countries argue that there may be no "public opinion" in those countries or that "opinion" may be restricted only to certain areas. The logic of this position as applied to the domestic scene was hammered home years ago by Herbert Blumer[76] and has been empirically verified by Converse, who found that even issues considered to be salient to wide segments of the American population had relatively small publics.[77] The Blumer thesis is further documented by Riesman: "We see here one of the problems of a national survey, namely, that coverage and comparability mean that the same questions will be asked of those who are virtually 'know-nothings' and those who could write a book on each theme."[78] He concludes that "on a national survey there is always danger in the assumption that we are in fact one country, and that issues relevant to one part of the population are or could become meaningful to another."[79]

One of the solutions recommended by Jones for counterbalancing the courtesy bias may be appropriate as a methodological device for neutralizing any known cultural distorting potential. I have argued elsewhere the merits of employing deliberately loaded questions, rather than supposedly neutral ones, in survey research.[80] Jones suggests the use of pictures depicting people engaged in what may be defined as "discourteous" acts (e.g., turning off a radio) and then asking the respondent why the person pictured might be committing such an act. In addition, she suggests the construction of deliberately loaded questions which take the onus off of the respondent, e.g., "Many people say that. . . ."[81]

I also commented in an earlier paper on the tendency of survey re-

[74]Wuelker, op. cit., p. 37.

[75]Mitchell, op. cit., pp. 672–73, and Keesing and Keesing, op. cit.

[76]Herbert Blumer, "Public Opinion and Public Opinion Polling," American Sociological Review (1948), 13: 542–49.

[77]Philip E. Converse, "New Dimensions of Meaning for Cross-section Sample Surveys in Politics," International Social Science Journal (1964), 16: 19–34, cited by Robert E. Mitchell, op. cit., p. 673.

[78]Riesman, op. cit., p. 360.

[79]Ibid., p. 365. See also footnote 9, pp. 275–76.

[80]"Public vs. Private Opinions: The 'Real' and the 'Unreal,'" paper read at the annual meeting of the Eastern Sociological Society, Philadelphia, April 1966 (mimeographed), p. 17–18.

[81]Jones, op. cit., p. 72.

search technicians to view discrepancies resulting from variations in interviewer characteristics or the interview situation as sources of error to be disposed of. I prefer to view such discrepancies as revealing the way different peoples perceive and relate to one another in different settings.[82] The tendency of survey researchers to view any discrepancy not directly attributable to the content of the instrument *in reliability terms* carries over into their interpretation of discrepancies in the back-translation process. Anderson criticizes Schacter's use of back-translation on these very grounds: he fails to make optimal use of the results. "The procedure indicated by Schacter was to 'eliminate the differences.' A more desirable procedure . . . would be to recognize these as alternate forms which approach measurement of the same conceptual realm with somewhat different linguistic irrelevancies."[83]

Another step, then, toward the solution of problems of comparability in cross-lingual research is to interpret the discrepancies uncovered by the back-translation technique in creative ways. For example, such discrepancies can suggest that a concept is more salient in one culture than another or even that it is absent in one. Or they might enable us to discover the way different cultures lead people to perceive differently what we assume to be the same phenomena. The culture of the survey research technician seems to lead *him* inevitably to the assumption that unexplained differences are unwanted differences—that similarities are more informative than differences, that consistency is more desirable than inconsistency.

A final word of advice to the cross-lingual researcher, whether he be anthropologist, psychologist, sociologist, or whatever, is that he consider seriously the wisdom of the Arab proverb, "With every language a (different) man," and its less subtle Italian counterpart: "A translator (traduttore) is often a traitor (traditore)."[84]

THE LOCAL SCENE

The salience of language in cross-cultural research is clear, but within our own society our sensitivities to this dimension are dulled by the dubious assumption that everyone is speaking the same language. It is probable that most of the kinds of errors in translation and interpretation—most of the semantic slip-ups—which occur in cross-lingual situa-

[82]Deutscher, "Public vs. Private Opinions," *op. cit.*, pp. 9–12.

[83]Anderson, *op. cit.*, his criticism refers to Stanley Schacter, "Interpretive and Methodological Problems of Replicated Research," *Journal of Social Issues* (1954), 10: 52–60.

[84]Both proverbs are mentioned by Blanc, *op. cit.*

tions also occur between interviewer and interviewee within our own society.[85] The real tragedy of "the one-hundred dollar misunderstanding," is not so much that Kitten and Howland could not understand each other, but rather that *they did not know* that they could not understand each other.[86] This is what it means to have a "misunderstanding," and I submit that there may be many misunderstandings between interviewer and respondent in our own domestic research. The potential for semantic breakdown or "misunderstanding" between the "English-speaking" teenaged Negro prostitute and the "English-speaking" Babbit-like college sophomore, differs only in degree from what occurs when an American who speaks French interviews a Moroccan whose French was learned on the streets of Casablanca.[87]

It is hard to say how much misunderstanding occurs, since, by the nature of it, it frequently passes unrecognized. Aaron Cicourel has advised that "the sociologist . . . when interviewing, cannot afford to treat his own language from the perspective of a native speaker, but must adopt the position of a cryptanalyst approaching a strange language."[88] This is a fair description of the stance taken by David Riesman in his analysis of the interviewing of a national sample of college professors for *The Academic Mind*. After interviewing both survey interviewers and survey respondents, Riesman allows that "for the most part, our methods lack the subtlety to catch the myriad ways in which (as in the novels of Henry Green) people can talk past each other, while believing themselves to be understood—or vice versa."[89] Anderson goes so far as to define problems of interviewer-interviewee relations as translation problems: "Translation is involved whenever our research requires us to ask the 'same' question of people with different backgrounds."[90]

There is empirical evidence that phonetic differences exist among social classes and among various speech contexts in New York City.[91]

[85]In his unique analysis of the interviewing process in a domestic survey, Riesman identifies many of the communication problems we have suggested occur in international research. See David Riesman, *op. cit.*, pp. 162, 275, 295–96 (footnote 27), 316 (footnote 55), 332 and elsewhere.

[86]Robert Gover, *The One-Hundred Dollar Misunderstanding* (New York: Ballantine Books, 1963).

[87]This example is from Haim Blanc, *op. cit.*, p. 207. When I suggest a difference "in degree" between the two cases, I do not pre-judge which of the two has the higher "potential."

[88]Aaron V. Cicourel, *Method and Measurement in Sociology* (New York: The Free Press of Glencoe, 1964), 175.

[89]Riesman, *op. cit.*, p. 273.

[90]Anderson, *op. cit.*

[91]William Labov, "The Effect of Social Mobility on Linguistic Behavior," in Stanley Lieberson (Ed.), *Explorations In Sociolinguistics*, special issue of *Sociological Inquiry* (Spring 1966), 36(2): 186–203. Or William Labov, "Phonological Correlates of Social Stratification," in the *Ethnography of Communication, op. cit.*, 164–76.

There is evidence that syntactic styles vary among different classes of Arkansans[92] and Londoners.[93] And, although one study of semantic variations between American sailors and college students found none,[94] another comparison between Negro and white college students suggests wide areas of semantic variation.[95] Within a society, as well as between societies, the sociologist seeks information from and about people who operate verbally with different vocabularies, different grammars, and different kinds of sounds.[96]

It is remarkable that sociologists have managed to so great a degree to avoid consideration of linguistic phenomena. When Hughes and Benney suggested that the interview as a form of social rhetoric is not merely a tool of sociology but part of its very subject matter, they were reminding us that the peculiar thing about human interaction is its symbolic nature and, in large part, that the symbols employed are linguistic ones. The unique quality of human conduct is its symbolic mediation through language—both verbal and nonverbal. Sociologists generally understand that this is the heart of George Mead's imagery of human nature. Perhaps we have failed to understand that no thoughtful observer of human conduct can reach any other conclusion.[97]

[92]Leonard Schatzman and Anselm Strauss, "Social Class and Modes of Communication," *American Journal of Sociology* (January 1955), 60(4): 329–38.

[93]Basil Bernstein, "Elaborated and Restricted Codes: An Outline," in *Explorations in Sociolinguistics, op. cit.,* pp. 254–61. Or Basil Bernstein, "Elaborated and Restricted Codes: Their Social Origins and Some Consequences," in the *Ethnography of Communication, op. cit.,* 55–69.

[94]David R. Heise, "Social Status, Attitudes, and Word Connotations," in *Explorations in Sociolinguistics, op. cit.,* pp. 227–39.

[95]Ernest A. T. Barth, "The Language Behavior of Negroes and Whites," *Pacific Sociological Review* (Fall 1961), 4(2): 69–72.

[96]There is not space here to discuss the importance of language in understanding the microsocieties within which we all move in our daily routines. These are the social situations—cocktail parties, bull sessions, family dinners, lectures, waiting rooms, and interviews—within which we routinely and sometimes unknowingly alter our vocabularies, sounds, and grammars. As Goffman asks rhetorically, "Where but in social situations does speaking go on?" (Erving Goffman, "The Neglected Situation," in the *Ethnography of Communication, op. cit.,* p. 134.)

[97]See for example, I. P. Pavlov, *Conditioned Reflexes: An Investigation of the Psychological Activity of the Cerebral Cortex* (London: Oxford University Press, 1927), pp. 357–409, quoted by Dan I. Slobin, "Soviet Psycholinguistics," in N. O'Connor (Ed.), *Present Day Russian Psychology* (Oxford: Pergamon Press, 1967). I am indebted to Slobin for my introduction to psycholinguistics through his lectures at Berkeley during the Spring of 1966.

PART V

ILLUSTRATIVE METHODS: SURVEY RESEARCH AND PARTICIPANT OBSERVATION

9

Survey Research and Participant Observation: A Benefit-Cost Analysis

DONALD P. WARWICK

A critical decision facing the social scientist interested in comparative research concerns the choice of methods for data collection. Given the strength of professional socialization in the various social science disciplines, this question is often never raised. Either because he has never considered an alternative or because he feels comfortable with only one method, the researcher may automatically move ahead with a survey or participant observation or some other approach currently in vogue. This paper argues that every study, comparative or otherwise, should explicitly raise the question of alternative methods, asking what is obtained from one that is not available in others. To highlight the various costs and benefits at stake, the paper provides a set of dimensions that can be used in evaluating the relative contribution of various methodological options. The approach is then illustrated with two methods: survey research and participant observation.

Social scientists have long been divided over the respective merits of quantitative and qualitative approaches to data collection. The symbolic poles of the debate are usually represented by the methods considered here. The general lines of argumentation are familiar enough: the survey is more "scientific" and produces more "hard" data; participant observation brings the social scientist closer to the front lines of research—to the "real people"—and catches details missed by the more gross and blunt survey instrument. Each camp also has its endemic conceits: survey re-

This essay is published for the first time in this volume. The author is indebted to Professor Renée Fox of the University of Pennsylvania for providing numerous insights into the process of participant observation. Many of the points raised here were suggested by her presentations to my seminar on comparative research in the Department of Social Relations at Harvard University. I am also indebted to the student members of this seminar for several stimulating discussions on the uses and limitations of various research methods, including those discussed in this paper.

searchers sometimes see themselves as more rigorous and their work more germane to "big" issues of public policy; participant observers often regard their approach as more creative, intuitive, artistic, and human and themselves as more sensitive, perceptive, and flexible. What truth is there in these claims? And, more importantly, what does one gain in one method that he loses in the other?

Every method of data collection is only an approximation to knowledge. Each provides a different and usually valid glimpse of reality, and all are limited when used alone. The essential question is not which method is best in the abstract, but which is most appropriate and feasible for the problem at hand. The relative advantages and disadvantages of survey research and participant observation can be highlighted by evaluating each with five criteria commonly accepted as desirable in social research: appropriateness of the method to the problem studied; accuracy of measurement; generalizability of the findings; administrative convenience; and avoidance of ethical or political difficulties in the research process.

APPROPRIATENESS

The choice of research methods resembles the selection of an accessory lens for a camera. It is almost meaningless to ask in the abstract which is better: a wide-angle or a telephoto lens. The answer depends completely on the type of picture that one wants—broad, panoramic coverage or more intense concentration on expression and detail. Similarly, although both types of lenses may offer great advantages for his study, if the photographer cannot afford either he must rest content with the range of detail provided by the original "middle-ground" lens on his camera. And even when he has both types of lenses and every conceivable filter he may still not be able to use them in a given study, perhaps because of poor lighting, the pressure of public opinion, or his own inexperience with the equipment. These issues of objectives, resources, and possibilities also weigh heavily in choosing between the survey and intensive observation.

Under what conditions is the sample survey an appropriate and useful means of gathering information? The conditions are three: when the goals of the research call for obtaining quantitative data on a certain problem or population; when the problems in question are reasonably specific and familiar to the respondents; and when the investigator himself has considerable prior knowledge of these problems and of the range of responses that will be obtained. All these conditions are met in the areas of research that have been traditional strongholds of survey research—studies of public opinion, voting, attitudes and beliefs, morale, and economic behavior.

Participant observation is usually more appropriate when the study requires an examination of complex social relationships or intricate patterns of interaction, such as kinship obligations or gift exchange in tribal villages; when the investigator desires first-hand *behavioral* information on certain social processes, such as leadership and influence in a small group; when a major goal of the study is to construct a qualitative contextual picture of a certain situation or flow of events; and when it is necessary to infer latent value patterns or belief systems from such behavior as ceremonial postures, gestures, dances, facial expressions, or subtle inflections of the voice.

Under these conditions the sample survey is of limited value when used alone. First, it assumes that the investigator knows enough about the situation to ask the right questions and that the respondents are willing and able to provide the appropriate answers. In many cases people are simply not conscious of what is happening around them, or they may not be able to translate their experiences into words. Second, the typical survey is arranged so that the interviewer arrives, spends an hour or two asking questions, and then departs. In many parts of the world the notion of a short, structured interview conducted by a relative stranger is foreign and may arouse hostility or suspicion. Third, because the survey draws upon the report of a single respondent at a single moment in time, it is much better for obtaining a picture of reality at that moment in time than for assessing causal connections or describing the flow of events. It is true that survey data, especially when based upon repeated questioning of the same individuals, can provide leads to causality, and that respondents can give their interpretations of social processes, but these are not the major strengths of the survey method. Finally, while one of the prime advantages of the survey lies in the structure it provides for classifying information, this structure is necessarily attained at the expense of intricacy and complexity in the data. Various compromises can be worked out between open-ended and close-ended questions as a means of capturing more of the complexities, but these fall far short of the freedom enjoyed by the participant observer to develop organizing schemes on the spot. Thus in methods, as in *The Mikado*, the punishment should fit the crime.

ACCURACY OF MEASUREMENT

A second goal of social research is to obtain accurate measurements of the phenomena under study *within* a given group or sample. *Accuracy* may be defined as the generalizability of the measurements taken to all the relevant measurements that might have been taken on the phenomena in question, such as social class, political power, or quality of housing. The essential question here is one of sampling: Are the measures or observations used as the source of data a representative sample of the broader universe of measurements and observations from which they were drawn? For example, there are many ways of measuring the distribution or concentration of political power in a local community. One of the simplest is the "reputational technique"—asking citizens who has the power. Another involves the analysis of the influence exercised by different individuals on key decisions made in the community. To determine whether or not a given set of measures is accurate we must first define the universe to which they refer, such as "community power," and then decide whether or not these measures are a fair sample of this universe. It should be emphasized that the concept of accuracy applies to participant observation as well as to the sample survey, though in different ways. In the former it is especially important to consider the generalizability of the observer himself—How representative is he of the universe of observers who might have been employed?[1]

Two aspects of accuracy are commonly discussed in the literature on psychological testing: reliability and validity. In the language of this chapter *reliability* may be defined as the extent to which a measure can be generalized to other measures of the same phenomenon. More specifically, reliability refers to the consistency of a measure with itself over time (as when an intelligence test is repeated with the same person a week after the first administration), or with equivalent measures of the same phenomenon (such as an alternate form of the intelligence test). *Validity* is more concerned with the generalizability of a measure to a broader universe of behavior which it is intended to reflect. It is seen when a test, a survey question, or an observation measures what it purports to measure, such as intelligence, power, quality of housing, or aggressiveness. An intelligence test is valid only if its results can be used to predict other behavior in the domain covered by "intelligence," including success in school, performance on one's job, and so on. In practice the distinction between reliability and validity is blurred, partly be-

---

[1]Cf. L. J. Cronbach, N. Rajaratnam, and G. C. Gleser, "Theory of Generalizability: A Liberalization of Reliability Theory," *British Journal of Statistical Psychology*, 16, 2 (1963), 137–63. These authors write: "An investigator asks about the precision or reliability of a measure because he wishes to generalize from the observation in hand to some class of observations to which it belongs. To ask about rater agreement is to ask how well we can generalize from one set of ratings to ratings by other raters. To ask about the reliability of an essay examination grade is to ask how representative this is of grades that might have been given to the same paper by other markers, or of grades on other papers by the same subject" (p. 144).

cause reliability is a precondition of validity, and partly because validity is often appraised by determining its consistency with measures of related phenomena.

Accuracy in measurement is enhanced by many favorable conditions in the research process. Some of these are present in survey research and comprise its distinctive assets, while others are more commonly found in participant observation. Since it is never possible to determine with certitude that a measure is accurate, the best that a social researcher can do is to draw together the evidence at his disposal to make a plausible case for the generalizability of his measures. Four conditions that are crucial in establishing accuracy are quantification, replicability, qualitative depth, and control over observer effects.

Quantification

The development of soundly based empirical indicators is a critical step on the road to accuracy. Statistical measures such as income scores, prestige ratings, and intelligence quotients allow for the objective comparison of individuals, communities, and even total societies. Such quantitative indicators also have the great advantage of permitting the investigator to use numerical estimates of accuracy, such as reliability coefficients and correlations with measures of other behaviors assumed to be related to the phenomenon in question. The sample survey usually has the edge over participant observation on quantification, though there is no inherent reason why participant observers cannot count, classify, and report at least some of their findings in tabular form.[2] This advantage of surveys should not be overstated, however, for the problems studied through participant observation often do not lend themselves to quantitative analysis, for reasons already noted.

Replicability

Accuracy in social research further requires that to the extent possible, the measuring instruments and conditions of research be so arranged that they can be repeated either in the same place at a later date or in a different setting. There are several reasons why replicability is desirable. First, it is an important precondition of validity, for it permits

[2]Cf. H. S. Becker and B. Greer, "Participant Observation: The Analysis of Qualitative Field Data," in *Human Organization Research*, ed. R. N. Adams and J. J. Preiss (Homewood, Ill.: Dorsey Press, 1960), p. 21. These authors suggest methods, for example, of checking the frequency with which certain expected incidents actually occur. However, these quantitative findings are rarely shared with the reader in final research reports.

other investigators to determine whether a given measuring instrument (including an observer) taps the same behaviors in other relevant situations. For example, if a paper-and-pencil test of hostility is found to be related to observers' ratings of hostility in Boston but not in Chicago, serious questions can be raised about the general validity of the measure. But to be able to make this comparison it is necessary to know *exactly* how and to whom the test was originally administered. Second, replicability contributes to both reliability and validity by allowing identical measurements to be taken on the same group at a later date. If the time interval is short and the group has not changed, this repetition will ordinarily serve as a measure of reliability or consistency. If the time interval is longer and the group has changed in some significant way, the new measurements may provide a basis for assessing validity. For example, if a test is intended to measure age-related changes in children, a valid test should yield different results on the second administration. Third, exact information on the original conditions of data collection is helpful in applying the measuring instrument to a situation known to be different, such as another country or culture. When the investigator is specifically concerned with differences, he must match the original conditions as closely as possible in order to separate cultural effects from other sources of variation. Finally, replicability allows the outsider to separate the process of data collection from the process of inference used in analysis. This is particularly important in participant observation, where the two processes are often fused. It is evident that the sample survey offers greater possibilities of replication on all counts. Because of the highly personalized and intuitive nature of the participant observer's work, it may be difficult for him to specify the exact conditions under which he collected his data and to lay bare the chain of inference used in reaching a certain conclusion. However, even here replicability could be increased if the observer published a detailed account of his field experience, as has been done in the anthropological novel *Return to Laughter* and in Berreman's account of his research in a Himalayan village.[3]

Qualitative Depth

Accuracy is also enhanced by the availability of qualitative material about the individuals, groups, or events under study, including historical analyses, ethnographic reports, clinical impressions, and thumbnail sketches provided by survey interviewers. The ultimate test of validity in

[3]E. S. Bowen, *Return to Laughter* (Garden City, N.Y.: Doubleday & Company, Inc., Anchor Books, 1964); and G. Berreman, *Behind Many Masks: Ethnography and Impression Management in a Himalayan Village* (Ithaca, N.Y.: Society for Applied Anthropology, 1962).

social research comes down to a feeling that the entire body of available data somehow "fits" or "sounds right." Decisions about the validity of even quantitative indicators, such as a measure of income, are often based upon a qualitative assessment of the congruence between this and other information. Thus the greater the range of data available on a given subject, the more sound will be the assessment of validity. Even in the most quantitatively oriented survey, qualitative data are always helpful and often essential in interpreting the findings. Data do not interpret themselves—they must be set in an analytic context of some sort, and this context is often suggested by qualitative interviews and observations.

While a well-designed survey can obtain a great deal of qualitative information through open-ended interview questions, probes, and the summary impressions of the interviewers, participant observation offers greater possibilities on this score. Its major advantage lies in the great flexibility enjoyed by the observer in adapting his approach to the problem at hand. As Bennett and Thaiss point out:

> . . . the informal, probing techniques associated with holistic-depictive research are typically flexible and eclectic, whereas the techniques in survey research are highly disciplined. Field work as a method is typically unpredictable because the movement of the researcher in the natural society is to some extent unpredictable. Hence he may find it difficult to accept the particular discipline of a particular methodological procedure. Rather than resisting discipline, however, he is in a position to try out many disciplined approaches, discarding or keeping them on the basis of a single pragmatic test—whether they contribute to general enlightenment, or secure a needed slice of data.[4]

Greater flexibility means greater exposure to qualitative cues—verbal and nonverbal—that may elude the net of the survey researcher. Through his continued presence in the group, the participant observer can develop an intimate understanding of the context of relationships and events, and he has the decided advantage of being able to match word against deed. Rather than just ask villagers about the distribution of power and prestige in the community, he can actually observe who wields power of different sorts, who receives honor and deference in village meetings or on ceremonial occasions, and who enjoys the highest standard of living. These advantages are partly offset by the reduced scope of most observational studies, the inherent difficulties in replication, and the increased necessity of personal judgment in interpreting the results of the study.

[4] J. W. Bennett and G. Thaiss, "Survey Research and Sociocultural Anthropology," in *Survey Research in the Social Sciences*, ed. C. Glock (New York: Russell Sage Foundation, 1967), p. 279.

Control Over Observer Effects

Accuracy was defined earlier as the generalizability of the measurements taken to all the relevant measurements that might have been taken on the phenomena in question. A major factor leading to reduced generalizability in both survey research and participant observation is the effect of the interviewer or observer on the measurements taken. If generalizability requires a reasonable fit between the "test" sample of behavior and the "true" reality, we must always ask how the observer affects this fit. In other words, does the presence of an observer or interviewer change the reality observed to such an extent that the sample obtained is not representative of normal conditions?

In the survey the effects of the interviewer can be controlled to some degree by having him adhere to standardized instructions and asking him to develop and maintain rapport with the respondent. These procedures are only partially successful in encouraging the respondent to "be himself" and describe his situation as it is. In some cases unfamiliarity with surveys, suspicion of outsiders, mistrust of the purposes of the research, and racial or class differences can lead to distortions. When the climate for research is essentially favorable these effects need not be serious, and they may be randomized to some extent by the use of many different interviewers. Also, in studies where precision is not essential, even information that is somewhat biased may still serve the purposes of the investigator, as happens when a sociologist requires only very gross data on income (e.g., in categories grouped in intervals of $5,000) or education (e.g., some college vs. no college). The picture becomes more complicated when an observer becomes part of a community for weeks, months, or even years. On the one hand his continued presence means that he has direct access to the daily round of community activities and opportunities for intimate contact with the residents. He sees important events as they happen and can obtain instant clarification of those phenomena he does not understand. Yet he always remains marginal and is not automatically allowed to view the "back regions" of the community.[5] In fact, his presence may have the unintended effect of changing the balance between the front and the back regions of the group, encouraging members to adjust their behavior to the observer's standards of what is correct for persons in their situation. This process of constant shifting is well illustrated in Berreman's account of his work as an ethnographic participant observer in a Himalayan village. He writes in his concluding remarks: "Impression management is a feature of all social interaction.

[5]Berreman, *Behind Many Masks*, organizes much of his discussion around the concepts of front and back regions in human affairs.

An understanding of its nature and of the resultant performances is essential to competent ethnography. Methodological procedures must be employed which will reveal not only the performance staged for the observer, but the nature of the efforts which go into producing it and the backstage situation it conceals."[6] This remark applies as well to the survey interview. In short, both the survey interview and participant observation are vulnerable to observer effects, and it is difficult to say in general terms which is more so.

GENERALIZABILITY OF THE RESULTS

In addition to the generalizability of the measures taken to other measures that might have been taken, most social research (except a census) involves the generalization of results based upon one group to a broader universe or population. This is true by definition in the sample survey where a fraction of a group is used as the basis for conclusions about the whole, but it also applies to participant observation. The anthropologist who observes a remote village usually wishes to generalize not only about that village but also about the entire tribe, that region of the country, the nation, social structure, or even human nature. Thus quite apart from the accuracy of the measures obtained from a sample or group, it is essential to know if the group itself is sufficiently representative of the population about which conclusions will be drawn.

The greatest single advantage of a well-designed sample survey is that its results can be generalized to a larger population within known limits of error. The greatest weakness of most observational studies is that the limits of generality are unknown. An intensive study of a single community may be beautifully designed and masterful in its portrayal of social life (a good example is W. F. Whyte's *Street Corner Society*), and yet we can never be sure of how well it represents other communities. Some writers, of course, are not interested in generalizing beyond their particular domain, but these are a distinct minority in the social sciences.

Generalizability is limited in most observational studies for three reasons. First, participant observers rarely follow the survey researcher's strategy of defining in advance the universe about which conclusions are to be drawn and then using random methods to pick the specific group to be studied. In anthropological studies it is common practice to choose a village that is not too close to a city, mission, or other contaminating influence and that is judged to be reasonably similar to other villages in the area. Similar processes of *ad hoc* "expert" selection are followed in

[6]*Ibid.*, p. 24.

sociological surveys carried out in a local factory or school that happens to be convenient. In all these cases generalizability is severely curtailed at the first stage of sampling. Second, even if probability methods were used at this first stage, generalizability would be further limited by the fact that the sample consists of a single case. There is ample evidence that villages and other social groups assumed to be alike, such as Indian communities in highland Peru, actually show great differences in social structure, conflict, mutual trust, and capacity for community action. One can never assume without further evidence that *his* village really represents some broader universe. Finally, generality is reduced by the sampling of observations within the unit studied. Where the data are gathered by a single observer and perhaps a local assistant, unknown "sampling error" will be introduced by their selective perceptions and their distinctive impact upon the group. All of us see different things when we enter a new group, especially when our mandate is as broad as that provided by participant observation. This is the point at which the accuracy of measurement, especially the problem of replicability, is closely related to the generalizability of the findings. The conscientious observer can help us estimate the extent of selectivity by honest and open reporting of the details of his fieldwork, but this does not solve the problem completely. Selective perception and personal impact are also found in the survey interview, but they are reduced to some extent by the use of structured questions and randomized by the use of several interviewers.

ADMINISTRATIVE CONVENIENCE

Decisions about which method or combination of methods will be used in social research usually hinge on three administrative considerations: cost, speed, and organizational complexity. The sample survey is generally a more expensive method of data collection than participant observation, both because of the large number of people directly involved (study directors, interviewers, coders, office staff, and perhaps even computer programmers) and because of the relatively high overhead costs. If the study is carried out by an established research institute, such as the Survey Research Center at the University of Michigan or the National Opinion Research Center, the budget must include not only the salaries and travel expenses of those who execute the survey but also the indirect costs of maintaining a highly specialized corps of field supervisors, sampling experts, specialists in data processing, and the like.

On the question of speed, both surveys and participant observational studies can range from a few weeks to several years. There is no accurate information available on this subject, but it seems that surveys have a slight advantage in this case. While both methods typically require several months for planning and data collection, the structured data provided by the survey are more readily amenable to rapid statistical analysis on standard computer programs. The period of interpretation following this analysis can also vary enormously, but the total time involved seems, on the average, to be shorter in surveys.

In addition to being more costly, surveys require more elaborate organizational arrangements than observational studies. In a large household survey, the efforts of many people must be coordinated—the study directors themselves, who may have other matters to attend to, the interviewers, the coders, and the travel agents. These complexities are multiplied in cross-national surveys where interview questions must be developed that are equivalent in meaning from culture to culture. Peculiar administrative and political difficulties arise in each research site, and adequate communications must be maintained across several continents.[7] Some of these problems would also plague participant observers engaged in the study of the same phenomena in different cultures, but they would normally be less severe because of the high degree of autonomy accorded to each observer.

ETHICAL AND POLITICAL PROBLEMS

A final yardstick of social research lies in the extent to which a study avoids ethical or political difficulties in the research process. Certain of these difficulties are inescapable in both survey research and participant observation, but they are somewhat different in each case.

Ethics

Any study involving direct contact with individuals faces an ethical dilemma arising from the clash of two social values: the freedom of scientific inquiry and the right to privacy.[8] The first flows from the twin conviction that men have a right to know and that systematic knowledge is the foundation of social progress. Pitted against this in social research is the parallel belief in individual liberty and dignity, with the corollary rights to freedom from invasions of privacy and manipulation. Both sur-

[7] Cf. G. Almond and S. Verba, *The Civic Culture* (Princeton, N.J.: Princeton University Press, 1963), Methodological Appendix.

[8] E. Shils, "Social Inquiry and the Autonomy of the Individual," in *The Human Meaning of the Social Sciences*, ed. D. Lerner (New York: Meridian Books, Inc., 1959), pp. 118–21.

veys and participant observation can be defended on the grounds that they will be used in programs of public welfare or economic development. The survey researcher might also argue that the infringements of privacy occasioned by his studies are more than compensated for by providing respondents with an opportunity to express their opinions on important issues or simply to unburden themselves to strangers who will protect their confidences. Participant observers could offer similar justifications for their work.

Nevertheless, several ethical problems are common to both methods. The first concerns the techniques used to gain the cooperation of those being studied, especially ingratiation and deception. This is a particularly serious problem in participant observation where the demands upon the "respondents" are greater than in the survey and the observer's personal impact deeper (one thinks of anthropologists who have become permanent personal advisers to the groups they have studied). In reflecting on her anthropological fieldwork among the Tiv in Northern Nigeria, E. S. Bowen (a pseudonym) writes: "Many of my moral dilemmas had sprung from the very nature of my work, which had made me a trickster: one who seems to be what he is not and who professes faith in what he does not believe."[9] The feeling of hypocrisy and of being a "sly ambulance chaser" was most acute as she sat up with the sick or attended funerals to learn about the meaning of illness and death in the community. Similar problems arise when the survey interviewer simulates warmth and friendship or ingratiates himself with the respondent as a means of extracting better information.

Second, both surveys and participant observation may result in invasions of privacy or produce other questionable effects on the respondent or the community. Although there are no sharply delineated "legal" norms on invasions of privacy in social research, it is clear that many respondents *feel* that certain studies have intruded too far with detailed questions on income, sexual behavior, or other highly personal matters.[10] Serious questions have also been raised about the propriety of using covert devices such as projective techniques (e.g., responses to ambiguous pictures) in the survey.[11] Similarly, both the survey and participant observation may have ethically dubious reactive effects upon the individuals involved. One such effect might be called *informational*, as when a study on fertility indirectly conveys information about contraceptive methods, or research on politically sensitive topics is used to "soften up"

[9]Bowen, *Return to Laughter*, p. 290.

[10]E. L. Hartmann, H. L. Isaacson, and C. M. Jurgell, "Public Reaction to Survey Interviewing," *Public Opinion Quarterly*, 32, 4 (1967), 296–98.

[11]R. O. Carlson, "The Issue of Privacy in Public Opinion Research," *Public Opinion Quarterly*, 31, 1 (1967), 1–8.

the population for subsequent action programs. Another type of impact is *affective*, involving emotional responses such as fear, anxiety, guilt, and shame. Such responses might be seen in studies of death among the fatally ill or research on homosexuality using "normal" subjects. These latent effects of social research are considered reactive in the sense that the last state of the respondent is different from the first.[12]

Third, ethical questions arise in the use of the data obtained by both methods, especially when promises of confidentiality have been made. These problems are particularly serious when the study is conducted in a single community or organization where the findings might be detrimental to political leaders, factory supervisors, or groups of the upper class, or identifiable social units such as dissident work groups in an organization. In organizational research the difficulties of maintaining confidentiality are compounded when the study is sponsored by the management and they receive detailed reports of the findings. Here the critical problem is that the administrators of the organization can make direct use of the results in sanctioning individuals or groups, such as those with low morale. In such cases the investigator is faced with a basic conflict between the sponsor's desire for useful information and the respondent's right to confidentiality. Sometimes in this type of research it is possible to maintain the confidentiality promised to individuals and yet jeopardize the interests of supervisors, work groups, or others when the data are aggregated. An attitude survey may show, for example, that the job satisfaction of a certain work group is lower than the average for the organization as a whole. Here even though no individual responses were revealed in the report, this information could be used against the supervisor, the factory manager, or the work group itself. In short, both surveys and participant observation may infringe upon individual rights; at the moment it is difficult to say whether the risks incurred in one method are greater than the other.

Politics

Just as social research entails a potential conflict of individual rights and values, so may it provoke a clash of interests. The sample survey is especially vulnerable to political difficulties because of the nature of the topics it covers, its high visibility, and the complexity of its administrative arrangements. Large surveys often focus on sensitive or controversial topics within the public domain, thus raising questions about sponsor-

[12]E. Webb, D. T. Campbell, R. D. Schwartz, L. Sechrest, *Unobtrusive Measures: Non-Reactive Research in the Social Sciences* (Chicago: Rand McNally & Co., 1966).

ship, intentions, and probable use of the results. If the study is sponsored by a public agency, such as a city, it may become the object of political attack by opponents of the agency, however well designed it may be and however aboveboard its intentions. This is especially true when the subject of research is a volatile problem such as race relations, urban renewal, or bomb shelters. Moreover, conflicts often arise between the sponsor and the research team on how a problem is to be defined (e.g., "revolution" vs. "insurgency" in a study sponsored by the army), how the questions are to be phrased, how the data are to be analyzed, where the results are to be published, and whether the final report should be written to summarize and describe the findings or persuade and convert a certain set of readers.[13] Since the ill-fated Project Camelot, United States-sponsored surveys overseas have increasingly met with charges that they infringe on national autonomy, perpetuate a kind of "scientific colonialism" by treating foreign collaborators as "hired hands," facilitate armed intervention in the affairs of other countries by gathering "intelligence" for military agencies, and so on.[14] Whatever the truth of these charges, they illustrate the heightened political sensitivity of large-scale international surveys.

The political problems faced in participant observation tend to be less dramatic and more local. It is true that anthropologists using this method have also been accused of international imperialism, mostly because their fieldwork was heavily dependent upon the cooperation of the former imperial powers. Kathleen Gough Aberle writes: "Until World War II most of our fieldwork was carried out in societies that had been conquered by our own governments. We tended to accept the imperialist framework as given, perhaps partly because we were influenced by the dominant ideas of our time, and partly because at that time there was little anyone could do to dismantle the empires."[15] Very often, however, the most immediate political problems arise from pressures to identify with a faction or interest group in the local community. Once the observer is accepted as part of the community, he may be asked to take sides on disputed issues or, even when not asked, may feel compelled to do so because of his own pattern of obligations and attractions. When the group under observation is literate and conscious of its interests, he

[13]Cf. G. Sjoberg, ed., *Ethics, Politics, and Social Research* (Cambridge, Mass.: Schenkman Publishing Co., 1967), esp. Chaps. 1 and 4. See also L. Rainwater and W. Yancey, *The Moynihan Report and the Politics of Controversy* (Cambridge, Mass.: The M.I.T. Press, 1967).

[14]I. L. Horowitz, ed., *The Rise and Fall of Project Camelot: Studies in the Relationship of Social Science and Practical Politics* (Cambridge, Mass.: The M.I.T. Press, 1967).

[15]K. G. Aberle, "Anthropology and Imperialism," in *Newsletter*, Radical Education Project, Ann Arbor, Michigan, 1, 1 (1967), 1.

may also be subject to the same pressures as the survey researcher in defining the focus of the study, analyzing and interpreting the data, and publishing the findings.

Thus there is no magic to either of these methods. Each is useful under some circumstances and not under others. The strength of the sample survey lies in its greater potential for quantification, replication, and generalization to a broader population. Participant observation normally has the edge on qualitative depth, flexibility for the observer, and appropriateness for the study of social processes and complex patterns of relationships. In this regard the following advice from two anthropologists sympathetic to survey research merits serious consideration:

> If anthropology has a message for survey research, it is this: delay the construction of schedules of all kinds until something is known about the cultural context of the phenomenon under study; do not assume that all slices of social actuality are always identically responsive to theoretical constructs; remember that all constructs are, in the last analysis, human conceptions of the social situation at one place and time, and their relevance to a new situation must always be a problem for investigation. If survey research has a message for anthropology, it is this: first, often context can be known in general terms, known sufficiently well to permit the use of instruments which will materially aid in the checking of particular hypotheses, or hasten the collection of certain kinds of data. It is not always necessary to know the culture in detail; the intelligent and well-educated observer can operate on the basis of our growing comparative knowledge of cultures and social systems. Second, whenever specific hypotheses are to be tested in fieldwork, the anthropologist has an obligation to construct and utilize instruments which will adequately represent the population under study.[16]

The same general reasoning could be applied to other methodological combinations, such as surveys and historical data or participant observation and content analysis. The next opportunity for breakthroughs in the various social sciences may lie precisely in kinds of mixtures proposed here. Both in comparative research and elsewhere the time has come to move away from methodological tribalism to fruitful experimentation with new options.

[16]Bennett and Thaiss, "Survey Research and Sociocultural Anthropology," pp. 302–03.

10

Survey Materials Collected in the Developing Countries: Sampling, Measurement, and Interviewing Obstacles to Intra- and Inter-National Comparisons

Scholars, government officials, and commercial interests in the developing countries are increasingly recognizing that survey research methods provide the only means by which systematic information can be collected and analysed for a wide range of purposes of both scholarly research and policy-making. American and European scholars and policy-makers are also becoming increasingly interested in using survey materials collected in developing countries for intra- and inter-national comparisons [12, 28]. However, there is ample reason to suspect that many of the materials—perhaps the vast majority—are of such questionable quality that they cannot be used for research on numerous topics. For example, validation checks conducted in the course of fertility studies sometimes reveal major discrepancies in simple factual information [9]; a validation check performed in the course of a study of capital forma-

Reprinted from Robert Edward Mitchell, "Survey Methods Collected in the Developing Countries: Sampling, Measurement, and Interviewing Obstacles to Intra- and Inter-National Comparisons," *International Social Science Journal*, 1965, 17, no. 4. Reprinted by permission of UNESCO and the author.

This paper may be identified as a shortened version of publication No. A-54 of the Survey Research Center, University of California, Berkeley. The paper was written for two related programmes at Berkeley, both initiated co-operatively by the Institute of International Studies, the Survey Research Center, and the Survey Research Center's International Data Library and Reference Service. One project is concerned with Comparative National Development, whereas the other concerns the collection, methodological evaluation, and distribution of existing survey materials collected in the developing countries.

The author is deputy director and co-ordinator of international research at the Survey Research Center of the University of California.

The figures in brackets refer to the bibliography on page 225–26.

tion in a rural area of a developing country showed a 15 per cent discrepancy in basic economic figures; other studies of household budgets and economic surveys have disclosed extremely sloppy work and serious inaccuracies in the reported figures [25].

Despite the criticisms which can be made of those who conduct survey research in the developing countries, and also those which can be made of their data and the ways they are used, there is no indication that the growth of this research approach will be curtailed by the existence of methodological and technical obstacles. Rather, with governments expressing more and more demands for information, and with scholars expressing an increasing interest in basic social science research, there will very likely be an accelerated rate of reliance on survey research methods.

The present paper attempts to outline and catalogue some of the major issues involved in the conduct of survey research in the developing countries. A concern with the use of existing materials for purposes of secondary analysis, especially for international comparative purposes, initiated this review. In addition, however, the lessons learned from this examination of the strengths and weaknesses of existing materials are of particular relevance for those wishing to collect original data.

The analysis of available materials is under three headings or types of bias: sampling, measurement, and interviewer bias.

SAMPLING ERRORS

Poor Workmanship

In many countries it is only an analytical fiction which permits one to discuss sampling and non-sampling errors separately, for the same staffs and procedures used in interviewing respondents are also used in preparing the samples. This is the situation in particular with regard to preparing samples of certain specialized populations for which no locator or parameter information is available. In these instances, the interviewing staffs frequently prepare the information which is used in drawing the sample.

Relatively few countries have adequate sampling information even for their major metropolitan centres, and, as a consequence, various incomplete, outdated maps are used, or, in the absence of alternative registers (for example, voting or housing registers), agencies will pre-list their sampling areas. Some studies in non-urban areas employ random-walk procedures [8] without the benefit of pre-listing and, therefore, the interviewer is at the same time a sampler. Interviewers also often select the respondent within the household, although it appears to be an increasingly common practice to have the interviewer first list the members of the household and then use a table of random numbers to select the actual person to be interviewed. Interviewers, of course, play a crucial sampling role in studies based on quota samples.

Unfortunately, there is abundant reason to question both the competence and honesty of interviewing-sampling field staffs in many countries, and, consequently, to question the adequacy of the samples which are drawn. Perhaps samples drawn by government agencies are of less dubious quality than others, but the sampling resources of these agencies are seldom made available to those involved in non-governmental social science research.[1]

An example of shoddy workmanship was discovered in a major Asian city where the leading (and in many ways most competent) research agency prepared house listings which were subsequently used in drawing a number of samples. The listings consisted of house addresses. Approximately eight months after the listings were prepared, they were loaned to a local university research group for a government-sponsored study, when it was discovered that approximately one out of the four addresses did not exist. The agency which prepared the listings must surely have been aware of their limitations as a sampling frame. However, this did not deter it from using the frame for a number of studies. Such practices, it is suggested, are not uncommon.

Coverage and Comparability of Sampling Frames

Given the lack of sampling resources available in developing countries, and given the sampling obstacles created by poor and often mobile populations, it is probably inevitable that sampling frames often fail to include large segments of the population within a single country and that samples used for international comparative purposes are typically based on noncomparable sampling frames.

These difficulties can be found in the valuable and interesting five-city (Tokyo, Manila, Singapore, Bangkok, and Bombay) general public opinion study called the 'Asia Poll,' a regional equivalent to earlier 'World Polls.' The sampling procedures differ considerably in these cities,

---

[1]Once prepared, a listing, no matter how incomplete, can serve as a useful device for controlling interviewers. Agencies with such lists typically require the interviewer to report information—for example, which floor was the unit on, how many doors in the house, how many adults, colour of the house, construction of the house— which the pre-listing obtained and which can be used to see if the interviewer actually visited the predesignated sampling unit.

with quota procedures being used in some and probability samples in others. Even if all five research agencies drew probability samples, the comparative researcher would still encounter difficulties, since the frames in each city would differ in their coverage. For example, a voting registration list might include 70 percent of one city's population, a housing registration list might include 80 percent of another city's population, and an area probability sample might be 90 percent complete in another city. In this situation, the researcher would have problems in deciding whether on some items—for example, occupational mobility—the apparent differences between two cities were significant (if he were to dare ask such a question of his data).

Similar problems of comparability can be found in the recent international comparative study of social stratification and mobility conducted in Rio de Janeiro, Montevideo, Buenos Aires, and Santiago. These are exceedingly interesting and worth-while studies, although local scholars have raised serious questions about the completeness of the various samples used.

These problems of the comparability of frames between countries are no less serious within single nations. For example, one might question the comparability of Rio de Janeiro samples with samples of São Paulo. Since survey studies in most developing countries tend to be conducted within the major city or in the city where the major research agencies are located, the sampling resources are differently distributed throughout the nation. Therefore, a so-called 'national urban sample' based on a number of cities will utilize sampling frames which differ considerably in their completeness. Differences can even be found between two agencies in their samples for a single city, and, furthermore, one agency will differ in samples it prepares at different times for a single location. For example, in evaluating the adequacy of existing materials it acquired, the International Data Library and Reference Service of the University of California's Survey Research Center discovered the following discrepancies in three separate samples drawn by two agencies in the same city: one study found no respondents earning less than ten (U.S.) dollars per month; another study found approximately 9 percent; and a third, which seems to be the most accurate, found 70 percent in this category.

Maintaining adequate sampling frames is an especially difficult problem in rapidly expanding cities such as exist in most developing countries, especially in Africa and Latin America. For example, in some African cities there has been a rapid change in housing from huts to flats, a process which destroys the sampling value of carefully prepared city maps [5]. The expense of keeping these frames up to date is usually prohibitive, and, in fact, it is not uncommon for agencies to use outdated frames.

Since adequate parameter data are seldom available, the researcher is not able to assess the exact nature and extent of the sampling biases in his materials. Too often, as will be noted again later, the only available checks are provided by results produced in earlier studies by the same agency. Misleading information in these instances is used to corroborate deficient data.

Cluster and Quota Sampling

Unfortunately, descriptive terms such as "national probability sample" or "quota sample" based on certain criteria are so general and vague in meaning that the consumer and user of data cannot determine the degree to which his sample is representative of some larger population or the degree to which two samples in the same or different countries are comparable. Only three of many issues relevant to these problems will be mentioned here: the ultimate sampling unit, clustering procedures, and quota sampling procedures—all of which are closely related to problems of sampling frames as discussed earlier.

Critical but ill-informed opponents of sample surveys and quantitative procedures for research in developing societies have argued that sampling necessarily leads to studies based only on individuals considered independently of the social networks in which they are involved [20, 23]. Evidently, these critics are unaware of the possibility of interviewing all members of a single household, of a kinship line, or of any collectivity; nor are they aware of snowball sampling. Furthermore, they fail to recognize the possibilities of various kinds of relational analysis, analytical procedures which have been given a welcome fillip by recent computer developments.

Although these criticisms are not well taken, at least they turn our attention to sampling units and the assumptions underlying their use. There are obvious differences in sampling units based on voting registers and those based on households; the former may consist primarily of men who are highly politicized, whereas the latter may have a surplus of apolitical women. The latter might also include a much higher proportion of all adults in the total universe. However, there may also be problems in the use of the household. Often, the household is defined as a group of people eating around a common kitchen or kettle, whereas in random-walk procedures it might refer to a single hut, regardless of the eating arrangements. Still other samples define a household as all those who share their earnings. After a household has been selected, standard procedures may or may not be used to select the respondent to be interviewed.

Often the average size and complexity of the household differs in different parts of the interviewing area, for example, between rural and urban areas or areas populated by families with different kinship systems. In these cases, the sampling units and ratios used to select respondents may overweight certain portions of the population, and alter the selection probabilities of various segments of the universe.

Obviously, the sampling units used in a study must be relevant to the research purposes and to sociological reality. It would be folly for any researcher to proceed blindly to draw his sample without first becoming thoroughly familiar with the major features of the local scene, including kinship structures. However, for the most part, it seems that the use of different sampling units is admittedly only a minor issue in a more complicated problem of sampling.

A key element, as described by Philip Converse [6], relates to the clustering procedures used in preparing samples. Very often the term "national probability sample" simply means that the study was conducted in more than one metropolitan area (Converse was referring to European practices, although the same remarks apply to the developing countries). Since research agencies in these countries often face serious transportation problems, as well as cost and supervision difficulties, the rural areas included in the sample are typically adjacent to the major metropolitan sampling points. Even when several sampling points are selected, the clustering procedures which are used add greatly to the error margins for materials, especially for items such as education, sophistication, and political involvement—items which tend not to be homogeneously distributed across regions. Given these considerations, the researcher is limited in his ability to project his findings to larger populations; he is limited in the importance he can attach to rural-urban (or centre-periphery) differences; and he is limited in his ability to subdivide his materials statistically by various criteria, especially those criteria highly associated with the major clusters defining the sample. Since scholars are generally unaware of these problems, they may tend to over-interpret their findings.

A number of difficulties involved in comparing two sets of probability samples have been noted by others [1]. For example, the two major commercial polling agencies in Great Britain disagree as to the proper base for national samples, and, as a result, the two agencies are reported to differ consistently in their electoral predictions. They also differ in the criteria used in determining socio-economic position, thereby making it hazardous to compare blue-collar workers from one agency's sample with blue-collar workers from the other agency's sample.

When sampling resources are not adequate and funds are scarce research agencies typically resort to quota sampling. Much research needs to be done comparing the relative merits of quota and various kinds of probability samples in the developing countries. As survey research, especially commercial research, expands in the developing countries, it is quite likely that there will be an increasing number of opportunities to do this. One confidential study shown me recently made such a comparison for two samples used in two commercial surveys in a large Latin American metropolitan city, and the comparisons indicated a very close congruence on many relevant items. However, this one example is countered by other experiences. An investigation by the Organization for Economic Cooperation and Development concluded that quota sampling procedures used in different European countries were so divergent and uncontrolled that one could not compare results obtained from the various samples [15].

Preliminary investigation of quota sampling procedures in the developing countries tends to support the OECD's conclusions. For example, some agencies will select their respondents by house calls made only during the day; others interview outside factories and office buildings, while others use various other techniques. Research agencies naturally defend their samples, but often on entirely erroneous grounds. On the basis of accepted parameter or universe data, the agency selects its various quotas—so many working women between the ages of 35 and 45, so many male blue-collar workers between the ages of 40 and 50, etc. When the interviewing materials are tabulated, the marginal distributions on demographic items typically agree with the distribution of these items in the universe. However, to claim, as some agencies do, that this agreement guarantees the representativeness of the sample is merely to confirm the predetermined consequences which bear no logical relationship to the degree to which the sample is truly representative.

Since research agencies have trained their clients to compare their sample figures with the known universe data, an apparent discrepancy in the sample can prove embarrassing. It is partly for this reason, and partly from a genuine interest in producing quality samples, that research agencies resort to various *post hoc* weighting procedures, or return to the field to pick up the needed extra respondents for particular population segments. Again, a comparison between the universe and sample figures —whether from a quota or a probability sample—need not be relevant at all as far as the representativeness of that sample is concerned.

Social and Cultural Accessibility
(Non-Completion Rates)

Even if a researcher is satisfied with the sampling frames and procedures prepared for his study, he will still have to overcome obstacles created for him by non-respondents, an especially acute problem in comparative studies. Non-respondents are typically not distributed randomly throughout the sample but differ according to variations in the cultural and social accessibility of distinct population segments. On an international scale, Almond and Verba's recent five-nation study (*The Civic Culture*) [2] provides an example of this problem. Their non-completion rates range from 17 percent to 41 percent. It is not clear whether the non-respondents are the same in all countries. In some countries, they would not be. For example, females account for 64 percent of the Mexican sample in the Almond-Verba study. According to the contractor, which is surely one of the best agencies found in any developing country, such ratios are not unusual and do not differ significantly from what has been discovered in a number of parallel or interpenetrating replicate sub-samples which have been drawn in Mexico.

Unfortunately, the 1960 Mexican census does not support this assumption: only 52 percent of the Mexican population living in cities of 10,000 (the smallest city sampled in the five-nation survey) or more are women; this figure varies by only a couple of percentage points for different size cities, and different adult age groups. Furthermore, parallel samples can be deceiving here. For example, no matter how many parallel sub-samples are drawn in India, men will usually constitute approximately 80 percent of the interviewed respondents for some agencies. That is, a number of studies and research experiences in Asia indicate that women are culturally and socially inaccessible to interviewers,[2] whereas the experience elsewhere indicates that men are relatively inaccessible, and, as the Almond-Verba study suggests, there are national differences in the availability of different types of respondents even within the Western world.

These same problems arise for samples within a single country, since groups may differ in their degree of accessibility to interviewers in different parts of a nation. In Latin America, some of the major intra-national differences in response rates seem to occur for members of the upper class, since they are difficult to interview in urban areas.

Intra-national as well as inter-national differences in response rates have implications for the way the data can be interpreted. As will be indicated again later, there is good reason to believe that respondents and non-respondents differ in their ability to provide equally good and complete information; therefore, certain comparisons—such as rural-urban or centre-periphery—will typically introduce biases. For example, the absence of members of the urban upper class may lead to an understatement of rural-urban differences (this understatement may be further com-

---

[2]However, in one South-East Asian country, two commercial agencies differed in their estimations of whether men or women had the higher refusal rate.

plicated if the rural sampling points are closely adjacent to the urban sampling points, as noted previously in the discussion of sampling procedures). If weighting procedures are used to give the correct proportions of upperclass respondents in the sample, some of the bias in single, one-variable marginals may be reduced. However, intensive multivariate analysis based on weighted cards can be highly misleading, especially if the samples are relatively small.

Even these very abbreviated remarks regarding sampling problems should be enough to alert the researcher to the limitations of any one study, let alone several studies which he might wish to use for comparative purposes. Furthermore, the issues discussed in this section should suggest some questions which researchers might ask themselves before beginning a study. For example, is it realistic and relevant even to aim for a national sample when the sampling resources are so inadequate and response-rates so flexible? Should some respondents receive only one call-back, thereby releasing resources to permit more call-backs on specified kinds of respondents?[3] The researcher certainly should collect information on the number of call-backs, on replacement procedures used, if any, and the degree to which respondents are self-selected; he should also be thoroughly familiar with the nature of the sampling frame and the procedures used in drawing his samples.

MEASUREMENT ERRORS

Sophistication and Meaningless Evidence

Until recently, social science research in the developing countries was conducted almost exclusively by anthropologists, as it is today in a great many areas. Anthropologists have made a number of cogent criticisms of survey research, especially opinion studies. Two criticisms are especially relevant: doubt as to the existence of any such thing as private or public opinion, the mechanisms for decision-making and opinion formation being thought to be absent in lower-class roles, especially in tradition-directed societies. Second, the critics imply that even if the native does harbour personal opinions, it is not possible to measure these opinions by means of standard interviewing techniques.

While it might be argued that the proponents of these views tend to

[3]One commercial agency in Asia reported that a 40 percent call-back rate is common for samples with pre-specified respondents, whereas replacement procedures which permit the interviewer to select a replacement among the other adults in the household will typically require only a 20 to 30 percent call-back rate. The latter procedure of course could possibly lead to major sampling biases, especially if interviews are held only during the day when men are at work.

generalize experiences gained from observation of primitive societies to the kinds of problems which are likely to be encountered in modernizing areas, and although these critics sometimes ignore the fact that survey research methods are used for gaining factual as well as attitudinal information, still there is considerable general support for their criticisms. For example, almost any study which includes consistency checks within the research instrument will discover a very high proportion of inconsistent responses. Studies being analysed by the International Data Library and Reference Service report very high proportions of "no answers," "don't know," "no opinion," neutral positions on attitude scales, and undifferentiated responses to manifestly different questions, such as attitudes toward the United States, the U.S.S.R., and China. Our preliminary inquiries into the opinion structures of certain groups suggest that the often overtly sophisticated questions framed by many researchers are eliciting meaningless opinion from respondents who have no opinion or only very unstable opinions. Philip Converse has systematically investigated some of these problems [7]. Using panel data for what might be considered élite American population segments, he raises serious questions regarding the stability of opinion in the "advanced sections of the most advanced societies." Even issues considered to be salient to wide segments of the American population were found to have a small public. "Issue publics" in the developing countries also are likely to be even more minuscule and limited to a small proportion of the educated. (However, as will be noted again, "issue publics" as used by Converse should not be confused with "basic" values.)

The second criticism raised by anthropologists also has apparent support, for there is little doubt that asking questions, as in a personal interview, is alien to many societies. Keesing, among others, has argued that to answer a question is to make a decision, which only certain individuals in a society have a right to do [16]. Other studies—for example, Lerner in the use of the concept "empathy" [21]—have amplified this issue by noting that lower-class respondents typically are unable to answer questions which require that they take the role of others. These difficulties have encouraged some researchers to sample only known opinion holders (the élite), whereas other researchers, less concerned with general public opinion than with specific behaviour and basic values, have interviewed unsophisticated respondents with considerable success. Family planning studies have probably been most conspicuous in this regard [10].

While recognizing the value of these various criticisms, it seems that they are perhaps too general and that, in fact, they suggest a number of dimensions which, once isolated, can help future researchers improve their ability to obtain accurate and meaningful information. Unquestionably, current attempts to measure public opinion and behaviour in the developing countries are imperfect. For example, little or no distinction is made among (a) topics about which the respondent has no opinion or is unable to give an adequate factual answer, (b) topics which are culturally sensitive, and (c) topics which need greater conceptual, linguistic, and measuring sophistication in order to draw out information.

Researchers and critics of research seem to be most aware of the "no opinion" dimension. They claim that research instruments are often so constructed and administered as to elicit meaningless responses. Many studies, of course, are not concerned with general opinions but, rather, with factual information and basic values. One might expect that there would be relatively minor difficulties involved in obtaining factual information on household expenditures and income, media exposure and voting behaviour, and family control techniques and family size. Many of the obstacles to obtaining factual information have been observed by others; for example, demographic surveys have difficulty in obtaining correct information in societies which do not have the Western concept of time; and economic surveys in largely non-monetary markets and in rural areas have discovered that employment, income, debt, and consumption vary in size over the farming year,[4] thereby making it impossible to generalize about the economy on the basis of the limited information that respondents are able to recall at only one time period. Even studies which seriously attempt to determine the reliability and validity of their information have discovered fairly serious errors.

Opinion studies which include consistency checks will probably discover even larger "error rates." At the present time, no standard method has evolved for handling such instances. One might delete the inconsistents from the sample, or the whole study might be abandoned if the error rate is high.[5] Some researchers simply treat inconsistency as a finding, and then disregard it in the subsequent analysis [4]. Still others, as will be noted again later, feel that it is best, at least for the key variables in the study, to obtain multiple indicators for a single dimension so that undue reliance is not placed on the answers to any single question.[6]

Of course, some of these suggestions can refer to issues for which respondents have opinions and information just as well as they refer to

[4]Some of the problems involved in these studies derive from the selection of inappropriate recall periods. That is, one cannot expect a respondent to remember the economic details of his life for very long.

[5]One study in Africa discarded two-thirds of the sample because the reported expenditures of these respondents exceeded their known income.

[6]For this approach, as applied to the use of aggregative statistics for purposes of international studies, see bibliographical reference n° 27.

issues for which this is not the case. For example, it is common practice in media-exposure studies in the United States for the questionnaire to repeat a single question several times and in several variations, a technique designed to help respondents remember whether they were exposed to particular media.

Some non-survey workers have argued that interview studies, especially those which use pre-coded and leading questions, structure respondents' frames of reference in such a manner as to encourage them to provide answers which under normal circumstances would not be within their capabilities to formulate. However, this is precisely what a well-designed interview schedule is supposed to do, and it presumably has many advantages over traditional research procedures. Rather than collect masses of partially relevant and irrelevant materials, the survey researcher attempts by prior inquiry to isolate major dimensions he wishes to study. And, rather than pore over his notes in an attempt to substantiate (more typically, to illustrate) his major hypotheses, and rather than be in a position where no information is available to test alternative hypotheses, the survey researcher, in the ideal situation, collects data permitting him to perform both of these tasks.

Many of the criticisms against survey research focus specifically on pre-coded questions, since they obviously provide the answers which respondents might not otherwise be capable of formulating for themselves. To avoid the dangers involved in these questions, as well as similar problems which might arise in open-ended questions, Converse suggests that the respondent be encouraged to volunteer that he has no opinion on a particular topic [7]. There is no reason why such an invitation or filtering technique could not precede pre-coded questions, although the general approach could possibly be overly effective in societies where respondents are eager to give the answer they think you want from them. They would volunteer "no opinion" when in fact they had one. (See the later discussion of "courtesy bias.")

The second of the three distinctions made earlier refers to culturally sensitive topics, something quite different from topics for which respondents can be said to have "no opinion." Culturally sensitive topics raise special problems for the comparative researcher, since what is sensitive in one country may not be in another. For example, it is said to be extremely difficult to obtain religious information in Moslem Pakistan, but relatively easy to do this in Hindu India. In some African areas, as well as in other parts of the world, there is a reluctance to talk about dead children and the number of people in a household—obstacles to demographic researchers. In the Middle East there is a reluctance to discuss ordinary household events [26], and Chinese businessmen in any country are reported to be especially secretive about any and all facets of their work and personal lives. In many countries, respondents are reticent about political topics in general and party preference in particular. On the other hand, it is by no means clear that family planning is nearly as sensitive an issue in the developing countries as might be expected.

Questions raised with regard to both meaningless opinions and opinions on culturally sensitive topics suggest the need for new measuring devices, especially devices to measure basic values. To this end, some studies have experimented with projective tests, role-playing, and various sentence-completion techniques, but, unfortunately, the relative merits of these approaches were not reported [3]. If different measuring devices have varying powers to elicit complete and accurate responses from different population segments, then questions might be raised with regard to the choice of sampling units. For example, for some purposes, husbands seem to be better respondents than are their wives when it comes to family-planning practices [17].

It will be some time before we can be assured that various segments of a population are offering responses which are comparable in terms of amount and quality. For even though respondents are willing to answer questions asked of them, there remain cultural differences regarding respondents' abilities to express themselves. For example, if one examines marginals from studies conducted in Malaysia, one will notice that the Chinese, when compared with the Indians, have a much higher proportion of "no answers" to pre-coded questions and fewer answers to open-ended questions. One of the reasons for this is that the Chinese are quite reticent, whereas the Indians are loquacious. This creates problems in comparing the two groups; and, of course, if the Chinese, Indians, and Malaysians are treated as a single national sample, the Chinese will be underweighted and the Indians overweighted.

Another example of this same kind of problem is suggested by the Almond-Verba five-nation study. They report that the Italians seem reticent about political topics. And, as was noted before, the Mexican sample has a very high proportion of women respondents least capable of responding to a personal interview. Since this study included a very high proportion of open-ended questions, a much higher proportion than is found in typical American studies, it would seem that the biases arising from cultural differences in sophistication, loquacity and articulateness are especially exaggerated.

Mention might be made of some additional means by which these various obstacles can be overcome, or at least means by which measurement errors of these kinds can be statistically controlled in the analysis of survey materials. For example, if respondents have a short span of attention, then interviewing might be conducted in several sessions, although this might be too expensive a procedure for most project budgets. At least the consequences of a short span of attention could possibly be measured by charting the proportion of "poorly answered questions" at different phases of the interview session. The proportion should increase towards the end of the session. Another obvious approach is to spend much more time and resources on the pre-testing of the research instrument, even if this requires that a smaller sample is interviewed in the final study. Researchers might also establish beforehand the amount of error they will tolerate in their materials, and then, on the basis of a small follow-up survey, decide whether the materials fall within the stated error limits. If not, then the materials and the research project might be abandoned entirely. Another procedure is to include numerous measures of verbosity, sophistication, credulity, conformity, extremism in responses, inability to differentiate, filter questions, information questions, items to measure the strength with which opinions are held, and various reliability or consistency checks. These measures can be used to differentiate population groups whose answers are biased and who need separate consideration. Finally, the researcher might develop various meta-languages which, although they limit the topics which can be studied, help to by-pass numerous measurement problems. Charles Osgood has been most intimately associated with attempts to develop such languages [22].

The third dimension which was mentioned—that is, the need for greater conceptual and linguistic sophistication—has a number of components. At the core of many of them, as with sampling, is poor workmanship and lack of trained competence among survey practitioners. This lack of expertness can be seen in research instruments which include questions such as "What was the reason you left your country and came to start work in the plantations; why did you not stay at home?" Even the basic skills of asking the question 'Why?' are rare among overseas researchers. Furthermore, it would seem that much of the criticism against survey research in the developing areas is based on what practitioners in the United States would consider poor representations of the method.

Poorly worded questions are found very frequently in the materials to be used for purposes of secondary analysis. This is especially true for the open-ended questions. Of course, this considerably detracts from the value of these data, for the researcher has no assurance that a question elicits the full range of dimensions implicit in the question, a problem which is further complicated by the typically poor coding schemes developed for categorizing the answers to these questions.

Conceptual and Linguistic Equivalence

Problems of conceptual equivalence are especially troublesome to the comparative researcher, since he will often find that the concept he is working with is not found in the local culture. Researchers have discovered this difficulty with regard to concepts of time, of the future, of distance or height with regard to visual scaling devices, and of a number of concepts which have clear evaluative overtones, such as "table manners." In one recent study, the English word 'aggressive' was used to describe various groups. This created problems in at least one country, since it was later discovered that "aggressive" had to be expressed either with a negative term or a positive one (one which implied pioneer). The positive one was used, which created some confusion on the part of the client.

Considerable knowledge of the local culture and language is needed in order to gain conceptual equivalence, or, as some call it, "functional equivalence." Agencies in the field which are aware of this are becoming increasingly opposed to what some of them refer to as " 'canned questionnaires' sent from the United States." They feel that a client's attempt to preserve the exact form of his questions, especially pre-coded ones, can only lead to major errors. One agency now insists that clients attach a paragraph of explanation or a *rationale* to each question submitted. Once the agency discovers the intention behind a question—that is, the kind of answer which is desired and how the question will be used—it formulates its own version.

This approach deserves further exploration, for it attempts to gain functional equivalence with regard to the information which the researcher wants to elicit rather than with regard to the form of the questions used to elicit this information. (For the latter approach see Almond and Verba's five-nation study.) To attempt to gain functional equivalence in answers may require four questions in one country but only one question in another. While these four questions certainly would add to the value of the information from that single country, obvious difficulties are created for the researcher who wishes to make international comparisons. Not only are different procedures used in gaining the same kind of information, but also, the key terms in the questions are often different. This would occur in studies asking questions about decision-making and authority structures, since the relevant issues and reference groups would be different in different areas [13].

There is general agreement on how the actual translation of the questions should be made. First, the original instrument is translated into the local language, and then another translator independently translates this translated version back into the original. The original and re-translated versions are compared and the discrepancies are clarified.

A fair amount of linguistic resources are required in order to follow these translation procedures in some countries. For example, a national study in the Philippines will require about nine languages; at least nine are required in India; about thirty are necessary in Indonesia; only two would be required for a national study in Canada or Belgium.

Unfortunately, relatively few research agencies have these linguistic resources. The implications of this are suggested by a recent study using a number of language versions which the contractor had prepared and discovered that approximately one-fourth of the translations made for any one language would have led to major biases.

In some areas, no attempt is even made to prepare a translation into the local language. Rather, this is left to bilingual interviewers. This seems to be a fairly common practice in Africa, where many of the languages do not have alphabets. So far as I have been able to discover, some of these African projects do not even decide on common terms for key concepts. Apparently, if the respondent speaks the Western language in which the questions are written, this is the language used in the interview. In other multilingual areas, research agencies interview in the language which the respondent speaks in his home.

Needless to say, the language used in an interview may have important implications for the information elicited, for languages may differ considerably in their richness and expressive quality. These problems arise even in a single-language culture, as shown in the class differences in language behaviour in the United States [18]. Since those who prepare and translate questionnaires are typically from the middle and upper classes, the instruments they produce are likely to be somewhat inappropriate for large segments of the population.

INTERVIEWER BIAS

Clinical Witnesses

It seems that the personal interview—that is, where an interviewer interviews a person in private—is relatively rare in a great many countries. For example, it has been estimated by some of my informants that at least 50 percent of the European interviews are conducted in the presence of third parties, whereas in many areas of the developing countries —for example, in non-urban Pakistan—almost all interviews are conducted in the presence of other people. Some researchers have referred to these other people as "clinical witnesses."

The implications of these third parties for the data which are obtained seem to depend on a number of factors, including the content of the question, the status characteristics of the third parties, and the general cultural rules defining interpersonal relations. Reports by people working in the field suggest that the "third-party" effect is considerable in societies characterized by sharp status and authority cleavages. In part, this is because the most important people are often interviewed first.[7] Field workers report that after each answer given by the first interviewed, the assembled crowd nods its approval, saying that the answer also represents the views of others. Not only does this create or help crystallize consensus, it also often produces resistance to being interviewed on the part of others.

As with many other topics previously mentioned, third parties sometimes have a mixed effect. For example, in studies seeking information rather than attitudes, third parties may help keep the respondent honest and also help him to remember the requested information. In other instances, especially with women and younger people, respondents may refuse to be interviewed unless a third person is present. It is common practice in many areas at least to obtain the permission of a third party —the local headman—before commencing field work.

These various examples raise general issues related to sponsorship and privacy in conducting interviews. If consent of local leaders is required, then respondents are likely to feel that the leaders also are sponsoring the study, thereby affecting the respondents' willingness to express certain feelings, especially "minority" or deviant feelings. A whole range of issues needs to be studied with reference to the other topic, privacy. Certainly, if attempts to secure privacy are associated with witchcraft, as they evidently are in some places, then a public interview is the only means by which information can be obtained. Also, if being asked for one's private opinion gives a respondent prestige in the local community, to deny him the privilege of being questioned in public may seriously reduce the likelihood that he will be willing to be interviewed.

Several procedures have been developed to avoid the assumed consequences of third parties. For example, for some questions the respondent is asked to cast a ballot rather than to give an oral reply. This procedure could possibly reduce biases in politically oriented studies; for example, the presence of third parties in Italy may have played a signifi-

[7] Respondents naturally have difficulty sometimes in understanding why they have been singled out to be interviewed. According to the local status and value scales, the community leaders feel that they "deserve" to be interviewed, and although the research team may not wish to waste resources in doing this, it is sometimes necessary to interview the local élite purely for public relations purposes.

cant role in the reticence reported by Almond and Verba. A second and administratively popular approach is to use teams of interviewers. The team saturates a village so that the field work is completed in a very short time [4, 8, 11]. The third approach, which is a more recent development, is to use resident interviewers. These interviewers, like the traditional ethnographer, live in the local community for a fairly long period of time. Some researchers, especially those who have worked in south-east Asia, claim that this is the only technique which can assure complete and un-biased information. The resident interviewer acquires knowledge and contacts to permit him to check on the information he receives; he recognizes errors and inconsistencies which can then be quickly clarified; he may be able to eliminate the recall problem; and by being a member of the community, he is able to overcome the natives' resistance to giving truthful information to outsiders. On the other hand, the use of resident interviewers and field-work procedures which assign a very large area to only one or two interviewers limit the number of sampling points which can be used and may, therefore, decrease the representativeness of the sample. Since interviewing assignments cannot be randomized, the entire information for a single sampling point is the product of one man's biases; also, spending long periods of time in one area may involve the field worker in community problems and provide him with so much "inside" information and so many personal contacts that his respondents refuse to provide him with information because they fear it will not be kept confidential. For larger studies, the period in the field is lengthened and the costs of the study are increased. Unless the field worker is a native of the region he is studying, it may require a prohibitively long time in residence before he is able to reap the benefits presumably associated with being a resident interviewer; and, it is not clear that this is the best procedure for obtaining many kinds of information. One study of American Indian tribes found that it is sometimes easier for an outsider to obtain certain information if the status of the information-seeking person is associated with what outsiders do [19]. Narrolls' study of the relationship between the length of time anthropologists spend in the field and the information they obtain indicates that length may not be important for some issues and that for other issues a very long period in the field is required [24]. Also, leaving a full-time interviewer relatively unsupervised may not be the best way to control cheating, although to disrupt a man's life by keeping him continually on the move may also create problems.

In any event, the comparative researcher will discover that field staffs and field-work procedures are organized very differently, often with very different implications for the quality and completeness of the information which is obtained.

Courtesy Bias

The second type of interviewer bias has been referred to as "courtesy" or "hospitality bias," a bias which seems to be especially common in Asia, everywhere from Japan to Turkey [13, 14]. Courtesy bias means that the respondent provides information which he feels will please the interviewer. He behaves this way because the norms governing interpersonal relations in general and relations with upper-class strangers in specific call for him to do so. However, courtesy bias might also be given a broader meaning, and be taken to refer also to respondents who provide information which they feel a person of their status in their country should give. This would include "ideological biases," as among refugees who exaggerate their opposition to their home country's regime; or, as in the discussion of culturally sensitive topics, it may inhibit respondents from admitting they voted for certain parties or exposed themselves to certain media channels.

There is some indication that the direction of the courtesy bias is different in different countries. For example, the humility of the Japanese is said to lead them to under-evaluate their own achievements, class positions, and the like. On the other hand, some researchers in the Middle East claim that respondents there tend to exaggerate their achievements, class position, knowledge of the world, and extent to which they are modern rather than traditional. In practical terms, this means that the type of question-wording appropriate to Western countries would be inappropriate to Japan, and what is appropriate in Japan and the West would be inappropriate in Turkey or Iran.

Some of the effects of the courtesy bias can be reduced by concealing the sponsorship of the study, by more effective training of interviewers, and by more careful wording of questions. With regard to wording, it is advisable to avoid the use of "moral" words which require either the respondent or the interviewer to pass judgement on the other. Above all, it is important to maximize the ease of giving a socially unacceptable answer, such as might be done through the standard practice of opening the question with "Lots of people feel this way . . . and lots of people feel the other way. Which direction do you lean toward in . . . ." Leading questions also might be appropriate here.

Perhaps courtesy bias is easier to control than its opposite, which might be called the "sucker bias." Sucker bias is found in areas where, according to Keesing in a study of élite communications in Samoa, all outsiders are considered fair game for deception [16].

Interviewer-Respondent Status Congruency

The third type of bias arises from communication obstacles created by the relative status characteristics of interviewers and their respondents. This interaction perspective of social relations has been studied in the United States with respect to age, sex, race, and class, and other characteristics. While these characteristics are important in the United States, they are likely to be critical in other countries. This is because the status of the interviewer is not well known (not institutionalized), which means that other ancillary status factors tend to structure the interviewer-interviewee relationship. These other status factors tend to be more significant than in the United States, since they also tend to maximize the before-mentioned courtesy bias.

In some countries, for example, interviewers are often considered as government employees, and since the local population does not readily differentiate policemen from tax collectors from political party workers, the interviewer has considerable difficulty in socializing the respondent into a new type of questioner-answerer relationship. In these situations, respondents are reported to be very reluctant to provide interviewers with accurate information. This may be one (but only a minor) reason why economic surveys often find that respondents exaggerate expenditures and under-report income, wealth, and savings. To overcome these suspicions, non-commercial research groups often seek an academic affiliation or sponsorship, denying any direct government connexion with their activities. Unfortunately, owing to the lack of local personnel, the field-work staff are often required to rely on government employees—not only on teachers but, as in some Asian countries, also on "moonlighting" secret police.

It is often very difficult to hide the political nature of many studies. For example, a poll in Latin America asking numerous questions about De Gaulle's visit, a German poll in Asia or Latin America asking a long list of questions about images of Germany, a poll in Africa regarding British radio programmes and the British Government, a poll in South-East Asia regarding views of Japan, or polls in various parts of the world regarding American prestige and foreign policy: all these research projects which never eventuate in scholarly publications may very likely raise questions in the minds of educated respondents regarding the purpose behind the studies in which they are asked to co-operate. A growing number of other countries conduct polls of their citizens, further adding to the suspicions which some groups no doubt have about survey research.[8]

Research agencies in many countries recruit their interviewers from among college students, which means that they come from middle- and upper-class backgrounds, and are themselves educated people. This type of interviewer creates a communication problem, since there are certain traditional ways in which members of different classes interact. For example, custom demands that lower-class persons use polite forms of address, be humble, and not express themselves freely to members of the upper classes. Recognizing this, some researchers have questioned whether the equalitarian-oriented interviewing techniques used in the West are appropriate in societies which have sharp status and authority cleavages. Respondents also might be confused if a non-native associated with the former colonial ruling group were not demanding in his questioning.

At the present time there is considerable variation in the composition of field staffs in the developing nations. In Japan, many agencies rely almost entirely on students; in the Philippines, students are used only rarely; one Indian agency has a staff composed primarily of full-time male interviewers, whereas another Indian agency relies primarily on part-time female interviewers; some agencies use only high school graduates, since they show less fear and moral repulsion with regard to interviewing members of the lower class, whereas others rely primarily on college graduates. It is very difficult to assess how well trained these interviewers are and how valid is the information that they collect. However, it is fairly clear that different kinds of interviewers are able to obtain different kinds of information; and, furthermore, it would seem that the different compositions of research agencies is yet another factor reducing the comparability of materials collected for cross-national studies.

Considerable research is needed on a whole range of issues related to biases arising from the interviewer-respondent relationship. Such studies should be of general interest to the social scientist, especially to the sociologist, since they touch on key issues of social relations. Research could be conducted on procedures most appropriate to different phases of the interview: the initiation, structuring, and terminating the interviewer-respondent relationship. Data on the relative effectiveness of different interviewing approaches with different respondent-interviewer combinations are also needed. Perhaps middle-class interviewers should alter their tactics radically, using equalitarian techniques with the upper class and authoritarian techniques with the lower class.

[8]It has been reported that some respondents refuse to talk unless findings are made known to the government. That is, the respondents see the interviewing situation as an opportunity to express an opinion and to influence governmental policy.

Almost any project can include information which can be used for methodological purposes. For example, future projects could obtain information on the status features of their interviewers, just as they do for their respondents, thereby making it possible to explore the apparent biases arising from different interviewer-respondent status combinations. In short, efforts are needed to define and measure interviewer effectiveness, as well as the relative effectiveness of different interviewing techniques when used in social relations which vary according to the status characteristics of the interviewer and respondent.

BIBLIOGRAPHY

1. ABRAMS, PHILIP. 'The production of survey data in Britain'. Paper delivered to Second Conference on Data Archives in the Social Sciences, Paris, 28 to 30 September 1964.

2. ALMOND, GABRIEL A.; VERBA, SIDNEY. *The civic culture*, Princeton, N.J., Princeton University Press, 1963, Chapter 2.

3. BACK, KURT W. *Slums, projects, and people*, Durham, N.C., Duke University Press, 1962.

4. BACK, KURT W.; STYCOS, J. MAYONE. *The survey under unusual conditions: a Jamaica human fertility investigation*. Monograph no. 1, 1959, published by the Society for Applied Anthropology.

5. BARBOUR, K. M.; PROTHERO, R. M. (eds.). *Essays on African population*, London, Routledge and Keegan Paul, 1961.

6. CONVERSE, PHILIP E. 'The availability and quality of survey data in archives within the United States'. Paper delivered to the International Conference on the Use of Quantitative, Political, Social, and Cultural Data in Cross-National Comparisons, held at Yale University, September 1963.

7. CONVERSE, PHILIP E. New dimensions of meaning for cross-section sample surveys in politics, *Int. Soc. Sci. J.*, vol. 16, 1964, p. 19–34.

8. FINK, RAYMOND. Interviewer training and supervision in a survey of Laos, *Int. Soc. Sci. J.*, vol. 15, 1963, p. 21–34.

9. FORTES, MEYER. A demographic field study in Ashanti, in: Frank Lorimer (ed.), *Culture and human fertility*, Paris, Unesco, 1954, p. 255–324.

10. FREEDMAN, RONALD. The sociology of human fertility: a trend report and bibliography, *Current Sociology*, vols. 10–11, no. 2, 1961–62.

11. FREY, FRED W. Surveying peasant attitudes in Turkey, *Public Opinion Quarterly*, vol. 27, 1963, p. 335–55.

12. HOFFMAN, MICHAEL. Research on opinions and attitudes in West Africa, *Int. Soc. Sci. J.*, vol. 15, 1963, p. 59–69.

13. HOLLSTEINER, MARY R. *The dynamics of power in a Philippine municipality*, Quezon, Community Development Research Council, University of the Philippines, 1963.

14. JONES, EMILY L. The courtesy bias in south-east Asian surveys, *Int. Soc. Sci. J.*, vol. 15, 1963, p. 70–6.

15. KAPFERER, CLODWIG. The use of sample surveys by OECD, *Int. Soc. Sci. J.*, vol. 16, 1964, p. 63–9.

16. KEESING, FELIX M.; KEESING, MARIE M. *Elite communications in Samoa, a study of leadership*, Stanford, Stanford University Press, 1956.

17. KISER, CLYDE V. (ed.). *Research in family planning*, Princeton, N.J., Princeton University Press, 1962.

18. LABOV, WILLIAM. Phonological correlates of social stratification, *American Anthropologist*, vol. 66, December 1964, Part 2, p. 164–76.

19. LANG, GOTTFRIED O.; KUNSTADTER, PETER. Survey research on the Uintah and Ouray Ute reservation, *American Anthropologist*, vol. 59, June 1957, p. 527–31.

20. LEACH, E. R. An anthropologist's reflections on a social survey, *The Ceylon Journal of Historical and Social Studies*, vol. 1, January 1958, p. 9–20.

21. LERNER, DANIEL. *Passing of traditional society*, New York: The Free Press of Glencoe, 1958.

22. MACLAY, HOWARD; WARE, EDWARD. Cross-cultural use of the semantic differential, *Behavioral Science*, vol. 6, July 1961 p. 186–90.

23. MERRITT, RICHARD L. *Symbols of American community*, forthcoming.

24. NAROLL, RAOUL. *Data quality control*, N.Y.: Free Press of Glencoe, 1962.

25. NEALE, WALTER C. The limitations of Indian village survey data, *Journal of Asian Studies*, vol. 17, May 1958, p. 383–402.

26. PROTHRO, EDWIN CAREY. *Child rearing in Lebanon*, Harvard Middle Eastern Monographs 8, Cambridge, Cambridge University Press, 1961.

27. RUSSETT, BRUCE; ALKER, HAYWARD R.; DEUTSCH, KARL W.; LASSWELL, HAROLD B. *World handbook of political and social indicators*, New Haven, Yale University Press, 1964.

28. WUELKER, GABRIELE. Questionnaires in Asia, *Int. Soc. Sci. J.*, vol. 15, 1963, p. 35–47.

11

Surveying Peasant Attitudes in Turkey

FREDERICK W. FREY

It is perhaps only appropriate that in developing countries survey research is itself developing. To make the survey results beneficial to the developing country, survey researchers must overcome difficult problems of organization, field work, untranslatable words, unfamiliarity of the population with some of the principal concepts employed in opinion research, and cooperation with the government. Here is a fine example, reported for the benefit of researchers everywhere, of a survey that went a long way toward overcoming these obstacles.

Policy maker and scholar alike are becoming increasingly aware of the vital attitudinal components in the process of "modernization" or "development." One community cuts the costs of school construction in half by getting voluntary participation in building activities, while another apparently similar community is unable to mount the same effort. In two nearby villages, one evinces great internal "demonstration effect" from the introduction of a new crop or novel tool, while in the counterpart village the innovation "doesn't take." In one region masses of people resist birth control, subsidize the shaman, shun the schoolteacher, suspect governmental offers of aid, and chafe under the mildest discipline of modern institutions, while seemingly similar masses in a comparable region do exactly the opposite. To understand such situations and alter them to advantage the policy maker urgently needs information about the relevant attitudes of the citizens of his concern. He also needs better theories about the relationships between one attitude and another, between attitudes and behavior, and between behavior and social organiza-

Reprinted from Frederick W. Frey, "Surveying Peasant Attitudes in Turkey," *Public Opinion Quarterly*, 1963, 27, no. 3, pp. 335–355. Reprinted by permission of the publisher and the author.

The author wishes to express his gratitude to Herbert Hyman, Ithiel de Sola Pool, Daniel Lerner, and Sloan Wayland, all of whom read the first draft of this paper.

tion. Consequently, his demand for studies of the social and political aspects of economic development is rapidly intensifying.

To secure such information, even in the most remote lands, the policy makers of the developing society (or those aiding it) have increasingly been turning to the social scientist—to the survey researcher in particular. Not occasionally, however, the help that he can readily offer is limited compared to what he can provide in the modern societies where his techniques were created and to which they presently are best adapted. In the underdeveloped world the difficulties in obtaining desired information are obviously great, and the difficulties in its interpretation are compounded by the dearth of supporting and background materials. As a result, there appears to be an especial need for those who have confronted interesting problems of survey design and execution in emerging nations to share their experiences, insights, and methods with others in the field. The present research report, acting on that principle, recounts some of the approaches employed by the author and his colleagues in carrying out during the past year a very large national survey of many important attitudes of the Turkish peasantry. Indeed, the reported research effort may well be the first intensive attitudinal survey, on a national scale, of the peasantry of any major emerging society.[1]

HISTORY AND SPONSORSHIP

A brief comment on the history of the project is perhaps useful, for it reveals something of the growth pattern of survey research in one de-

[1] The survey to be described was officially christened the Rural Development Research Project by the U.S. Agency for International Development. Elsewhere it has been styled the "Turkish Peasant (or Village) Survey." The present author first proposed the project to the Turkish government and AID in August 1961, strongly helped and encouraged by Dr. George W. Angell, Jr., and Dr. Paul Leubke, then of the AID Mission in Ankara. It is a simple truth and gratifying duty to state that without the imaginative, persistent, and venturesome support of both these men the survey would never have materialized.

The team of consultants created to guide the research effort consisted of Professors Herbert Hyman and Sloan Wayland of Columbia University and Professors Daniel Lerner and Ithiel de Sola Pool of M.I.T. The author was chief of the consultant party. The profound and pervasive contributions of Hyman, Wayland, Lerner, and Pool to nearly every facet of the investigation far exceed the possibilities of brief recapitulation here. Moreover, in addition to their expertise, the project profited in many ways from the great personal good will and esteem that these consultants had established in Turkey.

Another crucial figure in the main cast of characters was Dr. Sefik Uysal of the Research and Measurement Bureau of the Turkish Ministry of Education. Dr. Uysal performed with skill and devotion the extremely difficult role of the immediate Project Director. The Research and Measurement Bureau, advised by Dr. Angell and headed by Mr. Ibrahim Yurt, was the agency that carried out the project, handling innumerable difficult problems with great ability and energy in the process. Without its excellent facilities and staff to bear major responsibility for the effort, the survey might have been still-born.

veloping nation. The essential trend has been from small-scale, *ad hoc,* foreign-sponsored, and institutionally focused investigations to large-scale, continuing, domestically sponsored, and comprehensive researches. The milestones passed en route to the present study reveal this trend. In 1950, the Bureau of Applied Social Research at Columbia University commenced the series of studies of communications behavior in the Middle East that have been so ably reported in Lerner's *The Passing of Traditional Society.*[2] In Turkey some 300 interviews were obtained from urban and rural Turks resident in Istanbul, Ankara, and Izmir Provinces, sites of the country's three largest cities. Then, in 1957–1958, while Herbert Hyman of Columbia was a Visiting Professor at the Political Sciences Faculty of Ankara University, he and his associates carried out a comparative survey of the values of college students at the Political Sciences Faculty and at Robert College in Istanbul.[3] Building on this base, in 1959 the present author and his co-workers, with the cooperation of the Turkish Ministry of Education, proceeded to execute a national sample survey of the basic value systems of students in Turkey's public high schools (lycée-level schools).[4] This seems to have been the first national attitudinal survey performed in Turkey.

The success of these more limited but increasingly ambitious ventures led us to believe that it was possible to tackle an attitudinal study of the vital core of Turkish society—its peasant mass. More than two of every three Turks are villagers living in rural communities of 2,000 or less population. The nation is currently in the anxious "second stage" of its contemporary revolution; having largely accomplished the modernization of elite elements, it is attempting to bring its peasantry into active social and political participation on supra-village levels. Information about peasant attitudes and conditions of life—more profound than that obtained by the national census and more general than that garnered from the few good anthropological studies—is urgently required. Though the problems of a national attitudinal survey of the Turkish peasantry were numerous and recalcitrant, both the potential value of the results and the achievements of previous surveys argued for the attempt.

Support for the projected study of Turkish villagers was obtained

[2]Daniel Lerner, *The Passing of Traditional Society*, Glencoe, Ill.: Free Press, 1958.

[3]Herbert H. Hyman, Arif Payaslioglu, and Frederick W. Frey, "The Values of Turkish College Youth," *Public Opinion Quarterly*, Vol. 22, 1958, pp. 275–291.

[4]The final analysis and reporting of this survey carried out by Frederick W. Frey, George W. Angell, Jr., and Abdurrahman S. Sanay is currently in progress. A few political findings are presented in Frederick W. Frey, "Education and Political Development in Turkey," in Robert E. Ward and Dankwart A. Rustow, editors, *Turkey and Japan: A Comparative Study of Modernization*, Princeton, Princeton University Press, forthcoming. Copies of the instrument used will be forwarded on request to the author.

jointly from the government of Turkey and from the U.S. Agency for International Development.[5] About four-fifths of the total cost of the enterprise, which came to roughly $100,000, was borne by the Turkish government and the remaining fifth was financed by AID. The actual basis for the allocation of expenses was that AID furnished the team of United States consultants, provided certain data-processing materials, and covered part of the cost of statistical services.[6] All other expenses, particularly payment of interviewers, coders, and administrators, and the costs of instrument preparation and publication, were met by the Turkish government. The entire effort proceeded with near-exemplary cooperation on both sides—cooperation that was greatly facilitated by the prior smaller-scale survey experience that many of the key Turkish people had obtained in the course of the previously listed research efforts.

One further point regarding sponsorship may be of some interest. In any national survey of this scope there are bound to be a thousand contacts with various officials and organizations in the host country. This study was no exception. There was a dramatic bandit scare in several eastern provinces while the interviewers were in the field, stimulating one apprehensive governor to insist that gendarmes accompany our interviewing team into the villages (a service we were adamant in refusing). In another case, a county prefect (*kaymakam*), despite our explicit admonitions to the contrary, alerted the peasants in the selected village of his county to the fact that our team was coming. Once or twice local police raised questions about the operation even after being shown the elaborately official credentials with which we had armed our groups for just such emergencies. Queries were received from other sectors of the central government despite our advance notices of what we were about. Two minatory and misleading articles appeared in the popular press. Finally, we were constantly aware of the sensitive and possibly volatile character of the investigation, especially if a few unscrupulous individuals should espy a chance for advantage through attacking it.

[5]Though they were less directly involved in the details of the survey, the support of several other persons and agencies was crucial for the project. The Program Office of the AID Mission in Ankara, directed by Alexis Lachmann, spotted the proposal, saw the possibilities, and stuck its neck out to push it through official United States governmental channels. On the Turkish side, as will be explained in more detail, the Social Planning Division of the State Planning Organization, headed first by Dr. Necat Erder and then by Dr. Evner Ergot, was an invaluable source of strength and counsel. Finally, Dr. William Wrinkle, Chief of the Education Section of AID in Ankara, ably helped the enterprise over several crises.

[6]We are indebted to Milton Lieberman and Joel Tucker, statisticians working with AID in Ankara, for useful comments on the sample design. Tucker, in particular, was of great service in devising the proportionate sampling scheme.

To forestall untoward developments, to protect ourselves against a swarm of intrusions during our time of strenuous technical activity, and to summon expertise greater than ours in dealing with delicate political situations, we followed a pre-planned strategy of getting a well-located and powerful Turkish governmental agency to act as our official liaison and buffer in all such matters. We were extremely fortunate in having the Turkish State Planning Organization assume this burden and handle it masterfully, leaving our nascent survey organization generally free to concentrate on the demanding technical tasks of the research. Early attention to this inevitable political side of large-scale survey research in most emerging nations often can prevent the bitter and frustrating embroilments that seem always to erupt when other demands are most pressing.

SAMPLING

The basic population in which we were interested was, as has been said, the Turkish peasantry—the "villagers" (*köylüler*), as they are called in Turkish. Adopting the census definition of a "village," we desired a sample of all Turks sixteen years of age or over resident in legal communities of under 2,000 persons.[7] Itinerants, the institutionalized (including those in miltary service), and those mentally or physically incapable of responding to an interview were excluded from the defined population.

The fundamental sampling unit was to be the individual villager, or peasant, and not the family or the household head. Even so, the study was constructed so that we would emerge with three separate samples rather than merely the one sample of the peasantry. Our teams traveled to 458 different villages, completing in each case a separate schedule of information about the village as a whole, thus giving us, after some statistical adjustments, comprehensive data on a sample of Turkish *villages*. Moreover, in addition to the designated set of interviews with the sample of *villagers* in each of these villages, our teams also were instructed to obtain a series of *elite* interviews in every sampled village. These additional interviews were four: with the village head man (*muhtar*), with the village priest (*hoca* or *imam*), and with the legal wife of each, regardless of whether such individuals turned up in the regular sample. Thus, the investigation was constructed so as to yield (1) a regular sample of Turkish peasants, (2) an elite sample of certain formal village leaders and their spouses, and (3) a sample of the village communities of the country.

[7] The only legal communities of less than 20,000 persons that would not be included in our defined population would be those extremely few places that had become county seats (*kaza* or *ilçe merkezleri*).

The findings on the two added samples were obtained at a very low marginal cost and markedly increased analytic opportunities.

The sampling design was that of a two-stage cluster sample, with the first stage unit being villages and the second stage unit being villagers. We secured the village information blanks of the just-completed 1960 national population census from the Turkish General Directorate of Statistics in return for punching those data onto IBM cards. This provided us with a frame listing all 35,000 villages of the country along with the location and population of every listed community. Three bases of stratification were simultaneously applied to these villages: regional location, proximity to an urban center, and size. Actually, the first two criteria of stratification—region and urban proximity—produced fourteen strata when combined. Then, village size was taken into account in the fullest way possible by giving each village a probability of entering the sample proportionate to its size. In addition to accuracy, a cogent reason for using a proportionate sampling scheme was that we wanted to have an approximately constant "take" in each village visited, i.e., a constant number of interviews. This was necessary to ease administration and to enable us to structure the operation in such a way that our teams could go into a village and complete their assignment in the course of a single day, thereby greatly reducing the hazard of interrespondent contamination in these "little communities" of Anatolia. It served as well to simplify problems of housing and maintenance for the interviewers.

The desired sample size was deliberately set quite large—approximately 7,000 respondents in the regular sample plus another 1,500 in the elite sample. Behind this tactic was the realization that internal subgroup analysis was to be of prime importance. Complex, disproportionate sampling from many strata so as to yield enough crucial subgroups was impossible because of insufficient prior information about many aspects of the population and because we were not in a position at the beginning to identify with full confidence all the crucial groupings. Since the basic focus was to be the attitudinal modernization of a largely traditional population, it was clear that a good deal of deviant case analysis would be required. To maximize the opportunities for this type of analysis in a situation of considerable theoretical and practical uncertainty, a large sample seemed essential.

The over-all sample of villages was randomly divided into two *independent subsamples*. Several considerations urged this procedure even though it slightly increased travel costs. Probably the paramount reason was again our concern regarding the political sensitivity of the enterprise. It was always possible that some untoward event could occur during the two months we would be in the field and terminate the entire project. By establishing two independent subsamples and completing the first before commencing the second, we reduced the risk of such a calamity by 50 percent (assuming a probability of such an occurrence that was uniform through time). Once the first month of field operations was completed we would have obtained a satisfactory sample of well over three thousand interviews and could anticipate valuable results even if an interruption should befall us in the second month.

Apart from this protection against a premature interruption of the survey, the division of the over-all sample into two equal and independent subsamples also provided several other advantages. It gave us a useful and economical estimate of variance. It provided all concerned in the project with a welcome intermediate goal which acted, both psychologically and operationally, to reduce the burden of such a large-scale venture. And it allowed us to produce reliable early results, based on the first subsample, that proved to be of great use to the policy makers supporting the project in their justifications of it before more skeptical colleagues and to us, as the directors of the survey, in getting a head start in laying out the detailed agenda for analysis. (In fact, the division into subsamples was even useful in dividing our computer operation into two parts of less than five minutes' running time each, thereby giving us more IBM 7090 time for less money.)[8]

The greatest sampling risk was that of the second-stage procedure. Initially, we were quite confident that we could sample the *villages* effectively. The outstanding problem was obtaining the second-stage sampling frame—the list of adult *villagers* resident in each of the 458 selected villages. No adequate listing of individual villagers corresponding to our defined population existed for all the villages in our sample, nor was it possible for us to construct such lists in advance. Hence, we relied on our ability to have our interviewing teams themselves generate the requisite second-stage sampling frame in the field on their arrival in any designated village. Much of our planning revolved about this calculated risk of the on-the-spot, team-generated second-stage sampling frame. Without an acceptable solution to this problem the whole enterprise would have been impossible.

Several factors influenced our thinking on this matter. First, we knew of three types of lists of villagers that were legally supposed to be maintained for each village in the land. One was a list of all adults over twenty-two years of age—the list of eligible voters. The second and third were listings of the entire population of each village, to be kept by the

[8]The data processing is being done at the Computation Center of the Massachusetts Institute of Technology, to whose personnel we are grateful for much special effort and useful advice.

nearest Vital Statistics branch of the central government and by the village head men. Detailed preliminary investigation indicated that the last two lists were frequently not kept at all or were in very haphazard condition. The voting lists were better maintained but were sometimes not available to us in time, for a wild variety of reasons. Moreover, they did not include the sixteen- to twenty-two-year-old age group, which we definitely wanted in our sample.

In any event, we secured wherever possible any or all of the three aforementioned lists and provided our teams with these before they visited the villages. In about 80 to 90 percent of the cases the teams were thus able to use previously furnished lists as a base and concentrate first on deletions from those lists (those dead, moved, or incapacitated since the list's preparation, errors, duplicate citations, etc.) and then on additions to the lists (those come of age, moved into the village, previously omitted, in a desired group not covered by the list, etc.). This information was obtained by going over the lists, name by name, with the village head man, the council of elders, and other knowledgeable villagers. Our confidence in this procedure increased when we discovered, not surprisingly, that the lists in the larger villages were the more complete and that in the smaller villages, where the lists were more likely to be faulty, every adult usually knew all other adults in the village. In fact, in the entire sample, 94 percent of the males reported knowing everyone else in their villages, and village leaders proved to be especially well-informed in this respect.

In about 10 percent of the villages, the teams had to prepare a complete new list—no list of any kind could be obtained in advance. The median-sized village in Turkey has approximately 260 persons aged sixteen or over. The villages without lists were almost invariably smaller than this. In such cases the team leader and his assistant sat down with the *muhtar*, the council of elders, and anyone else who was likely to prove helpful and prepared the appropriate list of adult villagers, prodding the memories of the respondents (as instructed) by pointing to houses and asking about occupants, by inquiring after relatives of those named, by asking after the young people (sixteen to nineteen) and the aged, by mentioning the possibility of outlying domiciles (most villages are tightly clustered, except in coastal areas), and so on. The teams were also greatly aided in this task by knowing in advance the census estimate of the total population of the village and that about 54 percent of that total population, on the whole, was likely to be sixteen years of age or over.[9]

[9]The timing of interviewer activities on arrival in the village worked out quite neatly. The team leader and one male team member, who acted as his assistant, con-

On completion of the listing, the team leader numbered the set of names obtained and then, using a random starting point and an interval that we had computed in advance on the basis of census information, drew the sample of respondents for the instant village.[10] Team leaders were cautioned about avoidance of trend and periodicity in the frame and were observed carefully during three major pre-tests to be sure of their comprehension of the entire process. Full written instructions as to sampling procedure were furnished to all team leaders. All other team members were also instructed in the sampling procedure, both as a check on the leader and as a form of personnel insurance should a team leader become incapacitated. Moreover, a detailed report form listing such things as callbacks, terminations, substitutions, interviewer assignments, etc., was completed by the team leader for each village and submitted to headquarters with the sampling frame and finished interview schedules for each village visited. Every list and report form from each village was carefully checked by the author as it came into the survey headquarters. Listing mistakes and other errors in executing the sampling were practically nil—just a handful of cases of failure to substitute when substitution was desirable.[11]

---

sulted the *muhtar* and the council of elders and prepared the sampling frame. While the *muhtar* was thus occupied, one of the female interviewers questioned the *muhtar's* wife, conveniently assured of noninterference from that matron's otherwise-occupied husband. The remaining male and female interviewers sought out the *imam* and his wife and interviewed them separately but simultaneously, again minimizing the possibilities of interspouse interference among this elite group. When these interviews (with respondents who could be identified before the village sample had been prepared) were completed, the interviewers returned to the team leader, who by that time had their regular sample assignments ready for them. Then, while the ordinary team members proceeded with their regular interviews, the team leader personally interviewed the *muhtar*, with whom he had already established considerable rapport during the list preparation, and also completed a schedule of ecological information about the village.

[10]The central computation of the sampling intervals and random starting points was simply another control over interviewer performance. We could easily have had the team leader himself compute the appropriate interval for use in the given village and select his own random starting point. In fact, we successfully employed such a procedure on two of the major pre-tests. In the actual field operation we chose to ensure a slight reduction in the risk of a sampling mistake by giving starting points and intervals to the team leaders even though the price of this was a very slight unwanted fluctuation in the constant "take" per village.

[11]Substitutions, according to a strictly prescribed rule, were permitted only in the rare cases when a person clearly outside the defined population had inadvertently entered the sample. For example, if an interviewer found, on locating the respondent, that he was deaf or mute and physically incapable of responding to the instrument, but had not been properly excluded from the list on this basis, the interviewer would consult the team leader and a substitution would be required. This occurred, as we have said, only rarely, and the few errors that did emerge in this procedure all were cases of failure to substitute rather than of faulty substitution.

No perfect check on the accuracy of this second-stage sampling frame is available, but several partially confirmatory procedures, both general and particular, were employed in addition to those just described. First of all, the obtained listings were checked against those predicted on the basis of the 1960 census returns. According to the 1960 census, we should have secured an average of sixteen desired respondents per village. However, the census estimate was based upon a defined population somewhat larger than ours in that it included soldiers, those physically or mentally incapable of being interviewed, transients, etc. We obtained an average of 15.3, which, considering everything, was extremely close to the census figure.

Second, several spot checks of the sampling procedure in particular villages also indicated a very low level of error, as did repeated conversations with assorted team members conducted individually while the operation was in the field. Third, the marginals already drawn from the study very closely match the relevant census and other statistical materials that exist. Hence, all in all, the placing of considerable confidence in the sampling procedure seems warranted. Over all, 94.8 percent of the desired sample was successfully interviewed, the refusal rate being especially low—less than 1 percent. Ninety percent of the interviews were obtained on the first visit and 10 percent on callbacks. The lack of geographical mobility in a relatively traditional population can be an important compensatory asset to survey research in developing countries.

The final aspect of the sampling that is of interest is that an *interpenetrating* sampling procedure was employed within each village. Since we were conducting a survey under novel and arduous conditions with previously inexperienced interviewers, we desired some special verifications of interviewer performance. One of these checks was obtained by assigning respondents to interviewers in a random fashion so that between-interviewer variations in results, beyond calculable chance expectations, would alert us to the possibility of faulty interviewer performance. Failure to find such extreme differences was another factor increasing our confidence in the findings.[12]

On the whole, the sampling design and procedures developed for use among the village population of Turkey—a country that lacked any previously established survey organization (other than a national census)—seem to have proved effective. It is indubitably true that certain fortuitous circumstances existed in Turkey and that in a number of developing countries this brand of research is manifestly impossible at the present time: there had been a recent and reasonably accurate census in

[12]The mode of interpenetration of course had to take account of the bounds of sex and region that delimited an interviewer's activity.

Turkey; the State Planning Organization was sympathetic and strategically located; a cadre of village teachers suitable for use as interviewers existed; and so on. However, *some* fortuitous circumstances of this type are to be found in most emerging nations, and the Turkish case presented its share of special difficulties as well as advantages (rough terrain, bandits, political sensitivity, zones of military security, etc.). Even more important, alternative approaches to adjust for the lack of the specific advantages that existed in the Turkish case can often be developed with ingenuity and perseverance. Though there may be no census, the Ministry of the Interior or some other ministry may well have a list of the nation's villages. If not, such a list can often be garnered by visiting each of the provincial capitals or contacting each county seat. No State Planning Organization may exist, but the Ministry of Education or of Agriculture, or some *ad hoc* combination of ministries or other governmental body may well be able to act as an appropriate sponsor. Village teachers may not be available, but organized scouting of rural areas may still yield a sufficient number of suitable interviewer candidates. The essential point we stress is that problems of the sorts described can be anticipated and that satisfactory solutions to these problems would frequently seem to lie in the *types* of action we mention, even though the specifics must be varied according to the situation. There would appear to be many emerging nations around the globe in which procedures analogous to those reported here could be applied with high prospects for success.

THE SURVEY INSTRUMENTS

Just as the sampling plan was designed to furnish three separate samples (of peasants, village elites, and villages), so the survey instruments utilized in the project were of three kinds: (1) a basic interview schedule applicable to all respondents, (2) supplementary interview schedules for each of the four types of elite respondents, and (3) a "village information sheet" (completed by the leader of the interviewing team) furnishing important ecological data about the village as a whole.

The basic schedule administered to every respondent was developed in order to ensure a broad and fundamental level of comparability among all groups sampled. Other interests that were specific to the elite subgroups were handled through the use of supplementary schedules.

The village information sheet had several special purposes in addition to the obvious one of yielding general information about a sample of Turkish villages. Among other things, it was arranged so as to provide independent, summary village information on many matters concerning which we had *also queried our individual respondents* (e.g., educational level, radio ownership, mosque attendance, etc.). Thus, besides granting the opportunity for a rough and gross check upon the accuracy of respondent reports, this device permits us, for example, to distinguish between the radio owner in a community of very few radios and the radio owner in a village with a substantial number of radios, or between illiterate men in villages of high and low literacy. In more general terms, since the extensive ecological information regarding his village was punched onto each respondent's set of data cards, one gets the valuable and all too rare opportunity to examine, in considerable detail, different types of peasants located *in different, independently ascertained, types of community settings.*

Finally, considering our approximately sixteen respondents from each of the 458 villages in the sample as a small, but random, representation of opinion in that village, and exploiting the large number of villages covered, the way is opened to a promising analysis of the conditions under which various types of intra-village agreement and disagreement are to be found.

The basic interview schedule that was forged after weeks of discussions (and even thought) can best be labeled an omnibus instrument. This is not simply a euphemism for the fact that "there is something in it for everybody." Since formulations of their interests were solicited from some twenty-eight different Turkish agencies, from more than a dozen AID sections, and from eight or ten other organizations, and since our own theoretical hypotheses concerning development were also supposed to occupy a prominent portion of the instrument, a torrent of suggested topics and questions inundated us at the start. Under scrutiny, however, many of these proposals were seen to coincide, overlap, or, at least, be mutually supportive. Condensation of the many desired topics of inquiry into eight basic areas proved feasible and rewarding. These areas, which consequently became "sections" of the basic interviewing schedule, were: communications, personal background, attitudes toward development, other relevant psychological traits, socialization, position in and conception of the environing social structure, politicization, and religiosity.

The underlying rationale for these classifications can be represented geometrically as a series of three concentric circles. In the innermost circle—the heart of the study—was the section on attitudes toward development. Here we investigated the respondent's experience of various social services, his demands for these services, and his assignments of responsibility for their provision. We ascertained his acceptance of innovation, both in general terms and in relation to specific types of activity and likely sources. We inquired after his conception of the most important problem facing his village and what could be done about it. His attitudes toward cooperation with his neighbors in community projects, as well as his past experience of such cooperation, were examined. More specific matters, such as his image and evaluation of urban life, his notions of ideal family size and ways to preserve it, his rating of the most useful portions of the primary school curriculum, his conception of the direction of changes, if any, in the distribution of wealth, and other similar topics were explored. In short, the crucial interests at the center of the instrument were: (1) What were the respondent's attitudes toward development, change, and innovation? (2) What was the nature of his social demands, expectations, and satisfactions? And (3) to what agencies, including himself, did he assign responsibility for fulfilling these expectations?

To comprehend any given type of peasant response to this central area of interrogation, additional information about other personal characteristics of the respondent seemed clearly necessary. Hence, the second, or middle, concentric circle can be considered as bearing the title "related personal characteristics." It contained the basic instrument sections on personal background (age, sex, mother tongue, education, etc.), on other relevant psychological traits (tolerance of nonconformity, tolerance of frustration, empathy, guilt or shame orientation, basic values, fatalism, etc.), plus the more limited sections on politicization and religiosity.

The outermost circle represents those sections of the instrument that sought information about the peasant's interactions with other people, looking in part to these for both causes and consequences of the attitudes and backgrounds already established. A village, for example, may have a number of potential innovators within its walls, but these more creative souls may be so poorly located in the social structure of the village that either no demonstration effect or even a negative demonstration effect is produced by their sponsorship of change. Hence, a section on social structure and the villagers' personal perception of it was included. So, also, was a section obtaining much information about the respondent's communications behavior, vis-à-vis both the mass media and his face-to-face contacts. Lastly, a section on the socialization of the villager—by whom and how he was raised and how he views the training of his own offspring—was included to complete the desired portrait of the peasant. Hopefully, from the total instrument of about 100 questions requiring just over an hour, on the average, to answer will issue information permitting a rather complete initial assessment of the attitudinal characteristics of the Turkish villager as they relate to modernization.

Naturally, in constructing the instruments we encountered the usual problems of cross-cultural research, namely, those centered on the efforts to maintain stability of stimulus and of response interpretation in divergent settings. Since these problems, and the main techniques for vanquishing or reducing them, are well-known, we shall not broadly enter into them here. One problem of this type that may warrant brief mention, however, is that we were confronted with the fact that a number of our respondents spoke only an *unwritten* language—Kurdish. Hence, a rather special translation problem presented itself. Fortunately, the Kurdish speakers were geographically highly concentrated. We secured a number of very able bilingual (Turkish-Kurdish) interviewers, trained them carefully as a unit, and relied upon their real prowess at simultaneous translation, though inevitably sacrificing, thereby, some control over interviewer performance.

Two other matters also caused us some extra concern worth recording. One was that illiteracy prevented the use of list cards by the respondents, which meant that we were restricted in the types of questions we could ask. In multiple-choice questions, the number of alternatives had to be kept especially low and their formulation exceedingly brief and simple. Second, besides many general problems of appropriate wording for an audience of highly limited experience, in crucial sectors of questioning we ran afoul of the fact that there was no nationally understood word, familiar to all peasants, for such concepts as "problem," "prestige," "loyalty," and so on. Even though Turkish dialectic variations are slight, different basic words with somewhat different connotations are used in various regions. Since the notions involved were often of utmost importance and could not justifiably be abandoned, two main research tactics were open to us: the use of synonyms or the use of explanations (definitions). Synonyms had the disadvantage of clearly admitting variations in frame of reference of unknown magnitude, while explanations seemed to carry dangers of response bias or appearing formidable. In the half-dozen questions where this problem was acute, we attempted, on the basis of a specific pre-testing of the alternatives, to select the least damaging procedure and then to continue to probe for possible warping of results throughout the field operations and the analysis. Personal consultations with interviewers and specific "fact sheet" reports on this matter were most helpful (indicating, for example, that the words "problem" and "prestige" were well handled through synonyms in one case and definition in the other, but that "loyalty" [*baglilik*] remained rather troublesome). Generally speaking, in a novel project of this type we devoted a larger proportion of our resources than is usual in the West not only to training and morale but also to furnishing ourselves with several sources of "feedback" about the nature and success of our operations.

TRAINING AND ADMINISTRATION

One of the best ways of forestalling trouble in survey research is clearly the careful selection, training, and use of personnel. Attention to personnel considerations is particularly important in developing nations with scant experience of survey techniques. A vivid gallery of negative illustrations springs to mind, perhaps the most recent being among the best. In Turkey, just prior to our going into the field with the project under discussion, a pilot study for a different enterprise—a forthcoming agricultural survey—was made in a mountainous region near the Black Sea. The sampling plan was very well prepared, but, unfortunately, regular Turkish census enumerators had to be employed for the interviewing, which was much more subtle than that of the census. When the survey directors delved into the interviewers' manner of operation they found that, despite explicit instructions to seek out the respondent in his immediate location, wherever that might be, the interviewers had developed a different procedure that yielded greater economies of effort (and, alas, of reliable information). On arriving at a village, the interviewers summoned the village head man (*muhtar*) to them in tones befitting their self-perceived station (that of important government officials) and dress (dark suit, white-on-white shirt, and necktie). The transaction with the head man was appropriately terse and economical. They simply inquired after the nearest ample and shady tree beneath which they could establish themselves. Then they presented the head man with a list of the villagers whom they wanted to interrogate, much like the Grand Jury at the Assizes. The head man thereupon scurried along to inform the selected respondents of The Call, and the alarmed peasants, pausing only long enough to don their own Friday-best, duly appeared, were questioned, prevaricated, and withdrew (one suspects, rear end first in the ancient Ottoman fashion). Despite an excellently prepared sampling plan, the pilot-study results were largely worthless.

Knowing that the interviewer-respondent relation, always the vital front line of survey research, was going to be more critical than ever in our effort to study an unsophisticated population using previously inexperienced interviewers, we devoted much work to the recruitment, training, assignment, and support of our interviewing staff. Looking at recruitment first, several considerations guided our planning. We knew from our familiarity with Turkish culture that it would be absolutely essential to have female respondents questioned only by female interviewers. We also knew that we could not send out one woman alone as an interviewer. Our female interviewers would have to work at least in pairs with one another. While, of course, interviewing female respondents singly, they would have to travel as members of a *team* consisting of at least one other woman and a comparable number of men. This fact actually meshed quite well with our other plans, since we were also led to the organization of interviewers into teams by our desire to minimize intravillage contamination and to secure all interviews in a given village during the course of one day. We therefore settled on a scheme of having sixteen five-person teams in the field at a time, plus retaining roughly two teams in Ankara for replacement and emergency use. Each team was composed of three men and two women, one of the men being designated team leader.[13] The reserve teams were used as coders.

It was imperative, we felt, that all interviewers be themselves people from village backgrounds. In no other way could the essential rapport be developed and the interviewer's report be validly used as an added check on the sincerity and veracity of the respondents. Nonvillage people would, moreover, be likely to find the conditions of work especially onerous.

On the other hand, the interviewers quite plainly had to be fully literate and reasonably sophisticated. They also had to be young and vigorous enough to withstand the very real physical strain of the job and they had to be, as explained, of both sexes. Considering these four main criteria of village origin, at least secondary education, youth, and sex, it became apparent that the group on which we would have to rely for the bulk of our personnel was that of the village school teachers. Happily, this was an occupational group whose summers were free and who were thus available at the only time when the field work could be done, owing to the inaccessibility of many mountain villages at other times of the year.

An initial interviewer pool of approximately 400 persons was recruited. The usual devices of circularizing appropriate institutions, such as schools of social work and teacher training, and placing advertisements in selected publications were utilized to locate candidates. One other special technique we used that paid great dividends needs individual mention here. A few months before field work was to begin we sent a team of our Turkish co-workers from the Ministry of Education out to the provinces on a talent-hunting expedition. This recruiting team concentrated particularly on the more remote and distinctive regions, calling upon local superintendents of education there, explaining the nature of the enterprise, and asking which of the village teachers in the area would

---

[13]The upper limit on team size was set by—among other things—the maximum number of people who could fit reasonably comfortably into a large Jeep or Land Rover.

be likely prospects for such work. These candidates were then auditioned on the spot and dossiers prepared enumerating their qualifications. From this procedure we obtained a highly disproportionate number of our very best interviewers. They knew the region and its idioms and mores well. Though they never were permitted to interview in the village from which they came or were selected, they usually returned to the same general region, where their talents contributed greatly to the success we had in obtaining very realistic and meaningful interviews. In the emerging nations, field recruitment of interviewers followed by central training, even though somewhat more expensive than easy reliance on readily available urban applicants, would generally seem to be a wise investment.

Of the 400 candidates in the initial interviewer pool, some 125 individuals who seemed to offer the greatest promise were brought to an interviewer-training course in the capital that lasted a little over two weeks. On the whole, the course was similar to those given by survey organizations in the United States. It included detailed familiarization with the instruments and sampling plan, lectures and discussions on interviewing techniques, model interviews, role playing, coding practice, and pre-test field work. The administrative labor in preparing and translating training materials where none previously existed was heavy and was aggravated by the very rigid and condensed time schedule under which we were operating. Also, we could not assume moderate initial awareness of the general nature of survey operations, so that some extra time had to be spent on emphasizing the nature and importance of research and surveys in general. On the other hand, we were able to refine the instruments by following suggestions that our village-sprung interviewer-trainees made during their training.

The pre-testing of the operation in the field was deliberately made more extensive than is normal in the West. One minor and three major full-scale pre-tests, the latter involving some 300 to 400 interviews each, were conducted. The training teams were first sent out in large busses to villages near main roads. Then they were sent out to more remote villages in microbusses containing two teams each. Finally, on the third, "dress rehearsal" pre-test, jeeps and microbusses were used and quite isolated villages were contacted. This intensive pre-testing experience proved invaluable for solidifying seemingly abstract course material in the minds of the interviewers, for increasing their confidence in themselves, and for revealing unanticipated operational flaws that required correction. In fact, I should say that the greatest loss in our preliminary programming was that time pressures forced us to cram the three field pre-tests too closely together. More opportunity to go over each interviewer's performance in detail with him after each pretest would have been immensely rewarding. It is hard to overestimate the precautionary worth of such concrete and realistic instruction.

On completion of the interviewer-training program near the beginning of July, the project moved into actual field operations. The country was divided into regions. To each region was sent a "regional coordinator," about a week in advance of the arrival of the teams. The regional coordinators, who were selected from the interviewer pool, were generally older, more experienced and established men. Many of them were educational inspectors. Once in the field it was their responsibility to contact the provincial governors and relevant county prefects in their region and establish liaison with these officials, to set up a centrally located regional headquarters to which the teams (one or two) working in the region could have constant emergency access, and to secure for each village in their region, wherever possible, the population lists, giving them to the team before it visited the village. The regional coordinator performed the logistical duties of delivering and collecting survey instruments to and from the team, helping the team arrange its jeep transportation, forwarding mail and wages, and procuring rooms for the team when it was in the city in which he was located. Finally, the regional coordinator acted as a communications link between the survey headquarters in Ankara and the teams. He was supposed to know the location of the teams in his region at all times, and to keep us informed about his views of team morale and performance. The regional coordinators did their jobs well on the whole. The main problem that arose regarding their role was to keep them walking the middle ground between meddling with affairs properly left to the teams themselves and not maintaining sufficient contact with the teams.

We devoted a great deal of energy and attention to the establishment and maintenance of high morale among the interviewing teams. The work was hard. Each team had to do 30 villages in 60 days—20 interviews per village (16 regular, 4 elite). Since it was summer, many of the villages had moved women, children, and part of the menfolk to mountain encampments (called *yayla*) that were difficult to reach. In over one-quarter of the villages, access by jeep was impossible; horses, donkeys, and human feet were the only feasible means of transportation. In at least one case the team of interviewers, women included, had to scale a cliff with ropes to reach a mountain *yayla*. In another case one of our best female interviewers, whose husband was the team leader, was killed when thrown from her horse after an exhausting day's work. A few people became ill for one reason or another and had to be hospitalized. A few of the original women found the walking and climbing too much for them and had to be brought back to Ankara to work as coders, and replacements were sent. In fact, a mild shortage of female interviewers developed in mid-passage, so that the recruitment and training of new personnel continued all summer long. All these occurrences raised difficulties, some trivial and some extremely grave, that had to be met. The central staff, which had emitted a huge sigh of relief when the teams finally completed their training and went into the field, had to revise its expectations of a respite and continue its activity almost unabated until the end of field operations early in September.

One of our most effective anchors enabling us to ride out these storms was the high morale of our interviewing corps. After concentrating on building these favorable feelings during training, we tried to do everything possible to sustain them while in the field. We diligently and promptly forwarded all mail, pay, and messages to the interviewers in order to prevent them from feeling forgotten or isolated. We developed a newspaper for them, a sort of house organ that informed the teams of what their friends and acquaintances on other teams were doing and acted as a device through which we could drop hints regarding common problems and relative performances. We encouraged the interviewers to contribute anecdotes, poems, and stories to this paper, which they did quite avidly. (Not surprisingly, many of the poems emphasized walking, tramping, marching, etc., though all with enthusiasm.) Some of the anecdotes from their survey experiences will be useful in the presentation of results, though the poems can thankfully remain the ephemeral product of a hot Anatolian summer.

It was accepted as a sacred duty for a responsible member of the survey staff in Ankara to visit every team while it was in the field, not only to check on them and investigate uncertainties, but also to show them that we were personally concerned with their problems, reactions, and experiences, and that we were not comfortably relaxing in Ankara while they toiled through the most torrid summer in forty years. We also arranged for a suitably embellished official certificate and a bonus to be given to each person successfully completing the entire field stint, and we were able, as planned, to make this stimulating announcement in the dog days of early August when the second subsample was begun.

All in all, the impressive accuracy of the results obtained would seem to be directly related to the high dedication of the interviewing personnel—a dedication we were at great pains to stimulate and support, though only they truly supplied it. One of the oft-cited side benefits of the project was that we would bequeath to Turkey a sizable group of well-trained and experienced village interviewers who would be of great use to the government in future work with the peasantry. All indications are that this aim was accomplished. In the long run it may be almost as important as anything else we did.

CONCLUSION

The processing and analysis of the results of our labors is presently in progress. The incidence of inappropriate "don't know" responses, refusals to answer specific questions, weird replies, guessing, dissimulation, and the like appears to be very low. Over the entire basic instrument, for example, including some information questions for which the "don't know" answer would be suitable and informative, the proportions of such replies still averaged only about 6 percent.[14] Over the same instrument the average percentage of question refusals, coded separately, was 0.2. Even more significantly, when we examine the responses to the individual questions of the basic instrument by each subsample, we find that the subsample percentages are almost never more than 2 percentage points away from the over-all sample figure or 3 or 4 percentage points from each other. Thus, the variance seems quite low.

The results available to date are highly consistent internally and dovetail closely with the most reliable outside information on related topics. It is gratifying to relate that the findings also conform to most of our strongly held convictions about the fundamental social characteristics of Turkish society, though less elementary notions have been jolted. In the few cases of major discrepancy, further investigation has unearthed new facts and relationships that open up the unsettling possibility of error in our preconceptions, or the existence of a previously unsuspected accommodation between the superficially incompatible observations, rather than casting suspicion on the survey information.

Hence, the early analysis of the results seems to portend a largely successful outcome for the project. Of course, the interest and merit of the final reports and the predictions based thereon will be the essential test of that judgment. We have indulged in it here for hortatory purposes. The problems and difficulties lurking in a massive village survey under uncertain initial conditions as described in this note loom so large

[14]This figure is elevated if we add the "blank" and "meaningless answer" categories to the "don't knows." This should probably be done, though the one area in which interviewer performance was least acceptable was that of recording poor responses—making sure that some stipulation of the nature of the respondent's answer was entered even though the respondent may have said "I don't know" or merely shrugged his shoulders. Rather too often items were left blank in such cases. However, even if we add the blank and meaningless categories to the "don't knows," the total remains less than 10 percent across the entire instrument.

that one is apt to be unduly intimidated. The thrust of our discussion has been that such surveys are important, can be done, and can be done not too badly.

Though it is probable that no single step in the reported research effort was original, the composite operation was perhaps an innovation of sorts. To the best of our knowledge, no similarly extensive attitudinal survey of the entire peasantry of a large developing nation such as Turkey has yet been accomplished. Be that as it may, the effort was certainly an innovation for that particular country and for the U.S. Agency for International Development. As such, its own demonstration effect seems to have been considerable. Responsible officials of the government of Turkey are currently considering a replication of the survey four years after the original, as well as a commensurate urban attitudinal survey (which in some ways will be more difficult). Planners in other developing nations have sought information about the procedures employed, and some early impact on our own American foreign aid outlook even seems visible. Actually, the use of survey research for the study of processes of modernization or development is just now expanding so rapidly and so broadly that a deliberate examination and sharing of experiences, together with a critical discussion of potentialities, seems to be highly in order. It is hoped that the present research note contributes something to that end.

12

The Survey Under Unusual Conditions: Methodological Facets of the Jamaica Human Fertility Investigation

KURT W. BACK AND J. MAYONE STYCOS

FIELD PROBLEMS AND THEIR SOLUTION

The bureaucratization of large-scale surveys compels the project director to be several steps removed from the raw data. He may "sit in" on a few interviews, and discuss problems occasionally with individual interviewers, but in general he relies on informal reports from the supervisors as to what actually happens in the field situation. Rarely is the voice of the interviewer herself "heard" in any systematic way. Thus, not only the problems which are encountered but the techniques which the *interviewer develops on the spot* to deal with them are lost to all but the individual interviewer.

Perhaps in this country the long cumulative experience of many surveys has made it unnecessary to give serious attention to the interviewers' experiences. Whether or not this is true, it would certainly not hold for surveys in underdeveloped areas, where the problems are different and the experience minimal.

As a beginning in the direction of listening carefully to the interviewer, we took special pains to assure that each interviewer regularly write in comments on each schedule immediately following the interview. In addition, at the end of the field work, each interviewer filled out a questionnaire which raised general questions about techniques in the field. The following section contains a rough classification of comments

From *Human Organization*, Vol. XXX, No. 1, 1959. Reproduced by the permission of the Society for Applied Anthropology.

stemming from both of these sources, using the interviewer's own words to illustrate each general point. While the procedure falls short of any rigorous systematization, it is presented in the hope that it may provide leads for more systematic analyses in future studies in comparable areas.

The section is divided into two parts, the major one referring to problems of gaining entree to the community and household; the other referring to problems of gaining privacy for the interview, once entree had been secured.

A. THE PROBLEM OF ENTREE

Because of the clustering of cases in each sample area, it was obvious that many respondents would be forewarned of the nature of the interview, since news would travel within the area faster than would the interviewer. Worse than news, however, we feared the build-up of rumors which could result in closed doors or worse. One alternative was to secure the cooperation of community leaders who would pave the way for the field workers and quash rumors. We decided against this for two reasons. First, the study was of such a delicate nature that we feared some community leaders might be opposed to it. If we then entered the area against their wishes, there would be little hope for success. Second, the sampled areas were not communities in any social sense, but rather a city block, a section of a town, or a rural spot of terrain whose boundaries were more or less arbitrarily drawn for the census. It would be no simple matter, therefore, to locate the leaders effective in the chosen area. Since, moreover, many of the rural areas were relatively inaccessible, it was felt that the time and cost involved would be excessive, particularly in the light of the risk of refusal.

Another alternative was to saturate the area with field workers, complete the interviews in one day, and clear out before rumors had a chance to spread. Logistic considerations, plus the fear of community reaction to the advent of an army of notebook-carrying women, caused us to compromise on this solution: Teams of four to five workers were sent to each area. We estimated three to four days per area. In reality, in the rural sections, it took from four to six. Clearly this was enough time for gossip to spread to some extent. What was the general reaction of the surveyed areas?

On the whole, the reaction was worse than we had hoped, but better than we had feared. In no area was it so hostile as to preclude completion of the work, but in a number of areas it was bad enough to require considerable effort and fast talking on the part of the teams. It is a tribute to the staff that, in the face of considerable initial suspicion and hostility, refusals were negligible. What were these suspicions and how were they overcome?

1. Typical Suspicions

VAGUE FEARS.   It was the rare area where suspicions of one kind or another were not rife. Occasionally the "hit and run" interviewing technique worked sufficiently rapidly so that rumors became serious only after the departure of the team, to be discovered weeks later by the second team concerned with the experimental program. On the whole, however, suspicion was rapidly aroused, although it was not always specific. In such instances it seemed to be felt that the interviewers could be up to "no good" and rather diffuse nefarious motives were ascribed to them, ranging from "Black Art" (Black Magic) to cases of "secret service work" as illustrated below:

> R. refused to give either her name or her husband's, stating she felt we were on a secret service mission. (6367)

> R.'s partner questioned me for one and a half hours despite my efforts to leave . . . . He said he wasn't exactly doubting our intentions but for all he knows it is some secret service thing being done under this name to trap people to voice their opinions. (X107)

FEAR OF INDECENT QUESTIONS.   As respondents spread the word about the nature of the interview, the intimacy of the questions became exaggerated. The field workers would then encounter an enraged respondent waiting to hurl abuse at any one who would ask such "slack" questions:

> I heard that you are telling the women to lie on their left side when doing it and use flannel to wipe when they are finished, and they must buy a pill called birth control for so many guineas. I think that is slackness . . . . (7143)

> During interview, the R's mother went to the shop and on returning, from [when] she reached the foot of the hill she started bawling for R. When near she said "You no hear what me hear down a road. Me hear say the women them what going around de ask a how much time a night oonoo [you] carry on in a bed!" Do you imagine how weak my knees felt?

> [One of the crowd of men] approached us to find our exact mission, as he was sure such "nice ladies" would not lend ourselves to such "slackness" as was reported. Just what the slackness was he was too embarrassed to report as he was a "staunch P.N.P. man." (Supervisor report)

That rumors had often exaggerated the nature of the questions seems indicated by the following remarks:

> . . . one woman was frankly disappointed because the questions were not more shocking. Heaven only knows what she suspected, but she said, "Cho! Is only them little foolish question you have to ask?" (Supervisor report)
>
> I had the satisfaction of hearing her exclaim to her friend before I left, "But Miss M., not a ting in it. How people come so! I don't see anything wrong with the questions them." (5366)

FEAR OF CONSCRIPTION. The age-old suspicion that the census taker's visit precedes conscription was also encountered in at least one rural area in the survey. Two variations are given below:

> She said many women in her area were not happy because they had heard a rumor that their husbands in England would be drafted and wouldn't be able to return home, and if so Government would send around to tell them, so she thought that was what we had come to do. (6201)
>
> Respondent was one of a few who heard that people were going around with papers to ask the women to sign so their husbands would go to war . . . the Sanitary Inspector came up here and put a mark on the houses and that makes them all scared. That is a sign that war starts and your husband will be taken from you. (6223)

In another area an even more threatening variation on this theme was spread—the *women* were to be conscripted.

FEAR OF COMPULSORY POPULATION CONTROL. The most dangerous rumors of all involved the belief that powerful forces were engaged in various drastic programs to cut down the population. The "forces" are of such potency that the people will be able to offer little effective resistance. They range from the diabolic supernatural to the all-powerful human organization—government.[6] The means to be used range from sterilizing injections to kidnapping and murder of children.

The way in which acts of the field workers were interpreted to support these notions seems almost fantastic. In one rural area, one of the Directors initially visited the district to verify its boundaries. He, therefore, asked a good many people about the location of a certain river. Later, the interviewing team began asking questions about family size and birth control. These two sets of data were interpreted as evidence of

[6]Birth control and the population problem are popular press topics in the island. Moreover, there has been a recent change of government, and, although the party in power has no "policy" on population, it is introducing many other visible social changes. Possibly these factors contributed to the interpretation of the field workers' questions.

a plan for mass killing of the children—the Boss had been around earlier looking for good river locations for disposition of the bodies.

In a remote rural area where no one turned up for the experimental group meeting, it was later discovered that a number had been hiding in the bushes watching the program preparations. When they saw the movie generator being moved in, they concluded that it was a machine for sterilizing the women. The quotations below give further variations of such fears:

> She told me a woman had told her we were a group of "black art" people in disguise who had come to take away all the babies in the district. (5425)
>
> People around are foolish. They say them [interviewers] want to take us away for Red Cross. That is why they take our names. They want to prevent people who have too many children from having. (4257)
>
> She said in her opinion the whole thing is that after a time they will be called in and given an injection to have a baby and then Government take the child as their own. (4387)
>
> She said we want the names to take up and when the higher ones see it they will come and give all the people whose names they have injections to prevent them from having children. She said she heard that too many people are in the island and place poor so they don't want any more children. (4366)

Such fears were usually dispelled on the spot, although not without effort. Indeed, the foregoing picture of the community reception may seem so grim as to raise the question as to how field work was possible at all. Partly, of course, we have presented the more dramatic cases. In most individual instances, suspicions were not so severe. But also important were the interpersonal skills employed by the field workers to relieve anxieties and replace them with positive rapport. Before discussing and classifying the techniques employed, let us discuss the one presumably standard technique with which they were all equipped—the introduction to the interview.

2. The Standard Introduction

A brief standard introduction was devised on a basis of experience in the earlier exploratory survey and in pretesting for the present survey. It was used during training and was supposed to be followed, although not rigidly, during field work. Each interviewer also had ready a typed letter of introduction on project stationery, signed by the Directors and Research Manager. The letter was to be used "where necessary." The introduction went roughly as follows:

> There is a group of American doctors in the Island doing a study of us Jamaican women. They want to study about our lives, how we Jamaicans live, and how we would like to live and all about our family life. As they don't know the island very much, they have sent me along with some other ladies to go around and talk with you people. This has nothing to do with Government, even though they know about it. Well, this is so important to the doctors I have to make sure to write down what you say, because, you see, it is your own ideas and feelings they want, and I don't want to make any mistakes.

It should first be noted that little stress is placed on "confidentiality"—an aspect usually covered in such introductions. This stems from a traumatic experience in the exploratory survey in which interviewers nearly lost their lives in a rural area after stressing confidentiality. The people were not as committed to the values of privacy as those in certain other cultures, and their experience with it was so limited that they assumed it must mean witchcraft. They consequently banded together and plotted the demise of the witches.[7]

A second aspect is the effort to disassociate the project from government sponsorship—a standard device which worked well enough in the exploratory stage.

A third aspect is reference to American doctors. It was felt that this would give prestigeful sponsorship—as both doctors and Americans are supposed to enjoy high prestige. Moreover, the "American" reference indirectly showed the respondent that the readers of this interview could not be anyone with power over her. It also allowed a flattering identification of respondent and interviewer in the "We Jamaican women" as opposed to "the American doctors." This was also used in the exploratory survey.

Finally, both the aims of the project and its possible benefits were made vague.

While it seems safe to say that the introduction was successful, or at least harmless in most instances, in particular instances it boomeranged. This was the case especially as regards the references to sponsorship. We would hazard the guess that with the change in government many of the lower class see new hope in the party in power. Therefore a number of people were disturbed at the stated lack of government sponsorship:

> He said if it was Government sent me it would be all right . . . he would feel that although Mr. Manley [Chief Minister] fooled them up, he was at last doing something good . . . But he don't see how America is going

[7]See J. M. Stycos, "Unusual Applications of Research: Studies of Fertility in Underdeveloped Areas," *Human Organization*, XIII, No. 1 (Spring 1954).

to help Jamaican women. What the ——— them think? He would have nothing to do with American white people. (4331)

She stormed at me and said Government is slack to allow this work to be going on without her consent, for "I am an executive member of the PNP and Mr. Manley is supposed to call a meeting and inform us what is taking place in this country, for Busta time done now when them could do as them like." (9560)

Moreover, both the "American" and "doctor" references occasionally caused adverse reactions:

She read the letter of introduction and didn't like the word "Doctor." I tried to allay her fears by telling her in this case it was simply a degree. She said she felt that when I wrote these things down and gave them to him, he would come for her. (4331)

I made sure not to use the word "Doctor" as I wasn't certain of the impression the word would give. Instead I said "American gentlemen." (4234)

The American Doctors she felt were out to keep down poor black people and wanted to know their business to make fun of. (3406)

A reading of interviewer comments on their schedules makes one conclusion inescapable. While the standard introduction rarely caused trouble, at the same time it was rarely sufficient. Between the introduction and the actual commencement of the interview came a great deal of further conversation in which the interviewers applied several kinds of techniques to obtain respondent cooperation. In the remainder of this section we shall classify those techniques which were recorded by the staff during the course of their employment.

3. Rapport Techniques

EXPANDING ON THE PROJECT'S PURPOSE. The admittedly vague wording on the purpose of the survey was inadequate to satisfy some respondents. This was especially true where the interviewer had to deal with males. In such instances, the workers drew on other fields of comparison. Favorites were the discovery of bauxite and research in medical fields:

I go on to tell them that research is a very detailed thing. I may cite instances of the Yaws Commission and Hookworm Commission who had to carry out research before they could help. (C)

Years ago when men came around boring in the earth and examining the soil, none of us knew where it would lead. Their study of the soil led to the discovery of bauxite. This is another study that can only lead to good. I can't be more definite than that. I don't yet know myself. (8464)

CATHARSIS.   On their final evaluation forms, interviewers were asked specifically whether they had used techniques of flattery or identification. (These had been discussed in training.) They were also asked "what else" had been of assistance in quelling suspicions and hostility. The most frequent single response, mentioned by half of the interviewers, was in terms of freely permitting the respondent to vent her aggressions or suspicions. Much of the secret of success here was just sympathetic listening:

> . . . throughout the hostile period I would just remain calm and listen attentively to what was being said. (M)

But perhaps even more important was letting the respondent know that her feelings, however far from being based on truth, were not stupid or wrong. Thus the technique might more properly be termed *supportive* catharsis. The unburdening was not only encouraged but accompanied by positive expressions from the interviewer such as praise and agreement—devices which opened up the respondent to the interviewer's point of view:

> . . . I have found it easier to let them talk until they are quite finished and pay the utmost attention to what they are really trying to say; then agree with them. Let them know their opinion is right and valuable, then put over your point agreeing with his as you go . . . . (F)

> Respondent who was highly suspicious was happy to hear that they were entitled to their own opinion and to voice it. When asked my feelings I might say "You know, I have never thought of that before. It is a good thing you spoke. That's something I must think about." If my true opinion was something complimentary or would help to establish rapport, I would gladly shower in bands of compliments and get cracking on my mission, and score as fast as I can. (K)

> . . . I had a tough case in which I made her do all the talking and then I quietly warned her about her blood pressure but I would be glad to tell my boss all she was saying. [He] wanted to hear that as much as the interview. She wasn't so bad after that. (B)

> I found it helpful to make people feel I was not surprised nor thrown off by any reaction of theirs. There was an instance of the respondent who told me she was only waiting my arrival to let me know her objections to the indecent questions . . . and that she had no intention of answering any. I agreed with her that she was right in feeling that way about "what she heard" but I was glad for the opportunity of explaining the truth to her . . . it took some time but I won over both herself and another respondent who happened to be present. (A)

IDENTIFICATION.   In anthropological or participant observational research the successful worker eventually establishes some role in the community which is both understandable and non-threatening. Moreover, while he rarely becomes completely immersed in the social structure, he shows by his actions that he understands the local point of view and can participate in the thinking and activities with some sympathetic understanding. If he is not "one of the boys" he must at least be "a regular guy." In some of the areas with which we are dealing, the advent of the middle-class Jamaican "lady" was about as unusual as the arrival of an anthropologist to a pre-literate community; and in all areas her arrival was enough of an unusual event to cause some suspicion. How could the interviewer bridge the gap between herself and the respondents within a few minutes? One suggestion raised in training was that of identification. The staff was told that it would probably be useful to establish some common ground between themselves and respondents in order to dispel somewhat the strangeness or foreignness which might surround them. Following the field work they were asked whether or not they used the technique and were asked to cite successful and unsuccessful instances. The consensus was that it was successful wherever it could be applied. The ways in which identification was established were varied and, occasionally, devious:

> She is a Roman Catholic and trying to guard her faith. Hearing that I am a Catholic made her speak freely. (Y951)
>
> With many . . . I told them that I was the same religion or from the same parish. (N)
>
> Identification as one who had traveled as some of them had, as well as the fact that my husband was an agricultural officer established rapport especially in the rural areas. (A)
>
> In Kingston an ex-soldier did not want me to speak to his wife. He was blind owing to a head injury. He was extremely pleased to hear I had also suffered a head injury . . . now we're buddies for life! (H)
>
> I used similarity of names, age, likes and dislikes, identification of relatives known to the area, color and nationality too. (G)

It would seem that the avenues to identification are numerous. The important thing is to establish *some* common ground to make the interviewer human and acceptable. Of course, the technique has its hazards:

> Once I told a respondent I know her teacher very well and thought him a fine man. She hates him very much! (B)

Another interviewer shows how it is sometimes highly difficult to convince a respondent that there can be any common ground between them. In the present instance, *deeds* presumably demonstrated what words could not:

I have had a few cases where the R's were not impressed with either of these techniques solely because of distrust. They refused to believe that you could understand their feelings or have anything in common with them. For example, there was a R. with eight children and expecting the ninth; she was unwilling to be interviewed, the reason for which I later discovered was that she was so fed up with life she was against the whole world. As it were, she felt there was no hope for better, and it wasn't worth the while trying. I told her that I quite understood her feelings, for I myself had children and know how difficult it is to care them well. She was not at all convinced that I had children, much more to understand what she was talking about. She said I was working for a good salary, so it was in my place to tell her or say anything to help me get through my work, but she had no intentions of speaking with me anymore. I quite realized by this time that if I am not careful, this will be an interview lost. I then closed the book and began talking with her. We talked about a lot of things including the children's progress in school. I displayed a lot of interest in this, going through some of the children's books and giving credit and encouragement where it was really due. I eventually got the interview. I don't know if she was impressed. (I)

PRAISE AND FLATTERY.   Flattery was another technique mentioned in training and the staff was subsequently asked whether they had used it and with what results. Virtually all interviewers replied affirmatively and, as with identification, the particular attribute or possession selected for praise varied greatly. Popular targets were such ego extensions as the respondent's name and children:

> In many rural areas I found out the names of respondents before I visited them and called to them from afar. Most were very pleased and wondered how I knew their names. (N)

> One technique I find effective, especially in a difficult area, is to find out the pet names of as many as possible, and enter her yard calling her by that name most pleasantly.(C)

> In the majority of cases the children were the best target. They would talk so much about them that if you are not careful you never get the interview completed. (I)

> Nothing seems to intrigue a mother more as when one takes particular notice of her children. (C)

Other successful objects for praise were horticultural or agricultural products.

> A difficult respondent became very cooperative when I noticed and commented on the size and beauty of her Dahlias. The same thing happened in ——. (H)

> Most of the time there was a nice kitchen garden or a good crop I admired. This was very effective. (K)

Particularly compelling was a kind of flattery through respondent identification with the project. That is, the respondent was made to feel that her cooperation and participation were *important*:

> Suggest how extremely helpful their opinions on these questions are to our work; that's why we travel all this distance to get it. There are people nearer us we could just pick up the phone and speak with. (G)
>
> . . . a skeptical respondent would often cooperate when told she was the kind of person who having accepted and understood my mission would be helpful in removing any false ideas from the minds of other women. (A)

The interviewers were careful to point out, however, that flattery must be used with care. It can easily backfire if it is not sincere—or at least plausible. Undoubtedly there is a danger in assuming that lower-class respondents are "simple" and will respond to praise from one of a higher status. The staff learned that such simplicity cannot be assumed:

> I used it when there was something genuine to flatter about. (K)
>
> In using flattery one has to be very discreet. Don't overdo it or the respondent becomes self-conscious and develops an attitude of suspicion, or mistrust. (C)
>
> I used flattery in cases where there was a genuine object for such. (L)
>
> I found flattery very useful but something that had to be handled with care as it could easily arouse suspicion with respondents of the critical type. (B)

BLUFF CALLING AND STRESS TECHNIQUES. One gets the feeling from a reading of the interviewer reports that expressed hostility or resistance was not always entirely serious. Respondents or others in the community would put on a show to test the extent to which an interviewer could "take it." In some instances they would seem to engage in leg-pulling for sheer sport. Perhaps it was gratifying to frighten, humiliate, or anger someone of higher status. But perhaps they were unwilling to carry it through when confronted by someone of still higher status, or someone willing to call the bluff or even "pull rank." The following are from a supervisor's notes on callbacks:

> . . . after joking with them for awhile, laughing and kidding about my size, they admitted they did not mean to give Miss X a warm time, but they were "only running a little joke with her and she got vexed."
>
> We ran into a spot of bother when a group of men prevented Miss Y from interviewing a woman . . . they laughingly told me they did not mean anything.

In the following instances, the husband of the respondent opposed the interview becauses of the "slack" questions he had heard occurred during the interview. The interviewer suggested he ask his wife afterwards if any of these questions were actually asked. His brother spoke up decrying the gossip:

> "Don't you know that's what these people are like? If you say one word to them they change it to their own way!" I took out my pencil and he said, "Never mind lady, don't write it down. We don't believe these things." (7143)

Other instances show how close the resistance was to a kind of joke—a slight incident would precipitate the mirth and open the doors to the interviewer.

> I called her by name from the road. Thinking it was a neighbor she answered quite nicely. When she looked out, she turned to her husband saying "Oh, it's one of them!"—so we three burst out laughing. He told me later he wasn't going to allow the interview. (6337)

> Respondent heard me next door so she locked herself in and would not answer when I called. But there was a pair of shoes on the step which made me realize someone was inside. I knocked and when they realized I was aware that someone was there, they opened up and laughed. (5397)

In instances where lack of cooperation was felt to be of this spoofing kind, good-humored bluff-calling tended to create a release of tension and subsequent cooperation. For example, one woman stoutly insisted she had no partners other than her present one. The interviewer put down her notebook and, with a broad grin, said, "Get off it honey. I'm not that innocent!" The respondent laughed and gave a detailed history. (Exploratory interview observed by Stycos.) A similar good-natured reprimand was successful in the following instance:

> (We started in a chilled atmosphere and around the middle of the interview) she jumped up saying, "I am leaving you ma'am." I held her hand and said, "Come on man, let's finish. Don't treat a stranger like that." She laughed and we continued. (6333)

Finally, we must consider those few cases, where, other techniques failing, the interviewer resorted to sterner measures. The first type was a high-pressured persistence or its threat:

> Respondent hid and took a lot of coaxing and friendly abuse from the partner and others around. Still would not come to be interviewed. I told her I might have to leave her out and asked her to show me the next

house. On the way I said, "You may as well let me interview you now." She then said yes. (7305)

After returning to this respondent she states she is not giving any more information as she is leaving for St. Ann. After telling her I'll be there to see her in St. Ann, she gave me the answers to the questions. (4385)

In the following instance, however, the interviewer expressed some qualms about the effects of her persistence:

> . . . after awhile I told her I realized that it was only politeness that prevented her from dousing me with the water with which she was washing, or putting her dogs at me. This was a risk, however, which I was prepared to take, I told her, rather than leave without her answers. She thawed, gave me the interview, and was rid of me. As a result of this technique, I cannot be sure of the validity of her replies, however. (A)

In two other instances, interviewers mentioned that the threat of withdrawing in a huff shamed the respondent into cooperation. But the strongest frontal attacks are those contained in the following cases:

> . . . If she remains hostile I become very serious and speak to her quite sternly. Invariably it works, but generally among the younger respondents. (C)

> . . . I was so fed up I committed a sin involuntarily. Out of my mouth came these words, "Well, I don't know how much interested you are in birth control although you say it is good. I am not even sure that you know what I'm talking about." It was then that she loosened up and [gave previously concealed information about birth control]. (7384)

> She felt questions on page 17 were shocking to speak about . . . women blush to hear them. I quoted scripture: "When I was a child I spoke like a child; but now I am a woman I behave like a woman." This made the respondent cool down a little. (Y932)

Whether such techniques are more harmful than valuable is difficult to judge. It can only be said that they were cited almost invariably as instances of *successful* techniques by interviewers who had had the dangers of biasing respondents drummed into them during training. Conceivably, they are effective among types of respondents found particularly in the lower class where an authoritarian approach from a person of higher status is expected. One must at least consider the possibility that such an approach seems more sincere than an equalitarian one which might give the impression of condescension or even of fawning as a means to an end. The writers feel that the whole assumption of the positive results of "ingratiating" oneself among peoples of lower status needs further examination. Unfortunately, we lack the data to do so here.

B. THE PROBLEM OF PRIVACY

The delicate nature of many of the questions made it especially important that privacy be obtained for the interview. However, the visit of the visibly middle-class ladies to lower-class and often inaccessible areas was enough of an event, and curiosity or suspicion sufficiently strong, so that privacy was rarely obtained with ease.

During training, interviewers were alerted to the problem and general suggestions made for its solution. Upon completion of the field work interviewers were asked what techniques they actually used for dealing with the presence of others. It is, first of all, of interest that the staff tended to write copiously in answer to this question, suggesting that the problem was a real one. Moreover, their ingenuity in devising techniques to meet specific situations went far beyond the suggestions made in the training sessions. We are here interested in the kinds of techniques which proved to be effective.

Diverting and Sidetracking the "Outsider"

The problem of the presence of children was virtually omnipresent but apparently simple of solution. In a culture where authoritarian relations prevail between generations, children may simply be dismissed by an older prestigeful person, if done in a kindly manner:

> I merely patted the children and told them nicely to go outside and play, their mothers always seconding me. (H)

Another sure-fire technique was the modest bribe:

> If small children tend to be interested it is a lot easier to give them a penny to buy sweets and get them off. (F)

The diversionary technique was occasionally applied to adults, although with greater subtlety. In at least one reported case, outsiders were engaged in lengthy conversation by a second interviewer, while the first worked with the respondent. One interviewer favored leading the outsider away from the site, and, in a sense, stranding her.

> I usually directed my conversation to them, got them worked up to the point where they wanted to show me a hill or pig or something. Then I quietly slipped away and told the respondent I wished to see her alone. (B)

The reverse procedure (detaching the respondent from the outsiders) was also used:

I would ask most of the intimate and affectionate questions, seem to complete the interview and bid good-bye. I would then tactfully ask respondent to walk with me down the track or to the gate when I would tell her there were a few questions I had not asked, they were about herself and I did not want partner to hear. (K)

In an unusual instance, the diversionary bribe was used successfully, if exhaustingly, on an adult:

Her husband refused to leave the yard, hovering around weeding grass within hearing distance. To get him away, I bought three dozen oranges from him and sent him four times to pick different amounts. When I was through with oranges I sent him to pick pears and peppers. (6165-9)

"Freezing" the Outsider

This technique calls for considerable self-confidence and "nerve." The social atmosphere is made so painfully cold that the outsider leaves the scene rather than face it:

. . . an eloquent silence got rid of him. (6-5371)

I address all remarks pointedly to the respondent, not even glancing in the direction of the other. If the other made a remark about the weather, etc., I smilingly replied as if to the respondent. After a time the other would remove. (L)

Satisfying the Outsider's Curiosity

The explanation of the nature of the project was often given simultaneously to the respondent and outsiders who happened to be present at the time. Since the sample design made it likely that the outsider's household would be interviewed, or at least canvassed, the statement, "I'll be calling at your house later" was often sufficient to remove the outsider following the introduction. In other instances, however, deeds rather than words were needed to satisfy the outsider's curiosity—or to bore her into departure:

If reluctant and curious, ask all the simple questions in their presence and they leave satisfied that it is nothing harmful. (J)

If she was not satisfied with [my explanation] I would go on to ask a few questions like, "To what church do you go?" or, "Have you ever lived in Kingston?" Intruder usually commented, "Oh is that you a ask?" and walked away. (K)

Role-Educating the Outsider

The most frequently mentioned technique, cited by eight out of seventeen interviewers, was the most surprising. It consisted of the bald truth—that the presence of another might bias the respondent's answers to questions. Although interviewers had been told that this was the major reason for privacy, it had not occurred to the project directors to suggest it as a technique. The frequency of mentions, however, indicates that it was quite successful. We are, therefore, especially interested in the manner in which interviewers translated the rather sophisticated concept of bias into terms meaningful to the respondent.

1. One interviewer used the analogy of the classroom:

> I had no trouble whatever . . . I simply told them that I could question the respondent in his or her presence but perhaps they would answer before the respondent and she might hear and give the same answer, and that would not be her own opinion. I told them it would be like a class in school when those who did not know the answers to questions got it from others who spoke out of turn, but when there was private tuition one teacher to a pupil, the teacher got the pupil's own answer to questions. (N)

2. Two interviewers employed an age-status explanation when dealing with older outsiders:

> In cases where there were mothers around I told them they had had all the experience they needed, and as their daughters did not have it yet I was talking to help them along the way. As they know that the young people don't like to say certain things before them, that is why I would not mind speaking to them alone. In most cases they politely withdrew. (J)

> You know we are really working on the younger people first. We don't want to mix the both of you, for you will agree with me that older people must be shown more respect. (F)

3. Another suggested that human nature prompts all listeners to answer a question:

> I explain that I like to talk to each individual by herself as I want to get her opinion that as the human nature is zealous other people present will be inclined to answer for her and that would not be her opinion. They generally leave with a broad grin and "A-right nurse." (C)

4. Another used a doctor-patient analogy:

> In other cases I assumed a professional attitude, telling my unwanted

hosts that if respondent had been to a doctor they would have to leave her alone, as she would not feel so comfortable or vice-versa. (J)

5. Husbands were flattered by reference to their powers of influence over their wives:

> The presence of others was a challenge but always easy. First I'd be very friendly and rattle off in one breath almost something like: "I'm working on a Jamaica Family Life project and would like to hear your [wife's] [daughter's] opinion on certain points we women are interested in." Then very slowly: "There is nothing really private or mysterious about this, your wife will tell you; but what I really want is her *own* opinion. For example, one question is, "What do you think is a large family?" Now you may feel that five is large whereas your wife may feel that three or ten or any amount is. If she knows what you think about it, she might not want to say what she really feels, but what she feels that *you* feel, and that would not help me at all . . . . I'd love to talk to you as well, but it's a job and I have to carry out the boss's orders. (H)

In all of these cases there is an attempt to educate the respondent and outsider in the behavior and interpersonal setting appropriate to the role of respondent. This is done by means of analogies to social roles familiar to the respondent. In this way, the notion of privacy is made less threatening, and the rationale for privacy is made clear. Morever, and this may be equally or more important, the simple but careful and intellectual explanation may have given an ego-boost to the audience. According to the last interviewer cited above:

> It was a bit longwinded but it flattered the person's intelligence and after all that they were generally very happy to leave us alone.

Getting the Respondent to Expel the Outsider

While most techniques were applied directly to the outsider, perhaps the most ingenious system, mentioned by two interviewers, was that of motivating the respondent to effect removal of the outsider. In both instances cited, the respondent's interest and curiosity is first aroused; then by subtle cues (delaying the questions or tactfully threatening withdrawal from the scene) the respondent is "told" that the interview will occur only when privacy has been arranged:

> A curious young man was circling the house and trying to listen in . . . I was a bit uncomfortable and spoke on other subjects for awhile praising an awful-looking piece of embroidery the respondent was doing and asked her how to do a funny little stitch she was doing . . . . She eventually

asked the man to go up to the star apple tree and join the other men. (4234)

With stubborn elders, if frankness does not do the job, then work up the respondent until she is quite curious, then just suggest you will have to leave and come back when it is more convenient. Respondent usually makes it quite convenient! (F)

Male Outsiders

In passing, we have already made a few references to techniques employed in getting rid of males. However, since some interviewers commented that males caused more problems than the respondents themselves, it would seem worthwhile to single out techniques applied especially to them. The problem with males was twofold. First, they wield more authority than the women both in the community in general and as regards their mates in particular. Hence, if they were on the scene at the time they had to be contended with. Second, and closely related, they often felt that they should be the spokesman for the family, or at least that they should share in speaking. Since males were *not* interviewed, the interviewers often had the ticklish problem of securing their permission, while simultaneously removing them from the scene. In general, the most successful technique was flattery. First the male was flattered by sheer attention and by asking for his permission:

> I think that on a survey such as this, the men don't like to be ignored completely, so by asking for them just after identification and having a little talk with them helps to break the ice; for most of the Jamaican women are dependent on their partners' reaction, and establishing good rapport with them nearly always gives a truthful respondent. (F)

> One of the best techniques was to get the partner to cooperate. If there was a man in the yard I would approach him—"Good morning sir, do you live here? . . . I have come to talk to the ladies in the neighborhood and I'm sure you would like me to talk to your wife." Usually the poor man was highly flattered and would call out, "Mary, there's a lady to see you." As long as she had his permission, she did not mind talking at all. (H)

Second, the male was more directly flattered by reference to masculine and feminine roles. "Woman talk," after all, is of no *interest* to males (being unimportant) and women are naturally shy (unlike males) in the presence of an audience:

> I told him, "It's not because you can't hear, my good sir, but just look at this. Supposing a man comes to spray your bananas. He would talk with you and then both of you would walk to look at them. Wouldn't you do that without paying your wife any mind?" He agreed. I said, "Well if I

want to talk to your wife about pots and plates and things, there is no need to keep you around when she knows of such things." (6337)

I had to get rid of her husband by explaining that men's opinions were easily got as they seemed never shy to talk in public as most women were, but, as it was important to get the woman's point of view, it was just as important to see his wife personally and alone.

One interviewer felt that even grosser flattery could melt the male:

Flattery more so for husbands . . . . He was a crude, caveman-like type. I commended him on how he seems a very nice husband and . . . had everything that a woman wanted from a good man. After speaking a little more to him, he did not even question my mission but took me home, called his wife, showed me all his private papers, and gave me great assistance to do my work. (J)

Generally speaking, what evidence do we have that the techniques described were successful in their objectives? We shall postpone the questions of reliability and validity, and focus our attention on the two immediate objectives toward which the foregoing techniques were directed—establishing a level of rapport sufficient to gain permission for the interview; and maintaining a level of rapport sufficient to complete the interview and leave the respondent favorably disposed toward the experience.

Our evidence is general and somewhat circumstantial, but, when two pieces of data are considered together, a favorable conclusion seems justified.

First, only six-tenths of one percent of the eligible women refused to be interviewed.[8]

Second, when the interviewers were asked how the reception they received on their post-interviews compared with that of their pre-interviews, the distribution of responses was as follows:

Much cooler or much more hostile	0
Somewhat cooler or somewhat more hostile	1
Just about the same	5
Somewhat friendlier	7
Much friendlier	1

The majority felt the respondents somewhat friendlier and only one felt them at all cooler. Nor was it the case that interviewers were evalu-

---

[8]Six and a half percent of the eligibles were not interviewed because they could not be located, even after repeated callbacks. Some of them, of course, may have been hiding from the interviewers.

ating their own respondents. Since post-interviewers were never allocated the respondents they had had in pre-interview, they were evaluating the rapport work of other workers. As summed up by a supervisor:

> Second visits, except in one area, found families more interested; information had been spreading and people were beginning to lose any "treasured fears" they had by the time the project had reached the final stage. The project car could not come to a halt before it was surrounded by welcoming residents—male and female—who insisted on being given the proper information which their friends had previously got. There were overt acts of friendship by way of gifts, good wishes, requests for return visits, etc.

Although we can never know, we would hope that many respondents were left with the kind of sentiments expressed below:

> Her husband told me that what we are talking is good talk and nobody has ever spoken to them like that before and made them feel like human beings instead of cattle. (6286)

In so many cases there emerged the statement:

> Nurse, I am so happy you came to talk with me. For years I have wanted to talk my mind to someone like you! (S)

The importance of high interviewer competence should by now be apparent. The unusual physical difficulties of field work, the initial hostility and suspiciousness of the respondents, the delicate nature of the questionnaire and the heavy work demands all required that the field staff be both skilled in interpersonal relations and characterized by dedication and high morale throughout the work.

Behind Many Masks: Ethnography and Impression Management in a Himalayan Village

GERALD D. BERREMAN

PREFACE

Ethnographers have all too rarely made explicit the methods by which the information reported in their descriptive and analytical works was derived. Even less frequently have they attempted systematic description of those aspects of the field experience which fall outside of a conventional definition of method but which are crucial to the research and its results. The potential field worker in any given area often has to rely for advance information about many of the practical problems of his craft upon the occasional verbal anecdotes of his predecessors or the equally random remarks included in ethnographic prefaces. To the person facing field work for the first time the dearth of such information may appear to be the result of a conviction, among those who know, that experience can be the only teacher. Alternatively, he may suspect ethnographers of having established a conspiracy of silence on these matters. When he himself becomes a bona fide ethnographer he may join that conspiracy inadvertently or he may feel obligated to join it not only to protect the secrets of ethnography, but to protect himself. As a result of the rules of the game which kept others from communicating their experience to him, he may feel that his own difficulties of morale and rapport, his own compromises between the ideal and the necessary, were unique, and perhaps signs of weakness or incompetence. Consequently, these are concealed or minimized. More acceptable aspects of the field experience such as those relating to formal research methods, health hazards, transportation facilities and useful equipment suffice to answer the queries of the curious. This is in large measure a matter of maintaining

Reprinted from Gerald D. Berreman, *Behind Many Masks: Ethnography and Impression Management in a Himalayan Village* (Ithaca, N.Y.: Society for Applied Anthropology, 1962), 24 pp. Reprinted by permission of the publisher and the author.

the proper "front" (see below) before an audience made up not only of the uninitiated, but in many cases of other ethnographers as well.

As a result of this pattern "Elenore Bowen" shared the plight of many an anthropological neophyte when, according to her fictionalized account she arrived in West Africa girded for field work with her professors' formulae for success:

> Always walk in cheap tennis shoes; the water runs out more quickly, [and] You'll need more tables than you think.[1]

This monograph is not an exposition of research methods or field techniques in the usual sense. It is a description of some aspects of my field research, analyzed from a particular point of view. As such, it is an attempt to portray some features of that human experience which is field work, and some of the implications of its being human experience for ethnography as a scientific endeavor. It is not intended as a model for others to follow. It tells what happened, what I did, why I did it and with what apparent effect. As in all field work, the choices were not always mine and the results were frequently unanticipated. But the choices and results have proved instructive. I hope that this account will be of use to those contemplating field work and that it may stimulate more ethnographers to make available their knowledge and views of the field experience.[2]

INTRODUCTION

Every ethnographer, when he reaches the field, is faced immediately with accounting for himself before the people he proposes to learn to know. Only when this has been accomplished can he proceed to his avowed task of seeking to understand and interpret the way of life of those people. The second of these endeavors is more frequently discussed in anthropological literature than the first, although the success of the

[1]Elenore Smith Bowen, *Return to Laughter* (New York: Harper, 1954), pp. 3–4.

[2]The research upon which this report is based was carried out in India during 1957–58 under a Ford Foundation Foreign Area Training Fellowship and is reported in full in the author's dissertation, *Kin, Caste and Community in a Himalayan Hill Village*, Cornell University, 1959. The present monograph was prepared during a summer research appointment with the Himalayan Border Countries Project in the Center for South Asia Studies, Institute of International Studies, University of California, Berkeley. The author is grateful to these institutions and the individuals in them for their support. He would like to thank Aaron V. Cicourol, Erving Goffman, Dell Hymes and William L. Rowe for their helpful comments on earlier drafts of the manuscript. He is deeply grateful to the people of Sirkanda for their friendship and forbearance during his research.

enterprise depends as largely upon one as the other. Both tasks, in common with all social interaction, involve the control and interpretation of impressions, in this case those conveyed by the ethnographer and his subjects to one another. Impressions are derived from a complex of observations and inferences drawn from what people do as well as what they say both in public, i.e., when they know they are being watched, and in private, i.e., when they think they are not being watched. Attempts to convey a desired impression of one's self and to interpret accurately the behavior and attitudes of others are an inherent part of any social interaction, and they are crucial to ethnographic research.

My research in a tightly closed and highly stratified society will serve as a case study from which to analyze some of the problems and consequences inherent in the interaction of ethnographer and subjects. Special emphasis will be placed upon the differential effects of the ethnographer's identification with high-status and low-status groups in the community.

THE SETTING

The research upon which this account is based took place in and around Sirkanda, a peasant village of the lower Himalayas of North India. Its residents, like those of the entire lower Himalayan area from Kashmir through Nepal, are known as *Paharis* (of the mountains). The village is small, containing some 384 individuals during the year of my residence there in 1957–58, and it is relatively isolated, situated as it is in rugged hills accessible only on foot and nine miles from the nearest road and bus service.

I

Strangers in the area are few and readily identifiable by dress and speech. People who are so identified are avoided or discouraged from remaining long in the vicinity. To escape such a reception, a person must be able to identify himself as a member of a familiar group through kinship ties, caste (*jati*) ties and/or community affiliation. Since the first two are ascribed characteristics, the only hope an outsider has of achieving acceptance is by establishing residence and, through social interaction, acquiring the status of a community-dweller; a slow process at best.

The reluctance of Sirkanda villagers and their neighbors to accept strangers is attested to by the experience of those outsiders who have dealt with them. In 1957 a new teacher was assigned to the Sirkanda school. He was a Pahari from an area some fifty miles distant. Despite his Pahari background and consequent familiarity with the language and customs of the local people, he complained after four months in the village that his reception had been less than cordial:

> I have taught in several schools in the valley and people have always been friendly to me. They have invited me to their homes for meals, have sent gifts of grain and vegetables with their children, and have tried to make me feel at home. I have been here four months now with almost no social contact aside from my students. No one has asked me to eat with him; no one has sent me so much as a grain of millet; no one has asked me to sit and talk with him; no one has even asked me who I am or whether I have a family. They ignore me.

He fared better than the teacher in another village of the area who had to give up after three months during which he and his proposed school were totally boycotted.

Among the forestry officers whose duty it is to make periodic rounds in these hills, villagers' lack of hospitality is proverbial. They claim that here a man has to carry his own food, water, and bed-roll because he cannot count on villagers to offer these necessities to him on his travels. Community development and establishment of credit cooperatives, two governmental programs in the area, have been unsuccessful due largely to their advocates' inability to establish rapport with the people. My assistant, who had worked for more than a year in an anthropological research project in a village of the plains, was constantly baffled at the reticence and lack of hospitality of villagers. As he said:

> In Kalapur when you walked through the village men would hail you and invite you to sit and talk with them. Whether or not they really wanted you to do so, they at least invited you out of common courtesy. Here they just go inside or turn their backs when they see you coming.

The reasons for such reticence are not far to seek. Contacts with outsiders have been limited largely to contacts with policemen and tax collectors—two of the lowest forms of life in the Pahari taxonomy. Such officials are despised and feared not only because they make trouble for villagers in the line of duty, but because they also extort bribes on the threat of causing further trouble and often seem to take advantage of their official positions to vent their aggressions on these vulnerable people. Since India's independence, spheres of governmental responsibility have extended to include stringent supervision of greatly extended national forest lands, rationing of certain goods, establishment of a variety of development programs, etc. The grounds for interfering in village affairs have multiplied as the variety of officials has proliferated. Any stranger, therefore, may be a government agent. As such he is potentially troublesome and even dangerous.

Villagers' fears on this score are not groundless. Aside from the unjust exploitation which such agents are reputed to employ in their activities there are many illegal or semi-legal activities carried on by villagers which could be grounds for punishment and are easily used as grounds for extortion. In Sirkanda, national forest lands and products have been illegally appropriated by villagers, taxable land has been under-reported, liquor is brewed and sold illicitly, women have been illegally sold, guns have gone unlicensed, adulterated milk is sold to outside merchants, children are often married below the legal age, men have fled the army or escaped from jail, property has been illegally acquired from fleeing Muslims at the time of partition. Any of these and similar real and imagined infractions may be objects of a stranger's curiosity and therefore are reasons for discouraging his presence in the village.

Paharis are thought by people of the plains to be ritually, spiritually, and morally inferior. They are suspected of witchcraft and evil magic. In addition they are considered naive bumpkins—the hill-billy stereotype of other cultures is shared by Indians. Paharis try to avoid interaction with those who hold these stereotypes. Alien Brahmins may seek to discredit their Pahari counterparts by finding evidence of their unorthodoxy; alien traders may seek to relieve them of their hard-earned cash or produce by sharp business practices; scoundrels may seek to waylay or abduct village women; thieves may come to steal their worldly possessions; lawyers or their cohorts may seek evidence for trumped-up legal proceedings which a poor Pahari could not hope to counteract in court. Christians may hope to infringe on their religious beliefs and practices. Strangers are therefore suspected of having ulterior motives even if they are not associated with the government.

The only way to feel sure that such dangers do not inhere in a person is to know who he is, and to know this he must fit somewhere into the known social system. Only then is he subject to effective local controls so that if he transgresses, or betrays a trust, he can be brought to account. The person who is beyond control is beyond trust and is best hurried on his way.

This is, therefore, a relatively closed society. Interaction with strangers is kept to a minimum; the information furnished them is scanty and stereotyped. Access to such a society is difficult for an outsider.

II

Within this closed society there is rigid stratification into a number of hereditary, ranked, endogamous groups—castes—comprising two large divisions: the high or twice-born castes and the low or untouchable castes. The high castes, Rajputs and Brahmins, are land-owning agriculturists who are dominant in numbers, comprising ninety percent of the population. They are dominant in economic wherewithal in that they own most of the land and animals while the other castes depend on them for their livelihood. They are dominant in political power, for both traditional and new official means of control are in their hands. They dominate in ritual status as twice-born, ritually clean castes while all other castes are untouchable (*achut*). In most villages, as in Sirkanda, Rajputs outnumber Brahmins and so are locally dominant, but the ritual and social distance between them is not great and the economic difference is usually nil.[3]

The low castes, whose members are artisans, are disadvantaged in each respect that the high castes are advantaged. They are dependent upon the high castes for their livelihood and are subject to the will of the high castes in almost every way. Ideally their relationship to the high castes is one of respect, deference, and obedience. In return high-caste members are supposed to be paternalistic. In practice there is a good deal of tension in the relationship, and it is held stable largely by considerations of relative power.[4]

In addition there are non-hierarchical cleavages within the high castes and within the low castes based upon kinship ties (lineage and clan lines being paramount) and informal cliques and factions.

As a result of these factors the community is divided within itself. While there is consensus on some things there is disagreement on others. Acceptance by one element of the community does not imply acceptance by the whole community and frequently, in fact, precludes it.

THE RESEARCH

It was into this community that my interpreter-assistant and I walked, unannounced, one rainy day in September, 1957, hoping to engage in ethnographic research. On our initial visit we asked only to camp there while we visited a number of surrounding villages. We were introduced by a note from a non-Pahari wholesaler of the nearest market town who had long bought the surplus agricultural produce of villagers and had, as it turned out, through sharp practices of an obscure nature, ac-

[3]Cf. M. N. Srinivas, "The Dominant Caste in Rampura," *American Anthropologist*, LXI (February 1959), 1–16.

[4]G. D. Berreman, "Caste in India and the United States," *American Journal of Sociology*, LXVI (September 1960), 120–127.

quired land in the village. He asked that the villagers treat the strangers as "our people" and extend all hospitality to them. As might have been expected, our benefactor was not beloved in the village and it was more in spite of his intercession than on account of it that we ultimately managed to do a year's research in the village.

The note was addressed to a high-caste man who proved to be one of the most suspicious people of the village; the head of a household recently victorious in a nine-year court battle over land brought against it by virtually the entire village; the leader of a much-resented but powerful minority faction. That he gave us an unenthusiastic reception was a blow to our morale but probably a boon to our chances of being tolerated in the village.

I

The interpreter-assistant who accompanied me was a young Brahmin of plains origin who had previously worked in a similar capacity for a large research project carried out in the plains village of Kalapur. I shall hereafter refer to him as Sharma.

For the first three months of our stay in the village, most of our time was spent keeping house and attempting to establish rapport, both of which were carried out under trying circumstances.

According to their later reports to us, villagers at first assumed that we were missionaries, a species which had not previously invaded this locality but which was well known. Several villagers had sold milk in Mussoorie, a hill station sixteen miles distant that is frequented by missionaries. When we failed to meddle in religious matters or to show surprise at local rituals, this suspicion gradually faded. We had anticipated this interpretation of our motives and so were careful not to show undue interest in religion as a topic of conversation. We purposely used Hindu rather than areligious forms of greeting in our initial contacts to avoid being identified as missionaries. As a topic for polite and, we hoped, neutral conversation, we chose agriculture. It seemed timely too, as the fall harvest season began not long after our arrival in the village. Partly as a result of this choice of conversational fare, suspicion arose that we were government agents sent to reassess the land for taxation purposes, based on the greater-than-previously-reported productivity of the land. Alternatively, we were suspect of being investigators seeking to find the extent of land use in unauthorized areas following the nationalization of the surrounding uncultivated lands. My physical appearance was little comfort to villagers harboring these suspicions. One man commented that

Anyone can look like a foreigner if he wears the right clothes.

Gradually these fears too disappeared, but others arose.

One person suggested that our genealogical inquiries might be pre-liminary to a military draft of the young men. The most steadfast op-ponent of our presence hinted darkly at the machinations of foreign spies —a vaguely understood but actively feared type of villain. Nearly four months had passed before overt suspicion of this sort was substantially dissipated, although, of course, some people had been convinced of the innocence of our motives relatively early and others remained suspicious throughout our stay.

One incident nearly four months after our first visit to the village proved to be a turning point in quelling overt opposition to our activities in the village. We were talking one afternoon to the local Brahmin priest. He had proved to be a reluctant informant, apparently because of his fear of alienating powerful and suspicious Rajputs whose caste-fellows outnumbered his own by more than thirty to one in the village (his was the only Brahmin household as compared to 37 Rajput households in Sir-kanda) and in whose good graces it was necessary for him to remain for many reasons. However, he was basically friendly. Encouraged by our in-creasing rapport in the village at large, by his own feelings of affinity with the Brahmin interpreter, Sharma, and by the privacy of his secluded thresh-ing platform as a talking place, he had volunteered to discuss his family tree with us. Midway in our discussion, one of the most influential and hostile of the Rajputs came upon us—probably intentionally—and sat down with us. The Brahmin immediately became self-conscious and uncommunicative but it was too late to conceal the topic of our conversation. The Rajput soon in-terrupted, asking why the Brahmin was telling us these things and inquiring in a challenging way what possible use the information could be to an American scholar. He implied, with heavy irony, that we had ulterior mo-tives. The interview was obviously ended and by this time a small crowd of onlookers had gathered. Since a satisfactory answer was evidently de-manded and since most members of the audience were not among the people we knew best, I took the opportunity to answer fully.

I explained that prior to 1947, India had been a subject nation of little interest to the rest of the world. In the unlikely event that the United States or any other country wanted to negotiate regarding mat-ters Indian its representatives had merely to deal with the British who spoke for India. Indians were of no importance to us, for they were a subject people. They, in turn, had no need to know that America existed as, indeed, few did. Then in 1947 after a long struggle India had become independent; a nation of proud people who handled their own affairs and

participated in the United Nations and in all spheres of international relations on a par with Britain and the United States. Indians for the first
time spoke for themselves. At once it became essential for Indians and
Americans to know one another. Consequently India sent hundreds of
students to America, among other places, and we sent students such as
myself to India. We had worked at learning their language and we also
wanted to learn their means of livelihood, social customs, religion, etc.,
so that we could deal with them intelligently and justly, just as their
students were similarly studying in and about America. Fortunately I had
an Indian acquaintance then studying a rural community in Utah, whom
I could cite as a case comparable to my own. I pointed out that Indian
and American scholars had studied Indian cities, towns and villages of
the plains so that their ways were well known, but that heretofore the
five million Paharis—residents of some of the richest, most beautiful, historically and religiously most significant parts of India—had been overlooked. I emphasized that Paharis would play an increasing role in the
development of India and that if they were to assume the responsibilities
and derive the advantages available to them it was essential that they be
better known to their countrymen and to the world. My research was
billed as an effort in this direction.

I would like to be able to report that on the basis of this stirring
speech I was borne aloft triumphantly through the village, thereafter being treated as a fellow villager by one and all. Needless to say, this did
not happen. My questioner was, however, evidently favorably impressed,
or at least felt compelled to act as though he were before the audience of
his village-mates. He responded by saying that he would welcome me in
his house any time and would discuss fully any matters of interest to me.
He also offered to supply me with a number of artifacts as exhibits of
Pahari ingenuity to be taken to America. I might add, anticlimactically,
that in fact he never gave me information beyond his reactions to the
weather, and that the Brahmin, evidently shaken by the experience, was
never again as informative as he had been immediately prior to this
incident.[5]

The Rajput challenger, however, ceased to be hostile whereas formerly he had been a focus of opposition to my presence. General rapport
in the village improved markedly and the stigma attached to talking with
me and my interpreter almost disappeared. One notable aftereffect was
that my photographic opportunities, theretofore restricted to scenery,
small children, and adolescent boys in self-conscious poses, suddenly expanded to include a wide range of economic, ritual, and social occasions

[5]This is partly attributable to the substitution, soon afterwards, of a low-status
interpreter in place of Sharma, a circumstance to be described below.

as well as people of all castes, ages and both sexes. Photography itself soon became a valuable means of obtaining rapport as photographs came into demand.

The degree to which I was allowed or requested to take photographs, in fact, proved to be a fairly accurate indicator of rapport. One of the more gratifying incidents of my research in Sirkanda occurred at an annual regional fair some eight months after the research had begun. Soon after I arrived at the fair a group of gayly dressed young women of various villages had agreed to be photographed when a Brahmin man, a stranger to me, stormed up and ordered them to refuse. An elderly and highly respected Rajput woman of Sirkanda had been watching the proceedings and was obviously irritated by the fact and manner of the intervention. She stepped to the center of the group of girls, eying the Brahmin evenly, and said,

> Please take my photograph.

I did so, the Brahmin left, and my photography was in demand exceeding the film supply throughout the fair.

The incident described above, in which the Rajput challenged my interviewing of the Brahmin priest, came out favorably partly because of the context in which it occurred. For one thing, it occurred late enough so that many people knew me and my interpreter. Having no specific cause for doubting our motives, they were ready to believe us if we made a convincing case. Also, there was a sizeable audience to the event. My explanation was a response to a challenge by a high-status villager and the challenger accepted it gracefully. It was the first time that many of these people had been present when I talked at any length and my statement was put with a good deal of feeling, which fact they recognized. It was essentially an appeal for their confidence and cooperation in a task they knew was difficult and which I obviously considered important. They were not incapable of empathy.[6] As one man had said earlier,

> You may be a foreigner and we only poor villagers, but when we get to know you we will judge you as a man among other men; not as a foreigner.

[6]An effective appeal for accurate responses from villagers was to picture my academic examining committee in America as made up of relentless and omniscient task-masters who would unerringly detect any inadequacies or inaccuracies in my report and perhaps fail me on that basis so that I could not pursue my chosen profession. This evoked sympathy and cooperation from several informants, one of whom said he would assume personal responsibility for the accuracy of all information obtained from or checked through him.

With time, most of the villagers demonstrated the validity of his comment by treating me as an individual on the basis of their experience with me, rather than as the stereotyped outsider or white man.

Most important, my statement placed the listeners in a position of accepting what I said or denying their own importance as people and as citizens—it appealed to their pride. They have inferiority feelings relative to non-Paharis which account in large measure for their hostility, and my presence as defined in this statement counteracted these feelings. It was especially effective in response to the Rajput who put the challenge; a man with an acute, and to many aggravating, need for public recognition of his importance. He had gained some eminence by opposing my work; he now evidently gained some by eliciting a full explanation from me and magnanimously accepting it.

Although I remained an alien and was never made to feel that my presence in the village was actively desired by most of its members, I was thereafter tolerated with considerable indulgence. I became established as a resident of Sirkanda, albeit a peculiar one, and no one tried to get me to leave. I have heard strangers en route to or from further mountain areas inquire of Sirkanda villagers as to my identity, presuming that I was out of earshot or could not understand, and be left to ponder the succinct reply,

He lives here.

II

Other, less spectacular rapport-inducing devices were employed. Unattached men in the village were considered, not unjustly in light of past experience and Pahari morality, a threat to village womanhood. This fear with regard to my interpreter and myself was appreciably diminished when our wives and children visited the village and when a few villagers had been guests at our house in town where our families normally resided. We won some good will by providing a few simple remedies for common village ailments. One of the most effective means of attracting villagers to our abode in the village during this period was a battery radio which we brought; the first to operate in this area. It was an endless source of diversion to villagers and attracted a regular audience, as well as being a local attraction for visiting relatives and friends from other villages.

At first there had reportedly been considerable speculation in the village as to why two people of such conspicuously different backgrounds as Sharma and myself had appeared on the scene as a team if, as we claimed, we were not sent by the government or a missionary organization. The plausibility of our story was enhanced when Sharma made it clear to villagers that he was my bona fide employee who received payment in cash for his services.

Villagers never ceased to wonder, as I sometimes did myself, why I had chosen this particular area and village for my research. I explained this in terms of its relative accessibility for a hill area, the hospitality and perspicacity of Sirkanda people, the reputation Sirkanda had acquired in the area for being a "good village," and my own favorable impression of it based on familiarity with a number of similar villages. The most satisfactory explanation was that my presence there was largely chance, i.e., fate. Everyone agreed that this was the real reason. Villagers pointed out that when the potter makes a thousand identical cups, each has a unique destiny. Similarly, each man has a predetermined course of life and it was my fate to come to Sirkanda. When I gave an American coin to a villager, similar comment was precipitated. Of all the American coins only one was destined to rest in Sirkanda and this was it. What greater proof of the power of fate could there be than that the coin had, like myself, found its way to this small and remote village.

All of our claims of motive and status were put to the test by villagers once they realized that we planned to remain in Sirkanda and to associate with them. Sharma's claim to Brahmin status was carefully checked. Extensive inquiry was made about his family and their origins. His behavior was closely watched. His family home was inspected by villagers on trips to town. Only then were villagers satisfied that he was what he claimed to be. When all of the claims upon which they could check proved to be accurate villagers were evidently encouraged to believe also those claims which could not be verified.

That suspicions as to our motives were eventually allayed did not mean we therefore could learn what we wanted to learn in the village. It meant only that villagers knew in a general way what they were willing to let us learn; what impressions they would like us to receive. The range of allowable knowledge was far greater than that granted a stranger, far less than that shared by villagers. Although at the time I did not realize it, we were to be told those things which would give a favorable impression to a trustworthy plains Brahmin. Other facts would be suppressed and if discovered would be discovered in spite of the villagers' best efforts at concealment, often as a result of conversation with some disaffected individual of low esteem in the village. Our informants were primarily high-caste villagers intent on impressing us with their near conformity to the standards of behavior and belief of high-caste plainsmen. Low-caste people were respectful and reticent before us, primarily, as it turned out, because one of us was a Brahmin and we were closly identified with the powerful high-caste villagers.

Three months were spent almost exclusively in building rapport, in establishing ourselves as trustworthy, harmless, sympathetic, and interested observers of village life. In this time we held countless conversations, most of them dealing with the weather and other timely and innocuous topics. A good deal of useful ethnographic information was acquired in the process, but in many areas its accuracy proved to be wanting. Better information was acquired by observation than by inquiry in this period. We found cause for satisfaction during this frustrating and, from the point of view of research results, relatively fruitless time in the fact that we were winning the confidence of a good many people which we hoped would pay off more tangibly later. When the last open opponent of our endeavor had evidently been convinced of our purity of motive in the incident described above, we felt that we could begin our data collecting in earnest.

Until this time we had done all of our own housekeeping, cooking, dishwashing, carrying of water and firewood. These activities gave us an opportunity to meet people in a natural setting and to be busy in a period when rapport was not good enough to allow us to devote full time to research. As rapport improved we found our household chores too time-consuming for optimal research. We attempted to find assistance in the village but, unable to do so, we added as a third member of our team a 17-year-old boy who was of low-caste plains origin but had lived most of his life in the hill station of Mussoorie and was conversant with Pahari ways and the Pahari language. His role was that of servant and he assumed full responsibility for our housekeeping in the village. His informal contacts with some of the younger villagers were a research asset and his low-caste origin was not overlooked in the village, but otherwise he had little direct effect on our relations with villagers. His contribution to the research was primarily in the extreme reliability of his work and his circumspection in relations with villagers.

At this point of apparent promise for productive research, Sharma, the interpreter-assistant, became ill and it was evident that he would be unable to return to our work in the village for some time. Under the circumstances this was a disheartening blow. It plunged my morale to its lowest ebb in the fifteen months of my stay in India, none of which could be described as exhilarating. I cannot here go into the details of the causes for this condition of morale: the pervasive health anxiety with which anyone is likely to be afflicted when he takes an 18-month-old child to the field in India, especially if, as in this case, he is away from and inaccessible to his family a good share of the time; the difficulties of maintaining a household in town and carrying on research in an isolated village; the constant and frustrating parrying with petty officials who are in positions to cause all kinds of difficulty and delay; the virtual lack of social contact outside of one's family, employees, and the villagers among whom one works; the feeling of being merely tolerated by those among whom one works and upon whom one is dependent for most of his social interaction. In such circumstances research is likely to become the primary motivating principle and its progress looms large in one's world view. Therefore, to lose an assistant whose presence I deemed essential to the research when I was on the threshold of tangible progress after a long period of preparation, was a discouraging blow. I shall not soon forget the anxiety I felt during the five-hour trek to the village alone after learning of Sharma's illness and incapacity. To await his recovery would have been to waste the best months for research because his illness came at the beginning of the winter slack season when people would, for the first time since my arrival, have ample time to sit and talk. In two months the spring harvest and planting season would begin and many potential informants would be too busy and tired to talk.

III

After a period alone in the village, I realized that I could not work effectively without assistance due to my inadequate knowledge of the language. Although I dreaded the task of selecting and then introducing a new and inexperienced assistant into the village, this seemed to be a necessary step to preserve the continuity of the research. My hope and intention was to utilize a substitute only until Sharma would be able to work again. Not wishing to spend too much time looking for a substitute, and with qualified people extremely scarce, I employed with many misgivings and on a trial basis the first reasonably promising prospect who appeared. Happily, he proved to be an exceptionally able, willing, and interested worker. He differed from Sharma in at least three important respects: age, religion, and experience. Mohammed, as he will hereafter be called, was a middle-aged Muslim and a retired school teacher who had no familiarity with anthropological research.

These facts proved to have advantageous as well as disadvantageous aspects. I was able to guide him more easily in his work and to interact more directly with villagers than had been the case with Sharma simply because he realized his inexperience, accepted suggestions readily, and was interested in helping me to know and communicate directly with villagers rather than in demonstrating his efficiency as a researcher and his indispensability as an interpreter. As a result of his age he received a certain amount of respect. As a Muslim he was able to establish excellent rapport with the low castes but not with the high or twice-born castes. Perhaps most importantly, he had no ego-involvement in the data. He was interested and objective in viewing the culture in which we were working whereas Sharma had been self-conscious and anxious to avoid giving an unflattering view of Hinduism and of village life to an American in this unorthodox (to him often shockingly so) example of a Hindu village. Moreover, the Brahmin, almost inevitably, had his own status to maintain before the high castes of the village while the Muslim was under no such obligation.

Since it seemed probable that Sharma would return to work after a few weeks, I decided to make the best of the situation and utilize Mohammed in ways that would make most use of his advantages and minimize his disadvantages, for he was strong where Sharma had been weak, and vice versa. While high-caste people were suspicious of Mohammed on the basis of his religion, low-caste people were more at ease in his presence than they had been with Sharma. Furthermore, low-caste people proved to be more informative than high-caste people on most subjects. I therefore planned to utilize this interpreter to get data about low castes and from them to get as much general ethnographic data as possible. I was counting on the return of Sharma to enable me to return to the high castes and my original endeavor to secure information from and about them. However, after several weeks it became evident that Sharma could not return to work in the village. By then we were beginning to get a good deal of ethnographic material with the promise of much more. In addition to remarkably good rapport with the low castes (greater than that Sharma and I had had with anyone in the village) we were also winning the confidence of some high-caste people. In view of these circumstances I felt encouraged to continue with Mohammed and to broaden our contacts in the village in the remaining months of research.

I had not anticipated the full implications for research of the differences in status of my associates, Sharma and Mohammed. For example, villagers had early determined that Sharma neither ate meat nor drank liquor. As a result we were barely aware that these things were done by villagers. Not long after Mohammed's arrival villagers found that he indulged in both and that I could be induced to do so. Thereafter we became aware of frequent meat and liquor parties, often of an inter-caste nature. We found that these were important social occasions; occasions from which outsiders were usually rigidly excluded. Rapport increased notably when it became known that locally distilled liquor was occasionally served at our house. As rapport improved, we were more frequently included in such informal occasions. Our access to information of many kinds increased proportionately.

Mohammed's age put him virtually above the suspicion which Sharma had had to overcome regarding possible interest in local women. Mohammed's association with me in my by then generally trusted status, precluded undue suspicion of missionary intent or governmental affiliation. Probably his most important characteristic with regard to rapport was his religion. As a Muslim he was, like me, a ritually polluted individual, especially since he was suspect of having eaten beef. For most purposes he and I were untouchables, albeit respected for our presumed wealth and knowledge.

With this description as background, the differential effects which my association with these two men had on the research can be analyzed. In discussing this topic special attention will be given to the implications of the status of each of them for the impressions we gave to villagers and received from them. Some of the more general problems of research in a tightly closed and highly stratified system will also be considered.

ANALYSIS: IMPRESSION MANAGEMENT

Erving Goffman, in *The Presentation of Self in Everyday Life*, has presented a description and analysis of social interaction in terms of the means by which people seek to control the impressions others receive of them. He has suggested that this "dramaturgical" approach is a widely applicable perspective for the analysis of social systems. In this scheme social interaction is analyzed "from the point of view of impression management."

> We find a team of performers who cooperate to present to an audience a given definition of the situation. This will include the conception of own team and of audience and assumptions concerning the ethos that is to be maintained by rules of politeness and decorum. We often find a division into back region, where the performance of a routine is prepared, and front region, where the performance is presented. Access to these regions is controlled in order to prevent the audience from seeing backstage and to prevent outsiders from coming into a performance that is not addressed to them. Among members of the team we find that familiarity prevails, solidarity is likely to develop, and that secrets that could give the show away are shared and kept.[7]

The ethnographic research endeavor may be viewed as a system involving the social interaction of ethnographer and subjects. Considered as a basic feature of social interaction, therefore, impression management is of methodological as well as substantive significance to ethnographers.

[7]Erving Goffman, *The Presentation of Self in Everyday Life* (New York: Doubleday, 1959), p. 238.

I

The ethnographer comes to his subjects as an unknown, generally unexpected, and often unwanted intruder. Their impressions of him will determine the kinds and validity of data to which he will be able to gain access and hence the degree of success of his work.[8] The ethnographer and his subjects are both performers and audience to one another. They have to judge one anothers' motives and other attributes on the basis of short but intensive contact and then decide what definition of themselves and the surrounding situation they want to project; what they will reveal and what they will conceal and how best to do it. Each will attempt to convey to the other the impression that will best serve his interests as he sees them.

The bases for evaluation by an audience are not entirely those which the performer intends or can control.

> Knowing that the individual is likely to present himself in a light that is favorable to him, the [audience] may divide what they witness into two parts; a part that is relatively easy for the individual to manipulate at will, being chiefly his verbal assertions, and a part in regard to which he seems to have little concern or control, being chiefly derived from the expressions he gives off. The [audience] may then use what are considered to be the ungovernable aspects of his expressive behavior as a check upon the validity of what is conveyed by the governable aspects.[9]

In their awareness of this, performers attempt to keep the back region out of the range of the audience's perception; to control the performance in so far as possible, preferably to an extent unrealized by the audience. The audience will attempt to glimpse the back region in order to gain new insights into the nature of the performance and the performers.

An ethnographer is usually evaluated by himself and his colleagues on the basis of his insights into the back region of the performance of his subjects. His subjects are evaluated by their fellows on the basis of the degree to which they protect the secrets of their team and successfully project the image of the team that is acceptable to the group for front region presentation. It is probably often thought that his presentation will also satisfy the ethnographer. The ethnographer is likely to evaluate his subjects on the amount of back region information they reveal to him, while he is evaluated by them on his tact in not intruding unnecessarily into the back region and, as rapport improves, on his trustworthiness as

[8] Cf. Arthur J. Vidich, "Observation and the Collection and Interpretation of Data," *American Journal of Sociology*, LX (January 1955), 354–60.

[9] Goffman, *op. cit.*, p. 7.

one who will not reveal back region secrets. These tend to be mutually contradictory bases of evaluation. Rapport establishment is largely a matter of threading among them so as to win admittance to the back region of the subjects' performance without alienating them. This is sometimes sought through admission to the subjects' team; it is more often gained through acceptance as a neutral confidant.

The impressions that ethnographer and subjects seek to project to one another are, therefore, those felt to be favorable to the accomplishment of their respective goals: the ethnographer seeks access to back region information; the subjects seek to protect their secrets since these represent a threat to the public image they wish to maintain. Neither can succeed perfectly.

II

One must assume that the ethnographer's integrity as a scientist will insure the confidential nature of his findings about the individuals he studies. Those individuals, however, are unlikely to make such an assumption and in fact they often make a contrary one. While I think it practically and ethically sound for the ethnographer to make known his intention to learn about the way of life of the people he plans to study, I believe it to be ethically unnecessary and methodologically unsound to make known his specific hypotheses and in many cases even his areas of interest. To take his informants into his confidence regarding these may well preclude the possibility of acquiring much information essential to the main goal of understanding their way of life. I think here of my own interest in the highly charged sphere of inter-caste relations, where admission of the interest to certain persons or groups would have been inimical to the research effort.

Participant observation, as a form of social interaction, always involves impression management. Therefore, as a research technique it inevitably entails some secrecy and some dissimulation, unless the latter is defined very narrowly. If the researcher feels morally constrained to avoid any form of dissimulation or secrecy he will have to forego most of the insights that can be acquired through knowledge of those parts of his informants' lives that they attempt to conceal from him. With time, a researcher may be allowed to view parts of what was formerly the back region of his informants' performance, but few ethnographers can aspire to full acceptance into the informants' team in view of the temporary nature of their residence and their status as aliens. In a society where ascription is the only way to full acceptance, this is a virtual impossibility.

If the ethnographer does not gain access to back region information he will have to content himself with an "official view" derived from public sources publicly approved, and his research interests will have to be sharply limited. An out for those sensitive on this point may be, of course, to do the research as it must be done but to use the findings only with the explicit approval of the subjects.[10] In any case, the ethnographer will be presenting himself in certain ways to his informants during the research and concealing other aspects of himself from them. They will be doing the same. This is inherent in all social interaction.

III

Impression management in ethnographic research is often an exhausting, nerve-wracking effort on both sides, especially in the early phases of contact. Ethnographers may recognize themselves and their informants in this description:

> Whether the character that is being presented is sober or carefree, of high station or low, the individual who performs the character will be seen for what he largely is, a solitary player involved in a harried concern for his production. Behind many masks and many characters, each performer tends to wear a single look, a naked unsocialized look, a look of concentration, a look of one who is privately engaged in a difficult and treacherous task.[11]

The task is especially difficult and treacherous when the cultural gap between participants and audience is great. Then the impression that a given action will convey can not always be predicted; audience reaction is hard to read and performance significance is hard to judge. Misinterpretation occurs frequently and sometimes disastrously in such circumstances. Anyone who has been in an alien culture can cite *faux pas* resulting from such misinterpretation. Inadvertent disrespect is a common type. Although no vivid example occurred in the research being reported

[10]For a discussion of many of the issues involved here see, Edward A. Shils, "Social Inquiry and the Autonomy of the Individual," in *The Human Meaning of the Social Sciences*, D. Lerner, ed. (New York: Meridian Books, 1959), pp. 114–57.

[11]Goffman, *op. cit.*, p. 235. The pressures which commitment to a team performance may exert to prevent a person from behaving spontaneously, or from freely choosing the kind of impression he will strive to make, are exemplified in an insightful description by George Orwell: "Shooting an Elephant," in *Shooting an Elephant and Other Essays* (New York: Harcourt, Brace and Company, 1950), pp. 3–12. As a police officer in Burma, Orwell once shot an elephant against his better judgment, solely in order to sustain the image of himself as a "sahib" before an expectant crowd. "For it is the condition of his rule that the sahib shall spend his life trying to impress the 'natives,' and so in every crisis he has got to do what the 'natives' expect of him. He wears a mask, and his face grows to fit it" (p. 8).

here, largely due to an exaggerated caution on this score, the author experienced such a misinterpretation in the course of research among the Aleuts. He once amused local children by drawing cartoon faces on the steamy windows of the village store. These were seen by an adult who interpreted them as insulting caricatures of Aleuts, and he reacted bitterly although they were in reality generalized cartoons, totally innocuous in intent. The adult audience saw them in the light of unhappy past experience with arrogant non-Aleuts. Strained relations resulting from this incident could well have halted research had it not occurred late in the research effort, after most villagers had been convinced of the ethnographer's good intentions and friendly attitude.

In a tightly closed and highly stratified society the difficulty of impression management is compounded. In a closed society the outsider may be prevented from viewing the activities of its members almost completely. The front region is small and admittance to any aspect of the performance is extremely difficult to obtain. Pronounced stratification makes for many teams, many performances, many back regions (one for each performance group as well as for each audience) and considerable anxiety lest one group be indiscreet in revealing the "secrets" its members know of other groups.

In Sirkanda the ethnographic team consisted of the anthropologist, an interpreter-assistant and, as a peripheral member for part of the time, a houseboy. This was a team in that it constituted

> . . . a set of individuals whose intimate cooperation is required if a given projected definition of the situation is to be maintained.[12]

Villagers considered it to be a team. In their eyes the actions of each member reflected on the others.

IV

The initial response to an ethnographer by his subjects is probably always an attempt to identify him in familiar terms; to identify him as the performer of a familiar role. The impressions he makes will determine how he is identified.

In Sirkanda several roles were known or known of, under which strangers might appear and each—missionary, tax collector or other government agent, spy—was for a time attributed to our ethnographic team by one or all villagers as being our real, i.e., back region, role. None of these was a suitable role for accomplishing our purposes and it was only

[12]Goffman, *op. cit.*, p. 104.

by consistently behaving in ways inconsistent with these roles that we ultimately established a novel role for ourselves: that of students eager to learn what knowledgeable villagers could teach us about Pahari culture. I drew heavily on the familiar role of student, and my associates on the familiar role of employee or "servant." Foreign origin was an important aspect of my status, for I was at once a "sahib" and an "untouchable"; a person of relative wealth and influence but of ritually impure origin and habits.

For me the former was a more distressing status than the latter, but an equally inevitable one. I was always referred to as "the sahib" by villagers, although I succeeded in getting them not to address me as such. Goffman comments on the differences between terms of address and terms of reference in this context noting that

> . . . in the presence of the audience, the performers tend to use a favorable form of address to them . . . . Sometimes members of the audience are referred to [in their absence] not even by a slighting name but by a code title which assimilates them fully to an abstract category.[13]
>
> Perhaps the cruelest term of all is found in situations where an individual asks to be called by a familiar term to his face, and this is tolerantly done, but in his absence he is referred to by a formal term.[14]

Had I been alone in the village I would have had a relatively free hand in attempting to determine whom I associated with, so long as I did not infringe too freely on village back stage life or on matters of ritual purity. However, since I was in almost constant association with an assistant whose performance was closely tied to my own, my status and his were interdependent. The definition of ourselves which we cooperated in projecting had to correspond to known and observable facts and clues about ourselves and our purposes. Since to villagers my assistant was more conventional and hence comprehensible as a person than I, it was largely from him that impressions were derived which determined our status. It is for this reason that the characteristics of the interpreter-assistant were of crucial significance to the research effort.

V

Sharma, the Brahmin interpreter, was able to establish himself before villagers as a friendly, tactful and trustworthy young man. As such he was well-liked by high-caste villagers and was respected by all. Once his plains Brahmin status had been verified, it affected the tenor of all his

[13]*Ibid.*, pp. 172–73.
[14]*Ibid.*, p. 174.

relations, and consequently of the ethnographic team's relations with villagers. The effects of these relations on the research derived from his own attempts at impression management as a performer before several audiences, and from the attempts by villagers to control his impressions of them.

Most importantly, Sharma was a Brahmin of the plains. As such he felt obliged to convey an acceptable definition of himself in this role to the villagers among whom he worked and to the ethnographer for whom he worked. Before villagers he was obliged to refrain from extensive informal contacts with his caste inferiors. He was expected to refuse to participate in such defiling activities as consumption of meat and liquor, and was in general expected to exemplify the virtues of his status. He was, in this context, acting as the sole local representative of plains Brahmins, a group with which he was closely identified by himself and by villagers.

Before the ethnographer he joined a larger team or reference group of high-caste Indian Hindus. In this role he wished to convey a definition of Hinduism that would reflect well on its practitioners in the eyes of the foreigner. When possible he demonstrated an enlightened, sophisticated, democratic Hinduism quite unlike that indigenous to the village. Since, as a Hindu, he considered himself a teammate of villagers, he felt obliged to convey to the ethnographer an impression of village affairs that was not too greatly at variance with the notion of Hinduism which he wished to convey. He was, therefore, reluctant to discuss matters which might contradict the impression he had fostered—especially high-caste religious practices and inter-caste relations, the areas of most flagrant deviation (from his point of view) from his Hindu ideal. He tended, probably unconsciously, to color his accounts and structure our interactions with villagers so as to bias the impressions I received in this direction. On behalf of the ethnographic team, he was intent upon winning the villagers' acceptance and confidence, a fact which colored his accounts of us to them. His skill at impression management was evidenced by the rapport he achieved with both the ethnographer and the villagers and by the fact that I, as ethnographer, was largely unaware of his manipulation of impressions until later when I had access to information without his management.

VI

Villagers, too, had particular definitions of themselves that they wished to convey to the ethnographic team determined, to a large extent, by their interpretation of the nature and motives of this team. With a Brahmin in an important position on the team, low-caste people were reluctant to have close contact with it. High-caste people, on the other hand, were eager to demonstrate the validity of their claims to high-caste before this patently high-status outsider.

Pahari Brahmins and Rajputs (the high castes of this area) customarily do many things that are unacceptable in high-caste plains circles. As a result they are denied the esteem of such people. The appellations "Pahari Brahmin" and "Pahari Rajput" are often used in derision by people of the plains. Among other unorthodox activities, these Paharis sacrifice animals, eat meat, drink liquor, are unfamiliar with the scriptures, largely ignore the great gods of Hinduism, consult diviners and shamans, fail to observe many of the ceremonies and ritual restrictions deemed necessary by high-caste plainsmen, take a bride price in marriage, remarry their widows, are not infrequently polygynous (and in some areas are polyandrous), occasionally marry across caste lines, share wives among brothers, sell women to men of dubious character from the plains. In order favorably to impress a plains Brahmin they must conceal these activities in so far as possible, and this they indeed do. Just as Sharma wished to convey an impression of enlightened Hinduism to the ethnographer, villagers wished to convey their idea of enlightened Hinduism to Sharma. The two aims were complementary. Both resulted in projection of an exaggerated impression of religious orthodoxy. This exaggeration of behavior indicating adherence to the "officially accredited values of the society" is a feature characteristic of impression management before outsiders.[15]

Impression management of this kind is especially difficult when the intended audience, as in the case of the ethnographic team, has a known or suspected interest in the detection of back region attitudes and behaviors, and when it is in intimate association with the performers.

Virtually the entire village of Sirkanda was at first a back region for the ethnographic team; a great deal of the conventional behavior therein was back-region behavior. Attempts were made by villagers to avoid "inopportune intrusions" which Goffman describes as follows:

> When an outsider accidentally enters a region in which a performance is being given, or when a member of the audience inadvertently enters the back stage, the intruder is likely to catch those present *flagrante delicto*. Through no one's intention, the person present in the region may find that

[15]Cf. *Ibid.*, p. 35. I am indebted to Thomas S. Chambers for calling my attention to the following apt definition by Ambrose Bierce; a definition which might serve as a motto for this monograph: "Interpreter, *n.* One who enables two persons of different languages to understand each other by repeating to each what it would have been to the interpreter's advantage for the other to have said" (Ambrose Bierce, *The Devil's Dictionary* (New York: Dover Publications, Inc., 1958), p. 69).

they have patently been witnessed in activity that is quite incompatible with the impression that they are, for wider social reasons, under obligation to maintain to the intruder.[16]

When, for instance, an opportunity arose for the ethnographic team to move from a buffalo-shed on the periphery of the village to a house in its center, villagers' desire to maintain a modicum of overt hospitality wavered before their covert alarm until an untouchable was induced to place an objection before the potential intruders. The objection had the desired effect although it was immediately repudiated by its high-caste instigators who blamed it upon the irresponsible meddling of a mere untouchable. They thus assured the continued privacy of the village while maintaining their front of hospitality. The untouchable who voiced the objection had been coerced and bribed with liquor to do so. He later commented that villagers had said that people, and especially women, would be inhibited in the performance of their daily rounds if strangers were to be continuously in their midst; that is, the back stage would be exposed to the audience.

Before the ethnographic team the village at this time presented an apparently united front. Villagers of all castes cooperated not only in concealing things inimical to the high-caste performance, but also those thought to reflect adversely on the people as a whole. For example, an intra-caste dispute among untouchables came to a head at a high-caste wedding where the disputants were serving as musicians. While the disputants were presenting their case to an informal council of high-caste guests which had convened one afternoon, a heated argument erupted. It was suppressed and the council disbanded with the explicit warning that the ethnographer would hear and think ill of the village.

During this period of the research, untouchables were usually relegated to an unobtrusive secondary role, largely in the back region. With a Brahmin on the ethnographic team and with high-caste people as our associates, low-caste villagers were disinclined to associate with us, much less to reveal back stage information. We were in their view associates of the high-caste team and as such were people to be treated cautiously and respectfully. High-caste villagers could not reveal such information to us either because we were, in their view, members of the plains Brahmin team and a source of potential discredit to high caste Paharis.

Ethnographic information that was acquired in this context was largely of a sort considered innocuous by villagers—observations about the weather and current events, agricultural techniques, etc. Much of it was distorted. For example, our initial genealogies omitted all reference

[16]*Ibid.*, p. 209.

to plural wives; accounts of marriage and other ritual events were sketchy and largely in conformance with the villagers' conception of plains orthodoxy. Some of the information was false. Most of it was inaccessible. The back region was large and carefully guarded. Yet relations between the ethnographic team and the village were relatively congenial.

VII

When after four months the Brahmin interpreter was replaced by a Muslim, there were important consequences for the villagers' conception of the ethnographic team and consequently for their performance before that team. The progress and results of the research reflected these changes.

Mohammed, the Muslim interpreter, was respected for his age and learning, liked for his congeniality and wit, but doomed to untouchable status by his religion. This did not disturb him. As an educated and not particularly religious Muslim he had little personal involvement in the caste hierarchy of the village and little vested interest in the ethnographer's impression of village Hinduism. As an individual he was objective and interested but concerned more with projecting to villagers a favorable view of the ethnographic team than any particular image of his personal status. As a performer he played a less prominent role than his predecessor. This was reflected in his interpreting. Sharma had preferred to interpret virtually all statements and to direct the course of conversation to keep from offending villagers (and embarrassing himself) by treading on dangerous ground. Mohammed was anxious that communication between ethnographer and subjects be as direct as possible; that conversation be as non-directive as possible except when particular topics were being pursued. Consequently interpreting occurred only as necessary; ethnographer and subjects determined its direction.

As an audience, the Muslim's effect on the village performance was drastically different from the effect of the Brahmin. High-caste people did not wish to associate openly with a Muslim, for he was by definition ritually impure. He was in no sense their fellow team member as the Brahmin had been; he was in some respects almost as alien as was the ethnographer himself. Consequently high-caste villagers' behavior became correct but distant. Informal conversations and visitations decreased in frequency. The ethnographer was told in private by some high-caste villagers that they could no longer associate closely with him.

Low-caste people, on the other hand, became less inhibited than formerly was the case. When by experimentation they found that the Muslim was apparently oblivious to caste, these people began to be friendly. In the vacuum of social interaction left by withdrawal of the high castes, they were not rebuffed. The effect was circular and soon the ethnographers' dwelling become identified as primarily a low-caste area.

Not all high-caste people were alienated, but most preferred to talk in their own homes, with low castes excluded, rather than in the ethnographer's house. Some would visit the ethnographer only when they had been assured that no low-caste villagers would be present.

In these circumstances the village no longer presented the aspect of a unified team. Now it became clear that the village was divided. From the point of view of the high castes there were at least two teams: low and high castes. The former feared the power of the latter; the latter feared the revelation of back region secrets that might be given by the former. From the point of view of low castes there seem to have been at last three teams: high castes, "our caste" and (other) low castes. High castes were feared and resented; other low castes were to some extent competitors for status before outsiders. Competition took the form of conflicting claims as to the type and nature of interaction with one another, each caste claiming to treat as inferiors (or sometimes as equals) others who, in turn, claimed equal or superior status. Actually, in the context of the closed village a good deal of interaction took place among low castes with few status considerations.

VIII

The position of low castes—the untouchables—was an interesting one relative to the village team and its performance. Untouchables were in a position such that they might easily admit an audience to back stage village secrets. They were members of the village team perforce, but they were uneasy and not fully trusted members. Goffman has appropriately stated that:

> One over-all objective of any team is to sustain the definition of the situation that its performance fosters. This will involve the over-communication of some facts and the under-communication of others. Given the fragility and the required expressive coherence of the reality that is dramatized by a performance, there are usually facts which, if attention is drawn to them during the performance, would discredit, disrupt, or make useless the impression that the performance fosters. These facts may be said to provide "destructive information." A basic problem for many performances, then, is that of information control; the audience must not acquire destructive information about the situation that is being defined for them. In other words, a team must be able to keep its secrets and have its secrets kept.[17]

[17]*Ibid.*, p. 141.

In Sirkanda, low-caste people are in a position to know high-caste secrets because all villagers are in almost constant contact with one another; they have little privacy. Castes are not separated physically, socially, or ritually to the extent that they are in many areas. Low-caste and high-caste cultures, including back region behavior, proved to be very similar among these hill people.[18] But, for low-caste people the back region—the part that is to be concealed—is much smaller than for high-caste people. They do not feel obligated to protect village secrets to the extent that high-caste people do simply because their prestige and position are not at stake. They do not share, or are not heavily committed to, the "common official values" which high-caste people affect before outsiders. High-caste men, for example, were careful to conceal the fact that, in this society, brothers have sexual access to one another's wives. However, a low-caste man who had listed for the ethnographer the name and village of origin of the women of his family, including his wife and his brothers' wives, was not embarrassed to remark, when asked which was his wife, that

They are all like wives to me.

A more striking contrast was evidenced in attitudes toward village religious behavior. After some time, low-caste people encouraged the ethnographer to attend their household religious observances wherein possessed dancing and animal sacrifice occurred. High-caste villagers did not want the ethnographer to be present at their own performances of the same rituals. Some of them also objected to my presence at the low-caste functions and exerted pressure to have me excluded. The reason was apparently that high-caste people felt such behavior, if known outside, would jeopardize their claims to high status. Low-caste people had no such status to maintain. High-caste people, recognizing that village culture was essentially the same in all castes and that I was aware of this, felt their position threatened by the performance of the low-castes.

Low-caste people, unlike their high-caste village mates, had little prestige stake in outsiders' conceptions of the Pahari way of life. They were not competing with plains people for status nor seeking acceptance by them to the extent that the high castes were. People assume the worst about untouchables so they have little to gain by concealment. This is not to say that there is no particular definition of their situation that untouchables try to project or that it takes no effort to perpetuate it. The lowest-status group in Sirkanda, for instance, has tried to suppress its

[18]Cf. G. D. Berreman, "Cultural Variability and Drift in the Himalayan Hills," *American Anthropologist*, LXII (October 1960), 774–94.

reputation for prostitution by giving up some of the activities associated with it. But the range of such back region secrets among low castes is limited in comparison to that among high castes. It does not extend to Pahari practices as such but instead is limited primarily to those few practices crucial to their status competition with other low castes in the village and, even more importantly, to negative attitudes toward the high castes; attitudes which must be concealed in view of the power structure of the society.

Goffman notes that

> . . . to the degree that the teammates and their colleagues form a complete social community which offers each performer a place and a source of moral support . . ., to that degree it would seem that performers can protect themselves from doubt and guilt and practice any kind of deception.[19]

It is because in this highly stratified society moral support and rewards are allotted on the basis of caste that high-caste performers cannot trust their low-caste colleagues to sustain the performance—to practice the deception—voluntarily. Low-caste people resent their inferior position and the disadvantages which inhere in it.[20] Not only are they uncommitted to the village performance which is largely a high-caste performance; they are in private often committed to discrediting some aspects of this performance. Both of these are facts of which the ethnographer must be aware. As a result of them, if low-caste members feel they can do so in safety, they are not reluctant to reveal information about village life which embarrasses high-caste villagers. They may also, of course, manufacture information intended to discredit their caste superiors just as the latter may purposely purvey false information to justify their treatment of low castes. The ethnographer must be constantly alert to the likelihood of such deceptions, using cross checks, independent observation and the like for verification. Eventually he can identify reliable informants and the subjects upon which particular informants or categories of informants are likely to be unreliable.

That high-caste people recognize the vulnerability of their performance and are anxious about it is revealed in their suspicion and resentment of low-caste association with outsiders such as the ethnographic team. Anyone who associates too freely with such outsiders is suspect of telling too much, but only low-caste villagers are suspect of telling those facts which will seriously jeopardize the status of the dominant high castes. The suspicion that low castes are not entirely to be trusted to

[19]Goffman, *op. cit.*, pp. 214–15.
[20]Berreman, "Caste in India and the United States," *op. cit.*

keep up the front is therefore not due to the paranoia of those they may reveal; it is a real danger. On the other hand, high-caste members encourage association between strangers and low castes by sending the latter to appraise strangers who come to the village and, if possible, to send them on their way. By so doing high castes avoid the risks of being embarrassed or polluted by the aliens. At the same time they increase low-caste opportunities for outside contact, acquisition of new ideas, etc., and they thereby increase their own anxieties about low-caste behavior and attitudes. They are apparently more willing to face this anxiety than to risk initial personal contact with strangers. As a result, some low-caste people are more at ease with strangers and more knowledgeable about them and their thought patterns, than are most high-caste people.

Since they are not willing to extend to low castes the status, power, and material rewards which would bring them into the high-caste team or commit them to the high-caste performance, high castes rely heavily on threats of economic and physical sanctions to keep their subordinates in line and their secrets, which these people know, concealed from outsiders. To the extent that low-caste people do sustain the performance they are evidently responding to their fear of high-caste sanctions more than to an internalized commitment to the performance.

IX

Even high-caste villagers do not present a united front or consistent performance on all matters. Bride-price marriage, for example, is traditional in these hills and until recent times only poverty would account for failure to pay for a bride. To high-caste people of the plains bride-price marriage is reprehensible; a dowry is always demanded. This attitude has had its effect in the hills so that Paharis, and especially those of high caste, not infrequently forego the bride price in a wedding. There was an interesting division of expressed attitude among high-caste villagers in Sirkanda on this matter. Although there was no consistent difference among families in practice, some claimed that their families would never accept or demand a bride price while others claimed that their families would never give or take a bride without an accompanying bride price. I was unsuccessful in attempting to account for this difference in terms of the economic, educational, or other readily apparent characteristics of those concerned. I finally realized that it was largely a function of the relationship of the particular informant to me and my assistant and, more specifically, the impression the informant wished to convey to us. Many wanted to convey a picture of plains orthodoxy and, not realizing that we knew otherwise or hoping that we would think their families were exceptions, they tailored their accounts of the marriage transaction to fit this. A few, notably some of the older men of the Rajput land-owning caste, wanted to convey their conception of the proper Pahari tradition, perhaps in view of the fact that they knew we were aware of their practice of bride-price marriage and that to conceal it was by then useless. They expressed disapproval of dowry marriage and disclaimed willingness to be parties to such arrangements. They explained that as Rajputs they would not take charity (as a Brahmin would) and would insist on paying for anything they got including a wife; conversely they would require payment for their daughters because one does not give charity to other Rajputs. Moreover, gift brides die young and do not produce heirs, they asserted. Some villagers were more frank than either of the above groups, when they got to know us, and described quite freely the specific circumstances under which bride price and dowry were and were not included in recent marriage transactions.

On at least one occasion highly controversial information was revealed by a Rajput because of an erroneous assumption on his part that others in his caste had been telling the ethnographer the story in a manner uncomplimentary to himself. Early in the research I learned that the village had been riven by a legal battle over land begun some twenty years previously, and although I knew in a general way who and what was involved, I had not ascertained the details. One evening the proudest, most suspicious and tight-lipped of the members of the winning faction appeared unexpectedly at my house, lantern in hand, and without introduction proceeded to recount the nine-year legal battle blow-by-blow. He was evidently attempting to counteract information which he presumed the losing faction had given me. I was subsequently able to check his version with several other versions from both sides in order to reconstruct approximately the factors involved in this complex and emotionally loaded episode.

Thus, high-caste members are not entirely free of suspicion and doubt regarding the extent to which they can rely upon their teammates to sustain their performance. Even among high castes there are different performances which various groups try to project to one another and occasionally to outsiders. Lines of differential performance and impression management among them most often follow kin group and caste affiliation. These high-caste performance teams are usually factional groups in the village, competing and disputing with one another. They often attempt to disparage one another within the high-caste context by such means as questioning purity of ancestry. The head of the largest family in Sirkanda, a member of one of the two large Rajput clans of the village, expressed doubt that the other large clan, to which his wife (the mother of his five adult sons) belonged, was actually and legitimately a Rajput clan. This was a recurrent theme. Often cleavages between high-caste groups involved long-standing disputes over land and/or women.

High-caste performance teams also differed from one another in the age, sex, education, and outside experience of their members. Groups so defined can be described as performance teams because they differ in the definitions of their own and the village situation which they attempt to project to various audiences. Rarely, however, do they desert the high-caste team before outsiders or low castes, the two most crucial audiences.

The same kinds of statements can be made about particular low castes, although the low castes as a group rarely cooperate to put on a team performance. Usually, each low caste sustains its own performance, attempting to substantiate its claims to status relative to other low castes adjacent in the hierarchy.

X

Until Mohammed became my interpreter, I was identified and treated by villagers as marginally allied with the high-caste team because of my association with Sharma. With the arrival of Mohammed this identification ceased. Before long he and I became identified more closely with low-caste villagers. Since low-caste people speak frankly about village "secrets" and many other topics only when they do not fear high-caste detection and reprisal (i.e., only before a low-caste audience), the change in interpreters enabled me for the first time to gain access to their knowledge. The cultures of low and high castes are similar in this area. The part of the culture that constituted a back region and that was therefore inaccessible to the ethnographic team was smaller among low castes than among high castes. As a result, more could be found out that pertained to both groups from the former than from the latter.

The threat of high-caste sanctions persisted as a deterrent to free communication between the ethnographic team and the low castes, but its effectiveness diminished as some low-caste individuals came to trust us and to take us into their confidence. Even those low-caste people who became willing to talk freely to us often took elaborate precautions to assure that no high-caste listeners were around. The ethnographer's house consisted of three connecting rooms, one of which was at all times occupied by two or more buffaloes. The buffaloes were usually tended by female members of the family of their high-caste owners. Low-caste informants frequently inspected this room to verify that no one might be listening and on occasion they even circled the house to check on possible eavesdroppers.

In a sense, these informants became members of a team including the ethnographer whose purpose it was to convince others that they were engaging in innocuous conversation and radio-listening when in fact they might be discussing village customs and secrets of various sorts. In this situation, "team collusion" became an established pattern. Goffman designates by this term

> . . . any collusive communication which is carefully conveyed in such a way as to cause no threat to the illusion that is being fostered for the audience.[21]

Collusion within the ethnographer's team took the form of signals to indicate when a topic of conversation should be terminated or an invitation declined. Collusion was detectable within groups of informants one of whom might stifle a comment to the ethnographer in response to a meaningful and imperfectly concealed glance from a colleague. Collusion between ethnographer and informants was exemplified by one low-caste man who requested that the ethnographer tell him an English word by which to indicate that he suspected someone might be overhearing or likely to overhear our conversation and hence that we should alter the topic of conversation or that his subsequent remarks should be ignored. Double meanings were useful for this purpose. The ethnographer's housemates were buffalo cows and in colloquial speech the term for buffalo cow may be used in unflattering reference to a woman (these facts, naturally, formed the basis for many weak jokes at the ethnographer's expense). Informants might comment that the "buffaloes" were in the next room, or were restless, to indicate that women were tending the buffaloes and hence were likely eavesdropping.

The presence of Mohammed did not affect our relations with high-caste villagers in an entirely negative way from the standpoint of data collection. In his presence high-caste people did not feel compelled to live up to the plains Brahmin standards to which Sharma's presence inspired them. The wealthiest Brahmin in the area, for example, had remarked to Sharma and me that while some high-caste Paharis might eat meat and drink liquor, as we had probably heard, he himself never touched these defiling items. Later, when everyone knew that Mohammed and I knew about and participated in the consumption of these things among high-caste villagers, the same Brahmin shared with us a boiled leg of goat and a quart of liquor which he brought as a gift. He had been uninformative about his family to Sharma and insisted that Paharis were conventional in all respects, but he once fed Mohammed

[21]Goffman, *op. cit.*, p. 177.

and me at his home without concealing the fact that he had three wives. There were, however, facts which he could no more reveal to Mohammed than to Sharma. He would have been disconcerted, to say the least, had he known that we knew of his youthful activities as a member of a notorious woman-selling gang and that he had spent some time in prison as a consequence.

Thus, although low-caste people were our best informants, as confidence in the trustworthiness of the ethnographic team grew some members of every village group took us into their confidence and discussed secrets which other members of the same groups would not have revealed. As a rule, and not surprisingly, people did not reveal facts or secrets which directly contradicted the impressions they wished to convey of themselves or members of their households. Many kinds of back region secrets were revealed only by people who were not members of the groups whose secrets they were.

XI

As rapport increased and back region information accumulated it became possible for the ethnographic team to accomplish useful research on a broader scale—to understand formerly incomprehensible activities and attitudes, to relate previously disparate facts, to make intelligible inquiries, to cross-check and verify information. The effect was cumulative. As we learned more, more information became accessible. By being interested, uncritical, circumspect, and meticulous about maintaining their trust, we won villagers' confidence. For example, high-caste people who avoided close contact with Mohammed in the village visited his home in town and even ate with him, with the plea that he tell no one in the village. No one ever discovered these indiscretions, and those who committed them were not unappreciative. Contrary to villagers' early fears, no missionaries, policemen, tax officers, or other outsiders came to Sirkanda as a result of what we learned there. We tried to show our increasing knowledge in greater comprehension of our environment rather than by repetition of items of information. As we learned more, concealment from us decreased because we were apparently already aware of, and largely indifferent to, many of the facts about which villagers were most self-conscious or secretive. We took for granted things some villagers supposed were "dark secrets" (i.e., things contrary to the impression they hoped to convey to us),[22] and far from our knowledge. When we had asked, in genealogical inquiry, what a man's wife's name was we always got one name. When we later found that polygyny was

[22]Cf. *Ibid.*, p. 141.

not uncommon we asked first how many wives a man had and thereby got accurate information. Most villagers were unaware that our interests went beyond formal genealogical records, economic techniques and ritual observances. Many secrets were revealed largely because of the apparent casualness of our interest in them and because villagers had become accustomed to our presence in the village so that we were not considered to be as critical an audience as had once been the case.

Some of the most revealing instances of social interaction occurred between people who were apparently oblivious to the fact that the ethnographer was present. Frequently this was a temporary lapse. A performance for the ethnographer would be abandoned as tension, conviviality, concentration on a topic of conversation, or some other intensification of interaction occurred among the erstwhile performers. Such instances of preoccupation with one another were conspicuous by the fact that attitudes were expressed or information divulged that would normally be suppressed. The breach in the performance would sometimes be followed immediately or after some time by embarrassment, apology, or anxious efforts to counteract its presumed effect on the ethnographer's view of the village or of those involved in the incident. Minor instances of the same phenomenon were frequent sources of insights into the functioning of the society, and sources of confirmation or contradiction of informants' data.

The accuracy of information on back region subjects could often be checked through informants who would not have intentionally revealed it, by bringing the subject up naturally in conversation as though it were a matter of general information. That is, it was defined by the ethnographer as no longer restricted to the back region of the performance to which he was audience.

Some "secrets," however, could not be adequately verified simply because to do so would precipitate difficulty for all concerned, especially for those who would be suspected of revealing the secrets. Such secrets ranged from gossip about various past transgressions and indiscretions by particular families or individuals, to the fact that villagers of all castes were reported to eat occasionally the flesh of animals such as deer and goats, found freshly dead or killed in the forest. One low-caste man told me there were secrets he could not reveal until I had my pack on my back and was leaving the village permanently. He was afraid that some intimation of my knowledge might leak out and he would be punished as the only one who would have revealed the damaging information. After I had said my final farewells this man journeyed sixteen miles to my home in town, primarily, to be sure, to get some utensils I had offered him, but partly to tell me some incidents which he had been afraid to tell or even hint at during my residence in the village and which he would not tell in the presence of my interpreter or any other person. These incidents had to do primarily with the sensitive area of inter-caste and other illicit sexual behavior among powerful members of the community.

To this man as well as to other low-caste people and to a few high-caste friends the ethnographer had become what Goffman refers to as a "confidant," one who is located outside of the team and who participates

. . . only vicariously in back and front region activity.[23]

In this role I had access to a range of information not often accessible to those who come from without the group. Where group membership is by ascription this seems to be the only feasible role for the ethnographer to strive for.

XII

Certain secrets remained too dark to be told even by those who trusted us most. The village remained a team, united in its performance, with regard to some practices or beliefs which were too damaging to all (or to certain powerful high-caste people) to permit their revelation to an outsider. Obviously, like the perfect crime, most of these remain unknown. Indications of a few of them were received, however. For example, one old dispute which resulted in a factional split among Rajputs would have escaped me had not an old man referred to it briefly, bitterly, and inadvertently. Despite my best efforts I learned nothing about it beyond his chance remark that it involved a man and woman of the disputing clans seen talking and laughing together at the water source some generations ago. Even the most willing informants would only say that

Those people are all dead now so it doesn't matter.

I learned that some Pahari villagers occasionally sacrifice a buffalo to their gods, but that this has never occurred in Sirkanda. I was convinced that this was the case when considerable inquiry and observation seemed to verify it. Then, shortly before my final departure, a dog deposited the embarrassing evidence of such a sacrifice on the main village trail shortly before I chanced by. Villagers of all castes refused to discuss the matter in which all were obviously implicated. My one opportunity for a candid explanation occurred at the moment of discovery when I

[23]*Ibid.*, p. 159.

asked a child at my heels which god the buffalo had been sacrificed to. A reply seemed imminent until his elder, a few steps back on the trail, caught up and silenced the discussion as well as all chance for future fruitful inquiry on the subject. Villagers thought that to plains people this would seem akin to cow-killing, the greatest sin of all, and so it had to be rigorously concealed.

The sacrifice had evidently occurred during my absence from the village.

> If an individual is to give expression to ideal standards during his performance, then he will have to forego or conceal action which is inconsistent with these standards. When this inappropriate conduct is itself satisfying in some way, as is often the case, then one commonly finds it indulged in secretly, in this way the performer is able to forego his cake and eat it too.[24]

It was six months after my arrival before animal sacrifices and attendant rituals were performed in my presence although they had been performed in my absence or without my knowledge throughout my residence in the village. Likewise, it was not until after Sharma left that I witnessed drinking and meat-eating parties in the village.

Since I left the village for two or three days every week or so, there was an opportunity for essential and enjoyable back region activity to be carried on quite freely in my absence, and this opportunity was not neglected. In fact, it probably made my research in the village much more bearable to villagers than if I had been there constantly. It was largely the threat to their privacy that motivated villagers to make sure that I did not take up residence in the center of the village (as described above) but continued instead to live on its periphery. No doubt one of the most anxiety-producing situations known to man is to make public that which he considers to be private, back region behavior.

XIII

During my presence in the village, high-caste people appeared to be always playing to the low-caste audience as well as to their outside reference group of high-caste plains people. Before the low caste their effort was to appear as undivided as possible in matters relating to that audience, primarily in matters considered necessary to maintain their status relative to the low castes. Before the outside reference group they tried to appear as conventional as possible, at least in their conception of high-caste plains conventionality.

There was little difficulty in maintaining the high-caste front relative

24*Ibid.*, p. 41.

to low castes when only villagers were involved. When outsiders appeared, however, the front was jeopardized to the extent that the strangers might fail to play the role of the caste group to which they belonged. Thus, there was fear that government officials of high caste might come and mingle too freely with untouchables or that officials of untouchable caste might come and expect or demand to mix with high castes. These fears were activated by the presence, as members of the ethnographic team, of Sharma and Mohammed respectively. Alleviation of the fears was a gradual process. It was feared that from contacts with the aliens untouchables might get disturbing notions as to their own status. Government advocacy of the abolition of untouchability and official promotion of an equalitarian ideal intensified these fears. The village council president was willing to conform to government rules and eat with other council presidents and government officials of unknown caste at District headquarters but he would not do so in the village or in the presence of villagers lest it set a dangerous precedent and also lower his own status in the eyes of others. More immediate than the fear of status loss or of the introduction of upsetting alien ideas to untouchables was the well-founded fear that potentially harmful or embarrassing back region information about the village would leak to outsiders—notably the ethnographic team—from the low castes, as discussed above.

The performances of each team described here were aimed toward particular audiences. Therefore "audience segregation" was essential to the performers.

> By audience segregation the individual ensures that those before whom he plays one of his parts will not be the same individuals before whom he plays a different part in another setting.[25]

Probably there is no more revealing or embarrassing situation in Sirkanda or elsewhere than when two audiences for whom different performances are appropriate are present at the same performance. An example was the incident described above wherein a hostile Rajput joined and thereby effectively terminated an interview between the ethnographer and a local Brahmin.

Audience segregation on the part of villagers was manifested in the fact that their behavior differed before Sharma and Mohammed; that it differed in my presence and in my absence; and that it also differed when they confronted us alone and in groups. The performance of low-caste people was different in the presence of the ethnographic team (when that team included Mohammed) and in the presence of high-caste people,

[25]*Ibid.*, p. 49.

the former apparently approximating their behavior among their fellows (i.e., their behavior when before us, whether as individuals and or in groups, was consistent and contrasted sharply to their behavior before us in the presence of high-caste villagers). The greatest difference was in their expressions of resentment against the high castes before us and their fellows as contrasted to their usual inhibition of such expressions or any hint thereof before high castes.

Exceptions occasionally occurred, some apparently stimulated in part by the presence of the ethnographer. One of the most memorable examples occurred when a young Rajput man of relatively low personal and familial prestige brought his axe to be sharpened by the blacksmith who happened to be listening to the ethnographer's radio. The blacksmith took the axe, inspected it with obvious distaste and announced,

> This axe is worth eight annas (10 cents). My file is worth 15 rupees (three dollars). It would spoil my valuable file to sharpen this worthless axe. Go find a flat rock and sharpen it yourself.

Further feeble entreaties brought nothing but refusal from the blacksmith, and the Rajput left, presumably in search of a flat rock. This was unusual, but not unprecedented behavior for a blacksmith. It would not have been tried with a more prestigeful or cantankerous Rajput or with a valuable client. It probably would not have happened in this case had the ethnographer not been present to inhibit, by his presence, any retaliation.

Such sallies occasionally occur without the presence of an outsider. They are long remembered, fondly by low-caste people and resentfully by high-caste people, although they do not always result in immediate overt retaliation.

Low-caste people occasionally expressed reluctance to become too closely identified with the ethnographer. They realized that I would be there a relatively short time and any advantages they might derive from my company would be small and transitory compared to the retribution which envious or suspicious high-caste villagers could exact from them over a lifetime. One or two high-caste people expressed similar sentiments.

Some high-caste people behaved differently in our presence than in front of low-caste villagers. As has been mentioned, they would eat with me and with Mohammed in town but few would do so in the village. They would never do so in the presence of low-caste people. In our presence some of them expressed bitterness toward low castes that they would not have expressed to low-caste people unless greatly angered. A few expressed privately to us a willingness to interact more freely with low-caste people than was possible in the village situation, or respect for individual low-caste members that would not have been acceptable to their caste fellows.

XIV

Finally, my own behavior was tailored for my village audience. I carefully and, I think, quite successfully concealed the range of my interests and the intensity of my interest in some matters such as inter-caste relations. I refrained from going where I was not wanted even when I could have gone without being challenged and when I very much wanted to go. One instance occurred when I decided not to move into the proffered house in the center of the village. As another example, I never attended a village funeral. On the two occasions upon which I could have done so, I found that there was considerable anxiety lest my presence upset guests from other villages, though Sirkanda villagers claimed they would welcome my presence. There was evident relief when I stayed home.

In the village I concealed the extent of my note-taking, doing most of it at night or in private. I felt free to take notes openly before only a few key informants, and then only after considerable time. I recorded some kinds of detailed information such as genealogies and crop yields in the presence of all informants when I found that I could do so without inhibiting responses appreciably. This, too, took time and circumspection. Some subjects, such as ceremonial activities, could be freely recorded before some informants and not at all before others. I discarded my plans to use scheduled interviews and questionnaires because I thought they would do more harm in terms of rapport than good in terms of data collection in view of village attitudes and my relationship with villagers. I never took photographs without permission. I concealed such alien practices as my use of toilet paper—a habit for which foreigners are frequently criticized in India. I simulated a liking for millet chapaties and the burning pepper and pumpkin mixture which makes up most of the Pahari diet. Even more heroically, I concealed my distaste for the powerful home-distilled liquor, the consumption of which marked every party and celebration. Such dissimulations were aimed at improving rapport and they were worth the trouble. In this behavior a front was maintained in order to sustain a particular definition of my situation; a definition which I thought would increase my access to village back stage life, thereby contributing to the ultimate goal of understanding the lifeways of these people.

CONCLUSIONS

The change from one interpreter-assistant to another during my research in the Pahari village seemed, at the time, seriously to threaten the progress of the research. In retrospect the change has been found to be methodologically instructive and substantively advantageous. I might well have been unable to establish rapport so as to obtain access to this closed, highly caste-conscious village if my initial contact had been in the company of a Muslim interpreter. With the Brahmin interpreter I doubt that I would have gotten information approaching that which I did receive in completeness and accuracy in most areas, and especially in those areas of greatest interest to me, interpersonal and intergroup relations.

I

In such a society the ethnographer is inevitably an outsider and never becomes otherwise. He is judged by those among whom he works on the basis of his own characteristics and those of his associates. He becomes identified with those social groups among his subjects to which he gains access. The nature of his data is largely determined by his identity as seen by his subjects. Polite acceptance and even friendship do not always mean that access will be granted to the confidential back stage regions of the life of those who extend it. The stranger will be excluded from a large and vital area if he is seen as one who will not safeguard secrets from the audiences toward which the performances are directed, and especially if he is identified as a member of one of those audiences.

Sharma was a high-caste plainsman and consequently a member of very important audiences to the village performance—audiences rigorously excluded from an extensive back stage area of their life by both high-caste and low-caste villagers. As such he could likely never have achieved the kind of relationship to villagers which would have resulted in access to much of the back region of Sirkanda. Access to that region was essential to the ethnographer because it constituted a large proportion of all village attitudes and behaviors in this closed group. Mohammed was able to gain substantial rapport with the low castes. In view of the attitudes of villagers and the social composition and power structure of the village, the low castes (those least heavily committed to the village performance) were the only feasible source of back region information. They were a reasonably satisfactory source of such information on the entire village because all castes were in such close contact that they had few secrets from one another and did not differ greatly in culture. This is not to say that the information obtained was complete or totally accurate, but only to assert that it was much more so than would have been the case had Sharma been the assistant throughout the research.

II

In a highly stratified society where members of a subordinate group know a great deal about a dominant group and resent the differential advantages inherent in their status, the subordinate group poses a constant threat of subversion in the eyes of the dominant group. They are dissidents largely uncommitted to, or even resentful of, the performance of their superiors.

> It is always possible for a disaffected colleague to turn renegade and sell out to the audience the secrets of the act that his one time brethren are still performing. Every role has its defrocked priests to tell us what goes on in the monastery. . . .[26]

The untouchable castes of Sirkanda are in an analogous but somewhat different situation from that of defrocked priests. Like defrocked priests they are the most willing informants on the back region of their society and especially of the group they know but to which they cannot belong. Unlike defrocked priests they have been denied rather than relieved of full participation in the performance with which they are familiar. They are what Barnett calls "resentful" members of their society, while defrocked priests would be "disaffected" individuals.[27]

One must, of course, weigh the testimony of the vindictive dissident informant as carefully as that of the chauvinistic committed one. This is just one phase of the general ethnographic problem of evaluating data in the light of informants' vested interests, sources of information, attitudes toward the ethnographer, and many other factors.

The "secrets" which high-caste villagers in Sirkanda were most anxious to conceal included many of the kind found in all groups, and some which were shared by all castes. It is probably frequently the case, however, that skeletons in the closet are especially embarrassing to those who pose as faultless or who are actively trying to change the public image of themselves (i.e., who have aspirations of upward mobility), while those whose position is generally regarded as degraded and fixed are less concerned with concealing their skeletons. They may not see skeletons as readily or in the same light as others. As a result they have less to conceal and are therefore more useful informants on many topics.

The condition of "untouchability" or pariah status may not be un-

---

[26]*Ibid.*, p. 164.

[27]H. G. Barnett, *Innovation, the Basis of Cultural Change* (New York: McGraw-Hill, 1953), pp. 389–401.

related to the fact that people in this status are often useful informants on back stage information. Such status is commonly ascribed to denigrated groups which are in unusually intimate contact with their social superiors in rigidly defined back region activities, or whose members perform defiling, despised services for them. (This status may be assigned to others as well; in such cases the following comments would not apply.) Such people move freely in and out of the back stage area of their superiors' lives in the course of performing their duties, seemingly without being noticed. Often it appears that the society would like to deny that their services are performed at all.[28] Members of such low-status groups know a great deal about the back region of the high-status group, yet they are not personally committed to upholding its performance. They are not neutral confidants and they are not people privileged to enter the back region under certain circumstances as a result of a position of professional trust, as are doctors and lawyers in our society. They are a threat and a potential embarrassment—in Goffman's terms a "performance risk." One way to alleviate the threat (and perhaps the guilt) is to define them as "non-persons," i.e., as not entirely human, or at least as a different order of humanity. In the context of their duties they are simply not an audience. They are among the stage hands necessary for the actors to put on their performance, but they are irrelevant to the performance as it is seen by the audience. As a result of such definition, they are not in a position to communicate freely or effectively with those to whom the high-status group's performance is directed. They are not defined as eligible or competent to comment on high-caste matters. If they venture to do so before an audience it is assumed or hoped that they will be ignored. The high-status attitude is frequently expressed:

> Don't pay any attention, it's only a ——— (fill in derogatory name of depressed group).

Richard Wright presents a good example of this when he describes his job as bell boy:

> I grew used to seeing the white prostitutes naked. . . . It was presumed that we black boys took their nakedness for granted. . . . Our presence awoke in them no sense of shame whatever, for we blacks were not considered human anyway.[29]

[28]"We find that there are many performances which could not have been given had not tasks been done which were physically unclean, semi-legal, cruel, and degrading in other ways. . . In Hughes' terms, we tend to conceal from our audience all evidence of 'dirty work,' whether we do this work in private or allocate it to a servant, to the impersonal market, to a legitimate specialist, or to an illegitimate one," Goffman, *op. cit.*, p. 44. Also see, Herbert Passin, "Untouchability in the Far East," *Monumenta Nipponica*, XI (1955), 27–47.

[29]Richard Wright, *Black Boy* (New York: Harper, 1945), p. 176.

Goffman cites children, drunks, and the indiscreet as performance risks who are frequently treated as non-persons.[30] There is always a danger that such people will communicate their knowledge and that it will be taken seriously by some audience. This makes necessary the maintenance of rigid controls over those who comprise a performance risk. Such controls often boil down to physical and economic sanctions, especially when the performance risks constitute a coherent group of dissidents. Under most circumstances, therefore, the "untouchable" group will not dare to expose the back stage life of its superiors, or will think twice before doing so. As a result of these factors there is a good deal of strain between such groups.[31] The ethnographer has to guard against revealing the back stage information he receives and the very fact that he receives such information, both to protect his sources from sanctions that may be invoked against them and to protect his own welcome in the community.

Barnett has noted that the socially displaced or dissatisfied members of a society are more likely than others to be innovators, at least in those contexts where innovation is not rewarded by social approval, because they are less likely to be heavily committed to the status quo.[32] For the same reason they are often the most willing informants on back region information. As has been indicated above, low castes were the most dissatisfied groups in Sirkanda and their members were the most willing informants. However, with caste held constant, back region information was more readily obtainable from women, children, young men and old men than from men in their prime—those who are responsible for the status and well-being of their families and castes. The most reluctant informants about their own groups were consistently the men between ages 35 and 55. They were frequently worried lest their children, wives, juniors, or elders reveal too much. The latter categories were noticeably more relaxed, interested and conversational when they were not in the presence of the male household heads, once they had gotten to know the ethnographic team. I would guess on the basis of this research and some research experience in my own culture and that of the Aleuts, that it is generally true that the most reluctant informants on subjects other than the "official line" or front region performance, are those who have the greatest responsibility for the production of the performance and hence the heaviest commitment to its success. In Sirkanda this was the group of active household heads of high caste (when their responsibilities decreased as they graduated to "old-man" status, they mellowed on this score as on many others). They were valuable informants but their in-

[30]Goffman, *op. cit.*, p. 91.
[31]Berreman, "Caste in India and the United States," *op. cit.*
[32]Barnett, *op. cit.*, p. 378 ff.

formation was biased and incomplete. Perhaps if they had been completely secure in their status they would have been free with their information for then they would have had little reason to be anxious and hence little to conceal. Since they were sensitive about the status of high-caste Paharis they had much to conceal and were consequently inhibited informants.

III

I have tried to show that there is more than one "team" which makes up Sirkanda; more than one definition of the village situation is presented or may be presented to the outsider. As the ethnographer gains access to information from people in different social groups and in different situations he is likely to become increasingly aware of this.

The question of whether the performance, definition or impression fostered by one group is more real or true than that put forth by another, or whether a planned impression is more or less true than the back stage behavior behind it, is not a fruitful one for argument. All are essential to an understanding of the social interaction being observed.

> While we could retain the common-sense notion that fostered appearances can be discredited by a discrepant reality, there is often no reason for claiming that the facts discrepant with the fostered impression are any more the real reality than is the fostered reality they embarrass. A cynical view of everyday performances can be as one-sided as the one that is sponsored by the performer. For many sociological issues it may not even be necessary to decide which is the more real, the fostered impression or the one the performer attempts to prevent the audience from receiving.[33]

The back region is the place where the impression fostered by the performance in the front region is regularly and knowingly contradicted.[34] As such it is not subject to inspection in the same sense as the performance itself, for it is not presented to the audience. Its accidental projection into the front region or the audience's unexpected intrusion into the back region constitute disruptions and generally provide the only indication an audience has of back region activities. The back region is important not because it is the total or true reality but because it is part of reality and a part that is essential to understanding the whole, yet one which may easily be overlooked or misconstrued. If the ethnographer does not understand it he gains an artificial and distorted picture of his subjects, at best.

Behavior that differs before different audiences is equally revealing, equally true, in each context. A villager who dances in the possession of

[33]Goffman, *op. cit.*, pp. 65–66.
[34]Cf. *Ibid.*, p. 112.

a local godling at a shamanistic rite and who tells the visiting Brahmin that he worships only the great god Shiva may "believe" in both or neither but in each case he is responding in part to his social environment so as to maintain or enhance his position in it. From his behavior, inferences can be drawn about the nature of the pressures upon him in each situation and ultimately about the social system in which he functions, if not about the "true" feelings he harbors.

By my use of the dramaturgical scheme in analyzing this research situation I do not intend to imply that dissimulation is exceptionally prevalent among Indian villagers or among ethnographers.

> There is hardly a legitimate everyday vocation or relationship whose performers do not engage in concealed practices which are incompatible with fostered impressions.[35]

Stephen Potter has made such concealed practices part of our popular knowledge.[36] Novelists such as Richard Wright have portrayed them vividly.

> While the performance offered by imposters and liars is quite flagrantly false and differs in this respect from ordinary performances, both are similar in the care their performers must exert in order to maintain the impression that is fostered.[37]

In a highly stratified society the opinions and behaviors of one stratum are insufficient for an understanding of the whole society. An ethnographer coming into such a group inevitably becomes more closely identified with one or more strata than with others, a fact which largely determines the information he acquires and therefore his analysis of the system. In choosing his employees and other associates he has to bear this in mind. In making his analysis he must be aware of the distortions in his data which result from the fact that he is identified by his subjects with certain groups or individuals and that the performance he perceives is largely determined by that fact.

Impression management is a feature of all social interaction. It is apparently a necessary condition for continued social interaction. An understanding of its nature and of the resultant performances is essential to competent ethnography. Methodological procedures must be employed which will reveal not only the performance staged for the observer, but the nature of the efforts which go into producing it and the backstage situation it conceals. This monograph has attempted to explicate these as they were employed in one field study.

[35]*Ibid.*, p. 64.
[36]Stephen Potter, *The Theory and Practice of Gamesmanship* (London: R. Hart-Davis, 1956).
[37]Goffman, *op. cit.*, p. 66.